FROM TOCCOA TO THE EAGLE'S NEST

Discoveries in the Bootsteps of the Band of Brothers

DALTON EINHORN

Copyright © 2009 Dalton Einhorn
All rights reserved.

ISBN: 1-4392-6479-1
ISBN-13: 9781439264799
Library of Congress Control Number: 2009905405

This book is dedicated to all of the men who fought and the families they left behind and with particular reverence for the young men who went to War and never saw the peace for which they sacrificed

And is also dedicated to my Screaming Eaglets, Olivia and Will. This book was written while I waited nine long months to meet you and over many nights after I put you to sleep in your cribs. I can't wait to take you to see the places about which I wrote.

*And to Mathieu Jans. Your wonderful new life was something your dad and I discussed for a long time as he advised me on this book. May you and Olivia and Will never have to fight and I hope that you
will share in preserving the legacy that brought your fathers together.*

And to Richard "Red" Falvey, whose friendship has meant so much, and Paul Keleher for convincing me to write this in the first place.

A Note on Photographs and Contacting the Author

Due to the limitations of self-publishing, I could not include many photographs in this book. On my Facebook page, which you can find under my name, I have a companion set of photos for every chapter of this book. You are welcome to look at them and comment, and feel free to contact me through the site. I am happy to help anyone looking for advice on travel in the bootsteps of the Band of Brothers.

Table of Contents

Prologue	3
I The Beginnings of the Story	*15*
Origins	17
Toccoa	29
II: Normandy	*49*
Crashes and Endings	57
Landings and Beginnings	81
Brecourt Manor	107
Angoville-au-Plain	121
Carentan	139
III: Holland	*165*
An Uncomfortable Feeling	167
The 82nd Airborne in Nijmegen	175
Son and the Island	195
IV: Bastogne	*211*
Bastogne: the First Visit	213
Bastogne: the Big Picture	227
Entering Combat	247
Bivouac and Resupply	257
Noville	265
The Bois Jacques	283
Foy	315
The Last Chapter in Bastogne	325
The 501st on the Southeast Perimeter	333
Reflections	347
V: Richard Red Falvey	*361*
VI: Germany and Austria	*403*
The End of the War and the End of Easy Company	405
Dachau Concentration Camp	413
In the Heart of the Reich	427

VII: *Legacies*	*443*
Legacies	445
Band of Grandfathers	451
The Post-War Lives of Easy Company	457
Other Eagles who Have Flown	481
VIII: *Resources and Maps*	*639*

Prologue

On September 9th, 2001, I sat down in my den with my two dogs to watch the beginning of a new HBO miniseries, "Band of Brothers." I saw the previews and was very excited because I considered myself a war buff. I knew the miniseries was based on a book written by the historian Stephen Ambrose, and that it was about one company that was part of the 101st Airborne. While I knew the Screaming Eagles parachuted into France on D-Day and were encircled at Bastogne, I never heard of the 506th Regiment or Easy Company or anyone named Dick Winters or Don Malarkey or Bill Guarnere.

The first episode gripped me, and when the miniseries aired, I watched each new episode the night it was broadcast. I played in a men's ice hockey league at the time, and on those nights when there was a conflict, I videotaped the episode and rushed home from my game to watch and sometimes re-watch, occasionally not getting to bed until two to three in the morning. There were some rough next days at work.

Often when I see a historical movie or documentary, I want to know more about the subject. I'll go online and do some research, or even read a number of books. When I saw the miniseries, "Son of the Morning Star," I read the book upon which it was based and also read Ambrose's, "Crazy Horse and Custer." I think Ambrose wrote that book in 1975, and when I read the book in 1990, I actually thought he was a western historian.

Then "Band of Brothers" came along and did something to me unlike any other previous military history book or movie: I became engrossed. I am certain that a lot of it had to do to what was going on in the world at the time. The terrorist attacks of September 11th occurred shortly after the miniseries began. They hit me very hard because I was born in New York City and saw the World Trade Center burn from a hill in New Jersey.

When the attack on Pearl Harbor occurred 60 years earlier, the country went to war and able-bodied men were expected to enlist. In 2001, I was 33 years old and had horrible eyesight. There was no draft and there really was no clear way to contribute to the cause. I think the miniseries gave me a way to funnel my energy at a time when I felt the need to do something patriotic. My outlet became to immerse myself in the story of a group of heroic men who, along with hundreds of thousands of others, served the country and helped win World War II in Europe.

Another important appeal of Band of Brothers was that this was the first series or movie I saw that connected me to the men, not necessarily the actors who portrayed them. In all of the movies I previously saw about World War II, such as Patton, The Longest Day, Twelve O'Clock High and The Sands of Iwo Jima, the actors themselves were larger than the history. George C. Scott *was* Patton. Gregory Peck, Robert Mitchum, John Wayne, they were the stars.

Band of Brothers was different. The series focused on many different people and small stories within stories, not just Dick Winters. In the combat scenes, war was never glamorized and the soldiers were not supermen, except for Ron Speirs in Foy. There were interviews with the actual veterans at the beginning of each episode which really made them the stars; the largely-unfamiliar cast of actors who portrayed Easy Company brilliantly never stood out to me as much as those men did in the vignettes at the beginning of each episode.

I would say that I was, in the true sense of the word, inspired, which is pretty unusual because I'm normally a cynical person who would be the first to tell myself to stop being melodramatic when I say such things. But in this case, there was no self-criticism. I went well beyond just reading a few books about Easy Company and the 101st. I contacted professors of history at West Point and authors of books about World War II. And I decided to travel to the places where Easy Company trained and fought.

Luckily, my work allowed me quite a few chances to visit Europe and I made the most of those trips, taking time to do things that I never imagined, like hiring battlefield historians, and exploring places such as the Bois Jacques on my own, with a bag full of history books, maps and cameras. I definitely never pictured trying to run Mount Currahee by myself, which I did with a stress fracture in my leg. And, yes, that hurt a lot.

While I had a lot of opportunities to travel through work, I paid for several of my own trips and was not able to afford a visit to every single place where Easy served. I focused on what I felt were the critical sites: Camp Toccoa, Normandy, Holland, Bastogne, the Dachau concentration camp (Easy liberated a subcamp of Dachau), Berchtesgaden (the site of Hitler's Eagle's Nest) and the final two stops for Easy, Zell Um See and Kaprun in Austria. Perhaps in the future, I will visit Aldbourne or Haguenau, but as I will explain later, I do not think I missed much.

Just as I was very fortunate that I had the means to travel, I was equally lucky to meet several veterans. I was especially fortunate to befriend an original member of the 506th when it formed in Toccoa in 1942, Richard "Red" Falvey. Red served in the Headquarters Company of Easy's Battalion, the Second, and was with the 506th until it was disbanded in Austria in 1945. Not only did Red share with me many stories and artifacts, but he also accompanied me on a 2008 trip to Belgium, Austria and Germany to visit some of the places he saw for the first time holding a bazooka during the War.

As I traveled, I took a lot of pictures thanks to continuously upgrading the digital cameras I carried. I loved capturing the battlefields, and it occurred to me that a lot of other people might enjoy the pictures and also some historical information, so I posted them on the Yahoo! online photo community, Flickr. The response to my postings was enthusiastic and motivating. The pictures were viewed half a million times within the site and on internet searches and hundreds of comments were posted from a variety of people. I was glad to see the interest, and over time I noticed a pattern that got me thinking.

Some people commented that they would never be able to visit these places I photographed and appreciated getting to see some of the battlefields for the first time, or in such vivid color and with such good photography (I worked extremely hard to get good shots, sometimes at the expense of a hedgerow in my nose or feet soaked from walking through a wet field).

Another group of comments came from people who reached out to me for travel advice. Either they were planning trips, or they decided to take trips in the future, and they wanted to know how to find some of the battlefields and other sites that I visited. Then there were the Airborne enthusiasts, who often corrected my many mistakes, and traded information with me. Dozens of people offered advice on places to visit and shared their passions for the subject.

The most touching comments came from a small group of people who were relatives of veterans of World War II or of men on active duty today. The most emotional comments for me came from people who posted comments on photographs of grave markers, explaining that the soldier was their grandfather or great-uncle.

Among all of the several hundred people who contacted me were dozens who suggested that I should take what I posted online and turn it into a book. At first, my response fell into the category of "Who? Me?" But some good friends kept up their suggestions, and I realized that other people seemed to like what I was doing. And, after all, I wish I had a book that I could have used when I was going around visiting this place and that. That was the genesis of this book: what did I wish I knew when I made my first trip?

Great! Write a book. How?

By way of background, I minored in American history in college, so I knew what a history book looked like, and I was generally familiar with what made a good approach. I had some writing background from working for the National Hockey League's magazine. And I thought I was a decent story-teller, at least when beer started flowing. So I wasn't a lost cause as a potential author.

But then I ended up trapped in a paradox when it came to writing. I wanted to produce something that was truly unique, but how do you do that when there are hundreds of books about World War II and about the Airborne, as well as hundreds of websites? And many of those resources were written by people who spent decades living with the history, not just a few years.

I wrestled with the approach to take for about three months, during which I asked myself, what didn't I find in any of those other books? Or what factual elements did it take me several books to piece together? In the end, I think I came up with several things that are pretty unique, and a couple of things I know I've never seen anywhere else in print.

Most simply, this is the first Easy Company travel essay and guide that I have ever seen, and it's the only one of which I know that has directions and maps for the key battlefields. Second, I think that it is the only book on Easy Company that attempts to really tell the story of other units as well. While this book was motivated by the story of Easy Company, and that unit is the focus of my writing, I found I made a big mistake early on.

In the beginning, I charged around with a picture in my mind of Easy Company being the best unit of any in the war and Dick Winters being the best unit commander there was. Not only did Band of Brothers laud the successes of Easy Company, but there was little mention of other units, or a few, somewhat negative allusions or remarks. Then I started learning about what Easy Company did and what other units did. And I learned about the sacrifices and bravery of other American troopers. As I learned more, I felt that I had an unrealistic version of Easy Company and the rest of the American Army.

I learned that Easy Company was one of only nine rifle companies in the 506th Regiment, and that the 101st Airborne also had the 501st and 502nd paratroop regiments, the 327th and 401st glider infantry and also the 326th engineers, as well as field artillery and surgical units. Then I read the books of Don Burgett, a soldier in A Company of the 1st Battalion of the 506th. From him I learned that while Easy Company suffered nearly 15 combat deaths in the entire month of the Battle of the Bulge, the three companies of 1st Battalion had nearly 215 casualties in the first 24 hours outside Bastogne. I learned about the 82nd Airborne and how its' 507th Regiment fought a Waffen SS armored unit in an Alamo-like last stand in a small town south of Carentan shortly after D-Day. And how the 82nd's 504th Regiment made two amphibious assaults, despite being an Airborne unit.

And, with much shame, I learned about the units that I thought were running away from Bastogne as Easy Company headed as was portrayed in the miniseries. I learned that this was not a cowardly rabble, but a column that included men of the 4th and 28th Infantry divisions who were redeployed to the Ardennes after losing half their strength in the Huertgen Forest campaign. And despite their weakened numbers, they faced overwhelming German forces and held their ground before finally pulling back.

As I learned about other unit histories, I learned of the skill and bravery of officers I had never heard about in Band of Brothers. While my high opinion of Winters remained intact, I realized that I made a bad mistake in assuming he was the best of the bunch. He was an excellent officer, but one of many. I realize that sometimes this led to mixed feelings on my behalf as I traveled. I appreciated Easy's role but felt that it was critical that I share what I learned about other units in certain places and during various battles.

Another unique aspect of this book is that I did my best to try to share more information about men who died than I saw in Ambrose's book. Plus, I did something that I think was kind of novel. World War II lasted for only four years, and that time period represented a fraction of the lives of many of the surviving veterans. I created a collection of biographies on nearly 300 men who came home from World War II and I think it's interesting hearing what happened to these men after they got back from Europe, not just what they did in combat.

As I put all of this together, I began to get exposed to a lot of complexities running within the community of the surviving veterans, their families, their fans and others. I learned there are a lot of people trying to make a personal profit off of Band of Brothers and there are a lot of people with a lot of motives. There are some veterans groups who feel that that Easy Company got the spotlight at the expense of others. There are hard feelings among some family members towards individuals and other veterans.

I tried to avoid any of the controversy by focusing on my experiences, especially from my travels and research. While I share a few stories about personal interactions with veterans, families and the extended circle, I've tried to focus on my travels and the history that I learned. I think certain things may have been shared with me on a confidential basis and I will let them remain that way.

Accuracy is extremely important to me, especially when writing about a historical subject that is as well-documented as is World War II. I think that is important to establish that I am an enthusiast and an amateur historian, but not a professional. Stephen Ambrose was a history professor in addition to an author.

Contemporary historians such as Marty Murray and Hans Wijers have encyclopedic knowledge, relationships with veterans (and time in the field with many of them) and access to extensive official documents and other materials. You could spend days going through Mark Bando's website, let alone his books.

I did my absolute best to make sure that my information is correct, although I know that I must have made some errors. In no case did I proceed knowing I had a mistake in the book. If you knew me, you'd know I love the subject and have deep respect for the men who fought. Plus, I am the kind of person who kicks himself for getting 99.5% right, but still having a mistake. To that extent, I encourage those who want to know more to read books by some of the better-known historians or to spend time with battlefield travel guides.

After determining the content and facts, I thought about the tone of the book. The best travel guide I have ever read, Dayton Duncan's, "Out West," was written based on his several trips following the trail of Lewis and Clark. He took a conversational approach and combined humor, emotion and history. Duncan seemed like the kind of guy with whom you could sit down and grab a beer and hear some fantastic stories. I tried to emulate him. I wrote this book in a first-person tone in many cases, and often included anecdotes about my travels and people whom I met.

It took me nearly two years to write the book, the first few months of which were spent waiting for my twins to be born. Then, the process of writing and editing became more difficult, trying to balance sleep deprivation with feedings and a day job. In the end, I chose to self-publish because I felt it took long enough to get the book together, and I didn't want to be delayed by the process of submitting my manuscript to a lot of publishers. A downside of self-publishing is that I was limited in how many pictures I could include, so you will have to visit my Facebook site where all of my photos can be found. They are in full color, and are from all of my travels.

What I've written is a book that has a lot of unique content, some good pictures and a lot of useful practical advice and directions about visiting the places where Easy Company and other brave American units served. I think you will have a good idea of where to go and what you're seeing, and I hope it sparks an interest in learning much more.

Currahee!

. . .

I
The Beginnings of the Story

Origins

Origins: Dick Winters' Pennsylvania

Like many Band of Brothers fans, I found Dick Winters to be one of the most fascinating people in Easy Company. And while the miniseries steered viewers in Winters' direction and while it seems to me that Ambrose felt the story of Easy Company needed a central character, my interest didn't need any additional prompting.

Winters, like many men in the Airborne, came from modest beginnings and did not attend one of the military academies. Yet as a 26 year-old when he jumped into Normandy, he had instincts as a combat commander and as a person that were more mature than in many people twice his age at the time.

Long after the War, men under Winters' command continued to talk about him with tremendous reverence. Don Malarkey's book is a touching example with many examples of his genuine love for his former commanding officer. Floyd Talbert, shortly before his death (and after a prolonged disappearance from the Easy Company veteran's community) wrote to Winters about his bravery in Carentan. Letters that were sweetly shared with me by Burr Smith's daughter, Susan, showed that the love and respect for Winters lasted for decades.

There is so much that stands out in terms of his leadership, actions and character. Winters took his job seriously. He led from the front including charging by himself ahead of his men towards the German positions at the Crossroads on the Island in Holland, and it is a miracle that he wasn't killed while exposing himself to fire while moving the men into Carentan. He didn't take short cuts, either. I'm reminded of him reading his combat manual prior to attacking Noville and cannot imagine how the book made it with him given the scramble to get to Belgium. Winters also showed ultimate loyalty to the men, not his career. His decision not to send out a second patrol in Haguenau because he felt it could get his men killed for little gain fills me with admiration.

Actually, I imagine that Winters himself would be uncomfortable with the notion that he was the central character in Band of Brothers. In every book I read, or interview I saw, Winters consistently gave credit to the core group of men from Toccoa, especially the NCOs, to whom he referred as the backbone.

To be sure, Winters had his faults. He seemed to let both Harry Welsh and Lewis Nixon slide despite their drinking problems in combat. Also, he seemed to treat certain people, such as Buck Compton, harshly. His criticisms of General Taylor are somewhat beyond unfair at times.

Regardless, my impression of Winters is tremendously positive, and as really the first character I got to know in the miniseries, and after reading about his combat leadership, it seemed natural for me to start my book with my travels to the places where Dick Winters grew up: Lancaster and Ephrata in eastern Pennsylvania. Those towns are about 30 to 45 minutes from each other, and about two-and-a-half hours from New York City and about 90 minutes from Baltimore.

Dick Winters' Origins

Richard Davis Winters, Jr. was born on January 21, 1918 in Lancaster, PA at Lancaster General Hospital, which still is located at 555 North Duke Street. When he was three years old, Dick's father, moved the family to the small town of Ephrata, in northern Lancaster County. In 1927, his father moved the family back to Lancaster, to a two-family house where Dick grew up and lived when he went to college at nearby Franklin & Marshall University. That house in Lancaster is where the family waited for Dick to come home from World War II, and at least one book mentions that he sent money back to his family to help pay the mortgage.

Ephrata

The day of my first trip to Ephrata was one when I had a lot on my mind, and I started the trip from my New Jersey home distracted by a number of aspects of life. My wife and I were planning a family, I hated my job and had yet to hear about two new jobs for which I interviewed. The weather was horrible and I slept poorly the previous night. Not exactly the way I wanted to drive to a town where I had never been to look for where Dick Winters grew up!

There are many ways to get to Ephrata, but for me, all of them began with heading west from New Jersey on Interstate 78 into Pennsylvania. For those of you who have not driven on a highway in Pennsylvania, you should know that the rule is that every road can be under construction at any time. But by construction, what I mean is that on any highway, I-80, I-76, I-78, you can find yourself clawing through seven miles with one lane blocked by concrete barriers screaming "why are there no workers?"

And on this day, I was one of hundreds of drivers muttering to themselves about being in a seven-mile long traffic jam caused by one of those phantom work zones. Thunder and lightning ripped overhead and my car dehumidifier could barely keep the windshield from fogging over. I had no radio reception because of the static from the storm, and I was bored out of my mind and just wanted to move!

However, just after emerging from the pouring rain and traffic delay, I got a call on my cell phone – I was getting a job offer! Suddenly, the traffic didn't seem so bad, the weather was a minor inconvenience and the ride was getting downright enjoyable. In a better mood, I decided to get off the highway and reach Ephrata by going the most rural, and longest, route that I found.

Heading west into central Pennsylvania on I-78, through the beautiful valleys and farmlands of that part of the state, past the sign for Dietrich Meats and Pat Garrett's sheepskin outlet, I exited the highway at Bethel. I turned south, cutting through seas of rolling cornfields and grazing pastures along Route 501. With the windows down, there was a wonderfully relaxing smell of the road fresh from a recent rain, corn and also ranches. Many of the towns do not have street lights, and some have little more than a convenience store and a NAPA auto parts outlet. I was in real farm country, where animals outnumbered people. Yet I was only 90 minutes from Newark Airport, at least when there was no construction.

About 18 miles south of Bethel is the small town of Brickerville, where I turned east on Route 322 until I came upon Ephrata, which is about 10 miles away. From the Interstate to Ephrata was approximately an hour, and I would estimate that you would probably need about three hours to get there from New York City.

Ephrata, PA is a town of 13,213 people according to the 2000 US census, and is about four times the size it was when the Winters lived there in the 1920s. An irony, given Dick Winters' combat career, is that Ephrata was founded by German immigrants from the city of Eberbach, which is located about three hours east of Bastogne.

I entered Ephrata on what is called West Main Street (which is the local name for route 322), passing small stores, taxidermy shops, car dealerships and the occasional Amish/Mennonite furniture store. Should you come into town from that direction too, you will eventually make a right turn. Ephrata has a number of one-way streets, so look for either South Oak Street or South State Street. If you take South Oak Street, then you will turn right and go about three blocks and then make a left onto West Fulton Street. Stay straight onto Fulton. If you take South State Street, Fulton is your first left.

Whatever way you take, you will reach 41 East Fulton Street, where Dick lived with his paternal grandmother for nine years. Fittingly, the house where Dick Winters spent part of his childhood is adjacent to the Fulton Elementary School. Winters, as a commander, taught his men and prepared them for combat. His attack on the Germans at Brecourt Manor is taught to the cadets at the U.S. Military Academy at West Point as a classic example of fire-and-maneuver tactics against a fixed emplacement.

At the time of Winters' childhood, this house was the edge of Ephrata Borough, and unlike the residential area that surrounds it today, it was largely wooded, with a stream running nearby. The road that intersects East Fulton at the corner near the house is Railroad Avenue, along which a train line ran, just yards from the Winters' house. Young Dick watched the steam locomotives pass by, transporting passengers, coal and freight, and, often, livestock. Near this intersection were stockyards, and Dick would watch the animals and play among the haybales.

In a mild July rain, with houses and streets laid out in a grid around Fulton Street and Railroad, I found only a sliver of woods. Ephrata grew up. But I saw what looked like a small stream coursing through high weeds and bushes and I walked up. I tuned out the noise of a nearby contractor who was hammering on a house. I tried to picture, in that spot of woods in front of me, a young boy playing and running through those bushes by that stream, and a smile spread across my face. When I came back to reality, I realized that the contractor and his assistant were looking at me with quizzical expressions, probably wondering why I was standing by some woods, with a book in one hand, camera in another, in the middle of a rainstorm without any sort of weather gear or umbrella.

Walking back to the Winters' old home, I found that the rain was pausing just long enough for me to take a few pictures. I kind of smiled to myself because I thought that if the walls of that house could talk, they wouldn't have much to say, given how straight-laced the family seemed! But I'm sure the house would be proud of its' former resident.

Perhaps it was me standing in the street with a camera (outside a school), or that I was looking at a house and smiling to myself, or that I hadn't noticed that the rain intensified and I was – again – outside without any protection, but I saw a woman in a car drive by and give me my second quizzical look of the stop. When a police car drove by and I got the same look, I figured it was time to go and try to find the Winters house in Lancaster.

Lancaster

I think when I went to visit Lancaster, I expected a charming, small college town, with tourists photographing Amish families coming and going in horse-drawn carriages. Maybe Harrison Ford being menaced by a local bully with an ice cream cone like in the movie Witness.

When I looked at the map before I drove there from Ephrata, I imagined that it would take just a few minutes to drive through town to reach the Winters' old home on South West End Avenue. I think that I even expected that the house would be something unique and special, perhaps with a plaque or some other recognition of the story of what happened there.

What I did not expect when I reached Lancaster was to find an area that was quite developed, with traffic choking Route 222, also known as Oregon Pike, and a large number of run-down, industrial-looking buildings, neighborhoods that seemed a little dangerous and drivers cutting off each other. Later, I would find online reports about rising home prices and taxes, overcrowding and a violent crime rate much higher than is the national average.

So, I was a little disconcerted as I drove into Lancaster, going south on North Prince Street past Clipper Magazine Stadium, home of the Lancaster Barnstormers of the Atlantic League of Professional Baseball. I was heading into a part of town where if you drew an equilateral triangle, with sides of one mile each, you would capture much of the life of Dick Winters as a young man.

As I got to the intersection with James Street, I looked to the left down East James Street, where, several blocks away is Lancaster General Hospital, the place where Winters was born. To the right, down West James Street, is another point on that triangle, Franklin & Marshall University, where Dick went to college.

With traffic on North Prince so bad, I went two more blocks, turning to the right on West Walnut. By the way, a lot of streets in Lancaster are one way, so pay attention to where you're turning! Heading about half a mile west, through what seemed like a solid middle class, tree-lined neighborhood, I was certain that Dick Winters must have walked these streets to and from Franklin & Marshall.

Luckily, there was not a lot of traffic behind me because I was doing something that normally infuriates me when others do this: I was slowing down at each intersection to check out the street name, then speeding up to the next block. The number of times I've yelled at someone to just pull over and let the rest of us go by. And use your turn signals! So with a twinge of guilt, I kept up this routine until I came to North West End Avenue, and turned to the left.

My heart raced a little as I drove down the street where I knew Dick grew up, and I started counting off house numbers as I noticed that North West End Avenue became South West End Avenue. I drove a quarter of a mile, three tenths of a mile, and the house numbers got closer and closer to 418.

I got closer and felt like I was breathing a little heavier, almost like I was winded. It might have been because I knew I was close, but it also might have been due to the grill of a tailgating pickup truck that filled my entire rearview mirror. Spotting a parking space up on the right, I pulled over as the truck roared past, and I saw there was an American flag in the back window of the cab and a yellow ribbon magnet that said

"Support Our Troops" on the tailgate. My reaction was to think that a bully in a pickup truck with flags and stickers doesn't know the first thing about patriotism, especially as he's burning gas and harming the environment! And he certainly wasn't as patriotic as were the men of Easy Company.

Shaking off my ranting and raving, I figured that since I was already parked, I would simply walk to the house and after grabbing my camera, I turned around and realized that the house I was staring at was 418 South West End Avenue! I had pulled over right in front of the house.

The Winters family moved from Ephrata to Lancaster in 1927 into a two-family house located at 418 South West End Avenue. Richard Winters Sr. had to take on a $6900 mortgage to buy this house, and it was fortunate that he was able to keep his job during the Great Depression. That said, Dick's mother sold home-made corsets door-to-door to help earn money for the family.

Dick went to high school near this home, and proximity was one of the reasons that he chose to attend Franklin & Marshall. To help pay for college, he worked at a couple of nearby grocery stores, including one that was a few blocks away where South West End intersected with Manor Street.

I was touched by the modesty of this house. The Winters were a hard-working family impacted by the Great Depression and they lived in a working-class neighborhood. There was nothing fancy or extravagant and I think that a lot of us who read Band of Brothers forget that save for Lewis Nixon, whose family was rich, many of the men in the Airborne and in the military were of modest backgrounds. Many of the Airborne troopers about whom I read stated that one of the reasons they wanted to be paratroopers was the extra $50 a month they would earn. As I think many fans of Band of Brothers know, when Dick was in the Army, he sent home money every month to help pay the mortgage.

A more confident visitor might have gotten a closer look at the house, but I chose to stay on the curb because if I lived there today, I would not be so thrilled about strangers walking all over my property. I wondered how many times Dick thought about the family in that home and about this house when he was in the military. How often he thought about 418 South West End Avenue while keeping warm in a foxhole in the Bois Jacques or during his days at Toccoa. And I wondered how many nights the family spent on the porch or inside listening to the radio for news about the war and about their son's unit. And I wondered what it must have been like when Dick came back from the War and walked through that door.

There was a lot to think about as I got back to the car.

That's when reality intruded. I had in mind to drive past the house where Dick's grandmother lived a few blocks away at 614 Manor Street. However, after driving two blocks, I saw that the neighborhood there was very different, and as I drove a block further, I got the feeling that I was in a poor, high-crime area, and I noticed that my slow driving was attracting a lot of attention, especially from young men. It occurred to me that they might have thought I was looking to buy drugs, and I decided to pick up the pace and head out of Lancaster. Reaching West King Street, I turned right, and picked up Route 222 North (South Lime Street) and headed back up to the highway.

As I drove north, I came up to the intersection with East James Street, and looked to my left and saw Lancaster General Hospital, where a huge part of the Band of Brothers story began. My next stop would be where the 506th began: Toccoa.

• • •

Toccoa

I was in Toccoa, where it all began for Easy Company and the 506th (as well as the 501st, 511th and 517th regiments). I was in the origin. Like standing on the spot of the Big Bang, I was at the exact source from where all of the upcoming history burst forth. I was in 1942 with the knowledge that Normandy, Holland, Bastogne, and the Eagle's Nest would all stream forward from here.

And like the primordial cosmic soup that formed the universe, it was really hot. And it was really humid. And it took energy just to breathe in the thick, moist air. I may have been breathless from the excitement of being in Toccoa for the first time, but I was also having trouble as scorching temperatures sucked the air from my lungs.

Like many of the original men of Easy Company, I stood on the platform of the train station in Toccoa, GA trying to get my bearings. I walked out onto the train tracks. There was no one to be seen in any direction, no train traffic, no signs of open stores or restaurants and only an occasional car. Then looking back at the station, I said aloud to no one in particular, "so here is where it all began."

Toccoa is about two and a half hours northeast of Atlanta, closer to the South Carolina border than it is to the chaos of Hartsfield International Airport, where I had flown in earlier on the day of my first visit. Getting off of Interstate 75 at exit 154 onto Route 106/Route 63 you quickly pick up the rural feel of the area, driving for miles without seeing another car, and past the occasional ramshackle home with multiple cars on the front lawn, some rolling hills and pastures. There was a loud, well-practiced symphony of cicadas providing a soundtrack to accompany the thick, warm breeze blowing through my open truck windows, carrying smells of hay, plowed earth and animals. Even today, Toccoa feels rural. To the men who trained there, it must have felt like falling off the planet.

I sped along in a rented SUV, windows down, air conditioner on and listened to Tom Petty's "Running Down a Dream." For me, there were a number of parallels to the song's lyrics. I knew something good was waiting down the road, and I felt like I was emerging from a stretch of rain and cold like Petty described. I had a family coming (I hoped), just announced my resignation from a job I couldn't stand, and I was days away from starting a new job.

I had two days in Toccoa ahead of me, no agenda, a fully-charged iPOD, some cash and a credit card. Days of bad weather had just given way to a hazy sun. And as Tom Petty gave way to Creedence Clearwater Revival, I drove a little faster.

Following Route 106, I passed green signs indicating that I was heading the right way to Toccoa. The distance to town shrank as I came upon each new sign, and I entered Toccoa from the south. Before I left home, I took a look at a map and knew that Toccoa had a main street, Route 123, that was paralleled on the north side by a railroad track.

I pulled up to a streetlight and saw the sign for Route 123. I was the only car at the long light, and as I looked around, I noticed the sign that said "Currahee Street."

Crossing over the road and under the railroad track, I made the first right to find the museum at 160 North Alexander Street. The museum is housed in the train station, which is still an active Amtrak stop, and I think the location is very appropriate. The train station was the place of debarkation for the majority of the men who went to Camp Toccoa. It would also be the place where many of them would return after washing out of airborne training.

The museum was expanded a few years ago to accommodate a number of exhibits about the paratroopers who trained at Camp Toccoa. Among many artifacts is the actual stable from Aldbourne, England, where Private David Kenyon Webster and a few other men from Easy Company were billeted. The stable was built in 1922 and was donated to the museum and dedicated as an exhibit on October 7, 2005. Information on the museum can be found on the Stephens County Historical Museum website, and I recommend taking time to go through it to plan a visit and make sure you know when the place is open.

I visited the museum on consecutive days, and to be honest, the first time I was there, I was kind of in a rush to just get oriented and then get on to see Mt. Currahee. I decided to scout out the place and understand what was at the museum and learn if there was any part of the old camp I could see, and get any advice on driving up the mountain. I figured that I would come back the next day and spend a lot more time there.

The museum was pretty sleepy when I went in. There was just one volunteer at the museum, and we talked for a while. She was fairly surprised that I visited all the way from New Jersey. I was surprised that she was surprised, as the subject matter – the origins of the Band of Brothers – made an inexpensive, two-hour flight from Newark a minor inconvenience at worst. I was doing my best to be polite, but I really wanted to see Currahee, so I excused myself.

I was very happy I went back a second time, because I was in store for one of those experiences where good timing, nice people and shared interests coincide. The next day, I returned having seen the mountain and the old camp grounds and I was not in any sort of a rush. The museum was packed with a full house of staffers, as well as a delegation from the Georgia Tourism board. The workers heard that someone came all the way down from New Jersey the day before, and lo and behold, in I walked as if on cue. I felt somewhat of a celebrity. The state tourism department representatives learned about my visit and asked me a number of questions, and I was eager and pleased to tell them that I was enjoying my trip and the wonderful hospitality of the people at the museum.

Shortly, I was given a private tour of the museum and was told many stories about the men of Easy Company, as well as a number of the other paratroopers who served in Europe. We traded stories about some of the places we visited, and they told me about the men they met, including some of their favorites.

I was asked who my favorite Easy Company man was. I really didn't have to think for very long: Carwood Lipton. He came from very modest roots, losing his father at an early age and helping his mother run a boarding house in West Virginia, and he seemed to be the kind of man who never asked someone to do something he would not do himself. Lipton seemed to be a born leader, great soldier and very reflective and articulate. After all, Lipton suggested the quote that led Ambrose to title his book, "Band of Brothers."

The volunteers told me they liked Lipton but that their favorite was probably "Shifty" Powers, because he was from the south and he was someone to whom they could relate very easily. I really enjoyed the moment and the community, all thanks to Band of Brothers. A bunch of strangers, sharing stories about a group of men who, 60 years after their service, inspired admiration and respect.

A special gesture of their hospitality was their willingness to make color photocopies for me of a number of one-of-a-kind tactical maps of the Battle of the Bulge. They certainly did not need to do that, and the fact that they were pleased to do so made me feel lucky to have met the people at the museum. Maps under one arm, I took the opportunity to buy a number of things from the gift shop at the museum, including several of the white 506th PIR tee-shirts that were replicated for the miniseries.

Back in 1942 and 1943, Toccoa was a bustling little town, crowded on the weekends with soldiers who had passes. Three blocks up Alexander Street from the museum, at the intersection with Savannah Street (and on the current site of the Toccoa library) was the USO building, where dances, musicals and other forms of entertainment were offered. In August 1942, 14,000 troops visited the USO Hall, and in 1943, Bob Hope entertained the 517th PIR there.

Looking at the town today, it is hard to imagine the bustle. It reminded me of ghost towns out west, once crowded with thousands of miners, and now home to a few residents and businesses, and lonely and forgotten. The town itself is tiny, with more vacant storefronts than going concerns. I imagine that most tourists are there to see Toccoa Falls, a waterfall about five miles outside of town. Or maybe they're coming from another district to play against Toccoa's tough high school football team. I hope that the wartime contribution of Toccoa will lead to a boost in tourism in the future.

From the train station, I drove one block down Doyle Street to Sage Street and made a right, and crossed over the railroad tracks. On the left side, at 111 South Sage Street is Royal Cleaners, in the building that used to be the Toccoa bus station during the War. After the train, the bus was the second-most popular way for would-be paratroopers to arrive in Toccoa. On the electrical pole in front of the cleaners is a metal sign depicting a parachute and the number four. This sign is one of several throughout the Toccoa area that represent stops on a driving tour, directions for which you can get at the museum.

Turning right onto Currahee Street, I followed the current Route 123, which back at that time was old Georgia Highway 13. Whether they arrived by train or by bus, many of the men walked this road for six miles until they reached Camp Toccoa. Six miles in that heat would have been miserable, but it was a lot shorter compared to two other walks the men made.

When the men first arrived at Camp Toccoa, it had only a small firing range, so the paratroopers sometimes had to march 40 miles to Clemson University to use the much larger range there. Then they had to march 40 miles back. That would have been a nightmare for me because it was done on several occasions.

Another long march was a special occasion. The Commander of Colonel Sink's 2nd Battalion, Colonel Bob Strayer, read that the Japanese Army set a record for the longest forced march during the capture of Singapore. Strayer suggested to Sink that the 506th break the Japanese record by marching nearly 80 miles to Atlanta in 80 hours. Sink loved the idea and two of the battalions made the march with full equipment. Some of the men doubted Strayer would or could make the whole march, but he led at the front of the column and made it all the way, earning the respect of men who earlier cursed him and his idea for the miserable affair.

As I headed out of Toccoa, I was looking for Mount Currahee and nearly drove off the road because I wasn't paying attention. My advice for visitors is not to worry about missing a first glimpse of Mt. Currahee from the town of Toccoa itself. Trust me: you will not miss the mountain. Mt. Currahee will eventually dominate your drive as you head to the old camp. As you drive through town and pass the church on the left, you will have your first good view, looming in the distance with radio towers on the top, and almost certainly some thick Georgia humidity to make the view a bit hazy.

Within a few minutes, you go down a steep hill to the intersection of Route 184 and Highway 123, and if you stop at the gas station on the right, you will have a great view of the mountain. You will also have your final opportunity to buy some liquids and some emergency provisions. For me, on that hot day, two bottles of Gatorade and two packages of Little Debbie chocolate wafer bars were lifesavers! Sugar and more sugar!

Continuing through the light, you go uphill and you notice how steep the road becomes. I was sensitive to the degree of incline because I knew that overloaded men had climbed these hills in all kinds of weather, most of it bad! Coming from New

York, anything over 72 degrees feels hot, especially when you add that heat and humidity.

I heard somewhere that in this area, between the intersection and the camp entrance, there were several bars, and that men from the camp would head over for a few drinks when they did not have the time to go all the way into Toccoa itself.

As the road straightens out, the remains of the camp emerge on the left, though in quite a modest fashion. A non-descript reddish dirt road on the left is flanked by a metal sign with a few American flags at the base. It's hard to imagine that is the road that the men ran to the top of Mt. Currahee. The infamous three miles up, three miles down road!

A few hundred feet past the dirt road and sign is a concrete road on the left, with a big sign for the Patterson Pump Company. If you make that left turn, you are going through the entrance to the former Camp Toccoa.

When I was there, I didn't see another car for at least five minutes. There were no billboards or much of anything. Only cicadas welcomed me to the trail to the top of Mt. Currahee and the entrance to Camp Toccoa.

On my first visit, there was a forecast for rain in the late afternoon so I headed straight for the top of Currahee. The camp could wait because the trail looked rough and I didn't want to get caught in bad weather. I had this feeling that not much changed from the old camp days: it probably still was not an easy mountain to get up and back down.

The sign by the dirt road to the top of Currahee is a marker to commemorate the Colonel Robert Sink Memorial Trail. "Colonel Bob," as the men called him, was the only commander the 506th ever had. Given an opportunity for promotion to general and a chance to command a division in 1945, Colonel

Sink refused because he did not want to leave his unit, an incredible sign of devotion to his men.

Colonel Sink, with the exception of asking for a second, pointless patrol in Haguenau, seemed to me to be the type of leader whom I would have liked to follow. In combat, Sink led from the front and was constantly near the action. In Normandy, Colonel Sink made a legendary reconnaissance himself and barely escaped with his life. He visited Noville on December 19th in the midst of intense fighting for the town during the Battle of the Bulge. It seemed he was always near the front.

My eye was caught by something on the bottom of the sign: his date of death, December 13, 1965. I stood there contemplating that he died before I was born. Solemnly, I reflected that many of the veterans, who seemed so alive from the actors' portrayals in the miniseries, were gone. Regret hit me and I wished that I had gotten interested in the history of Airborne when many of the men were still alive.

I walked back to my truck and got ready to drive the top. Sometimes, people listen to travel advice with a deaf ear, thinking that no matter what advice they get, nothing bad will happen. If you visit, do not drive the trail in a car and do not try to drive the road during bad weather. That advice is free.

Luckily, I knew about the rough condition of the road before I left New Jersey and I saw the forecast for rain in the afternoon, so I rented an SUV and felt somewhat confident as I headed to the top of Mt. Currahee, taking a quick look at the sky for any signs of storm clouds. I drove about 200 yards up the trail and pulled over to look at a long, white barracks-style building off of the right side of the road behind a chain link fence. That building is the only structure left from Camp Toccoa, and is now on the grounds of property owned by the Milliken Company. I read somewhere that Bill Guarnere thought that the building may have been a mess hall. Back when the camp was open, the building was situated on a road called Third Avenue.

With my back to the trail, the former camp grounds in front of me, the cadence of men singing while running and the stomping of boots on the rough road were not hard to imagine.

Twisting and turning up the road, taking the ruts and potholes with care (even though I was in a rental), I followed what essentially is a man-made scar in the Georgia forest covering the mountain. The road is extremely steep in some spots, and I groaned at the thought of running the mountain in 50 minutes, three miles up and three miles down or be kicked out.

There are very few places to turn around, so once you've decided to drive up, you're committed, and if you decide near the top that your car can't make it, you are in trouble.

As I reached the top of the mountain, I found a place to park near a utility shack next to a set of stairs to the base of the radio and cell phone towers. There were chain link fences and barbed wire around the equipment. Realizing that the forecast called for lighting, I looked at the towers and equipment and realized that I did not want to be there when the weather rolled in. What a way to go: electrocuted by lightning while visiting Toccoa.

The view from the top of Currahee was beautiful, even with the thick blanket of hazy humidity that hung over Stephens County. I knew that I had come to one of the most legendary spots of the Band of Brothers story, and I just enjoyed standing in the sun, looking at the hawks that circled overhead and just appreciated the place and the moment.

I took a few minutes to walk along the road, and I found myself looking down a lot to watch where I stepped because there were big potholes and loose rocks everywhere. Ankle sprains must have been rampant among the men. The road to the top of Currahee really is nothing more than a logging road, occasionally graded by a bulldozer or some other vehicle.

I drove back down towards the bottom of the road, and there was one thing that I had to do before I saw the camp: run part of the trail. I parked across from the remaining building from the camp, stretched awkwardly and ran about half a mile uphill before turning back around. I just wanted to have ran that road, albeit partially, stress fracture and all.

As I settled into the car, the forecasted bad weather began to roll in, and I decided that I would take a quick drive over to the former camp grounds, visit the memorial at the entrance to what was called Camp Drive at the time, and then get back to my hotel and review the materials that I collected from the museum and go online to get some history on Camp Toccoa.

Camp Toccoa

Construction of Camp Toccoa started in 1938 as a Works Project Administration initiative for the Georgia National Guard. When it opened in January 1940, it had the name Camp Toombs, in honor of a Southern politician who became a Confederate Civil War general. The Band of Brothers trained in a camp named after a man who thought he would be the president of the confederacy that seceded from the United States. A few books suggest that the camp's original name came from being located near a casket factory on Highway 13 (that would make it Camp Tombs, I suppose). However, that story is just a myth. Nonetheless, Colonel Sink did not like the way the name sounded, so he petitioned the Army for renaming, which happened in 1942. Camp Toccoa was the new, official name.

Among the first arrivals in Camp Toccoa was "The Cadre," a group of regular Army men who instructed the new recruits in military basics and also pushed them through physical training. Several veterans described the cadre as tough SOB's who were there to weed out men. I imagine that the abuse of the cadre, on top of Captain Sobel's methods, further bonded the Easy Company men who made it through training.

In July 1942, the 506th had 500 officers and 5,000 men begin training at Camp Toccoa. Among them were many of the central figures of Band of Brothers: Dick Winters, Lewis Nixon, Bill Guarnere, Carwood Lipton, Joy Toye, Chuck Grant, Ken Mercier, John Martin, Joe Liebgott, Frank Perconte, "Skinny" Sisk, Ed Tipper and others. Out of the original group, only 140 officers and 1,600 enlisted men were left to make the trip to Fort Benning, GA for jump training in December 1942.

After the War, the camp was turned into a prison, and then eventually sold to private companies. Two commercial sites sit on the former camp grounds today. The Milliken & Company, a textile manufacturer, occupies one part of the old camp and the other part belongs to Patterson Pump, a producer of industrial pumps.

On my second trip, I was rested and full from a big breakfast at my hotel. I drove the 40 miles back to Toccoa and based on the fog and the wet roads, it was quite clear that the forecast of the previous day was right. I wondered what that would mean for my visit to the camp grounds this morning. Would it be muddy and wet? As I drove, the clouds parted and the sun shone strongly, revealing Mt. Currahee against a brilliant blue sky. Inspired, I decided to try a new route, up Georgia 365/ US 17.

On my second visit, I spent a couple of hours walking around the remains of Camp Toccoa. Turning left on what is called Ayersville Road, which is flanked by the signs for the Milliken and Patterson companies, I parked on the shoulder and got out. Ayersville Road is actually the old Camp Drive. Some people have seen a picture of the entrance to the camp from the War years. I parked right near where the guard post stood. From my car, I could see the last building from Camp Toccoa on the other side of some fences on the Milliken property.

Adjacent to the road is a memorial to the four parachute infantry regiments that trained at Toccoa: the 501st, 506th, 511th and 517th. The 501st and 506th served in Europe as part of the 101st Airborne, the 511th served in the Pacific and the 517th served Europe. The memorial has several components including a symbolic parachute that is adorned with a monument for each regiment. In front is also a monument with golden jump wings, which symbolize the ones that the paratroopers earned when they achieved jump qualifications. On the bottom left is part of a pair of legs, the end of a rifle and a pair of boots. This seeming partial section of the monument symbolizes the dwindling number of surviving veterans who trained at Camp Toccoa. Like seeing the date that Colonel Sink died, I was hit by another reminder of the passing of the men of Band of Brothers. As I write now, I can't help but wonder when I might see a note about Bill Guarnere or Dick Winters, and knowing the sadness that I will feel when that happens.

While thinking about the dwindling numbers of veterans, I flashed back to Toccoa in 1942. When the men arrived there, they were young, healthy and vital, in their late teens or early 20s. At the museum in Toccoa, there are pictures of these young men before they went off to war, some of whom never came back. At the museum, you will see a War-era picture that you can also see on the 506th Airborne Infantry Regiment Association web site of the area around the memorial, which was the entrance to the camp. At this entrance were an MP station and a small tank, which Colonel Sink had removed, saying that he was running an airborne outfit, not a tank unit.

Getting back in the car, I paused to look at the sole remaining building from Camp Toccoa again. I thought about how that lone building, separated from the road by a parking lot and two sets of fences, used to be one of many buildings and row after row of tents. I'm sure that during training, no one stopped to look at that building with the nostalgia that filled me 65 years later.

As you head down the old Camp Drive, you see the Patterson Pump Company on your right, and along the road, by the company parking lot, there is a marker designated number 10. Marker 10 stands on an area that was the camp headquarters, quartermaster's office, motor pool, bowling alley, movie theater and warehouse.

Directly across the street is marker number 9, which is in front of a thick stand of trees and is on the site of the former Camp Toccoa Parade Field. Vivid evidence of the changes to the old camp grounds over time: what was once an open field used for training and reviews is now a thick growth of pine trees.

I thought about the young men of the camp going in and out of the headquarters buildings, or going to see a movie, perhaps complaining about Captain Sobel and joking with each other as they walked along. As I did, I heard the Patterson Pump public address system make various announcements about needing people in the warehouse or the loading dock. I wondered what the workers knew of the history of this spot and about the combat experiences of the men who passed through. Or did they just think of it as a place to work?

Further down the road, on the left side, are several fire hydrants that are remnants of the camp. There are also some street signs with names like Jumpy Johnson Way and Jake McNiece Path located where A through E streets used to be.

Jake McNiece is a name that many Band of Brothers fans probably do not know, but should. One website called McNiece a non-conformist, which is to put things quite mildly! McNiece was one of a group of Airborne soldiers called "The Filthy Thirteen" who were the real-life inspiration for the movie, "The Dirty Dozen." The men of The Filthy Thirteen were known for being extremely tough fighters, especially outside of combat. They were notorious for going AWOL, for not saluting or respecting officers, for raising hell, for not cleaning barracks and for going into combat with Mohawk haircuts. There is a famous picture of two paratroopers with Mohawks applying war paint before jumping into Normandy on D-Day. Those guys are Filthy Thirteens.

One thing is very important, though: the men were not murderers as was depicted in the movie. These men had incorrigible discipline problems and did not respect authority, but they were not criminals of the type portrayed by Telly Savalas and the rest in the movie.

One of McNiece's most critical assignments came as a Pathfinder for the first aerial resupply during the siege of Bastogne, but how he got there was ironic. McNiece went AWOL after the 101st was relieved from Holland after Market-Garden. He chose to stay on leave longer than he was granted, a decision he also made in England after the 506th returned from Normandy. His Captain, Gene Brown, felt that busting McNiece to private was not going to be enough, so he proposed something a little more drastic: McNiece should "volunteer" for the Airborne Pathfinders. The Pathfinders were the first men in on parachute operations and deployed equipment used to guide the main body of air transports to the landing zones. Needless to say, this was extremely hazardous duty.

According to one story that I read, McNiece reasoned that there would not be any drops during the winter, plus it appeared that the war in Europe was nearing an end. If he became a Pathfinder, he could sleep in warm, clean bunks in England, and eat better food than the paratroopers had. He agreed to volunteer. He was eventually joined by his fellow Filthy Thirteener, Jack Agnew, as well as others, and formed a crack Pathfinder group. The plan worked well until the Germans attacked through the Ardennes about three weeks later.

On December 22nd, McNiece was ordered to drop into Bastogne to guide the airborne resupply that would come the next day. At about 1500, he and a group of men took off for Bastogne, but the plane was ordered to return to base and the jump was delayed. The Pathfinders left for Bastogne on the morning of December 23rd before the main group of planes. Each C-47 carried 1200 pounds of vital equipment for the men trapped in Bastogne.

The Pathfinder planes were rocked by German antiaircraft fire, and McNiece and one of his comrades were nearly killed by a round that came directly through their STIC. At 0935, the pilot of McNiece's plane spotted a large cemetery in Bastogne, which stands today across from the Heintz military barracks, and the men went out the door, hit the ground and furiously went to work setting up their equipment to guide the transports following shortly behind them.

There is a famous picture of a Pathfinder setting up a transmitter antenna on top of a pile of bricks with four soldiers covering him. That man was identified as Jack Agnew, and the men covering him were from the 327th Glider Infantry Regiment. Shortly afterwards, the transports arrived, bringing desperately-needed supplies and a huge morale boost.

After the road signs and the fire hydrants, the curb on the left ends at the edge of the old base. About 100 before the end of the curb, on the left side of the road, a barrier lays across what looks like an old road or path. I headed there and parked. I ducked under the barrier and walked down the road a few feet, pausing to notice a sign behind a tree for Regimental Drive, a road that paralleled Camp Drive back in the old days. At the museum in Toccoa, one of the volunteers told me that he believed that barrier stood across C or D Street.

I walked in the heat and humidity of a summer Georgia morning with no other people around. Just me and the old camp grounds and a fair number of ticks (wear long pants). Although the street was somewhat visible, I saw only the barest trace of anything man-made. A small patch of road concrete here and there, a chunk of cement and a lone fire hydrant.

The street ends in a clearing, and the remains of another road are visible leading off to the left. This second street is Regimental Drive itself, despite what the sign back out by Camp Drive says. This part of the camp, while revealing faint signs of old streets, is largely overgrown by bushes and trees.

The trees were a stark reality. Every one of those trees, some 70 to 100 feet tall after decades of growth, were all younger than the men who passed through Camp Toccoa. Many of the men who arrived there for training were long dead when these trees were saplings. And now the trees overgrew the remains of Camp Toccoa, hiding the few visible traces that men had been there.

As I stood alone, filled with emotion thinking about the men who never made it back home, the veterans who passed and about the reclamation of the area by nature, I was startled by a crash in the bushes behind me. A deer trotted from between two bushes, paused on Regimental Road to look at me, and then ran up a near bank and disappeared into the forest.

I looked over my shoulder for signs of the deer, the only life I had seen in the whole area, as I headed back to my car with a thought-filled ride back to the airport ahead of me. I saw where it all began, walked the streets of Camp Toccoa, ran Currahee, drove to the top of the mountain, saw the museum and stood on the train tracks and at the bus station where so many of the men arrived.

For the men who were still left, the next stop was Fort Benning for jump training, then to Camp Mackall and then on to

New York. They briefly stayed in a military installation called Camp Shanks that is north of New York City on the western shore of the Hudson River overlooking the current Tappan Zee Bridge. A small museum stands on a tiny part of the old base but virtually nothing is left to see.

In September 1943, the 506th was taken south by train to Hoboken, NJ, where the men boarded ferries across the Hudson River to Pier 88, where the overcrowded S.S. Samaria, heaving in high seas, with poor ventilation and even worse food, would take them to England. Easy Company was going to war in Europe.

• • •

II
Normandy

By all rights, I shouldn't love Normandy as much as I do. My first trip there in 2003 was so bad that it should have scared me away for a lifetime.

Like the Steve Martin-John Candy movie, "Planes, Trains and Automobiles," I had bad luck, horrendous delays, multiple forms of transportation and bad weather, along with a really bad case of sleep deprivation for good measure.

What brought me there to Normandy was a conference that I was supposed to attend in the famous town of St. Malo in Brittany. I didn't know the geography of France very well so I looked at a map to find Brittany and a big smile broke across my face when I realized that Normandy was just to the east. I could take a nice side trip and see where D-Day took place.

My original plan was to fly into Paris, rent a car, drive through Normandy and then head to St. Malo after seeing the beaches, the airborne landing sites and the American cemetery. A simple plan that more or less would have taken me in a long arc by car at my own pace. Traveling into Paris gave me a lot of flexibility in terms of flights and finding a rental car with an automatic transmission at Charles de Gaulle Airport.

However, a British friend of mine told me that I'd regret my plans to go through Paris (oh the irony). According to him, a man whom I presumed was an expert, the French notoriously called airline strikes throughout the summer season. I could be stuck with no way to get to Paris or back home. I might have to figure out how to take a train from Paris to Germany and get a flight back to the US from Frankfurt or some other place. It didn't sound like fun. Plus, he said that there was a wonderful alternative – fly into London, take a leisurely train ride to Portsmouth and then take the Channel ferry into Cherbourg and then drive. His plan seemed like a lot of steps, but the idea of crossing the Channel, like the soldiers who landed at Omaha and Utah beaches did, really appealed to me, so I made the complicated arrangements online and away I went.

The planning was the only good and easy part of the trip. My overnight flight arrived into Gatwick Airport nearly two hours late due to a massive North Sea storm. I got no sleep on the overnight flight, which meant that I was awake for about 20 hours upon touchdown and I wasn't in the best of moods. I rushed to Victoria Station and got the train to Portsmouth. I was tired, but at least I had several hours before catching the high-speed ferry. Optimistically, I thought I would be able to catch a glimpse of Nelson's HMS Victory, which is docked in Portsmouth harbor.

An hour into my 90-minute train ride, an announcement came over the PA system. The train was disabled and we had to get off at the next stop. Calling it a train station was generous. It was more like a small platform that hoped one day it would grow into a siding.

I wore a wool sweater with a tee-shirt underneath, and was quickly soaked by the sideways, cold rain from the storm that delayed my flight. The rain was so heavy it started to get the clothes in my bag wet. I felt like a miserable cat getting a bath. A train finally came along about 15 minutes later and I boarded to find the air conditioning on full blast as if there was meat being stored on board. I froze in my seat as I listened to an announcement that the train was not bound for Portsmouth and that I'd have to make a connection.

I made that connection and finally arrived in Portsmouth and walked around the dock to the ferry terminal. I just wanted to plop down in my seat on the ferry and sleep. Of course, the woman at the ticket counter told me that my high speed ferry was cancelled due to storm-driven rough seas in the Channel. It reminded me of the wave-off of the invasion on June 4, 1944 because of bad weather.

The agent then told me I was rebooked for another ferry that was bound for Le Havre, near Caen. Ground transportation to Cherbourg, where my hotel was, would be provided upon arrival. Without any reaction, I listened as I was told that I would have to wait several hours to leave, that the crossing would be about six hours long and that I would get into Le Havre around midnight. As I headed into the ferry terminal, I was delayed getting through security by some sort of ruckus. A Frenchman cut the line and walked through the X-Ray wearing all kinds of metal. It took about 10 minutes to settle everything down, and during that time I was separated from my bags. I checked to make sure my computer was still in my briefcase and I collected my stuff and headed in.

I got onto the massive ferry, which was filled with small sedans and other family cars, not tanks or other fighting equipment that the Allies brought over in 1944 on their LSTs. I sat down and looked into my bag, hoping to listen to a CD (these were the days before MP3 players) and I realized that my player, all of my CDs and a couple of other items were gone. I got robbed at some point. I suspected that it was back in the ferry terminal security area when I was separated from my bags during the commotion.

Staring at where my CD-player should have been, I lifted my head up and barely took in the captain's announcement that the seas were one to three meters and that we should be careful if we got out of our seat. He wasn't kidding. You didn't feel the heaving seas if you sat, but if you stood up, you stumbled around like in the movie, Weekend at Bernie's.

I didn't get a minute of sleep on the ferry, of course, and when I arrived, there wasn't a sign of ground transportation anywhere. The ferry staff spoke only French and didn't appear interested in helping me in the slightest. However, a British gentleman who spoke French screamed at them and he turned to me and another passenger and told us that they would have a car for us in 30 minutes and that it would take about two hours to drive to Cherbourg. Rain, thunder and lightning were constant throughout the ride. On the way, I chatted with them, and sat in awe of how eloquent were these two random British men, compared to a public school-educated American like me. At about 3 in the morning, I finally got to my hotel and fell asleep after being awake for about 40 hours.

At about seven in the morning, I woke up, went downstairs and grabbed breakfast, and then took a taxi to the Cherbourg airport to pick up one of the very few rental cars in the area that had an automatic transmission. I made my reservation online and it said the rental car desk was open from morning to evening. As the taxi drove away, I got to the door, and saw everything inside was closed. I found a woman who worked in the terminal and learned through my broken French and her broken English that the airport was closed because of the storm and that the rental car agencies were closed as well. I suppose they felt, who rented cars at the airport when there were no flights?

About the only stroke of luck that I had that day was that I asked for a receipt from the taxi driver. There were no taxis around, but the receipt had a phone number and I called for a taxi. The driver spoke no English, but somehow I was able to communicate to him that I needed to stop at an ATM and that I needed a rental car. He took me to a nearby cash machine, and then took me to Avis, which was sold out. Another agency, same result. A third stop was fruitless too.

Finally, we got to the only other place he knew and they had one car – a stick shift. Growing up in the US you almost never see a manual transmission, so I had no idea what to do. The agency owner spent 11 years living in Houston and he was certain that he could teach me how to drive a stick, so off we went on a driving lesson, until the car broke down in a storm. It turns out the car was just back from the garage and the mechanics hadn't fixed the problem.

At this point, exhaustion hit me. I never had so many things go wrong and I think I could have made a lot better decisions if I had been rested and if I had more international travel experience at the time (I've learned a lot about how to travel since then). I should have gone back to my hotel in Cherbourg and slept until I was somewhat lucid, and then called the rental car agency. I could have tried to call someone at the conference to come get me. But I was then at the point of getting only four hours of sleep in the previous 50 hours, and I just wanted to get the hell out of there.

I decided to go back to England. I went back to the ferry port and the woman behind the desk told me in French that she would not sell me a ticket: the ferry was full. I was despondent. I called the owner of the rental car agency who earlier gave me his number in case I had any problems. Within minutes, his wife, an elegantly-dressed petite woman, was charging through the door of the Cherbourg ferry station, yelling at the top of her lungs. By the time she reached me, the shocked agent already had my ticket printed.

I waited in the terminal for eight hours and was enveloped in a haze of second-hand smoke. I kept myself awake to avoid being robbed again. Around dinnertime, I finally boarded and found a seat in an interior room with no windows. Of course, the captain announced that because of the storm it would take longer than was normal and that it would be very rough. The crossing was tough and I didn't sleep a minute.

Figuring I was finally through with my ordeal, I went through passport control and enjoyed hearing the English language again. I felt better even though I was coming up on about 65 hours of sleep deprivation. That reprieve was short-lived. When I went through passport control, the guard looked at me and then directed me into a side room where I faced an immigration agent and a military officer. They wanted to know why I went to France and came back immediately. Unknown to me, earlier that day a terrorist attack was thwarted in London and everyone was on high alert. The officers looked very tense, but I went through my whole story. Each detail and bad turn caused them to wince. Their bodies slumped, they shook their heads back and forth. After I was done, they handed me my passport and asked me what I was going to do next. I told them that I was going to take the train back to London and try to find a hotel. Their bodies sank lower. It was well past midnight. The trains wouldn't run for another few hours.

I grabbed a taxi and told the driver to take me to the Hotel Intercontinental in Hyde Park. I had no reservation and with my luck I would find it full. Over a two hour period, the driver, Patty, and I talked about 9/11, New York and the British people and I began to relax and feel somewhat human. The ride cost a fortune but it was well worth it. The hotel had room for me and by about 3:00 AM, I was in a king-sized bed, freshly-showered, and, after nearly three days with only a few hours of sleep, I went to bed.

Fast forward to 2006. I was eating breakfast in the restaurant of my hotel in Bayeux, France which – oddly – was a Best Western, reading a copy of Band of Brothers. A distinguished-looking older gentleman came up to me and asked if I was American. I said that I was and he asked if he could shake my hand and wanted me to know how much the sacrifice of the Americans during the War was appreciated. He wished me the best of luck and walked on.

Fast forward to my visits to the American cemetery at Colleville-sur-Mer, which is kept immaculate by the local French workers, and visited regularly by many French people (and even Germans).

Fast forward to a winter's day in Angoville-au-Plain, where my wife and I were treated as special guests by one of the townspeople. Fast forward to a desperate visit to Carentan, where the mayor of the town bailed out my wife and me.

I treasure Normandy, and all of my thoughts of there leave me warm, and eager to take my children when they are old enough.

• • •

Crashes and Endings

It was the letter that brought me to Normandy to stand in a wintery, windy, cold rain looking at a soggy field surrounded by hedgerows. It was the letter made me feeling so sad, and the rawness of the North Sea storm made the setting seem appropriately funereal. The letter was the simplest evidence of the commitment, spirit and selflessness of the men of Easy Company and of the other volunteers of the Airborne. The letter personalized the sacrifices. And it was the letter that provided a stark insight into the heartbreak of the families back home.

This wasn't reading Stephen Ambrose describe the emotions of the men. These were the words of one of the men himself. It was the letter 1st Lieutenant Thomas Meehan wrote to his wife, Anne, on the evening of June 5, 1944. As he boarded his C-47 at Uppotery Field on the verge of embarking for Normandy, he handed the letter out the door to a serviceman who promised to mail it. And after receiving that promise, Tom Meehan, serial number O-437484, boarded STIC number 66, which was destined to crash about 90 minutes later in the darkness, 3,600 miles from home, killing all 22 men on board. And I was looking at the crash site.

"Dearest Anne,

In a few hours I'm going to take the best company of men in the world into France. We'll give the bastards hell. Strangely, I'm not particularly scared. But in my heart is a terrific longing to hold you in my arms. I love you Sweetheart, forever.

Your Tom"

I don't think any other artifact of Easy Company so concisely and so completely captures what it meant to go off to war. Not a battle, or a war trophy, or a medal. Nothing born of violence and fighting. Just a 50-word letter expressing the love of a husband for his wife, and a leader's confidence in the men of his company and his focus on the completion of the mission.

And it had me oblivious to getting soaked while I stood on a desolate lane looking at a now-empty field.

The letter haunts me every time I visit an area where Easy served, and fills me with a deep sadness that 23-year-old Tom Meehan never saw his wife again, and never saw a daughter who grew up without her father.

I wondered if his wife received that letter before getting the telegram telling her that Tom was dead. The telegram wouldn't have been sent right away because the scattered drop of the paratroopers made it difficult to determine who was missing, wounded or dead. Did she read and re-read that letter many times as she listened for news about the 101st on the radio or try to find information on the Division in the newspaper?

I picture Anne reading that letter and feeling loved and wanting to send her love to Tom. I picture Anne bringing her hands to her mouth and squeezing her eyes shut as hard as she could and saying something like, "just please come home." I picture her reading that and crying, despite his confidence.

Looking at the soggy field, next to Beauzeville-au-Plain, a hamlet over 1,000 years old, I now understand exactly what the veterans mean when they say that they are not heroes. The heroes were the men who never came home.

The letter and the crash give me a different perspective on Band of Brothers than many other people have, I think. Yes, the book is a celebration of the men who lived to tell the tales such as Dick Winters, Carwood Lipton, Shifty Power, Babe Heffron, Don Malarkey and Bill Guarnere.

But to me the significance of Band of Brothers is that it documents and brings back to life the men who never returned. That's the most important part: the introduction to men like Tom Meehan, Easy's original combat commander, Skip Muck, from Tonowanda, NY (who swam across the St. Lawrence River near Niagara Falls), Alex Penkala (from South Bend, IN and one of 13 children), John Julian (a good friend of Babe Heffron's), Don Hoobler (one of the most-liked men in Easy Company), and the other real heroes.

The book Band of Brothers is more about bonds, brotherhood, friendship and love than about what were the tactical elements of a given attack. It's about men who volunteered for risky duty, leaving wives, parents, children and siblings back home to wonder if they were safe. It's about men who endured arduous training that bonded them as close as family, and then went to war during which their numbers decreased with every battle.

That's why I think Band of Brothers is so remarkable. It's not about what kind of weapons they used or about the battle tactics or the combat depictions. It's that the book and the miniseries allowed us to get to know the men so well. By going through the episode and chapters about training in Toccoa and Aldbourne, we know the men well by "The Day of Days." And then we watch them die or get wounded as the war, as the miniseries, unfolds.

We often celebrate the survivors, but in Normandy, on a cold, miserable day, I found myself honoring the heroes of STIC 66. Of the 22 men on the plane, five were the flight crew and 17 were paratroopers. The latter were among the 4,500 casualties, including 546 killed and 1,907 missing that the 101st Airborne suffered from June 6th to July 1st. 2,500 families who would receive the briefest of telegrams saying their sons were killed or missing in action.

Walking back to the 11th Century Norman church of Beauzeville-au-Plain, whose 1,000-year-old stones were as gray as the slate-colored sky, I entered the small parking lot on the eastern side to look at a memorial to the 22 men killed. The memorial was dedicated in 2000, a year before Band of Brothers aired. To the right of the memorial is an unmarked dirt road, leading back to the third field on the right where the plane crashed early in the morning of June 6, 1944.

On D-Day, the C-47s carrying the men of Easy Company were part of a fleet of 81 transports that took off from Uppotery Field, which is located about 10 miles inland from the English Channel. The planes flew to the southwest, low on the deck to avoid enemy radar, turned to the east, passing over the islands of Jersey and Guernsey, and gained altitude for the drop. As the planes crossed over the coast, anti-aircraft batteries opened up. Seconds seemed like hours as the men waited anxiously to get out of their transports before being blasted out of the sky.

STIC-66 was one of the unlucky ones. The pilot of the plane flying behind Meehan's saw it get hit by antiaircraft fire and then plunge down below the clouds and out of sight. Like many of the C-47s, STIC-66 carried several equipment bundles on its belly that could be released over the drop zone. STIC-66's bundles contained explosives, and the anti-aircraft fire may have hit one of them. Other planes carried equipment that wouldn't explode, such as carts and medical and communications equipment.

The role of luck is astonishing. Perhaps those explosives could have been on another plane, and at least some men might have gotten out of STIC-66. But that would have meant another plane might have gone down, hit in an explosives bundle, not a cart. Bad luck for one plane; good luck for another.

For two men of Easy Company, luck would be particularly important. STIC-66 was overloaded with men and equipment, and two of the troopers who were supposed to board her, Sergeant Robert "Burr" Smith and Private "Red" Hogan, were told at the last minute to fly in a different plane. Band of Brothers mentions that they flew in Dick Winters' STIC (number 67), but Smith's family found evidence that he flew in STIC-68 with Bob Rader and Frank Perconte instead. They survived the war.

STIC-66 disappeared from the view of the other pilots in the air, but men already on the ground saw the plane trying to land, with its' landing lights on and gear down, indicating the pilot was trying to save the men on board. Some accounts suggest the pilot may have had a chance, but with the plane crippled and little visibility, it hit the ground at high speed, skidded into a hedgerow and exploded instantly. The munitions on board burned among the wreckage of the plane for nearly three days.

On D-Day+1, Easy Company trooper Forrest "Goody" Guth came across the crash site. Guth and several Easy men landed near Ravenoville, and fought with elements of the 502nd Regiment. The next day, they broke off from the 502nd and headed to their original jump objective, Ste Marie DuMont. Moving through Beauzeville-au-Plain, they saw the wreck of a C-47, and Guth stopped to take a few pictures, not knowing that his commanding officer and 16 other men from his company lay dead around them.

Even if Guth and his group knew who was on board, combat in the area prevented anyone from gathering at the crash site and reflecting. Sniper fire, German counterattacks, plus the need to complete the expansion of the beachhead were matters of survival. Nonetheless, I find it sad that the plane and the charred bodies lay there with no one to look after them.

In the rain, I said a few private thoughts for the men of STIC 66:

> 1st Lieutenant Thomas Meehan
> 1st Lieutenant Harold Capelluto (Pilot)
> 2nd Lieutenant John Fanelli (Co-pilot)
> 1st Sergeant William Evans

Staff Sergeant Murray Roberts
Sergeant B. Friedman (Navigator)
Sergeant Albert R. Tillotson, Jr. (Crew Chief)
Sergeant Norman E Thompson (Radio Operator)
Sergeant Elmer L. Murray, Jr.
Sergeant Richard E. Owen
Sergeant Carl N. Riggs
TEC 5 Herman F. Collins
TEC 5 Ralph H. Wimer
PFC Sergio G. Moya
PFC Gerald R. Snider
PVT Georges L. Elliott
PFC William T. McGonigal
PFC John N. Miller
PVT Earnest L. Oats
PFC Elmer L. Telstad
PFC Thomas W. Warren
TEC 5 Jerry A. Wentzel

The letter and the visit to the crash site made me want to know more about 1st Lieutenant Thomas Meehan, III. From Band of Brothers, I knew that Tom Meehan became the C.O. of Easy Company after the "Sobel Incident," which was made famous in the book and the miniseries. Captain Sobel was removed as C.O. of Easy in the wake of a mass resignation by the Company's Non-Commissioned Officers (NCOs). The men had been motivated by a poorly-conceived Court Martial of Lieutenant Winters by Sobel, and by the feeling that their commander was an incompetent combat leader who would get them killed. Colonel Sink was furious and ripped into the sergeants, but he recognized that he had a serious problem, and he transferred Sobel to the jump school at Chilton Foliat. To lead Easy Company, Sink selected Meehan, who was in the Regiment's B Company.

There is little in the book or miniseries about the man who was Easy Company's first combat commander. A few scenes in the miniseries were devoted to Meehan, including a briefing during which he confidently announces to the men that Easy will achieve its' D-Day objectives.

But in Band of Brothers, Ambrose wrote only briefly of Meehan, saying:

> "Meehan was Sobel's opposite. Slender, fairly tall, willowy, he had common sense and competence. He was strict but fair. He had good voice command. "Under Meehan," Winters said, "we became a normal company.""

Winters offered a little bit more information in his book, "Beyond Band of Brothers," in describing the Company's morale after Meehan took charge:

> "In any event, with Lieutenant Meehan in command, a far more conducive command climate permeated Easy Company as we entered the most intense period of training since our days at Toccoa."

Winters also wrote of a brief encounter before the 101st took off for Normandy that perhaps made Joe Toye and Dick Winters among the last men to see Meehan on the ground. Toye noted that Meehan announced to the men that they would not take prisoners. Winters said that Meehan stopped by his plane, and the two men shook hands and nodded to each other, a gesture of wishing good luck, did not say anything, and then turned to board their aircraft.

Those small bits of information were nice, but I decided to try to find out more. When I met Buck Compton, I asked him about Meehan. Compton told me with a warm smile that Meehan "was a nice guy."

On the 506th Parachute infantry website I found a picture of Meehan, along with a picture of the mass grave where he is buried. I also found the pictures Guth took in a book he wrote.

Then I found an interesting website maintained by the American WWII Orphans Network. On the site was a post from Tom Meehan's daughter, Barrie Meehan Meller, who said of her father:

> "Born in Philadelphia on July 8, 1921, Tom was an artist from the start. He later trained at the Philadelphia School of Industrial Art to become a commercial artist, but the war intervened. Always a fine horseman, he joined the Cavalry while it was still mounted, but found himself in a tank, not so much to his liking.
>
> When the opportunity arose to go into the newly formed 506th Parachute Infantry, he made the switch. Rising from the ranks to 1LT, he became E Company commander about six months before the Invasion of Normandy. His plane, with 21 men aboard, was loaded with Bangalore torpedoes and blew up when hit by enemy fire in the first hours of D-Day, the remains crashing to the ground southeast of Ste. Mere-Eglise. I cannot think of a better tribute than to offer one of his last letters home:
>
> England,
> May 26, 1944
>
> "Well, I see in the papers that the Anzio Beachhead is no longer that, and that Cassino has fallen. Looks like "we ain't losin'".
>
> Looking back at the grim days of '40-'41-'42, it seems hardly possible that we should have come so far. Those were grim years and we in the States hardly realized it. Now the shoe is on the other foot and the war has probably been decided in Europe.
>
> Yet, somehow I wonder about this "peace" as all the writers are describing it. I'm afraid that I am a pessimist

with little faith in the realization that any peace will be compromise, not everlasting. I suppose that people, being as they are, have thought and tried world peace for thousands of centuries, but war, like the unwanted cat, comes back.

All we want is our way of life and all the handshaking and backslapping in the world won't change our ideas to conform with the other fellows'. The question is not, "How can we insure a permanent peace", but "how can we have peace for the maximum length of time and still be ourselves, unyieldingly?" Natural, human, inevitable. And so, generation after generation has its day of crawling in filth and extracting the life of some other joker that only wanted peace, but a different brand of it.

We're fortunate in being Americans. At least we don't step on the underdog. I wonder if that's because there are no "Americans" - only a stew of immigrants, or if it's because the earth from which we exist has been so kind to us and our forefathers: or if it's because the "American" is the offspring of the logical European who hated oppression and loved freedom beyond life. Those great mountains and the tall timber; the cool deep lakes and broad rivers; the green valleys and white farmhouses; the air, the sea and wind; the plains and great cities; the smell of living – all must be the cause of it. And yet, with all that, we can't get away from the rest. For everyone of our millions who has that treasure in his hand there's another million crying for that victory of life. And for each of us who wants to live in happiness and give happiness, there's another different sort of person wanting to take it away. Those people always manage to have their say, and Mars is always close at hand.

We know how to win wars. We must learn now to win peace. Stick our noses in the affairs of the world. Learn politics as well as killing. Make the world accept peace whether they damn well like it or not. Here is the dove, and here is the bayonet.

May we never see the day again that "World Peaceways" and like organizations dull our senses and make us anything but realists. If I ever have a son, I don't want him to go through this again, but I want him powerful enough that no one will be fool enough to touch him. He and America should be strong as hell and kind as Christ. That's the only insurance until human nature becomes a tangible thing that can be adjusted and made workable."

Clearly, by the age of 23, Tom Meehan was a remarkable young man.

The remains of the men were collected in 1946 and buried in a mass grave in Ste. Mere Eglise. In 1952, the men were reinterred in a mass grave at the Jefferson Barracks National Cemetery south of St. Louis, MO. The mass grave is located at plot 84 0 25-31. (The pilot, Harold Capelluto is buried in the American Cemetery in Colleville-sur-Mer, plot A, row 9, grave 19). I am hopeful that someone in the St. Louis area will read this and place flowers on the mass grave. I know that the next time I am in Normandy, I will place an American flag on Lieutenant Capelluto's grave.

In 1991, two men from the Forced Landing Association conducted an excavation of the crash site. Digging as deep as three feet, the men found a wealth of artifacts from the crash, several which were identified as belonging to Lt. Meehan. A charred watch with its hands frozen at the time of impact (0112), a ring with the initials "TM" engraved inside the band and Lt. Meehan's dog tag were among the discoveries, which also included parachute harnesses, a flattened helmet, a cricket and many other dog tags.

Knowing that the fate of the young men of STIC-66 was to die violently and helplessly without ever having a chance to fight and having insight into the impact back home juxtaposed against the timelessness of the thousand-year-old-church at Angoville-au-Plain makes the site one of the most profound and important places in Normandy to me.

Endings

The 506th suffered the highest casualties of any Airborne regiment in Normandy, according to Band of Brothers, with a rate of 50%. Many bodies were found, while other men who were never seen again were classified as missing and presumed dead. Many bodies were returned to the U.S., but others remained in Europe for burial in American military cemeteries there.

Using the American Battle Monuments Commission website, I found the following men of the 506th who died on D-Day and are buried in Europe or listed as missing (there are many more men of the 506th, such as Salty Harris, who died later on in the campaign. The following represents only June 6, 1944):

William H. Atlee, Technician Fifth Class, U.S. Army
Service # 17068781
Entered the Service from: Iowa
Buried at: Plot E Row 14 Grave 44, Normandy American Cemetery,
Colleville-sur-Mer, France
Awards: Purple Heart

Dale H. Atwood, Private, U.S. Army
Service # 19030209
Entered the Service from: Minnesota
Buried at: Plot E Row 17 Grave 27, Normandy American Cemetery
Colleville-sur-Mer, France
Awards: Purple Heart

George R. Bailey, Corporal, U.S. Army
Service # 11070500
Entered the Service from: Rhode Island
Buried at: Plot C Row 23 Grave 30
Normandy American Cemetery
Colleville-sur-Mer, France
Awards: Purple Heart

Raymond O. Barkey, Private, U.S. Army
Service # 35139764
Entered the Service from: Indiana
Buried at: Plot G Row 2 Grave 7, Netherlands
American Cemetery
Margraten, Netherlands
Awards: Purple Heart with Oak Leaf Cluster

Kenneth A. Beatty, First Lieutenant, U.S. Army
Service # O1285532
Entered the Service from: Georgia
Buried at: Plot B Row 16 Grave 26
Normandy American Cemetery, Colleville-sur-Mer, France
Awards: Purple Heart

Donald E. Bignall, Corporal, U.S. Army
Service # 19138691
Entered the Service from: California
Buried at: Plot H Row 9 Grave 23
Normandy American Cemetery, Colleville-sur-Mer, France
Awards: Purple Heart

Robert A. Boehm, Private, U.S. Army
Service # 18110326
Entered the Service from: Texas
Buried at: Plot C Row 22 Grave 3
Normandy American Cemetery, Colleville-sur-Mer, France
Awards: Purple Heart

Keith K. Bryan, Private, U.S. Army
Service # 17068435

Entered the Service from: Iowa
Missing in Action or Buried at Sea
Tablets of the Missing at Brittany American
Cemetery, St. James, France
Awards: Bronze Star, Purple Heart

Harry L. Burg, Jr., Private First Class, U.S. Army
Service # 15117552
Entered the Service from: Ohio
Missing in Action or Buried at Sea
Tablets of the Missing at Brittany American
Cemetery, St. James, France
Awards: Bronze Star, Purple Heart

James G. Campas, Private First Class, U.S. Army
Service # 12130524
Entered the Service from: New York
Buried at: Plot G Row 3 Grave 38
Normandy American Cemetery, Colleville-sur-Mer, France
Awards: Purple Heart

Colin Campbell, Private First Class, U.S. Army
Service # 6904258
Entered the Service from: New York
Buried at: Plot I Row 21 Grave 28
Normandy American Cemetery, Colleville-sur-Mer, France
Awards: Purple Heart

Warren K. Carney, Private First Class, U.S. Army
Service # 17068499
506th Parachute Infantry Regt, 101st Airborne Division</ H3< td>
Entered the Service from: Iowa
Buried at: Plot G Row 18 Grave 36
Normandy American Cemetery, Colleville-sur-Mer, France
Awards: Purple Heart

Franklin A. Cato, Private, U.S. Army
Service # 34575103

Entered the Service from: Georgia
Buried at: Plot B Row 17 Grave 31
Normandy American Cemetery, Colleville-sur-Mer, France
Awards: Purple Heart

Freeling T. Colt, First Lieutenant, U.S. Army
Service # O-363413
Entered the Service from: New York
Buried at: Plot D Row 22 Grave 26
Normandy American Cemetery, Colleville-sur-Mer, France
Awards: Purple Heart

Floyd J. Corrington, Sergeant, U.S. Army
Service # 19127607
Entered the Service from: California
Buried at: Plot E Row 8 Grave 16
Normandy American Cemetery, Colleville-sur-Mer, France
Awards: Purple Heart

James J. Farrell, Private, U.S. Army
Service # 33254402
Entered the Service from: Pennsylvania
Buried at: Plot C Row 25 Grave 12
Normandy American Cemetery, Colleville-sur-Mer, France
Awards: Purple Heart

Frederick J. Feneran, Private First Class, U.S. Army
Service # 12129872
Entered the Service from: New York
Buried at: Plot G Row 10 Grave 15
Normandy American Cemetery, Colleville-sur-Mer, France
Awards: Purple Heart

George V. Fernandez, Private, U.S. Army
Service # 20228814
Entered the Service from: New York
Missing in Action or Buried at Sea

Tablets of the Missing at Normandy American Cemetery, Colleville-sur-Mer, France
Awards: Bronze Star, Purple Heart

Bryce L. Fountain, Private First Class, U.S. Army
Service # 39098854
Entered the Service from: California
Buried at: Plot F Row 15 Grave 5
Normandy American Cemetery, Colleville-sur-Mer, France
Awards: Bronze Star, Purple Heart

Philip Germer, Private, U.S. Army
Service # 17091587
Entered the Service from: Colorado
Buried at: Plot C Row 28 Grave 30
Normandy American Cemetery, Colleville-sur-Mer, France
Awards: Purple Heart

Arthur M. Goodrich, Jr., Technician Fifth Class, U.S. Army
Service # 13104267
Entered the Service from: Maryland
Buried at: Plot D Row 3 Grave 12
Normandy American Cemetery, Colleville-sur-Mer, France
Awards: Purple Heart

Walter J. Gunther, Jr., First Lieutenant, U.S. Army
Service # O-426647
Entered the Service from: Massachusetts
Buried at: Plot E Row 24 Grave 25
Normandy American Cemetery, Colleville-sur-Mer, France
Awards: Purple Heart

Soini A. Hall, Private, U.S. Army
Service # 39100392
Entered the Service from: California
Buried at: Plot E Row 18 Grave 18
Normandy American Cemetery, Colleville-sur-Mer, France
Awards: Purple Heart

John D. Halls, Private First Class, U.S. Army
Service # 17091542
Entered the Service from: Colorado
Buried at: Plot C Row 10 Grave 32
Normandy American Cemetery, Colleville-sur-Mer, France
Awards: Bronze Star, Purple Heart

Andrew F. Hill, Warrant Officer Junior Grade, U.S. Army
Service # W2124538
Entered the Service from: New York
Buried at: Plot F Row 13 Grave 5
Normandy American Cemetery, Colleville-sur-Mer, France
Awards: Bronze Star, Purple Heart

Bryant L. Hinson, Private First Class, U.S. Army
Service # 14130253
Entered the Service from: Mississippi
Buried at: Plot G Row 25 Grave 32
Normandy American Cemetery, Colleville-sur-Mer, France
Awards: Purple Heart

James Drayto Holstun, First Lieutenant, U.S. Army
Service # O1030157
Entered the Service from: Louisiana
Buried at: Plot E Row 21 Grave 20
Normandy American Cemetery, Colleville-sur-Mer, France
Awards: Purple Heart

Julius A. Houck, Sergeant, U.S. Army
Service # 16100659
Entered the Service from: Indiana
Buried at: Plot F Row 19 Grave 17
Normandy American Cemetery, Colleville-sur-Mer, France
Awards: Bronze Star, Purple Heart

Joseph M. Jordan, Private First Class, U.S. Army
Service # 15107761
Entered the Service from: Indiana

Buried at: Plot D Row 24 Grave 37
Normandy American Cemetery, Colleville-sur-Mer, France
Awards: Purple Heart

James D. King, Private, U.S. Army
Service # 39528067
Entered the Service from: Arizona
Buried at: Plot C Row 11 Grave 9
Normandy American Cemetery, Colleville-sur-Mer, France
Awards: Purple Heart

Robert C. Kinzy, Private, U.S. Army
Service # 35754486
Entered the Service from: Ohio
Missing in Action or Buried at Sea
Tablets of the Missing at Normandy American Cemetery, Colleville-sur-Mer, France
Awards: Bronze Star, Purple Heart

John J. Kittia, Private First Class, U.S. Army
Service # 6877969
Entered the Service from: Pennsylvania
Buried at: Plot C Row 25 Grave 43
Normandy American Cemetery, Colleville-sur-Mer, France
Awards: Purple Heart

Salvatore Laferrera, Private, U.S. Army
Service # 12099723
Entered the Service from: New York
Buried at: Plot A Row 10 Grave 34
Normandy American Cemetery, Colleville-sur-Mer, France
Awards: Purple Heart

Hector A. Lefebvre, Private, U.S. Army
Service # 31263088
Entered the Service from: Massachusetts
Buried at: Plot A Row 13 Grave 37
Normandy American Cemetery, Colleville-sur-Mer, France
Awards: Purple Heart

Grover C. Loika, Private, U.S. Army
Service # 39103349
Entered the Service from: California
Buried at: Plot D Row 12 Grave 19
Normandy American Cemetery, Colleville-sur-Mer, France
Awards: Purple Heart

Robert C. Machen, First Lieutenant, U.S. Army
Service # O-367482
Entered the Service from: Maryland
Buried at: Plot I Row 15 Grave 35
Normandy American Cemetery, Colleville-sur-Mer, France
Awards: Purple Heart

Ralph W. McClellan, Private First Class, U.S. Army
Service # 14134645
Entered the Service from: Tennessee
Buried at: Plot F Row 17 Grave 32
Normandy American Cemetery, Colleville-sur-Mer, France
Awards: Purple Heart

William E. McCrory, Private, U.S. Army
Service # 39312927
Entered the Service from: Oregon
Buried at: Plot G Row 2 Grave 38
Normandy American Cemetery, Colleville-sur-Mer, France
Awards: Purple Heart

Vester B. Millard, Private, U.S. Army
Service # 36481858
Entered the Service from: Missouri
Buried at: Plot J Row 2 Grave 11
Brittany American Cemetery, St. James, France
Awards: Purple Heart

Carl T. Monson, Sergeant, U.S. Army
Service # 39531402
Entered the Service from: Arizona

Buried at: Plot C Row 9 Grave 24
Normandy American Cemetery, Colleville-sur-Mer, France
Awards: Purple Heart

Warren W. Perkins, Private, U.S. Army
Service # 16073039
Entered the Service from: Illinois
Buried at: Plot A Row 22 Grave 10
Normandy American Cemetery, Colleville-sur-Mer, France
Awards: Purple Heart

John Pinchot, Private First Class, U.S. Army
Service # 15321068
Entered the Service from: Ohio
Buried at: Plot F Row 13 Grave 15
Normandy American Cemetery, Colleville-sur-Mer, France
Awards: Purple Heart

Steve Radovich, Private, U.S. Army
Service # 33439585
Entered the Service from: Pennsylvania
Buried at: Plot F Row 14 Grave 30
Normandy American Cemetery, Colleville-sur-Mer, France
Awards: Purple Heart

Leslie B. Riley, Technician Fifth Class, U.S. Army
Service # 17091581
Entered the Service from: Colorado
Buried at: Plot F Row 10 Grave 42
Normandy American Cemetery, Colleville-sur-Mer, France
Awards: Purple Heart

Othis C. Shepherd, Staff Sergeant, U.S. Army
Service # 14023173
Entered the Service from: Mississippi
Buried at: Plot C Row 16 Grave 32
Normandy American Cemetery, Colleville-sur-Mer, France
Awards: Purple Heart

Christopher C. Smith, Private First Class, U.S. Army
Service # 12138478
Entered the Service from: New York
Missing in Action or Buried at Sea
Tablets of the Missing at Normandy American Cemetery, Colleville-sur-Mer, France
Awards: Bronze Star, Purple Heart

Robert L. Stewart, Private, U.S. Army
Service # 39530497
Entered the Service from: California
Buried at: Plot E Row 7 Grave 36
Normandy American Cemetery, Colleville-sur-Mer, France
Awards: Purple Heart

Stanley E. Stockins, Technician Fourth Class, U.S. Army
Service # 20616538
Entered the Service from: Illinois
Buried at: Plot H Row 1 Grave 21
Normandy American Cemetery, Colleville-sur-Mer, France
Awards: Purple Heart

Benjamin J. Stoney, Technician Fourth Class, U.S. Army
Service # 39530033
Entered the Service from: California
Buried at: Plot H Row 10 Grave 39
Normandy American Cemetery, Colleville-sur-Mer, France
Awards: Purple Heart

Jack Swinney, Private, U.S. Army
Service # 39532008
Entered the Service from: California
Buried at: Plot D Row 12 Grave 14
Normandy American Cemetery, Colleville-sur-Mer, France
Awards: Purple Heart

Robert L. Todd, Sergeant, U.S. Army
Service # 12131770

Entered the Service from: New York
Buried at: Plot C Row 10 Grave 45
Normandy American Cemetery, Colleville-sur-Mer, France
Awards: Purple Heart

George A. Trotman, Private, U.S. Army
Service # 37478444
Entered the Service from: South Dakota
Buried at: Plot B Row 1 Grave 15
Cambridge American Cemetery, Cambridge, England
Awards: Purple Heart

Victor A. Turkovich, Sergeant, U.S. Army
Service # 12131780
Entered the Service from: New York
Missing in Action or Buried at Sea
Tablets of the Missing at Normandy American Cemetery, Colleville-sur-Mer, France
Awards: Bronze Star, Purple Heart

John A. Vendelis, Private, U.S. Army
Service # 33066904
Entered the Service from: Maryland
Buried at: Plot C Row 16 Grave 46
Normandy American Cemetery, Colleville-sur-Mer, France
Awards: Purple Heart

Ardean D. Vernatter, Private, U.S. Army
Service # 13088786
Entered the Service from: Pennsylvania
Buried at: Plot F Row 5 Grave 15
Normandy American Cemetery, Colleville-sur-Mer, France
Awards: Purple Heart

Leslie E. Williams, Private, U.S. Army
Service # 39314670
Entered the Service from: Oregon
Buried at: Plot D Row 7 Grave 24

Normandy American Cemetery, Colleville-sur-Mer, France
Awards: Purple Heart

John A. Wright, Private, U.S. Army
Service # 37552915
Entered the Service from: Minnesota
Buried at: Plot F Row 11 Grave 5
Normandy American Cemetery, Colleville-sur-Mer, France
Awards: Purple Heart

The crash of STIC-66 was only one of thousands of personal tragedies and triumphs happening that night. While Lieutenant Meehan and other men of the Airborne were dying, thousands of others were dropping into Normandy, trying to get out of their parachutes and get to their objectives and complete their missions.

Among those men were Dick Winters, who did not know it at the time, but was now the C.O. of Easy Company, Carwood Lipton, Don Burgett, Forrest Guth, Colonel Bob Sink, General Maxwell Taylor and the other men of the Airborne.

• • •

Landings and Beginnings

"Where the hell am I?"

"Where the hell are the Germans?"

"Where the hell is my leg bag?"

"Where the hell is everyone else?"

I imagine that in the first few seconds on the ground, those four questions (and probably a thousand others) must have raced through the minds of nearly every paratrooper, though not necessarily in that order and perhaps with a little saltier language.

I am fascinated by beginnings and origins. Like seeing where Dick Winters grew up, or walking among the remains of Camp Toccoa and climbing Mount Currahee, there is something about seeing the beginnings of the legacy of the Band of Brothers that gives the story more meaning.

To stand in the spots where the men landed in Normandy, thus beginning Easy Company's combat history, is electrifying.

There is something that awes me when I think of the significance of standing in a place where I know a paratrooper landed. I realize I'm on the spot where everything I know about each of these men in combat started. It's almost like the clock started right where you are standing. Every minute before landing was training and preparation. Every moment going forward was the experience of those men in combat. And it all started with that first second on the ground.

At 0640 on June 6th, General Theodore Roosevelt of the 4th Infantry Division went ashore on Utah Beach and realized that he and his men landed in the wrong place. Faced with a choice of getting back aboard the landing crafts and going to the right spot, Roosevelt proclaimed, "We'll start the war from here," and moved his men forward.

General Roosevelt said that as the entire 4th Infantry Division swarmed the beach around him. There were 13,400 American paratroopers who dropped into Normandy of whom 6,600 were part of the 101st Division. The paratrooper who landed by himself in the dark, far from his drop zone and surrounded by Germans had to start the war from wherever "here" was.

Among the few veterans of the 506th whom I met personally, none could tell me exactly where they landed. They pointed out that they had bigger things to worry about than remembering where they landed. Most were too concerned about getting out of their parachutes, finding their weapons, figuring out where they were and forming up with other men. In books I read, a number of paratroopers remembered exactly where they landed, and I know several of the tour guides know the spots too.

Since I am so fascinated by beginnings, I've spent a considerable amount of time trying to figure out where "here" was for some of the men, and then follow what happened to them on D-Day. If you get to Normandy, I'd recommend spending time on a tour with Battlebus or Overlord Tours to see some of the landing sites for yourself.

And you might get a chance to see the precise spots of the landings of a few of the men of the 101st Airborne who were of interest to me. And get to see where the beginnings of their combat legacies started.

Drop Zone C: The Intended Landing Site and the First Drop

Hiesville is a collection of houses and estates surrounded by the fields of Drop Zone C, the general area where the 1st and 2nd battalions of the 506th Regiment and one battalion of the 501st should have landed. Should have. The location between Hiesville and Ste. Marie DuMont was chosen because it was near Causeways 1 and 2, the southernmost roads leading inland from Utah Beach. Securing the roads was vital in order for the 4th Infantry Division, landing at Utah at about 0645, to move inland. Germans flooded the fields just west of the beach, and road traffic was limited to the narrow, vulnerable causeways. The two battalions of the 506th had to secure the exits, which you can still travel down to the beach.

The misdrops of D-Day are legendary and at Drop Zone C, only 10 of the 81 planes found their mark. It has always been said that it was a blessing in disguise for so many planes to miss their targets, because it gave the Germans the impression that a much larger force was landing than just two Divisions. But that wasn't any consolation to the men landing in Normandy that night.

There were actually three landings scheduled for Drop Zone C on D-Day. Dick Winters and Easy Company were in the second one, on board the big air fleet of C-47s that carried the majority of the paratroopers. A few hours after Winters and the men jumped, a glider landing occurred. But about 90 minutes before all of the main activity started, a daring group of men known as Pathfinders jumped into Normandy in order to set up a combination of radio beacons and lighted panels to aid the navigators of the main armada. Not only did they have to avoid the Germans, the Pathfinders had to figure out where they were, work quickly and hope their equipment wasn't broken.

One group of Pathfinders assigned to Drop Zone C was commanded by 1st Lieutenant Gordon C. Rothwell of the 2nd Battalion of the 506th. Rothwell flew on Pathfinder Plane 4, along with Easy Company men Richard Wright and Carl Fenstermacher. The plane skimmed the English Channel as it approached Normandy in order to avoid radar detection and climbed to reach jump altitude. Once Plane 4 made it over the coast, all hell broke loose. Anti-aircraft fire ripped it apart and set one engine ablaze. Too low to jump, the paratroopers were stuck on board the aircraft, which the pilot struggled to keep aloft.

Men threw equipment off the plane to try to lighten the strain on the one remaining engine, which grew redder and redder. Finally, the second engine gave out, and the plane ditched in the cold, heaving Channel. Amazingly, every man on the plane was rescued safely by HMS Tartar after half an hour in the water. Thankfully, the men removed the bulky, heavy equipment they wore and floated with help from their Mae West life preservers.

Other Pathfinder drops were more successful. Pilot Roy Kessler dropped his Pathfinders right on target and they set up some of their guidance equipment within half a mile of their intended drop zone, although one piece of equipment was damaged. But even so, the overwhelming majority of C-47s missed their marks.

Another group of Pathfinders arrived to guide in the two waves of glider transports that would land in Normandy after the parachute drop. The Pathfinders for the glider pilots came in right on target and 56 gliders began landing on Drop Zone C around 0400. Allied intelligence knew the fields around Normandy had hedgerows, but it did not know that many of these bushes were so tall and thick that hitting them was like running into a brick wall.

Brigadier General Don Pratt, the assistant commander of the 101st Division, was a passenger on the Waco glider piloted by Colonel Mike Murphy, the senior glider pilot in the European Theater of Operations. Pratt rode into combat sitting in the front seat of jeep chained in the back of the glider, which had been reinforced with some steel plate to protect the general from ground fire. Whether it was the extra weight or the wet grass, the wheels of the glider locked upon landing and it skidded into a hedgerow, killing co-pilot John Butler and Pratt instantly. Murphy was severely wounded, but survived the crash. Adjacent to the field where Pratt's glider crashed, at the intersection of the D329 and D129 roads is a monument to Don Pratt, the first American general killed in the liberation of Europe.

There are several roads that can take you to Hiesville, but one of the easier routes is to take the D913 to the town of Vierville, a few minutes west of Ste. Marie DuMont. Turn north, and follow the road through the hamlet of Culoville and turn left to reach Hiesville and the area of Drop Zone C.

Colonel Sink's Wild Ride

Somehow it sees totally fitting that of the mere 10 C-47s that landed men in the right place on Drop Zone C, one was carrying Colonel Sink. Could it be any way other than that Colonel Bob would be exactly where he should be on D-Day? I can't see the gods of fate that led the other STICs off-course daring to go up against Sink.

Sink established his CP in the tiny cluster of farmhouses known as Culoville, through which you pass as you drive to Hiesville from Vierville. Culoville is the place where Easy Company spent the night of June 6th, and it was there that Dick Winters thanked God for letting him live through that day and made his promise that if he survived the war, he would buy a farm and spend the rest of his life living in peace.

Expecting to have two of his battalions, plus one battalion of the 501st, plus his headquarters staff, nearly 2,000 men in all, Colonel Sink found himself two hours after landing in Normandy with only 40 men. Even worse, the planes who found Drop Zone C carried mostly regimental headquarters staff, not infantrymen. And even worse than that, Sink had no way to communicate to anyone: his radio team landed 22 miles off target, near Cherbourg, and he could not contact any other units.

Before dawn, Lt. Colonel William Turner of the 1st Battalion arrived at the regimental CP and checked in with Sink.

Sink ordered Turner to take his group of 50 men to clear Causeway 1, the southernmost exit from Utah Beach. Causeway 1 was the objective of Bob Strayer's 2nd Battalion, which hadn't showed up because it was scattered several miles to the north. Sink had no idea what was going on, not even word that the commanding general of the 101st Airborne, General Maxwell Taylor, already secured Causeway 1.

Turner got his orders and immediately departed with his men. The next day Turner was dead, killed instantly by a sniper's bullet to the head as he peered through a tank hatch. Ironically, Turner's replacement, Colonel James LaPrade, died six months later in Noville, within a few hours of the battalion's deployment near Bastogne. Two commanders of 1st Battalion died shortly after deploying into combat. There is little about Turner in the history books. Don Burgett, on his website forum, commented that Turner was a very quiet southerner, and also that he was brave and should not be forgotten for his sacrifice.

At the Regimental CP, Colonel Sink was frustrated by a lack of news. His patrols found nothing – no signs of Germans or any of his own men. Sink then did something that to me was so incredibly risky that he probably should have been court martialed, but on the other hand, so gutsy that I admired the hell out of him. Spotting a jeep and a driver sitting nearby, Sink decided to conduct his own reconnaissance. He commandeered the jeep and driver, Private George Rhoden of the 81st Antitank Battalion. Then he approached privates Amory Roper and Salvadore Cisneros, who stood nearby holding Tommy guns and told them that they had just "volunteered" for a patrol.

Rhoden drove with each "volunteer" holding onto the hood with one hand and with his gun in the other. Sink sat in the back armed with just a pistol, accompanied by his S-3, Major Hank Hannah, who had a carbine, a revolver and a lot of grenades. The jeep left the CP (on the right side of the road just before the left turn to Hiesville if you come up from Vierville, in what I believe is a horse farm today), and headed towards Vierville along a pastoral road through gorgeous countryside. Lovers driving through that road today would find it idyllic and romantic.

Meeting the current D913, they turned right (to the west), passing horses grazing in meadows. Suddenly, on the left, they spotted a German sentry who started to raise his weapon before Hannah dropped him with a single shot. Other German soldiers heard the firing and ran out towards the road. But the Germans dove into ditches as Sink and his men sped by and fired their weapons.

Near the first left turn, towards Angoville-au-Plain, the jeep came across a site that I can only equate to the scene in Star Wars where Han Solo, screaming like a banshee, chases a group of Stormtroopers on the Death Star until he turns the corner and sees hundreds more of them. The next scene you see is from Chewbacca's perspective – Han running at full speed, laser blasts hitting all around him.

There at the turnoff for Angoville, the road was blocked by a full battalion of German troops and several artillery pieces on their way to Utah Beach. Sink ordered Rhoden to turn around and go back the way they came. Rhoden raced as the troopers on the hood held on for dear life. Near Vierville, the German soldiers who ducked on Sink's first pass started to emerge. The jeep roared back a second time and the Germans again hit the deck as Sink's patrol opened fire a second time. The jeep raced back to Culoville, where the shaken men broke into laughter.

No one laughed later when the Germans realized from Sink's patrol that Americans were in Culoville, and pressed against the village. (That night, as Easy Company rested in the town, Winters went on a patrol by himself and heard hobnailed boots on the cobblestone road, ducked into the bushes and barely avoided a German patrol). General Taylor wasn't laughing either when he heard about Sink's reconnaissance. He chewed out Sink for going on the mission himself while leaving troopers relaxing back at the CP.

Taylor had good reason to be a little grouchy when he yelled at Sink because he had a tremendously busy day himself. Although many men in the 101st did not like Taylor on a personal level, the General spent D-Day in the middle of a lot of fighting, and made a number of quick, smart decisions that helped secure Causeway 1, allowing the 4th Infantry to break inland through the beachhead.

A Startled Pathfinder Meets General Taylor

Taylor landed with a group of men about halfway between Ste. Marie DuMont and Culoville, near the hamlet of Holdy, where the Germans had a gun battery. Taylor expected to find himself surrounded by 2nd Battalion of the 506th, but quickly figured out that it had been misdropped. Rather than sitting still and assessing the situation, Taylor organized 40 men of the 3rd Battalion of the 501st Regiment and their commander, Lt. Colonel Julian Ewell (who would later save the day in Bastogne), and headed in the direction of Causeway 1 to secure the landing beach.

The force moved south, crossed the D913 west of Ste. Marie DuMont, and cut eastward paralleling the road. When they reached the D14, the men turned south at a spot only a few hundred yards from Brecourt Manor. Then they turned east towards Pouppeville. If you take that road from the D14 to the beach, you will see a parking lot just past a 90-degree bend to the left. The road leading from the beach to the parking lot is Causeway 1.

Along the way, Taylor's group grew to about 150, infused by a large number of officers and a General, but few privates and corporals. The presence of so many officers and so few riflemen led General Taylor to quip, "Never have so few been led by so many." As the men approached town, they encountered an old couple in a farmhouse. Taylor spoke fluent French and learned that they were in Pouppeville and that the beach was near to the east. Soon they learned that the town was also full of Germans who were determined to fight. Machine gun and small arms fire opened up on the Americans and house-to-house fighting broke out.

Colonel Ewell was as fearless as was Colonel Sink on his drive around Vierville. Ewell personally led many of the advances in the clearing of Pouppeville and was repeatedly exposed to enemy fire. Looking around a corner, Ewell reeled back as a sniper's bullet hit his helmet, leaving a dent as a reminder of a close call with death. Three hours later, the men secured Pouppeville at the cost of 18 casualties, including 6 dead. Among the dead were Lieutenant Nathan Marks, medic Edwin Hohl and privates Bob Richards and Luther Gillick. Robert P. Richards was buried at Colleville-sur-Mer.

Taylor's force moved east and reached lead elements of the 4th Infantry Division who had just landed on Utah Beach. Leading the column streaming off the beach was a group of tanks that would later be commandeered by Lewis Nixon to help mop up the Germans at Brecourt Manor after the attack led by Dick Winters.

With Causeway 1 secure, Taylor traveled back to Culoville to make contact with Colonel Sink and then he went to Hiesville to establish the Divisional HQ. Between Culoville and Hiesville, on the right side of the road before you reach the Pratt Memorial, is an estate that has a Screaming Eagle plaque on the gatepost in front. This is the Le Cauday estate, the site of Taylor's HQ.

From the road, you can see on the first chimney from the right, a small antenna that was installed by a Pathfinder early on June 6, 1944. I always wondered if the Pathfinder who put it up was on Kessler's plane.

On a trip with my guide from Overlord Tours, Olivier, I was told a story that I laughed at and hoped was true. But my grandfather would, "never let the facts get in the way of a good story!"

As the story goes, the pathfinder who placed the antenna on the roof, after turning on his equipment, was overcome with exhaustion, probably from stress, and also possibly from the air sickness pills the men took. He crawled down into the house and fell dead asleep in one of the beds. He woke up to being shaken violently by a stern-faced American officer who told him to get out because that house was going to be used for General Taylor's HQ. Unsure for how long he slept, the trooper looked around and headed out into the night, trying to figure out what to do next.

Don Burgett, Forrest Guth and Other Men Drop Near Ravenoville

Part of the joy of traveling through Normandy is the spectacular countryside itself. It's so easy to get caught up trying to see every point of World War II history that you forget that the area was settled millennia earlier. 1944 was practically yesterday in the grand scheme of things.

Normandy was governed by the Romans before Christ was born, conquered by the Vikings in the 9th Century and was from where William the Conqueror launched his victorious attack over the English at the Battle of Hastings in 1066. In Bayeux, you can see the Bayeux Tapestry, the 1000 year-old chronicle of William's victory in England. When you are in Normandy, looking at landmarks from the war nearly 70 years ago, try to take a moment to remember the previous 2000 years of history around you.

Normandy is also a rich part of the French Romantic period, and is illustrated vividly in the music of Claude Debussy and Maurice Ravel, and in the art of Claude Monet, de Maupassant, and Courbet.

In the summer there, I look around and often think about Monet. You are surrounded by timeless, gorgeous pastoral scenes. Green meadows, flowers, animals grazing and butterflies, with a natural soundtrack of birds and the occasional tolling of church bells. It takes little imagination to see the area as a living Monet painting, and it should be of little surprise to know that he developed as a young painter in the area after his family moved there from Paris. Monet began painting outdoor scenes, an unusual practice at the time, and one of his first works was "Impression: Sunrise," which was inspired by his view of the Le Havre harbor. I only got to see Le Havre at night when my ferry arrived very late in the middle of a storm.

In the 1880s, Monet moved his family to Giverny, in southeast Normandy, and he painted the surrounding villages and fields. He also created a private garden, as well as his own water lily pond, subjects well-known to fans of his work.

In the winter, especially by the beach east of Ravenoville, it is music that comes to mind. My wife and I visited Normandy in January 2007, and as we were there, a storm blew through the North Sea and churned the English Channel. Waves swelled and crashed against the shore, sending ocean foam flowing inland. The Ravel piece "Une Barque sur l'ocean" (A Boat on the Ocean) played in my mind. It was easy to see that Ravel lived in Normandy, and that Debussy was inspired by the area, oceans and seascapes, towns and ancient cathedrals.

Driving near the town of Ravenoville, you are flooded with the romance of Normandy, and if you pause, it will seem amazing that these peaceful, pastoral lands were the scenes of such violence. But the ancient church there is where a pitched battle was fought, and the fields leading towards the beach are where many of the men of the 506th, including Don Burgett of A Company, and Forrest Guth, John Eubanks, Walter Gordon and Floyd Talbert of Easy Company landed.

Ravenoville is a few miles east of Ste. Mere Eglise. You can take the D15 east from Ste Mere Eglise until you come to a T-intersection with the D14. Before you make the left turn to go north, take a look straight ahead. You will see a small dirt road and may be able to make out a stone farm building on the right. That is the Marmion Farm, an important landmark to keep in mind. You might be tempted to drive straight ahead and take a look around, but it is private property and only some of the authorized tour guides have permission to go there. I asked Olivier what might happen if someone went there without permission and he looked at me, and made a sort of knowing grimace and reminded that this is farm country, and some people don't like trespassers. And would you want to get arrested in a foreign country? Good point.

Turning left (north) on the D14, you see the Ravenoville church on the left, and look for the first right and head down that road towards the beach about 1-1.5 miles. If you can pull over and look to your south and back towards the Marmion farm, you will be looking at the fields where many men of the 506th (and other units) landed.

Landing in the fields here was a mixed blessing. Looking out at the fields, you can see a lot of hedgerows, drainage ditches, bushes and other areas that would have provided a lot of cover for a man once out of his parachute. However, there was equal cover for Germans, who had many strongpoints in this area and it is no fluke that the Germans took a number of prisoners here. As Don Burgett pointed out in his book Currahee, the area also was well-marked for pre-set mortar and artillery fire.

Forrest Guth and the Easy Men Near Ravenoville

Forrest "Goody" Guth was one of the men of Easy Company who dropped in the fields east of Ravenoville. I met him briefly and had a chance to trade a couple of emails with him before he passed away, and I asked him if he could find the exact spot where he landed. He said that he couldn't be sure where he came down but that it was about a mile or so east of the Marmion Farm. A short distance from Ravenoville.

When Guth landed in the field, he realized quickly that he was not in the right place, though he did not know where he was. He followed a hedgerow until he ran into Walter "Smokey" Gordon, also of Easy Company. Shortly afterwards, they also found two other men of their company, John Eubanks and Floyd Talbert. Eubanks was lucky to be alive. He didn't respond to Guth's cricket signal and was almost shot. In the nick of time, he managed to blurt out something and was recognized by voice.

The men of Easy Company were soon doing what thousands of other paratroopers were doing at the same moment: forming up in increasingly larger numbers. Individuals met individuals, formed pairs, then met other small groups and become larger groups. Men of different divisions and regiments were forming makeshift fighting units and pursuing their objectives.

The four Easy men soon joined up with soldiers of the 502nd Regiment, the 82nd Airborne and the 377th Parachute Field Artillery, and eventually formed a group of about 50 and came under the command of Colonel John P. Stopka of the 3rd Battalion of the 502nd. Stopka identified a German strongpoint at the Marmion farm, and led the men in a successful attack, clearing out the Germans and setting up a headquarters.

It was at Marmion's farm that several of the most famous pictures of Easy Company men on D-Day were taken, with a camera that Guth smuggled with him despite orders forbidding troopers from taking pictures. For history's sake, it is a wonderful gift for all of us that Guth broke orders. As a result, we have the picture that appears on the cover of Band of Brothers, the men in front of the statue in Ste. Marie du Mont, as well as a series of pictures taken at Marmion Farm. The two pictures that readers of the book will recognize are one of Guth clowning around, wearing a Nazi helmet on top of his own, and the other is of Gordon and Eubanks holding a Nazi flag.

Don Burgett

Don Burgett, like Guth, came down in the fields east of Ravenoville. However, Don took a different route than did Guth and ended up on the road from the beach.

Burgett's STIC got the green light to jump at 0114 and he followed Lieutenant William Muir, a fellow Michigan native, out the door. Ending up in a field alone, Don got out of his chute and lay on the ground in time to see the tragedy of a full STIC of men jump at such a low altitude that not a single parachute deployed and every man hit the ground with a thud: 17 Americans killed by one American pilot flying too low. That same night, two C-47s gave the green light to their paratroopers over the English Channel. The men drowned in the freezing water in the dark, weighed down by 100 pounds of equipment.

Walking in what felt like a newly-plowed field, Don searched in vain for other men until he heard someone crawling in a willow grove nearby. He raised his rifle and pressed once on his cricket but got no reply. He clicked again, no reply, but now he could see a figure walking straight towards him. Six feet away from the muzzle of Don's gun, the figure was finally recognizable. It was Hunley from his company. Don swore at him and asked why he didn't reply, and all Hunley could scratch out was that he lost his cricket and that his throat was so dry that he couldn't give the password. Hunley, like John Eubanks of Easy, was lucky not to get shot after not responding to a challenge.

Burgett and Hunley were joined by two more A Company men, Red Knight and Slick Hoenscheidt. Red and Slick told Don that they heard him and Hunley talking from across the field, and were able to locate them easily. (Don would remember how sound travels at night when he was in Bastogne and kept very quiet when manning his machine gun on the perimeter during the frigid Belgian night).

The parallel of Don Burgett's experience to that of Guth is striking. A man nearly shot because he didn't respond to a cricket challenge. Four men from the same company finding each other in the dark, trying to get their bearings and then moving out and joining up with other men from different units.

Moving steadily through the fields, the four A Company men finally found a place to rest for a short time as morning broke. They moved out to the road that runs from Ravenoville to the beach (the road still exists today). They immediately met up with seven other men, including Lieutenant Muir, and headed west towards Ravenoville. Muir put two scouts, one of whom was named Archie Ponds, about a quarter of a mile in front of the main column, and placed Burgett, alone, about half-way between the two groups. Don wrote they proceeded west about half a mile and then came to a sharp bend in the road to the left, where the scouts disappeared from his view. When he reached the end of the curve, the scouts were nowhere to be seen. If you drive towards the beach and do a U-turn, you will come across this same bend about a mile from town.

Nervous and searching quickly in the field and hedgerow to the left, Burgett spotted the rifles and packs of the two men, but saw no sign of them. He reported back to Muir. Without any men to spare for a patrol for the two missing troopers, Muir ordered Burgett to patrol by himself 300 yards in front of the main body. I cannot imagine how isolated Don must have felt.

The small group reached Ravenoville and joined up with other troopers while receiving machine gun and sniper fire.

As Americans of every unit arrived at the town, Ravenoville became a series of small and large firefights, some in courtyards, some in houses, and some in orchards. Among the many preparations the Germans made included catwalks in some of the trees so that they could shoot down on invading troops.

After a series of firefights, Don and the men made positions in ditches on either side of the road right near the Marmion Farm. As darkness fell on June 6th, they strengthened their positions with piles of rocks at the end of the ditch to protect themselves in the event the Germans sprayed the ditches with fire. During what Don called the darkest part of the night, he spotted a shadow that turned out to be a German with a submachine gun who sprayed the ditches. Don wrote of the rock piles they built, "fifteen minutes of work had saved our asses."

To the northwest of the intersection is a small, thousand-year-old church. Several German snipers were holed up in the church and fired from there on the paratroopers. Burgett's friend, Hagenbuch, chased a German into the church, burst in, and saw about 20 enemy soldiers. Seeking help to rout the Germans, Hagenbuch was joined by two troopers and a first lieutenant who found a French light tank. The next time Burgett saw Hagenbuch was an hour later, lying on the deck of the tank, stunned during the attack.

On the morning of June 7th, Don and the men of A Company parted ways with the paratroopers of the other units and headed for their objective, Ste. Come Dumont. You can follow the path of the men by taking the D14 south towards Ste. Marie Du Mont.

As you head south on the D14, you will see a sign for St. Martin de Varreville on the left, and a small road heading west on the right. Just down this road, in the group of houses known as Mesieres, is the site of the famous attack on what was known as the XYZ complex. The XYZ complex is about a kilometer west of Ste. Martin de Varreville, and was the barracks for the Germans who manned a nearby coastal artillery battery. Lieutenant Colonel Patrick "Hopalong" Cassidy, CO of the 1st Battalion of the 502nd gave the task of capturing the complex to Sergeant Harrison Summers of B Company plus about 15 other men.

Harrison Summers is one of the most legendary men in the history of the paratroopers, although there is controversy about his exact exploits on D-Day. If the story is close to what Stephen Ambrose described in his book, "D-Day," then that Summers did not win a Congressional Medal of Honor, even after an effort was made following his death from cancer in 1983, is a tragedy. Ambrose wrote of Summers, "his story has too much John Wayne/Hollywood in it to be believed, except that more than ten men saw and reported his exploits." Later research suggests that other men played a bigger role than Ambrose knew, thus the controversy.

Ambrose and legendary historian SLA Marshall described Summers' attack on XYZ as mostly a one-man show. Approaching XYZ, Summers rushed into action, expecting the men with him to follow, but they didn't and he didn't wait. The story Ambrose and Marshall provide is that Summers knocked in the door of the first building and sprayed it with fire from his Thompson submachine gun, killing several Germans and sending others running out the back into another structure. Summers chased them and attacked that building alone. One of the Americans, inspired to action, joined the fight, and put his machine gun to work on a third building, which Summers then charged. The Germans fired at Summers as he ran forward, but he made it through without being hit, then knocked in the door and opened fire, killing several more Germans.

Exhausted, Summers collapsed, and his gawking squad moved up and gave him more ammunition. He rested for half an hour, when he was joined by a captain from another unit who offered to join the fight. Almost like a Hollywood movie, just as the captain uttered his offer to help, he was shot in the heart and killed instantly. Summers leapt up and charged the next building, killed several more Germans and took a few prisoners, who were turned over to his squad. At this point, a private joined Summers and the two of them advanced, providing each other with covering fire. They cleared another few buildings, killed several more Germans and then came to a large building that had a shed and a haystack on the side. The machine gunner set the haystack on fire with a tracer, and the blaze spread to the shed, which was being used to store ammunition, and it soon exploded, sending the Germans outside in a rush. Those who didn't surrender were killed.

After five hours of fighting Summers collapsed from exhaustion and had a cigarette. He killed at least 20 Germans and took over 30 prisoners. Nearly single-handedly, Harrison Summers defeated a German position of 100 men, so the story goes. While he received a battlefield promotion to lieutenant and was awarded a Distinguished Service Cross, he never won the Congressional Medal of Honor. Supposedly, the paperwork was submitted during the war, but was lost. An effort made to have him awarded the MOH posthumously after his death was unsuccessful.

The controversy around the Summers story is not small. Accounts from other men may have not emerged until years later. Plus, a few historians pointed out potential errors in the stories, including descriptions of the interiors of building that do not match the actual layouts of the structures.

For me, I have come to accept that every combat story is likely to have errors and inconsistencies when retold after combat. Stories are not captured during or right after a battle. How could anyone have a photographic memory, completely unblemished by emotion, adrenaline, hate and fear flowing through their system simultaneously? Who knows what personal bias and self-image does to stories? Didn't Oedipus purposely overstate the number of men who attacked him? How many Roland Wearys from Slaughterhouse Five are out there, exaggerating their own roles?

Harrison Summers is a hero. He volunteered and he served. He went to Normandy and risked his life, and there is no doubt that he was in the middle of combat at XYZ. I think that even if one tenth of what he did is true, he deserved the Silver Star, and any more than that, he deserves the Medal of Honor. And, of course, there is the small matter of the fact that a bunch of men who served with him tried to get him the Medal posthumously, and they must have known something.

Back on June 7th, 1944 Burgett and his group headed south along the D14 past the turnoff for XYZ, receiving small bursts of fire along the way, until they reached the intersection with the D913, which is just south of a small farm road leading the right. Today, that farm road has a small sign that says, simply, "Brecourt."

Dick Winters, Carwood Lipton and the Men Around Ste. Mere Eglise

Of the 81 planes transporting the 506th Regiment to Normandy, eight of them, STICs 66-73, carried Easy Company. STIC-67, piloted by Lieutenant William M. Sammons, carried Dick Winters and 16 other Easy men, including Burt Christenson, Jeeter Leonard, Joe Hogan, Woodrow Robbins, William Howell, Carl Sowosko, Richard Bray and Robert Van Klinken and Bull Randleman.

The miniseries did a great job of portraying the D-Day jump, although some liberties were taken with Winters. In real life, the co-pilot was not killed causing Sammons to panic and give the green light. Sammons was actually hit in the foot by anti-aircraft fire, and perhaps from shock gave the jump signal, and with a shout of "Bill Lee," Dick Winters was out the door at about 0130.

Winters landed on the northern end of Ste. Mere Eglise, but I have not been able to find anyone who knows the exact spot. Some speculate it was on the northwestern edge, some on the northern edge. We know Winters could see the church, so it could not have been too far from town, but the exact location probably could not have been found again by Winters himself. He landed very hard and was probably rattled, plus he was concerned about losing his leg bag and rifle and then was fired upon by a machine gun.

Other more significant liberties were taken in the miniseries scenes after Winters landed. The man who landed next to Winters was not John Hall but a supply sergeant from F Company. And the ambush scene during which Guarnere disobeys Winters and fires before getting orders is complete Hollywood fiction.

We know that Winters started north and then headed east, and a map in George Koskimaki's book suggests that the eastward route was the present Route de Beauzeville-au-Plain. However, after seeing the area, I think that it was probably the present Rue de Beauvais, especially because Winters mentioned in one book that they started out heading northeastward.

Soon after moving east, Winters and the supply sergeant encountered Carwood Lipton, who landed in Ste. Mere Eglise in a walled-in area behind the City Hall (Hotel de Ville), about a block north of the church.

One day, I walked from the church along the Rue Cap de Laine, the main street in Ste. Mere Eglise, and I found the City Hall building. I sped up as I walked around the corner to see if I could find a courtyard. After turning the corner from the Rue Cap de Laine, I walked about a block and saw a road leading towards the back of the City Hall. Heading towards the City Hall itself through a parking lot, I looked to my left, and saw a small building with a walled-in area. About a block away was the church. I was looking at where "here" was when the war started for Carwood Lipton.

Winters landed around 0130, and by about 0230 was clear of Ste. Mere Eglise with a group of 12 men, including a couple of stragglers from the 82nd Airborne. At about 0300, the small group met about 50 men, mostly of the 502nd Regiment, under the command of Lt. Colonel Robert Cole, C.O. of that regiment's 3rd Battalion. For Winters, meeting Cole was ironic. A decision was made by the American staff that only one man from each division could win the Congressional Medal of Honor. Colonel Sink recommended Winters for the Medal for his actions at Brecourt Manor. However for leading a bayonet charge across an exposed causeway near Carentan dubbed "Purple Heart Lane," Colonel Robert Cole was awarded the lone medal for the 101st. Cole never lived to receive the medal. He was killed in Holland in Operation Market Garden, and his Congressional Medal of Honor was awarded posthumously.

The hodgepodge of men turned south onto the present D115. Again, it seems to me that they reached the D115 via the Rue de Beauvais and then headed south, passing the intersection with the Route de Beauzeville-au-Plain. Near the intersection, on the left, is a small estate called the Artilly farm, which was being used as a German barracks.

A few hundred yards south of the turn-off for Artilly is a T-intersection where the D423 meets the D115. This is the site of the ambush depicted in Band of Brothers. The ambush happened on flat ground, not under a railroad bridge and the men who shot the Germans were from the 502nd. Winters was not the only man who lost his weapon on the jump: Bill Guarnere did too. So, the miniseries depiction of the ambush was fictionalized. The Germans had been heading back to their quarters at Artilly when they were gunned down. In a wild frenzy of looting, the soldiers grabbed what they could, and Winters and Guarnere picked up small pistols.

As the first light of dawn warmed up the sky, the group of men reached the intersection of the D115 with the D14, near the town of Audoville. Winters and Cole wished each other luck, and the two groups parted. Cole was on his way to secure the northern Utah Beach causeways, and Winters was going to bring his men to Ste. Marie DuMont to help secure the southern causeways, the original objectives of the 2nd Battalion of 506th.

Winters found an abandoned wagon on the D14 and underneath the seat was an M-1 rifle that he took, and after scrounging some ammunition, food and a canteen, he felt ready to fight. He would have a chance to do that shortly, along with a considerably larger group of men. A few minutes after heading south, Winters' small group met up with about 40 soldiers under the command of the D Company, C.O., Jerre Gross. (Like Colonel Turner of 1st Battalion, Gross was killed in action the next day, near Ste. Marie DuMont). Unit strength increased even more as the platoon-sized unit linked up with the battalion staff, including Colonel Strayer, his executive officer Major Oliver Horton, his S-3, Captain Clarence Hester, his S-2, Lewis Nixon and a number of other men, including Otto Sykes and Red Falvey.

Largely overlooked in Band of Brothers, Clarence Hester was instrumental in assembling many 2nd Battalion soldiers. Hester was quick thinking and resourceful. Realizing the jump had scattered the men, he put a flashlight bundle in a tree and went out in search of paratroopers. Others, seeing the lights, headed to them and assembled there.

According to a couple of stories that I was told, Colonel Strayer knew that they had dropped in the wrong place, but he had no idea of his location (which was actually near Ste. Marie de Varreville). Hester ordered Nixon, who spoke fluent French, to find a nearby farmhouse, talk to the residents, pinpoint their position and report back. While Nixon scouted, the battalion staff assembled many men of the 506th who had been misdropped onto what was really Drop Zone A. After two hours, Hester hadn't seen Nixon and decided he couldn't wait any longer. Hester conferred with Colonel Strayer who ordered the men to move out at around 0330.

Just then, a drunk Nixon staggered back to the assembly area and told Strayer he was moving out in the wrong direction. Among the men, Nixon was well-known for his drinking. Don Malarkey, in his 2008 book, called Nixon the resident lush. Malarkey wondered how a straight arrow like Winters could be such good friends with a drunk like Nixon.

While it is true that many of the paratroopers, as well as many of the Germans, drank copious amounts of Calvados, the local apple brandy, which was available in vast quantities, Nixon's drunkenness in combat is an attribute that has always made me wonder if Stephen Ambrose gave him a free pass in Band of Brothers. I also can't help but feel that Dick Winters had a double-standard when it came to his friend, Lewis Nixon, as compared to other officers, such as Buck Compton. Winters' criticism of Compton's close relationship with his men seems to me to be misdirected given his shielding of Nixon.

Oriented with the information gained from Nixon, Strayer headed for his objective: Causeway One. On the morning of June 6th, 1944, the large column of men from the 2nd Battalion of the 506th moved south along the D14. At 0930, they reached a tiny collection of houses known as Le Grand Chemin.

Le Grand Chemin is French for, loosely, the big path. It consisted of a number of stone buildings that housed the workers at a nearby estate called Brecourt Manor.

• • •

Brecourt Manor

Olivier looked at me with a serious expression on his face and said "don't get out of the car, and don't lock the door."

He saw the first three dogs. It was the other 10 that he didn't see that really worried him. "Do they bite?" I asked. "Yes," he said as he looked around. And with that, he got out of the car, lit a Cuban cigarillo and stood with his hands on the top of the door, looking for signs of the other dogs, his eyes squinting, smoke coming out of the sides of his mouth.

Warily looking over either shoulder, Olivier took a few steps down the road.

The first three sentries barked, and an older gentleman in a jacket and sunglasses emerged from a barn flanked by seven or eight more dogs. The pack, now 10 or 11 strong, stared at Olivier as he walked towards the gentleman. I wondered how fast a battlefield tour guide smoking a cigarillo and carrying a book full of materials was. We weren't trespassing – the road leading to Brecourt Manor is a public, tertiary one – but the battlefield there is on private property.

Olivier waved and yelled in French, and the man responded with a wave and a shout back. Although I didn't hear any commands, I saw the dogs relax and some walked up to Olivier to be petted as he talked to the gentleman. Others wrestled with each other with those horrific snarling noises that roughhousing dogs make, a few went into the barn, and one simply sat down in the sun, sleepily satisfied that he did his job of alerting his master.

The gentleman was Mr. de Vallavielle, the owner of Brecourt Manor, where Dick Winters and Easy Company fought as an organized unit for the first time. Mr. de Vallavielle is a descendant of Colonel de Vallavielle, a retired French World War I veteran who led men against the Germans at the Marne and Verdun, where his army suffered a collective 1.25 million casualties. In the latest war, two of his own sons were killed fighting Germany in 1940. Now on D-Day, Colonel de Vallavielle's property was the site of a German gun battery, and 12 untested American paratroopers were preparing to evict a much larger Nazi force from that proud Frenchman's home.

Brecourt is a fight that I think captures the imaginations of the fans of Band of Brothers, because it was more than a successful operation: it was the first time Easy Company fought together as an organized unit. If the landing sites were where the war started for the individual paratroopers, Brecourt Manor was "here" for the beginning of the combat legacy of Easy Company.

The fight also inspires because it was the first test of Dick Winters as a combat commander, and he excelled. This was the beginning of Winters' record as an outstanding tactician who led from the front: the assault on Carentan, the charge at the Crossroads in Holland, the leadership in Bastogne. The combat lineage is traceable back to the D-Day attack at Brecourt.

I suspect that Winters would say that at Brecourt he did merely what he was trained to do, and that much of the credit should be given to the men who carried out the attack with him. Both may be true, but at Brecourt, with virtually no information, Dick Winters led an assault that was so textbook that it is taught today at West Point as a classic example of fire and maneuver tactics. And it is certain that the silencing of the howitzers saved lives on Utah Beach.

Brecourt was one of the first Easy Company battles that I committed myself to understanding, and I found it to be quite fascinating as a case study in learning about combat. The action took place in a small area and involved only a few men, whose movements against fixed positions were well-documented, and the tactics were textbook.

Those dynamics make Brecourt a highly-digestible topic. This wasn't some massive, epic clash, like Gettysburg. If you read Band of Brothers, plus one or more of the books by Buck Compton, Don Malarkey or Bill Guarnere (and Babe Heffron), you will understand the whole battle well, and since no section on Brecourt is more than a few pages, you can knock off the whole thing in an afternoon.

Studying Brecourt is also interesting from the perspective of relying on oral histories.

In college, I treated history books as bibles and just assumed they were all factually correct. Then when I read the books by Winters, Compton, Malarkey and the rest, I noticed differences in their accounts of the same action even though the overall theme is consistent. I found it interesting to find different descriptions of what happened by men who were nearly side-by-side during the battle.

At first, differences in descriptions of the fights had me nervous because I wanted to have "the truth" for this book, and I didn't think you could have more than one version of what actually happened. Not only did I want to honor the veterans by being correct, but I also know that there are hundreds of people who are Airborne history experts and I didn't want to have the book picked apart for factual errors.

I was stalled for a while, but then relied on some lessons I learned when I studied the history of the American west after I got out of college. I recalled what I learned about the benefits and limitations of oral history when I met the superintendent of the Little Big Horn Battlefield about 20 years ago. He told me that individual accounts give you the best description of what happened and what the fighting was like, and when witnesses can corroborate the stories, you have a very credible account of what actually happened.

But there are limitations to oral histories. Combat is ferocious, and only a rare person can be observant and objective when bullets are flying. You don't have time to stop and take notes when someone else is trying to kill you. Plus, adrenaline, hate, fatigue and other factors can affect what you remember. Soldiers have often told me that two men side-by-side in the same battle see different things and they may describe a battle with conflicting details, yet both men should be considered right.

Sometimes though, people aren't always right. Time changes memories, especially as one ages. And although we don't like to say this of our heroes, sometimes people bend the truth to make themselves sound braver, tougher and more important. I say that about oral history in general, and do not mean to imply any of the Brecourt stories were embellished.

Also, human nature is a major factor in terms of what the veteran says and what the interviewer hears. Marshall interviewed Winters about Brecourt for his book, "Night Drop," which does not treat the fight with much accuracy or enthusiasm. Perhaps Marshall ranked other fights as more important. With Ambrose, I do not know if he was told things that he did not include in Band of Brothers, although I imagine he had much more information than he could use. I am aware of one Battle of the Bulge book in which the author ignored official documents that would have detracted from his story. Again, I do not mean to detract from the heroism at Brecourt, and only mean to point out that sometimes interviewers can even be biased.

Also, I learned at Little Big Horn that history tends to be written by the winner. As an example, many historians wrote that no one lived to tell the tale of Custer's Last Stand. Actually, the Indians who killed him survived, yet no one thought to ask them what happened until many years later. To date, I have yet to read a German account of fighting against Easy Company.

So I reconciled the potential conflicting stories by focusing on making sure I had the big picture right. You can conduct research forever, but at some point the best you can do is work with what you have. If the general point is accurate and has extensive documentation, then it is possible to feel comfortable about minor differences in the accounts of different individuals. That mindset is what I adopted throughout this book, but I had to come to that point by really thinking about Brecourt Manor first.

The Fight at Brecourt Manor

Olivier took us to Brecourt by driving south on the D14 until we reached Le Grand Chemin. This was the route taken by the large group of soldiers Winters and others joined after breaking off from Cole's force. When the group arrived in Le Grand Chemin at about 0930, machine gun fire erupted from the front and on the right. Men hid in ditches and rested and ate, or found other paratroopers at the temporary CP in the hamlet and exchanged news.

The German fire was probably the result of a reconnaissance of Brecourt by Lt. John Kelly of D Company. His scouting mission turned into a poorly-conceived frontal assault and Kelly was lucky to get all of his men out with no casualties. He returned to the command post and reported German artillery and machine guns.

Colonel Strayer ordered Winters up to the CP. There Winters learned that no one had seen Lt. Meehan and that he was in charge of Easy Company. Without any specific orders or any detailed intelligence, Winters was directed by Captain Hester to take Easy Company, which barely numbered half a squad, and eliminate the German position at Brecourt Manor.

The Germans were dug in front of the de Vallavielle's house in a seven-sided field on the west side of a hedgerow that parallels the D14. The field itself is like taking a rectangle that runs sort northeast-southwest and on the west side, adding a big "M" where the legs touch the corners of the rectangle. All of the sides are bordered by hedgerows, although on the southern end, there is a large opening along the road where we stood.

Winters crawled from Le Grand Chemin along an east-west hedgerow that led to the northeastern corner of the field at Brecourt and surveyed the situation. From Olivier, I learned that the owner of the farm from which Winters did his reconnaissance does not allow visitors on his property and gets very agitated by trespassers, so my own observations of Winters' approach were from the D14.

Winters saw a machine gun in the northeastern corner of the field, and at least one howitzer. He correctly guessed there were other German positions, and ruled out a frontal assault as too dangerous. I agree with Winters' belief stated in Band of Brothers that had Captain Sobel led Easy into combat, a frontal assault is exactly what he would have chosen, and probably at the cost of nearly every man in the charge. When you see Brecourt, you understand: unless you kept your head low and in the trenches, you would have been a sitting duck for machine guns on the other side of the field and on the flank.

The miniseries has a vivid, terrifying, intense portrayal of the fight at Brecourt. Winters sent Myron Ranney and Carwood Lipton to a flanking position on the north side, with orders to fire into the first howitzer position. Unable to see the Germans from the ground, Lipton made the very dangerous move of climbing into a tree to sight the enemy. Just south of Lipton's tree was a machine gun manned by Joe Liebgott and Cleveland Petty. Winters used the rest of his men to assault the German machine gun and howitzer on the northeast corner of the field. Classic fire and maneuver tactics.

Winters led an assault team that consisted of himself Joe Toye, Popeye Wynn and Gerald Lorraine from the regimental headquarters company. Another flanking team was comprised of Buck Compton, Bill Guarnere and Don Malarkey. On Winters' signal, his assault team opened fire, followed by Petty and Liebgott on the machine gun. Compton's team moved into position and when Winters saw them throw grenades into the machine gun position, he yelled "Follow me!" and charged forward. Winters led from the front.

Very thorough descriptions of the success of Winters attack are found in Band of Brothers and other books. Easy Company captured and destroyed three howitzers, and a small group that included Ron Speirs of D Company knocked out the fourth gun.

Some Interesting Things I Learned About Brecourt

The miniseries did a wonderful job of portraying the combat, and I get goosebumps every time I watch "Day of Days." However, there are some areas in which real life differed from the miniseries and there are some additional facts that I enjoyed learning.

The most important overall difference between real life and the miniseries was observed by Buck Compton who wrote in his book and told me in person that the on-screen depiction was different from what he remembered. Compton's account suggested that taking the first machine gun was a confusing and spontaneous brawl, whereas the miniseries depicted it almost as going according to a plan.

The most important specific difference between real life and the miniseries is the disappointing portrayal of Gerald Lorraine as a scared "jeep jockey." In the miniseries, a terrified Lorraine could not aim his rifle and missed a fleeing a German forcing Bill Guarnere to shoot the soldier down with his Tommy Gun. In reality, during the fight, Winters and Lorraine were deadly with their fire and it was Guarnere who had a problem with his accuracy before he finally got his emotions under control. Lorraine was awarded a Silver Star for his actions at Brecourt and won a second one for actions in Holland.

Aside from those two points, most of what I found in my research was just additional information that added more depth to the battle, such as the attack on the fourth gun.

The fourth howitzer was attacked by Speirs, Julian "Rusty" Houch, Len Hicks of F Company, privates Jumbo DiMarzio, Ray Taylor and an unidentified, trooper, as well as Bill Guarnere from Easy Company.

Moving in to attack the fourth gun, Hicks waited for Houch to throw in a grenade. Just as Houch raised himself to pitch the grenade, a German bullet slammed into him, killing him instantly. Speirs leapt forward into the attack, and both Hicks and the unidentified men were hit, but the gun was secured. Guarnere joined the assault, and cut down several Germans in the position and in the field.

Guarnere was filled with rage at the death of his brother, Henry, in Italy and fought wildly all morning. But the whole experience caught up to him at that fourth gun position. Guarnere wrote that after they secured the final gun, he leaned against the wall of the position to scout the area through binoculars and fell asleep. He crashed from the emotional and physical exhaustion of the previous few days. Joe Toye arrived and saw Guarnere, eyes closed, slumped over, and thought he was dead. Toye hit him in the back of the head to check and Guarnere jumped, scaring both of them out of their wits.

Another interesting aspect of the fight that I learned about is time. The battle for Brecourt Manor took nearly three hours, and was long enough for Winters to go back to battalion headquarters and yell at the senior officers for failing to supply the men with enough ammunition. Shortly after that, Captain

Hester, not Private Hall, joined the men at the howitzers with explosives that were used to blow the barrels.

As a postscript, the fight at Brecourt did not end with the withdrawal of Winters and his attacking force. After Winters yelled at the senior officers about not supplying enough ammunition, Nixon was ordered to link up with the tanks of the 4th Infantry Division and to try to bring a few back to help mop up the Germans. Nixon headed south in the direction of Pouppeville, and encountered several Sherman tanks that landed at Causeway 1 and directed them towards Brecourt.

One of the more amazing photographs I have seen is in a book published by The History Channel called, "Above the Battle: D-Day the Lost Evidence." In the book, there is an aerial reconnaissance photograph that was taken high enough to show Ste. Marie DuMont, Brecourt Manor and, on the road leading from Pouppeville, several Sherman tanks. The authors wrote that it was likely that those were the tanks that were brought to Brecourt.

By the time Nixon and the tanks rolled up to the assembly area, all of the guns were destroyed and Winters had the men back to in Le Grand Chemin, with Don Malarkey firing mortar rounds on the remaining Germans to suppress fire. At about the same time, lieutenants Harry Welsh and Warren Roush arrived with 30 men and a second attack was launched. Winters directed tank fire with hand signals as the troopers moved alongside to flush the Germans, who were routed with few prisoners or survivors. After the fight, Winters took his legendary first and only sip of hard cider.

Brecourt Manners

Visiting Brecourt is an absolute thrill, but it is also a privilege, thanks to Charles de Vallavielle, who permits visitors as long as they are respectful and accompanied by a tour guide.

Requiring visitors to go through one of the approved guides is more than fair given the number of people who would like to visit what is someone's private property.

Unfortunately, this requirement is necessary because there are always people who cannot behave themselves and ruin it for the rest of us. I nearly got into a fistfight confronting two men about to urinate in the bushes behind the gas chamber at Dachau, only a few feet from a public bathroom. I've seen litter in the foxholes in the Bois Jacques. It's impossible to understand how some people can be so thoughtless and selfish. To quote Gunnery Sergeant Hartman in "Full Metal Jacket," "if it wasn't for dickheads like you, there wouldn't be any thievery in this world."

The Surprise of Visiting Brecourt

When Olivier drove us down the D14 and pointed out Le Grand Chemin, a couple of things went on inside me. First, my heart raced, because I knew Brecourt Manor was nearby. Second, I was surprised: Le Grand Chemin wasn't what I expected. My original impression, and I have no idea what led to this, was that Le Grand Chemin was a small town, and was far away enough from Brecourt Manor for the Americans to gather without being noticed by the Germans and for the paratroopers not to have a clear sense of what waited for them at the estate.

In reality, Le Grand Chemin is a cluster of about six or seven large farmhouses and farm buildings on either side of the D14. There is a sign for the hamlet and I think the speed limit on the road is reduced there, but it is so unremarkable. And on a clear day with little wind, Tiger Woods could easily drive a golf ball from those farmhouses to the battlefield at Brecourt. It's that close: from the road, you can see the hedgerow behind which the howitzers were placed.

If Le Grand Chemin was smaller than I thought, Brecourt Manor was downright anti-climactic at first. We drove about 100 yards south of Le Grand Chemin and turned right down a country lane, and parked by the field. Olivier pointed to a pasture and said that was the battlefield. Drive down a road and turn right and there it is? That's it? In my mind, I had built up the significance of the fight there into a truly war-changing event where a group of not much more than a dozen men routed a German force five times their size and silenced guns that could have killed hundreds of men on Utah Beach.

Yet here it was so simply and so easily. The field and hedgerows looked just like hundreds of others that we passed by throughout the day. And this historic fight with so much significance happened on a field that I realized was much smaller than I pictured. The length of the field is not much longer than 200 yards, if even that long, and the width is so tight at spots, that you could probably see the faces of men on the other side.

And when I saw the small size of the field I was astonished, not by the success of the Americans but by the failure of the German defenders. How could the much larger German force, with multiple machine guns for suppressing fire, not launch a counterattack against the paratroopers? How did they sit by and allow the howitzers to be knocked out? A good shot with a rifle could have done a lot of damage. Winters remarked in several books that the Germans were almost nonchalant, and that several were shot while ambling back to their guns, oblivious to the firing around them.

But any feelings of things being anti-climactic vanished once we got out into the field. Once I walked the field myself, and stood in the exact spots where the howitzers were placed and stood on the site of the machine gun that was knocked out by Compton, Guarnere and Malarkey, it all slowed down and a big smile broke across my face. I looked out on the field and laughed at Malarkey's incredibly stupid dash out to try to pick up a "Luger" that turned out to be an artillery rangefinder. The feelings of things being anti-climactic were long gone. This was worth every penny of the cost of the trip to Europe and the guided tour.

That evening, the men of Easy Company spent the night in Culoville, where Dick Winters thanked God for surviving the day. That night's sleep in Culoville was the first he and the men had since they woke up in England on June 5th. Without knowing it, Dick Winters was the official commanding officer of Easy Company, and the men who were with him in Culoville fell asleep knowing that he was a smart, decisive combat leader.

That night, the dead men from STIC-66 lay among the wreckage in a field a few miles to the north.

. . .

Angoville-au-Plain

On a raw winter day south of Angoville-au-Plain, water flooded criss-crossing drainage ditches and pooled on the empty fields, where it rippled in the harsh wind. Empty, soggy, menacing, this was Drop Zone D, a key landing site for the 101st. And it looked much the way it did on D-Day when it was flooded by the Germans in anticipation of a paratrooper and glider landing on the field. Across the Cotentin Peninsula, the Germans flooded low-lying areas and the swollen rivers and ditches claimed scores of paratroopers who drowned, trapped by their chutes and heavy loads.

The moment was eerie, and not just because of the visual similarity to June 1944. The oddest part was that except for my wife, who sat in our car shivering from the cold and refusing to get out in the rain, there was not a soul around. Not even a car in the distance. The emptiness was a stark contrast to D-Day when this area had the highest concentration of landing paratroopers of any drop zone in Normandy. And back then there were an additional several hundred German soldiers in the immediate area.

Yet for all of the loneliness and emptiness, there was something familiar and comforting. To the north, peeking through the treetops beyond what was once the assembly area of the 2nd Battalion of the 501st Regiment, was the steeple of the thousand-year-old church of the hamlet of Angoville-au-Plain. The church was what I brought my wife to see.

We drove along the muddy roads to the church and parked and looked at its' gray, weathered stones. The weather was so awful that even a husband who is always too warm joined a wife who is always too cold in feeling miserable. This wasn't Bastogne cold, but it was one of those days when the temperature was just above freezing, it was wet and the wind blew right through you.

My wife sat in our rental car with the heater on high and her hands over the vents and shivered. But she was going to be a trooper. She wanted to see the 12th Century church after hearing me talk about how it stood in the middle of a raging battlefield, while inside two medics from the 501st Regiment manned an aid station for nearly three days straight. Those medics treated over 80 men from both sides as the town changed hands numerous times on D-Day. And she wanted to see the church pews that still remain stained by the blood of men who lay across them 65 years earlier.

I got out first, lifted the heavy latch on the metal gate of the yard in front of the church, and pushed, producing a symphony of creaks. I was the Pathfinder, and once the gate was open, I signaled to her to run from the warmth of the car and past the cemetery to the church. The tombstones in that cemetery told of a millennium of settlement; the founders of the hamlet gone a thousand years before their resting places became a pitched battlefield between hundreds of soldiers born far from Angoville-au-Plain.

I turned the massive, heavy handle on the ancient, pre-gothic church door and pushed. The door didn't budge. I turned the handle in the other direction and pushed as hard as I could. Same result. By the time that I turned to tell my wife the church was closed, she was already in full stride back to the car, the gravel of the courtyard crunching loudly as she ran for warmth.

But despite the crunching of the gravel under her boots and the whoosh of the blowing the wind, she could hear the woman's voice in the distance and stopped and looked around. I heard the sound and tried to localize it and in my peripheral vision caught the waving arm of an old woman in a window in the house across from the church. I waved back and the woman yelled something in French. I thought she said told us to wait a minute, but I wasn't sure because my French is so bad. Perhaps she was telling me the church was closed, but I was an optimist. A very cold optimist.

Soon, the woman emerged from her house, holding some papers and carrying a massive key. She shuffled across her driveway and the street, talking to us in French the whole time, waving and holding up the key. By the time she reached us, she was halfway through an elaborate greeting, gesticulating with her hands and laughing, much to our delight.

The woman arrived with a big smile, put her arm around my wife's elbow and brought her back to the church door. Although I told the woman "je ne parle pas" (I don't speak French), the woman happily continued talking in French, unlocked the massive door and pushed it open, and we entered the musty church. She handed us a booklet on the history of the church and the role it played during D-Day, and tugged on the arm of my wife, who was delighted by the kindness and the personal tour, "en Francais."

The woman gestured to a church pew to the left of the door, and I pointed out the deep, dark stains. This was one of the bloody pews. Across the bench a soldier once poured out a massive amount of blood. When I visit the church, I always wonder if the men who bled these stains lived, and if they did, if they ever returned to the aid station where they were saved.

Continuing her tour in French, the woman brought us over to a number of stained glass windows, several of which were dedicated in 2004 on the 60th anniversary of D-Day. I made out some of her words – that she was describing how Americans made the commemorative windows and they were installed in a ceremony that had the medics of D-Day as honored guests.

This special gesture of Norman hospitality is something that I am happy to say is not isolated, at least in my travels. I think it's fair to say that many Americans have negative views of the French. Some of those biases may be based in fact, especially if you have been in Paris, but my feeling is that the Parisians treat everyone badly. The paratroopers wrote of not finding the people of Normandy to be welcoming, especially when compared to the Dutch. But in general, I think that the people of Normandy are genuinely friendly and still tremendously grateful for the sacrifice of the Americans who liberated them. I wish every American could go to Normandy. They would see the immaculate American cemetery at Colleville-sur-Mer, which is maintained by French workers. They would see that the American landing beaches are still called Utah and Omaha. And they if they go to the church at Angoville-au-Plain they might meet a delightful grandmotherly woman who is proud of this treasure.

Angoville-au-Plain is only a small part of the Easy Company story in Normandy. Really, it was only a place for Easy to rest and wait for men who were misdropped to find their way in and bring the unit back to full strength. However, the story of this hamlet and what happened in the area would be a shame to overlook. I did not know from Band of Brothers or several other books that there was extensive combat in and around Angoville-au-Plain, and that there was a great deal of sacrifice and tragedy, and so when I visit Normandy, I always stop there.

I think that one of the best books on the actions in this area is "D-Day with the Screaming Eagles" by George Koskimaki. I remember wishing that if I read just a short account of the fighting around Drop Zone D, or I had the maps from that book on my first visit, I would have spent much more time there and tracked the history of the 501st Regiment and the 3rd Battalion of the 506th.

The Pathfinders and the Trap

Angoville-au-Plain isn't much more than a collection of houses and a church, and is quite easy to reach if you don't miss the turnoffs from the main road, the D913. Heading west out of the town of Vierville on the D913 for about 300 yards, look for the first left turn (to the south). That is where Colonel Sink's D-Day patrol ran into a battalion of Germans. If you miss this turn, you can get to Angoville-au-Plain by heading a few hundred feet further west on the D913 and making the next left.

When you get to the center of the hamlet, you will see the church and across the street is a memorial to the medics who ran the aid station. A few hundred feet west of the memorial (past a driveway and what looks like a small canal) is a road leading to the south. That road makes a sharp bend to the left at what was the middle of the assembly area of the 2nd Battalion of the 501st Regiment. If you keep going past the manor house and around a bend to the right, the road becomes a dirt track surrounded by empty fields and ditches. Welcome to Drop Zone D, the target for a Pathfinder drop and then the big drop of the 1st and 2nd battalions of the 501st Regiment and the 3rd Battalion of the 506th Regiment.

The men who landed on Drop Zone D had several objectives on D-Day: seize the canal locks at La Barquette (which were opened to flood the landing fields), capture the high ground near the town of Saint Côme-du-Mont, take key bridges near Brevands and destroy bridges over the Douve near Carentan that the Germans might use to attack the Americans in the Cotentin Peninsula.

The Pathfinders arrived in three planes about 45 minutes before the 100-plus C-47s carrying the men of the 501st and 506th arrived. Pathfinders were equipped with a number of signaling tools to guide the transports. Lighted panels could be placed in a "T" shape in depressions in the ground or ditches so that they were visible to pilots but not to enemy soldiers. Pilots would fly along the length of the T and drop their men at the crossbar. The panels were color coded (Drop Zone D was red) and blinked the Morse Code pattern for each letter. In addition, the Pathfinders also had "Eureka" radio beacons, which the men turned on as soon as they heard the approaching airplane motors.

The Drop Zone D Pathfinders were under the command of Captain Frank Brown of the 501st regiment, and their jump went badly, perhaps an omen of what would happen en masse 45 minutes later. Two STICs dropped their Pathfinders too soon, dispersing them over Saint Côme-du-Mont. The other plane was on target but dropped its' men right on Drop Zone D and into a trap.

The Germans expected the fields south of Angoville-au-Plain to be a landing zone and had machine guns and mortars set up in the adjacent fields. When the Pathfinders landed, the Germans attacked. Half of the Americans were captured or killed, and others were forced to hide, staying low as German flares illuminated the fields, preventing any use of the lighted signal panels.

Although the toll was terrible, the Pathfinders who weren't killed or captured did their job beautifully. Pathfinders knocked out two of three German machine guns and activated their Eureka beacons, contributing to the greatest drop concentration on any landing zone that night. Greatest did not meant perfect, though. Of the 45 planes carrying the 1st Battalion of the 501st, only 18 dropped their troopers on target.

The 501st and the 506th Arrive

On course thanks to the Pathfinders, a flotilla of C-47s roared towards Drop Zone D. Unknown to the paratroopers on board was what the Pathfinders already found out: the area around Drop Zone D was a deathtrap, and they were heading right in. As the transports reached the southern Cotentin Peninsula, heavy anti-aircraft fire opened up. At least six C-47s were shot down and dozens of others were riddled.

As the 501st and 506th paratroopers landed, the Pathfinders on the ground saw the next phase of the slaughter the Germans had prepared. Some of the paratroopers landed in the flooded ditches and drowned. Others spotted a burning house that the Germans set on fire to trick the paratroopers into thinking it was an assembly area. American troopers who showed were machine gunned up as the Pathfinders looked on helplessly.

The situation was even worse for the men on the STIC that carried Lt. Colonel Robert Wolverton, commander of the 3rd Battalion of the 506th Regiment. Many of the Pathfinders who landed on Drop Zone D dropped in the area *between* strong German positions. Some of the Pathfinders had a small chance. But Wolverton and his STIC landed on the main positions themselves. Wolverton and half of the men of his STIC were killed, and the other half were taken prisoner.

Only a few hours earlier back in England, Wolverton gathered his men before they headed for their planes. He looked at his assembled 3rd Battalion and said:

> "Men I am not a religious man and I don't know your feelings in this matter, but I am going to ask you to pray with me for the success of the mission before us. And while we pray let us get on our knees and not look down, but up with faces raised to the sky. God almighty, in a few short hours we will be in battle with the enemy. We do not join battle afraid. We do not ask favors or indulgence, but ask that if you will, use us as your instrument for the Right and an aid in returning peace to the world. We do not know or seek what our fate will be. We ask only this, that if die we must, that we die as men would die, without complaining, without pleading, and safe in the feeling that we have done our best for what we believed was right. Oh Lord! Protect our loved ones and be near us in the fire ahead and with us now as we pray to you."

The men stood in silence for two minutes, then Wolverton yelled, "move out!" Two hours later, he was dead, shot multiple times either as he descended or as he hung from his parachute harness, hopelessly caught in a tree among the Germans pouring out of their strongholds. Captured American paratrooper Joe Beyrle described seeing German guards use Wolverton's bullet-ridden body for bayonet practice

My edition of George Koskimaki's book has a picture of Bob Wolverton, posing in his full jump gear, with camouflage paint on his face, taken half an hour before he took off for Normandy. To look at the picture of a man who would die hanging from a tree in Normandy, never actually reaching the ground, is eerie. The picture is of him, ready for combat, ready to lead his men. Seeing it in the book, knowing his fate, is simply chilling. Bob Wolverton was a graduate of West Point and left behind a widow.

In general, officers paid a heavy price on Drop Zone D. By the morning, only one of the three battalion commanders was still alive. Lt. Colonel Robert Carroll, the commander of the 1st Battalion of the 501st was killed, as was Wolverton's executive officer, Major George Grant, and also Captain Van Antwerp of G Company. Major Philip Gage was wounded and captured, and captains Reed, Harwick and McKnight were captured (although Harwick later escaped).

Like the pasture at Beauzeville-au-Plain, where Lt. Thomas Meehan and the men on his C-47 were killed, this field I was looking at was telling me another story of endings. Of the deaths of dozens of men who never had a chance. Who died in their parachute harnesses or shortly after hitting the ground.

But just as the field I was looking at was a story of endings, it also told of beginnings. Near Drop Zone D were the locks at La Barquette that were jammed into the open position to allow water from the Douve River to flood the area. The locks were a key objective of the 501st. American soldiers began fighting for control of those locks, and among them was the legendary commander of the 501st Regiment, Colonel Howard "Jumpy" Johnson.

Johnson was born in 1903, the year the Wright Brothers made their first successful flight, and perhaps it was this coincidence that led him to jump out of planes. Johnson was admitted to the U.S. Naval Academy in Annapolis, but after two years there, he left to become an Army Air Corps pilot. His flying career didn't last long as he washed out of the training program due to a vision problem, but he stayed in the Army, moving from base to base in the U.S., and even to China.

When World War II broke out, Johnson was given command of the 501st Regiment, which was formed at Camp Toccoa. Johnson's 501st was known as the Geronimo Regiment, and was considered among the best of all of the parachute units in the entire Airborne. Much of their success was attributed to Johnson's ferocious and outgoing character. He had a reputation of not tolerating foul-ups in his unit and he demanded perfection. He constantly told his men that they were the best parachute regiment in the Army and he boasted constantly to others about his unit.

Johnson was known for being fearless (some would say foolish) in combat as he never sought cover from German artillery fire. While he may have been brave, and he may have been foolhardy, he was also severely hearing-impaired, and he remarked that he couldn't even hear the German firing.

Tragically, Johnson did not live to see the full story of the 501st in World War II. On October 8, 1944, Johnson went to inspect the positions of his 2nd Battalion on a dike near Heteren, Holland when a fragment from a German mortar or artillery shell tore through his abdomen. Before he died, he gave command of the 501st to Colonel Julian Ewell, telling him, "take care of my boys."

Colonel Johnson left behind a wife, a son and a daughter and was buried near Nijmegen, Holland. After World War II, Colonel Johnson's body was brought back to the U.S. and he was reburied in Arlington National Cemetery.

Back on June 6th, 1944, however, Jumpy Johnson and his men were earning their vaunted reputations by attacking larger, well-entrenched German forces around a critical objective, the lock at La Barquette.

Johnson hit the ground exactly on target by an amazing fluke. His pilot gave the green light prematurely, but because an equipment bundle was stuck in the door, Johnson was delayed in jumping. Once on the ground, he realized he was in the right place and quickly figured out that many of the men of his regiment must have jumped early because of the premature signal from his plane, and that many of them must have drowned.

He struggled to get out of his chute as a German soldier emerged from only 75 feet away and opened fire. Johnson returned fire with his Colt .45 and moved out in the darkness, quickly finding 15 soldiers, most of whom were part of Wolverton's battalion. Originally in command of nearly 2200 men, Johnson found himself on the ground with only about 150 soldiers by 0400. Nonetheless, he led the mission to take the locks himself.

Johnson set up his regimental CP near "Hell's Corner," a road junction just north of the locks and deployed his men into two groups. The first group, only 50 strong, was sent to seize the lock in a sprint across open ground. The second group, consisting of his remaining 100 troopers, deployed in a defensive perimeter around Hell's Corner.

During the course of the day, Johnson moved among the locks, Hell's Corner and the hamlet of Addeville, organizing the men and trying to redeploy the uninjured and walking wounded to positions that were in the most danger of being overrun. Attempts to seize other targets, including bridges leading to Carentan were repelled by German fire. Up and down Johnson's lines, men were engaged in fights with the Germans, and as the evening came, the paratroopers, though able to recover some equipment bundles and reinforced by stragglers, were short on ammunition and supplies. Nevertheless, they held, and unknown to them, the 4th Infantry Division was pouring inland from Utah Beach.

Colonel Ballard and the Attack on Les Droueries

Jumping ahead 63 years, I was about 1,500 yards to the north of where Colonel Johnson and his men were holding their own. I stood in the middle of where Johnson's 2nd Battalion was forming up in its assembly area between Drop Zone D and Angoville-au-Plain.

The 2nd Battalion was led by Lt. Colonel Robert Ballard, the only Drop Zone D battalion commander to survive D-Day. From this assembly area, several companies attacked westward toward German strongholds at Les Droueries, visible through the hedgerows in the distance. There are no markers in this area, and the only map I have ever seen of the fighting appeared in Koskimaki's book. The fight for Les Droueries is one of many battles that many people may not know about. In terms of size, it was much larger than the action at Brecourt Manor, but you have to dig deep to find out about it.

To people of my generation, the name Robert Ballard is probably almost always identified with the ocean explorer who found the wreck of the Titanic and the Bismarck. That Robert Ballard is not the Lt. Colonel from Florida.

Lt. Colonel Robert Ballard stood out from some of the other senior officers of the 501st, such as Johnson and Ewell, because he never attended one of the service academies. But Robert Ballard shared one thing in common with his peers: he served as the regimental commander. Ballard took command of the 501st from a seriously-injured Ewell during the Battle of the Bulge, just as Ewell took over for Johnson after he was mortally wounded during Operation Market Garden.

Ballard, like many of the men in the 101st, found himself alone on the ground when he landed during the D-Day jump. He had one advantage compared to many of the men scattered across Normandy: he figured out exactly where he was. After landing, Ballard realized immediately that he was near Saint Côme-du-Mont, and a little bit off target. He got out of his parachute harness quickly, and lay still for 10 minutes until he was sure there were no Germans around.

Ballard moved out along some hedgerows until he ran into one sergeant and then another and learned that there were many men in the vicinity, although some of them were separated by flooded fields and irrigation ditches. They could hear firing in the distance and moved to assemble the men of the battalion. The 2nd Battalion had a unique way of assembling during night drops. One paratrooper jumped with a large bronze bell, and another had a green lantern. Men oriented themselves by the sound of the bell and guided themselves by spotting the lantern, which was usually placed high off the ground so that it could be seen easily. Neither the bell nor lantern carrier was ever seen again after the jump.

By 0330 Ballard had only about 90 men of his battalion present, and two of them were about to become legends of D-Day. The only two Battalion medics present were Kenneth Moore and Bob Wright, who set up their aid station in the church at Angoville-au-Plain. Later, the force grew to about 250 as engineers, men from the battalion HQ Company and a few soldiers from other regiments filtered into the area.

Ballard's battalion had to destroy the bridges over the Douve River to prevent German reinforcements in the area of Carentan from hitting the Americans coming ashore on Utah Beach. With his 250 men, Ballard moved toward Saint Côme-du-Mont, from where he could advance to the bridges over the Douve.

In between the Battalion assembly area and Saint Côme-du-Mont is a small cluster of farmhouses and barns about 600 yards to the west called Les Droueries, which you can see from where the road from Angoville-au-Plain makes the sharp turn to the left towards Drop Zone D. The dirt road you see running to the right is one of the approaches the men took towards Les Droueries. From the entrance to the dirt road by the assembly area, you have a prime view of how the fight took place.

A group of paratroopers scouted Les Droueries, and observed Germans moving among the buildings and reported the activity to Ballard. It became clear that the attack on Saint Côme-du-Mont would have to wait. Unless Les Droueries was cleared, the 2nd Battalion ran the risk of being outflanked as it attacked Saint Côme-du-Mont. An attack plan was prepared quickly and at 0530, the order to move out was given to the two available companies, E and F.

E and F companies attacked les Droueries, but the attack bogged down quickly. By 0700, both companies had casualties and were unable to move ahead. Around 0900, Johnson radioed Ballard and ordered him to break off his attack at Les Droueries and head south through Basse Addeville to reinforce the men there and at the locks. That was impossible Ballard responded, as he now had Germans moving south of Fox Company's positions, cutting him off from Johnson's troops. Recognizing Ballard's tenuous situation, Johnson ordered him to do his best to join them to the south.

Unable to move south to join Johnson and with insufficient strength to move through Les Droueries or Saint Côme-du-Mont, Ballard realized that his attack was stalled. Just then, he heard firing coming from his rear in Angoville-au-Plain.

Kenneth Moore, Robert Wright and the Church at Angoville-au-Plain

On the morning of June 6th, Angoville-au-Plain was a battlezone that kept changing hands.

The town was secured by about 50 engineers from the 326th Battalion, who were driven out a short time later by a larger group of Germans. Those Germans were then driven out by men of the 3rd Battalion of the 506th, who were part of Bob Wolverton's force. The men of the 506th were driven out, but then men of the 501st retook the town. Throughout the day, the Germans called in 88 and mortar fire, and the Americans responded with mortar fire of their own. By some estimates, the Americans were driven out and retook Angoville-au-Plain three times, although some claim that the town changed hands even more than that.

I imagine that if the old woman who showed the church to my wife and I was in that house on D-Day, she would have been in the basement hoping that the firing would end. And I'm certain that as a young girl, she never would have been able to imagine all of the generations of Americans who would visit Angoville-au-Plain over the years.

In the midst of the chaos and danger, 501st medics Kenneth Moore and Bob Wright kept working. They treated men of both sides, and had only one rule – no weapons were allowed in the church. At one point, with pitched fighting raging around the church, three German paratroopers entered with deadly serious looks on their faces, their weapons drawn. The medics yelled at them to leave their weapons outside or to get out. Startled, they left. Another German patrol entered later, and when the Germans saw their comrades being treated, they nodded and left, so goes one of the stories.

As you enter the church you will see a large discoloration on the pew on the left. Across the aisle is another one. You are looking at a pew stained deep red from a young man's blood. Was he awake? What was he thinking of when he was lying there? Did he survive? This is the only place I know where the blood is the evidence of the war, not a crater or a bullet hole. Blood to me is the strongest evidence of how this was literally life and death.

Moore and Wright manned the aid station for nearly 72 straight hours. One of the stories I was told is that two of the soldiers treated there died and so did the small child of one of the families in town.

But nearly 80 wounded soldiers did survive, thanks to the tireless work of Moore and Wright, and their willingness to treat the men of both sides. The legacy of Moore and Wright inspired Americans and the townspeople alike 60 years later, when the residents of Angoville-au-Plain sought to restore the church where Moore and Wright performed their heroics.

In 2000, an American named Mark Patterson, who offers Normandy battlefield tours, stepped up and commissioned a stained glass window to be placed in the church (an experience that he chronicled on his website entitled, "The Angoville-au-Plain Stained Glass Project"). Patterson designed a wonderful window that I have had the fortune to see at the exact moment when sunlight shone through, illuminating all of the panels. His design included 15 red crosses, blue and white panels that represent the infantry and a bible verse. In addition, there is a Screaming Eagle logo, a pair of paratrooper jump wings and the insignia of the 501st Regiment. Patterson also honored France for its' gift of the Statue of Liberty to the United States in 1876 by representing the head of the statue. Finally, he honored the two men who ran the aid station, medics Wright and Moore. A ribbon courses along the bottom, and the men's names are embedded in it, separated by a red cross.

In an adjacent windowframe is another stained glass window, this honoring the paratroopers who landed there on D-Day. In the window is a paratrooper, flanked in the rear by two canopies and the small figures of men above the church. The dates June 6, 1944 and June 6, 2004, the 60th anniversary, are featured across the bottom of the frame.

Easy Company and Angoville-au-Plain

By June 7th, Angoville-au-Plain was secure, and that day, the men of Easy Company, which was still badly undermanned, moved in. They spent the previous night in Culoville, resting after the Day of Days and their actions at Brecourt. For the next several days, they rested up in Angoville-au-Plain and waited for Easy Company soldiers dropped all over the Cotentin Peninsula to regroup with them.

Behind the memorial to Bob Wright and Ken Moore is a fence. On the other side of the fence is the farmhouse where Colonel Sink kept his CP for several days. The property itself is private, and it's best to keep that in mind.

Easy Company and the 506th remained in this area until the order came in to attack and seize Carentan.

• • •

Carentan

Carentan is the strategic crossroads town that Band of Brothers fans know from the eponymous miniseries episode. It was attacked by multiple regiments of the 101st Division and it fell on June 12, 1944. It was the place where Dick Winters exposed himself to machine gun fire while moving his men out of ditches on either side of the road. It was the town where Albert Blithe experienced temporary blindness from fear. And it was near Carentan where the 506th fought its' first battle as an entire regiment in Bloody Gulch.

And my favorite memory of Carentan has nothing to do with World War II, and the story of it actually begins with a trip to the nearby town of Graignes.

Carentan is in the Manche "departemant" in Normandy and has a population of about 7,000. The town may have roots dating back to Ancient Greece, and is considered by some to be the ancient port town of Crociatonum. During the summer, the town is filled with tourists, and stores have flower-packed windowboxes, with open doors that allow the smells of fresh pastries and other foods to catch your nose as you walk down the street. In my case, when I walk past the boulangeries and smell the fresh bread, I salivate like Pavlov's dogs, which is exactly what the shopkeepers have in mind. Inevitably, I end up with a bag of one or two pain au chocolat (translation: "chocolate bread"). Restaurants are open late and the sun doesn't set until nearly bedtime.

But when my wife and I drove into Carentan one evening in the winter of 2007 with a car that had about a pint of gas left, we found nearly all of the shops and restaurants closed. Few people were on the street, and, more importantly, not a single gas station was in sight. Nearly 30 minutes away from our hotel, in a quiet French town, with a fuel gauge reading below empty, cold temperatures and no ability to speak the language fluently, we were both very, very concerned about what would happen. True, our fear was nothing compared to what the men must have felt on D-Day, but be that as it may, we were very nervous.

The problem was my fault to begin with. The fuel warning light came on early in the afternoon as we drove through the town of Tribehou on our way to Graignes, the site of one of the most dramatic stories of the D-Day invasion. I had seen the story on a History Channel documentary and read Marty Morgan's fantastic book, "Down to Earth," and was motivated to see the place for myself.

Only five minutes earlier, we passed through the southwestern corner of Carentan and drove by a gas station, and in the back of my mind, I thought to myself that I should stop and fill up the tank since it seemed low. But in-mid January, the sun sets early in Normandy. It was already late in the afternoon and I was determined to get us to Graignes before we ran out of daylight. We would have to get gas later, regardless of what the fuel gauge screamed at me. Fighter pilots would say I was target locked. I was so focused on seeing Graignes in the daylight that I forgot one of the most basic rules of travel in a foreign country: if you need supplies, get them when you can because you can never predict what will happen!

We drove along the D29, a road that was flanked on both sides by flooded fields. The recent January rains made the area look like the way it did on D-Day. We passed through St. Georges de Bohon, then Tribehou and saw the D57, the road to Graignes and took a left. I knew these were the areas where over 180 men belonging to the 507th Regiment of the 82nd Airborne were misdropped on D-Day, nearly 20 miles from their target. They were so far off course that Graignes was not even on their maps.

Graignes: the Alamo in the Swamp

Graignes holds a special place in my heart because it is the site of one of the most dramatic chapters of Operation Overlord, and very few people know about the battle there. The paratroopers in Graignes held off the Germans for five days before having to withdraw under withering fire from artillery, tanks and infantry. The Germans executed 20 wounded men who couldn't be evacuated and also 30 residents, including the parish priest. Then the Germans destroyed the town church, which was being used as an aid station.

The battle of Graignes began at about 1:30 AM on D-Day, when a few paratroopers of the 3rd Battalion of the 507th began appearing in the farmhouses in the area around the town. The villagers heard planes overhead, and quickly realized with the appearance of the paratroopers that an invasion was underway. By 0200, more soldiers arrived, both by parachute and by glider.

In all, about 12 planes dropped their men in the swamps around Graignes, about 20 miles away from their actual target, Amfreville. Many of the men landed in water, and a number drowned in the flooded swamp. Equipment bundles landed on dry land and in the water, and over the next several days, villagers made forays into the surrounding countryside and marshes to retrieve equipment.

The paratroopers had no idea where they were, but they saw the steeple of the 12th-Century church in Graignes and worked their way through the swamps to the hamlet. For the survivors of the fighting in Graignes, the route they took into town would later be the way they escaped to Carentan.

Among the men of the 3rd Battalion who made their way into Graignes was Corporal Benton Broussard, a French Canadian who was fluent in French. Broussard ended up at the farmhouse of the Rigault family, who continually exposed themselves to the risk of being executed by the Germans in order to help the Americans over the coming week.

Throughout D-Day, more paratroopers moved into Graignes, and the men were able to take stock. Thanks to the retrieval of equipment bundles, they were very well-supplied, including having several machine guns and 81-millimeter mortars.

Major Charles D. Johnson took command of the group, assembled the officers and asked their opinions about the situation. Johnson realized that while the men were not that far from Carentan and Ste. Mere Eglise in terms of actual distance, he felt that moving them through the swamps with enemy in the area was too risky. Johnson felt the best option was to stay put and harass any German units trying to reinforce the fighting to the north.

Captain Leroy Brummitt, the Battalion S-3, disagreed and proposed a nighttime march through the swamp, even if it meant crossing through chest-high water. Alternatively, they could skirt the coast to reach their original objective. Crossing the swamp would mean destroying their mortars and other heavy equipment that could not be carried through potentially deep water. Johnson rejected the suggestion and the beginning of the defense of Graignes was underway.

Since the Americans were undetected by the Germans, they had time to set up a tough defense, with mortars dug into the cemetery and spotters set up in the church belfry. Machine gun and rifle positions were established with interlocking fields of fire. Communications lines linked positions, and mines were placed outside the village.

As the men dug in, more paratroopers arrived, including additional soldiers from their HQ Company and about 20 men from the 501st Regiment of the 101st. Amazingly, even two men from the 29th Infantry Division who landed at Omaha Beach ended up as part of the American contingent, which numbered about 180 by the end of June 6.

The next day, the villagers of Graignes met and unanimously agreed to help and support the Americans, despite knowing that the Germans would execute them if they were caught. Colonel Johnson explained that while the soldiers were well-armed, they had insufficient food rations. The proprietress of the local grocery and café, Germaine Boursier, organized the women of the town and they prepared two meals a day. Madame Boursier even managed to visit other towns and collect food under the noses of the Germans. In some cases, the townspeople hid weapons, ammunition and other supplies in the backs of their horse-drawn wagons, using hay, feed and fertilizer as cover, and trotted past German soldiers as they made their way into Graignes. The danger was extreme, but the townspeople did not flinch from helping the Americans.

Things were quiet in Graignes until June 10th, the day the 502nd Regiment attacked Carentan to the north. When Colonel Cole and his 3rd Battalion attacked along Purple Heart Lane, the Germans moved additional units into the Carentan area. Patrols increased noticeably and the inevitable happened late in the day: a strong column of Germans approached Graignes from the north over the bridge from Port des Planques. A detachment of Americans from Graignes were in the midst of trying to blow the bridge when the Germans appeared. A small firefight erupted and the Americans waited for the bridge to be full of German soldiers when they blew it, killing many of the enemy.

A short time later, a different group of paratroopers shot up a German motorized patrol, and as they sifted through the identification papers of the dead soldiers, they found something that made them realize they were in big trouble. The Germans they killed were a reconnaissance patrol belonging to an SS armored division. After four days of relative quiet, the men realized they were about to be hit by an elite German armored division. The defenders of Graignes had no contact with any other American units and did not know if the invasion had failed or succeeded. They only knew that they were alone.

June 11, 1944 was a Sunday, and Colonel Johnson allowed some of his men to attend the 1000 mass at the town church, which was led by Father Leblastier. It would be the last mass ever held in the church and the last service performed by the Father.

As the townspeople and soldiers gathered in the church, firing was heard to the south. Soldiers ran back to the village yelling that the Germans were coming. Captain Brummitt, the man who argued for the soldiers to leave Graignes and head towards Carentan, realized that this was it: the full SS armored division was at their doorstep.

The first German unit to attack the town was a disorganized patrol that was routed by the Americans. Townspeople fled the village and were accosted by German soldiers, who made the civilians load the dead and wounded into trucks and carts.

Four hours later, the Germans hit the town with a barrage of mortar fire followed by infantry attacks on the flanks of the defensive lines. The Germans nearly broke through but were repelled with great losses. However, during the attack the Americans suffered serious casualties who were brought into the church which served as a makeshift aid station. The wounded were treated by Battalion surgeon Abraham Sophian, Jr., Father Leblastier and a Franciscan priest, Louis Lebarbanchon.

A few hours after the fighting died down, rumbling was heard outside of town. German armor was approaching Graignes and being sent towards Carentan as well. At 1900 on the 11th, Colonel Johnson told the remaining civilians in Graignes to leave town. He said that the Americans did not have enough ammunition to hold off the Germans much longer and that they would be safer outside of the area.

Shortly afterwards, American spotters in Graignes observed German forces setting up 88s south of town and the men knew that the first target would be the belfry of the church. One of the lieutenants ran to the church and yelled for the observers, Lt. Elmer Farnham and an assistant, to leave but they insisted on staying and vainly tried to direct mortar fire on the 88s. The men in the belfry were quickly killed by direct hits from the 88s. Within a few minutes, Major Johnson and 1st Lieutenant Lowell Maxwell were killed as well.

Ironically, with Johnson dead, Brummitt became commander: the man who advocated leaving was now in charge of the last stand. The end came at about 2300. Another German assault collapsed the American line and firefights broke out all over town as the paratroopers launched red flares to signal they were low on ammunition. Germans surged forward, overrunning some American positions and simply bypassing others. Defending Graignes was now impossible.

Brummitt gave the word to withdraw, but a difficult issue remained. There were over 30 wounded paratroopers in the church aid station who could not be moved. Dr. Sophian elected to stay and treat the wounded, knowing that he would be captured by the Germans along with all of the men. He did not know that he would pay for that decision with his life.

The armored unit that attacked Graignes was part of the 17th SS Panzergrenadier Division and of the 2,000 Germans who assaulted the hamlet, over 500 were killed and another 700 were wounded. The surviving Germans entered the village furious and bent on retribution. They entered the aid station and forced Sophian and 18 walking wounded outside in front of a wall. The men were separated into two groups. One group was escorted to the pond outside Madame Boursier's café and were bayoneted and shoved into the water. When the French found the bodies, all of the men were huddled together. The other group was forced to walk to the nearby village of Le Mesnil Angot and ordered to dig a pit. When completed, the SS shot each man in the back of the head and pushed his body into the pit.

A group of SS also gathered local civilians and accused them of aiding the Americans. They dragged Fathers Leblastier and Lebarbanchon behind the church and shot them to death. The church's housekeepers, including an 80-year-old woman, were shot in the rectory. Another 44 villagers were rounded up, but none would admit to helping the Americans. Amazingly, they were not executed.

When the villagers returned home the next day, they not only found their homes looted, but they also found the bodies of the two priests, burned with gasoline. The Germans also burned the church, the café, the boys' school and 66 homes to the ground and damaged another 160 houses.

But the story didn't end there. Over 20 troopers fled Graignes and sought shelter at the Rigault farm in Le Port St. Pierre. By noon, the group swelled to 80, as a large group under the command of Captain Brummitt joined them at the farm. That night, the men were taken by boat through the swamp and arrived in Carentan on the evening of June 13. Another group of paratroopers hid in the farm until the 15th, when they finally were taken by boat to Carentan.

The battle for Graignes cost the lives of over 30 American soldiers including the 19 in the church. There were also more than 30 civilian deaths from the executions and from being caught in the crossfire and shelling of the town. But the Germans suffered nearly two battalions' worth of casualties and had to divert some of their best armored infantry away from Carentan. Meanwhile in Carentan, not a single paratrooper knew of the sacrifice to the south that kept the better part of a division diverted.

Visiting Graignes

We reached Graignes with only about 30 minutes of daylight left, and as we drove towards the church, we passed a simple stone marker that said "Rue de 507[e] R.I.P. En Homage A

Nos Liberateurs" and went up a hill. At the crest, we had an incredible view of the flooded fields between the village and Carentan to the north, and the remains of the church to the right. Not a single person was in sight as we walked through the church cemetery, a pastel sunset to the west and a slight breeze occasionally blowing by.

Except for an occasional dog's bark or rooster's cock-a-doodle-doo, it was nearly silent.

A peaceful, idyllic moment on ground where brutal acts of unthinkable violence occurred. Like many other parts of Normandy, the pastoral beauty is so great, and the setting is so quiet and peaceful that it is nearly impossible to imagine the deaths of young men among the ancient hedgerows, farm pastures and beaches.

As the gravel of the cemetery crunched under my feet, I looked around at the remains of the church, thinking about how it must have felt for Captain Sophian, the surgeon who could have escaped, to wait for the arrival of the Germans. And I wondered what the wounded paratroopers expected. This was their first combat. I am sure some of them thought that there were rules of war by which the Germans would abide. I am sure that those who were more severely wounded were thinking of home. I also thought about what it must have been like for the men who were ordered to dig the pit or those who were marched to the pond.

For me, the digging of the pit is something that I wish I knew more about. Upon hearing the order, each man must have known he would die. Did he solemnly go along with it? What was he thinking about his death and about his family? Many of the men were so young that I wonder if they fully understood what was happening. I also wondered how many of them simply refused. What would go through your mind knowing the SS were going to execute you? Did they try to escape? Rush the guards?

In the church, a simple plaque memorializes the fate of 30 American men who were dropped way off target and ended up in the small hamlet by mistake: Major Charles Johnson; captains Loyal Bogart and Abraham Sophian; lieutenants Elmer Farnham, Richard Hoffman and Lowell Maxwell; sergeants Cyril McIntyre, Jean Tessier, Nelson Hornbaker, Harry Murray, Marvin Allen, George Baragona, Walter Choquette, Raymond Collabam and Kennith Gunning; corporals Jesus Casas, Reuben Lempke, Willard Lucas, James Noff, Leopold Parklom, Edward Pittis and Thomas Travers; and privates William Love, Arnold Martinez, Robert Miller, David Purcell, Lacy Reaves, Robert Rochwell, Jospeh Stachowiak and H. Weiss.

We stood in the churchyard looking over the flooded fields back towards Carentan and towards some of the lower-lying areas and dusk settled quietly around us. The areas where the men landed and walked into Graignes were in front of us and they fell into the shadows of a setting sun, and then hid, camouflaged, in the bluish light of early evening. My mind was filled with the thoughts of the execution as we got into the car and drove down the hill and made a left by the stone marker. That's when the fuel situation came back to me. I noticed the fuel light was on and the bar was at empty. And since it was a rental car, I didn't know how much gas was actually left in the tank.

Back to Carentan

For some reason, I thought that it would be better to enter Carentan from the southeast than go back the way we came, even though I saw a gas station earlier. The route that I picked looked like a major road on the map, and it was also the one that was followed by companies of the 327th Glider Regiment during the attacks on the flanks of Carentan on June 10, the day before Graignes fell. Lesson number two: never pick a new route when you know the first one has what you need.

By the time we reached the main road, it was completely dark and not a single store appeared open. We passed a closed gas station. We pressed ahead into Carentan and I kept an eye on the gas gauge, which was now below the empty line, the warning light shining brightly. Hitting Carentan, we came to an intersection with a street light and I thought it would be best to head into the center of town.

The center of Carentan has many shops, a train station, restaurants, homes and buildings but no gas station. Now the gas gauge was well below empty and I was sweating in the freezing January temperature, fearing we would run out of gas on a Sunday night, unable to speak the language and with no idea how we would get back to our hotel in Bayeux. Too worried about wasting any more gas, I parked in the center of town and approached some street workers. I didn't know the French term for gas station, but I asked in French where the Total Petrol was (Total is a brand of gas stations like Sunoco or Exxon in the US). They looked blankly at me and then at once, they all spoke in French and I didn't understand a single word. I pointed to the car and said "gasoline" and they shrugged.

I decided to go in a different direction and see if I could find a station by walking. My poor wife followed behind me, holding her coat shut while silently shivering, but not saying a word in order not to stress me out further. We got to the train station. Nothing. We walked another two blocks. Nothing. We headed back towards the car, and I was beside myself wondering what the hell was going to happen.

As we walked past a large open area that looked like a park with a parking lot, I saw the sign "Hotel de Ville" on a building at the far side. Hotel de Ville: Town Hall. I entered the building and prayed there would be an English speaker but at first I didn't find anyone at all. Walking further into the building, I entered an office, and at that moment, a distinguished gentleman in a three-piece suit came from out of the back, saw us, tugged down on the hem of his vest and approached talking in French. I explained in French that I didn't speak the language, but this time when I asked "ou est le Total Petrol du Carentan" (which was probably an insult the way I said it), the man looked at me and I knew he understood my dilemma. It was at that moment that I realized that the sign on his office door meant "Mayor." I was going to get directions to the gas station from the mayor of Carentan.

Just at that moment, though, another door opened and people poured out of a meeting room towards us. They started talking to the mayor and he evidently told them our story and they all started speaking to us in French. He commanded the audience and quieted them all down, and he did the most ingenious thing. He pointed to the street in front of the town hall, and then physically walked me as he gave directions. We went straight. Then he turned me by the shoulders, saying "une adroit" (a right turn), then he made a circular motion and said something like "rond point" (a traffic circle) then he walked me around the circle, using 90 degrees of arc and said "une adroit" (another right turn), turning my shoulders again. I repeated the directions but left out the second right and he did the whole dance with me again – forward, right, arc, right. Got it!

As we left the building, he led the crowd outside and they all waved to us. I could hear them saying things like "au revoir" and wishing us luck. It was a touching sendoff and made me feel wonderful about the people of Carentan.

We got back to the car and had a surprise in store for us. From where we parked to where the town hall was, the road workers had closed the street. We had to take another direction and I got turned around and was lost. So, I parked again, and walked my way back to the town hall and saw exactly how to drive to the traffic circle. Only one problem. Would the car make it?

We reached the traffic circle and I made the right, then made the next right and drove about 300 yards when on either side of the road, shining brightly, were two well-lit gas stations. Just beyond them was the street light that we hit when we came into town from Graignes. If we just went straight on our original course, we would have hit the gas stations right away.

In the end, our call was very close. I realized from reading the manual that our fill-up volume meant there was under a pint of gas left in the tank. Half a liter. If those gas stations were closed, or if we missed them, well, there are eight pints to a gallon, and if this car got 30 miles per gallon, that meant that we had enough gas left for four miles. And that was if the car had mileage that good.

Heading back to Bayeux, we laughed in the car and remarked how much we loved Carentan.

Purple Heart Lane

The sacrifice in Graignes alleviated some of the pressure that would have hit Easy Company when it took Carentan, an attack that was shown in the miniseries. However, for the 101st to take Carentan in the first place took an epic battle to drive out the Germans who were keeping the Americans on the other side of the Douve River. It was one of the bloodiest fights in Normandy for the 101st, and it isn't mentioned in Band of Brothers.

Easy Company had to attack Carentan because the original attack across the Douve River decimated the 502nd Regiment to the point that it could not seize the town. For two days the 502nd was devastated trying to take the fourth and final bridge across the Douve to allow other units to cross and hit Carentan. The 3rd Battalion had 65% of its men wounded, killed or missing, and one company was reduced to 12 men. In the end, to take the last bridge required the most chilling act of combat:

a bayonet charge led by the Commander of the 3rd Battalion, Lieutenant Colonel Robert Cole.

Once the Americans secured the area from Ste. Mere Eglise to Utah Beach, the next task was to link with the Omaha beachhead. That would allow one continuous front, and was vital for moving inland and breaking out into the countryside. But to link required seizing Carentan. Because of German flooding, the only way into Carentan was along a causeway from Saint Côme-du-Mont. The causeway begins just southwest of the present Dead Man's Corner Museum.

The causeway road is almost like a dike, elevated above the flooded fields by about five to ten feet, and is straight as an arrow. A soldier shooting from one end of the causeway could hit the other side, and there was virtually no cover for anyone on the road. It was a shooting gallery.

The 502nd Regiment was selected for the attack on the causeway and the original order was for the Regiment to seize all of the bridges and then take Carentan itself. The 502nd was under the command of Lt. Colonel John Michaelis, who replaced an injured Colonel George Van Horn Moseley. Michaelis kept his 1st Battalion as a reserve and decided to clear the causeway with his 3rd Battalion, which was under the command of Lt. Colonel Cole. Robert Cole was born in Fort Sam Houston, TX, on March 19, 1915, and graduated from West Point in 1939.

The 3rd Battalion had to pass over four bridges, the first just south of Dead Man's Corner, the second over the Douve River, the third over a smaller stream and the fourth over the Madeleine River. Each bridge was in full view of the Germans who were positioned on both sides of the causeway and at the end of the fourth bridge in the nearby farmhouse of the Ingouf family.

Cole's men organized before midnight on June 9th and moved out very early in the morning of June 10th. They crossed the first bridge, but they found that the second bridge was damaged and engineers could not make repairs due to German fire. A patrol led by Lieutenant Ralph Gehauf moved forward while a plan was drawn by Cole, and it made it all the way across the fourth bridge, where it found that the road was blocked by a large metal gate. The gate was large and narrow and men could pass through only in single file. After nudging their way through, the patrol members moved forward only a few feet when flares screamed into the sky and mortar and machine gun fire began coming in, especially from the Ingouf farmhouse.

Cole thought covering fire from the 65th Armored Field Artillery and its 105-mm guns, and the 907th Glider Field Artillery Battalion and its 75-mm pieces, could allow the engineers to repair the second bridge, but by noon they were still unsuccessful. Cole improvised and he and several men set planking across the wrecked bridge, and the Battalion moved in single-file over the river. German artillery fire hit around the men, but no casualties were reported. It took three hours for the last man to cross the plank bridge, by which time the leading elements of the Battalion were over the third bridge.

As the scouts crossed the third bridge, the Germans opened fire from around the Ingouf farmhouse. Soldiers tried to move forward, or dive into narrow ditches, but a German machine gun began hitting them and they crawled back to the third bridge. The 3rd Battalion was exposed in a long, thin column, and any attempts to charge would result in significant casualties as soon as the men stood, but they were receiving fire from the sides and there was nowhere to hide. Cole ordered an artillery strike and the covering fire allowed the Battalion to get across the last bridges and penetrate through the gate.

But again the attack bogged down, even though the bulk of 3rd Battalion was across the last bridge. Serious casualties were inflicted by German artillery, mortar, machine gun and rifle fire, as well as strafing runs. At about 0400 on June 11, Cole received orders to continue his attack, meaning his men were in continuous action with little sleep or food for over 28 hours. The Battalion now had all of its units forward and pressed against the Ingouf farmhouse, but the Germans repelled the paratroopers with significant fire.

An artillery barrage was called in right on the farmhouse, but despite the heavy caliber of the American weapons, the effect on the Germans was negligible. Cole felt the situation was desperate and that 3rd Battalion had no other option: the survivors had to fix bayonets and charge the stubborn Germans. Artillery fire pounded the German positions until 0615, when smoke rounds hit around the farmhouse to conceal the movements of the paratroopers.

With the smoke filling the air, Cole rose up, pistol in hand, and blew his whistle signaling the charge. However, many soldiers did not hear the order to charge because they were scattered. There are estimates that of the 250 men left in 3rd Battalion, only about 75 to 100 actually heard the order and charged.

As men ran towards the farmhouse, Private Edward Sowder of I Company was hit in the head with a mortal wound. Before he died, he passed his bayoneted rifle to Cole who continued ahead. Some controversy exists about whether Sowder actually passed his M-1 Garand to Cole or whether the Colonel picked up the weapon from the falling man, but in either case, it is documented that Cole ran forward with the Private's rifle.

Finally, 3rd Battalion took the farmhouse but it was so badly wrecked that taking Carentan was out of the question. Cole sent word back to have Colonel Pat Cassidy bring up his 1st Battalion. Cassidy's men took positions around the Ingouf farmhouse shortly before the Germans counterattacked. The Germans hit the Americans from the south and the southwest, with both thrusts coming through an orchard next to the farm.

The American lines held, and machine gun fire repelled the Germans. The Americans took advantage of a lull in the fighting to strengthen their lines. C Company of the 1st Battalion moved towards Carentan and dug into an area known as the Cabbage Patch. The marker that is there today is only a short distance from the gas station that saved my wife and me from our near-disaster in Carentan.

During this lull, the assistant commander of the 101st, General Tony McAuliffe, wanted to retrieve the wounded and directed his regimental surgeon, Major Douglas Davidson, to meet the German commander in Carentan and ask for a temporary cease-fire. McAuliffe replaced Don Pratt, who was killed in a glider crash on D-Day. The request for the cease-fire was misunderstood by some of the men of the 502nd. They thought that the Germans asked the Americans for a truce.

McAuliffe ordered all American units to cease fire until Davidson returned. Davidson was escorted by German soldiers into Carentan, but the Nazi commander refused to meet him and sent the doctor back to the American lines. As Davidson reached the 502nd positions near the Cabbage Path and Ingouf farmhouse, the Germans hit the American positions with the most intense barrage they had yet received. Artillery, mortars, machine guns and rifles blasted away at the American positions.

Despite McAuliffe's orders to hold fire, the 502nd roared into action. Regimental spotters observed that while Davidson was in Carentan, the Germans moved up men and equipment and appeared to be strengthening their lines for a counter-attack. That attack came from a number of directions, and with the artillery and mortar strikes, the American lines nearly buckled. The Germans were so close that the paratroopers could hear the enemy talking and working on rifle bolts.

The 502nd repelled the attack and fighting was especially fierce in the Cabbage Patch. Nonetheless, by 1830 on

June 11, Cole thought that his battered units would wilt under the pressure of another strong German attack. He called in a massive artillery strike that involved every gun in the area. After a walloping five minute barrage, the Germans were heard fleeing from the area around the 502nd. The artillery fire came so close to the American lines that two paratroopers were killed by friendly fire.

Finally, by the night of June 11, 1944, the 502nd Regiment secured the way into Carentan, in large part due to the sacrifice of the 3rd Battalion and the leadership of its CO. Cole had 400 men in his 3rd Battalion under his command when he began his attack. Only 132 were left on June 11.

Lieutenant Colonel Robert Cole was recommended for the Congressional Medal of Honor for his actions on Purple Heart Lane, but he did not live to receive the decoration. On September 18, 1944, the 29-year-old Cole was in Holland trying to take yet another bridge, when he was killed by a sniper. His Medal of Honor was awarded posthumously to his mother, Mrs. Clara H. Cole, who received it along with Cole's wife and two-year old son. Robert Cole is buried in the American Battlefields Monuments Commission Cemetery in the Netherlands.

The Congressional Medal of Honor awarded to Robert Cole has the following citation:

> "For gallantry and intrepidity at the risk of his own life, above and beyond the call of duty on 11 June 1944, in France. Lt. Col. Cole was personally leading his battalion in forcing the last 4 bridges on the road to Carentan when his entire unit was suddenly pinned to the ground by intense and withering enemy rifle, machine gun, mortar, and artillery fire placed upon them from well-prepared and heavily fortified positions within 150 yards of the foremost elements. After the devastating and unceasing enemy fire had for over 1 hour prevented any move and inflicted numerous casualties, Lt. Col. Cole,

observing this almost hopeless situation, courageously issued orders to assault the enemy positions with fixed bayonets. With utter disregard for his own safety and completely ignoring the enemy fire, he rose to his feet in front of his battalion and with drawn pistol shouted to his men to follow him in the assault. Catching up a fallen man's rifle and bayonet, he charged on and led the remnants of his battalion across the bullet-swept open ground and into the enemy position. His heroic and valiant action in so inspiring his men resulted in the complete establishment of our bridgehead across the Douve River. The cool fearlessness, personal bravery, and outstanding leadership displayed by Lt. Col. Cole reflect great credit upon himself and are worthy of the highest praise in the military service."

Despite all that sacrifice and heroism, there is, unfortunately, little left of the battle of Purple Heart Lane to see today. The road Cole's men crossed is the current D913 and there is a bridge over the Madaleine, but instead of the Ingouf farmhouse and orchard, there is a traffic circle. And heading down the Route de Saint Come, instead of the Cabbage Patch, there is a small monument on the west side of the road in front of industrial buildings and across from a new car dealership.

Finally, on the night of June 11, after about 48 hours of action, the 3rd and 1st battalions were relieved. With the 502nd shot to pieces and unable to take Carentan, the order was given for the 506th to seize the town.

Easy Company's Attack on Carentan

The attack on Carentan was a tale of two platoons, and the miniseries focused on the one led by Dick Winters. The 2nd Battalion of the 506th attacked Carentan on June 12 from the hamlet of La Billonerie, moving northeastward along the current D971 (it was the N171 at the time). Easy Company deployed with First Platoon led by Winters moving up a road called the Route d'Auvers, while another group, led by Buck Compton, conducted a flanking movement. Compton wrote in his book that while they saw signs of fighting, there was no action as they entered town and it appeared that the Germans withdrew from Carentan, or at least that sector.

For Winters' group, the story was different. As you move along the Route d'Auvers, you come down a hill where the road ends in a T-intersection (actually more of a Y-intersection) with Rue Holgate. There at the intersection, facing you, is a house where the Germans had a machine gun that fired on Winters' platoon coming down the road. A squad moved forward into town, and as the rest of the platoon advanced, machine gun fire erupted. The men dove into ditches on either side of the road and refused to move.

All of the men, that is, except for Dick Winters. The miniseries accurately portrayed how Winters yelled at the men to get out of the ditches while he was exposed to enemy fire, with machine gun bullets popping in the dirt around his legs. Winters screamed at the men, and to their astonishment, he even cursed, which was very rare. Finally, he resorted to grabbing men and throwing them out of the ditches.

At the intersection of the Route d'Auvers and Rue Holgate, you can look back along the road and wonder, like I do, how Winters was not hit. I have never read anything about whether it even occurred to Winters that he was in danger of getting hit. He led from the front and I doubt he thought about anything other than completion of his mission and getting his men to move up. His leadership from the front is one of those remarkable things that led me to go to Ephrata and Lancaster.

Bloody Gulch

Another prominent fight depicted in the miniseries episode, "Carentan," was the battle of Bloody Gulch. The 506th took Carentan with a number of casualties, but it appeared that the Germans pulled out of town leaving only a rearguard to harass the oncoming paratroopers. After the seizure of Carentan, the American command expected that the Germans would counterattack, because with Carentan in Allied hands, Omaha and Utah beaches could be linked.

With a German attack expected, the 506th was deployed to high ground west of Carentan near the hamlet of Douville. The 501st regiment was moved south of Carentan about a mile (about 500 yards past La Billonerie, where Easy began its initial push into Carentan), and the 327th guarded the east and southeast in an arc that included Montmartin-en-Graignes.

For the first time in combat, the entire 506th Regiment deployed as a single unit. All nine companies were abreast in a north-south line, with the HQ Company behind them a few hundred yards. Easy itself was dug in on the far right flank, near a railroad line. To the north of the railroad, the fields were flooded. The trap the Germans originally set for the Americans now worked against them. German armor had to funnel itself through a limited number of roads and through Bloody Gulch.

I know a lot of Band of Brothers fans who are interested in the Battle of Bloody Gulch. Personally, I don't feel very excited about the fight there, though perhaps that will change. For those who know only the miniseries, Easy Company is depicted as holding the line while other companies fled in panic, which simply wasn't true. During the battle, German armor hit D and F companies very hard. The two companies had only bazookas and mortars to stop heavy tanks and they were forced to pull back a few hundred feet, where they then reorganized and advanced back to their original positions. I am bothered that the producers of the miniseries felt it added something to suggest that Easy fought hard and stayed calm while other units bolted. And so Bloody Gulch has a sour connotation because of the embellishment.

Another reason why I am not so passionate about Bloody Gulch is that while researching the site of the Gulch, I came across people who wanted to keep the location to themselves. My feeling about the history of the Airborne is that it's for all to share, and that we should encourage everyone to learn as much as is possible. It honors the men who fought there. I've always been willing to give directions, share historical notes and other items with people who ask.

One person I met online would not share any information on Bloody Gulch because he said he offered tours of the area and did not want to give away what he called his secret spot. Another person, who originally reached out to me through Flickr, told me that he would take me there, but he was reluctant to give me directions because he did not want to see a lot of tourists. I was left with a bad taste in my mouth. Perhaps over time, I will take more interest in Bloody Gulch, but not just yet.

Reaching Bloody Gulch is a little bit tricky, but with a little patience, you can find it. One way is to head out of Carentan on the Route des Auvers, the road that Winters and First Platoon took on their attack. The road becomes the D223 and heads in the direction of Baupte and Cantepie. About 1000 to 1500 yards west of Carentan, you will come across an orchard on the right side of the road, followed by a farmhouse. There is an unmarked dirt road a few hundred feet past the farmhouse. Take the turn and follow the road to the north. Eventually, the dirt road will pass underneath a bridge. That bridge is the remains of the old rail line, which anchored Easy Company's right flank. An alternative way to get there is to take a right from the Route des Auvers onto the D971 and then a left at the traffic circle. When the road ends, bear right.

The Next Campaign

The 506th jumped into Normandy on D-Day with about 2,000 men. When it finally returned to England in July, over

200 were dead, 185 were missing or captured and there were 500 to 600 wounded. But the mission was successful: the Americans breached the Continent and were racing towards Paris and beyond. As other Army units joined the fight, Easy Company and the rest of the Regiment returned to England to recover and prepare for their next assignment.

After a number of aborted missions, orders were given for a daylight drop into Holland. The 101st Airborne was about to become part of Operation Market-Garden. Holland would prove to be a frustrating experience for Easy Company and the Americans. They fought well, but Market-Garden failed to produce an Allied victory by Christmas.

Perhaps there was karma because Holland was very frustrating for me as well. Like the Allies, I was plagued by bad weather, including a lot of raw, windy rain. The Americans did not encounter what they expected in Holland. They were told to expect to fight old men and boys and that they might be able to end the War by Christmas. Instead they ran into crack German armor and infantry. Holland wasn't what I expected either. I thought I would find an element of preservation like I saw in Normandy or Bastogne. Instead, I was frustrated by destroyed battlefields, traffic, overcrowding and overdevelopment.

And I also found that in Holland, the image I had of Easy Company as the best unit in the Army took a beating. It was humbling to learn that Easy was simply one of many very talented and heroic units in the American Army, and that other companies and divisions faced much worse scenarios in Holland. Not knowing about other units other than Easy Company was the worst part of Holland for me. And to set things straight, I had to tell the story of Holland by focusing on units other than Easy Company, even though my book was about Band of Brothers.

• • •

III
Holland

An Uncomfortable Feeling

Easy Company spent ten weeks in Holland, the longest deployment of the unit in any theater during the War. They landed in the town of Son (Zon), liberated Eindhoven, were caught in a German armored ambush and counterattack in Nuenen, endured one of their worst artillery barrages of the war in Veghel and defended the soggy, cold Island. Their deployment lasted from September 17 to November 25. There are many towns where they fought, and many places were terrible casualties were suffered, as well as a few places, such as The Crossroads, where fantastic victories were achieved.

Surprising to me is that despite all of the combat history of Easy Company in Holland, I have had a hard time being very enthusiastic about its' experience there. If someone handed me a plane ticket to Normandy or Bastogne or Austria, I'd go in a second. But if they handed me a plane ticket to Amsterdam, I would probably hesitate to think about going to the Netherlands on a whim.

There's something about Holland just doesn't feel right. Every once in a while, my wife will tell me that I'm projecting my feelings onto her, and I suppose that on occasion, but not often, she's right. So I may not be objective when I say that I feel that both the book and the miniseries lost steam when they hit Holland. I think it's especially the case if you compare the Holland episodes to those about D-Day, Bastogne or the concentration camp. It almost feels to me that in the book and miniseries, Holland is what happened after Normandy and before Bastogne.

I don't think it's the fact that Operation Market-Garden went badly that has me feeling that way about how Band of Brothers treats Holland. It seems to me that most of the miniseries focuses on Nuenen and at the Crossroads. While the book covers more than just two battles in a ten-week period, it takes reading other books to find out how violent and intense things really were in Holland.

Veghel is a good example of what I mean. Several Easy veterans said that the worst shelling they ever endured came not in the Bois Jacques, but in the town of Veghel on September 23, 1944. David Webster wrote a stomach-turning letter home about being in an apple orchard in Veghel as German shells bracketed foxholes before finally finding the men seeking shelter inside them. About digging foxholes desperately quickly under intense 88 fire. Webster's book will make you sweat, yet the book Band of Brothers mentions Veghel only briefly, and the miniseries omits the attack completely.

Alternatively, read Don Burgett's chilling account of his unit being hit by artillery fire near Son or Opheusden, or George Koskimaki's documentation of the constant and intense fighting experienced by the 101st throughout Holland. I think that you might get the same feeling that I had that Holland is a lull in Band of Brothers.

There is something else that contributes to my discomfort with Holland: Holland itself. Now my sour attitude is not at all based on any negative personal interactions with any of the Dutch; they are wonderful people and good hosts. But I don't think I've recovered from the shock of finding the whole country overdeveloped. Unlike Toccoa, Normandy and Bastogne, which are largely preserved, the small Dutch towns and fields where American paratroopers fought and died are disappearing rapidly and being covered by homes, parking lots, stores, roads and factories. And more development is planned and more battlefields will disappear.

In some cases, I feel like visiting Holland is like going to the southern tip of Manhattan to Fraunces Tavern, where George Washington gave his farewell address to his men after the Revolutionary War. You can visit the Tavern, and I've even had dinner there. But despite the rich history, it's impossible to picture what that part of Manhattan was like during the late 18th Century. The fragment of the American Revolution is lost in a maze of skyscrapers, Starbucks shops, concrete and dense traffic.

The city of Eindhoven is unrecognizable today compared to when Easy Company and the 506th Regiment liberated it in 1944 when the population was 100,000. Now, the greater metropolitan area is close to 800,000 and what were once towns past the outskirts, such as Nuenen, are now more or less suburban neighborhoods.

The church at Uden, where Dick Winters watched the Second Battalion, including most of Easy Company, get shelled in nearby Veghel is there, but so are hundreds of new homes. Hell's Highway, the vital road that was secured with great loss of life so that British armor could race northeast to support the British in Arnhem, is gone in many spots.

Given the reverence I have for places where Americans fought and died, I was simply unnerved a lot of the time I spent in Holland. That it rained every day I was there only made my discomfort stronger.

So Band of Brothers seeming to lose momentum and the overdevelopment are two big reasons why I feel uncomfortable in Holland.

But there is also another big reason and this one is self-inflicted, like being careless with a loaded weapon. It is in Holland where I really learned how wrong I was in my initial view that Easy Company (and the 506th) was the toughest, most noteworthy unit in the American Army. My visit to Holland was like a punch in the face or at least a swat in the ass with a gigantic history book.

I visited Arnhem, and saw the John Frost Bridge, better known as "The Bridge Too Far." I saw the Hartenstein, the iconic building that served as the British paratrooper headquarters (it was instantly recognizable from the movie). I saw the house where Major-General Robert Urquhart (portrayed by Sean Connery) hid in an attic to escape German patrols near the Hospital. I saw the Ter Horst house, which was immortalized in the movie as the makeshift aid station where a Dutch woman and her father treated over 300 wounded British paratroopers.

I saw an exhibit at the Arnhem museum next to the Frost Bridge that showed how the block-to-block fighting in the area took place and how the Polish paratroopers, led by Major General Stanislaw Sosabowski (who was portrayed in the movie by Gene Hackman) dropped into a German trap near Driel. Sosabowski had misgivings about the British plan of attack, but he led his men in anyway, only to be repaid by the British who made him a scapegoat for the failure of the paratroop landings. And when I visited, I couldn't believe how small the area was where the British and Polish landed and fought to the end. It was simply shocking.

I visited these and other areas, and could not believe the price of Montgomery's arrogance. Of the 10,300 men of the 1st British Airborne Division and the 1st Polish Parachute Brigade, only 2,500 made it out of Arnhem. At least 1,300 were killed, and another 6,500 were taken prisoner.

Compared to what happened to the British and Polish paratroopers during Operation Market Garden, the story of Easy Company is a lot less singularly important. That's no knock against Easy Company, but really against me for being narrow-minded.

And if I was uncomfortable being slapped in the face with my lack of appreciation for the British and Poles, I was downright embarrassed when I learned about the fighting that involved the 82nd Airborne in Holland.

So I am confessing my arrogance and my ignorance. Other than saying a couple of novenas, which would not work since I'm Jewish, I thought that the best penance I could offer was from an inspiration I received after being in the field in Holland, and it starts with the story of my first visit there.

A Real Education

On my first trip to Holland I arrived in a largely oblivious state. I got there at dusk after spending two days in the Ardennes, and really didn't spend any time in advance learning much about Nijmegen, where I would spend my first night in Holland. In fact, most of the preparation I did was getting a tour guide and reserving a room at the Best Western Belvoir. I think I probably spent more time worrying about finding the hotel than the history of the surrounding area.

When I finally got to the hotel, I was pleased that I got lost only once, given that I had no city map and no GPS. I wanted to celebrate my travels with a beer and a good meal since I was starved after spending a long day in the field in Belgium. I walked through the hotel lobby to the restaurant and saw a sign that said "Closed. Private Group." I was disgruntled. Couldn't I get a meal or a drink? The kitchen was obviously open. So was the bar. After all, there was a long table with a large number of people including some older gentlemen and whom I guessed were their wives. Some waiter was telling me no?

Then I looked closely and saw that the gentlemen were wearing caps with the insignia of the 504th Regiment. It then struck me that the date was September 16, the anniversary of the eve of Operation Market-Garden. The waiter looked at me and said "the restaurant is closed for their dinner. These people have been coming here for many years." And upon seeing these veterans, my heart filled with pride and gratitude and I quietly walked down the street to a nearby restaurant.

Approaching Holland

After returning home, I thought about what I learned on my trip, including seeing the 504th veterans and the site where they fought one of the most heroic battles of World War II. I felt that one of the ways I could make amends for my earlier ignorance about the role of the 82nd was to dedicate part of this book to the fighting of the All-American Division in Nijmegen.

I thought about those men who keep coming back to Holland from the US. And I also thought about 13 men of the 504th Regiment who stayed in Holland permanently: Private Anthony Bei, First Lieutenant Harry Busby, Private Peter Colishion, Sergeant Wilford Dixon, Private Francis Downs, Private Thadeus Gondela, Private Raymond Grummer, Private John Mullen, Private Walter Muszynski, Private John Rigapolous, Private Jack Seitinger, Private Robert Washko and Private Robert Wilson.

Those young men died during an amphibious assault known as the Waal River Crossing and are buried at the American Cemetery in Margraten which is located east of the Dutch city of Maastricht. The cemetery is not far from a hilly forested area known as the Ardennes.

And rather than complain about what parts of Easy Company's legacy in Holland are buried under concrete, I chose something more positive and inspirational. I decided to write about specific sites that still look a lot like they did back in 1944.

• • •

The 82nd Airborne in Nijmegen

I Learn About the 82nd Airborne

Frank, my tourguide, and I stood in the drizzle and fog and looked across a grassy flood plain at the gray, cold water of the Waal River near the Nijmegen Highway Bridge. The mood was appropriately solemn for viewing the site of a suicide mission called the Waal River Crossing, and we stood on the spot of a memorial to commemorate the event.

On September 20th, 1944, the 82nd Airborne's 504th Regiment and Company C of the 307th Airborne Engineer Battalion made a broad-daylight amphibious assault under the full view of German guns. Half of the men who crossed in the first wave towards the spot where I stood were killed, wounded or missing. Before they began their mission, many of those men in the first wave, upon seeing their task, handed their valuables to others on shore, certain they would never return alive.

Like the story of Graignes, I never heard about the Waal River Crossing when I was focused solely on Easy Company and the Band of Brothers. Just an hour before seeing the site of the Crossing, I was in a rush for Frank to take me to the Crossroads and other places in Holland that I learned about from Band of Brothers. Then, as I stood in the rain by the river, I became ashamed of myself for not knowing about the Crossing. I was mad that I was so naïve as to think that, basically, Easy Company won the war single-handedly.

So the discomfort I feel about Holland is without a doubt partly caused by the sheer guilt of not being aware of the sacrifices of thousands of other men who fought there.

The memorial was built on the dike on the north shore of the Waal River about two-thirds of a mile west of the Nijmegen Highway Bridge on the spot that the 504th had to seize. There were Germans in the area around the memorial and they had to be eliminated in order to allow the 505th Regiment to seize the southern end of the Bridge and so that British armor could take the span. And the Bridge had to be taken quickly in order to save the British and Polish paratroopers in Arnhem who were by that time in desperate straits.

Behind us to the west was a stand of trees where the SS had an artillery and mortar position. From where we stood, German infantry, machine guns and antiaircraft guns poured fire into the completely exposed Americans. It seemed like Omaha Beach, but even worse in a way. On Omaha Beach, there were a lot of targets. But in Nijmegen, the 504th was the only group crossing the river and every German could concentrate their fire. Plus, when the survivors finally got out of the boats, they had to run across a wide flood plain, still exposed to fire.

The memorial offers testimony to what happened. Two stone obelisks flank a plaque with the names of 48 dead Americans. It chilled me to look at the battlefield and the memorial and think about what happened.

Then as I looked back across the Waal River, Frank stunned me with a short sentence: "take a good look because this will all be gone in a few years."

This historic spot, like much of the Netherlands, will be sacrificed to development to accommodate the growing population of the country. The men who crossed this river did so to protect the Nijmegen Highway Bridge. Now, 70 years later, the very place of their sacrifice will be altered forever by the construction of a new bridge.

The 82nd Airborne Drops into Holland

North of Groesbeek are about the only woods and farmland that I saw in the entire Nijmegen metropolitan area. After driving through the expanding sprawl of neighborhoods and seeing nothing but traffic, I was amazed to see that the fields where General Gavin and the 82nd Airborne dropped into Holland were still there.

Just as I felt bad realizing that I never heard of the Waal River Crossing, I also thought that I really should have done a better job of appreciating the role of the 82nd Division in World War II. In Normandy, Easy Company went into action for the first time and I was certainly drawn into its' story. But I had no clue that by the time of D-Day, many of the men of the 82nd had already jumped into Sicily and Italy. It shocked me to learn that D-Day was the third combat operation for some men of the 82nd, whereas it was the first test for the 101st. It's a different perspective than what you get in Band of Brothers.

In Normandy, Ste. Mere-Eglise and the bridges over the Merderet were the sites of epic fighting involving the 82nd. In the story of the Battle of the Bulge, one reads about the 101st in Bastogne, but the popular stories do not talk much about the brutal offensive operations of the 82nd in the northern sector of the Ardennes. It was there that a Private Martin of the 325th Glider Regiment had one of the best quotes of the war. After asking a retreating tank destroyer crewman if he was looking for a safe location, he said: "Well buddy just pull that vehicle behind me. I am the 82d Airborne and this is as far as the bastards are going." But I guess "NUTS!" was shorter and sweeter.

Guilt. Stupidity. You name it, I felt it.

Groesbeek was where most of the All-Americans came down, and as was my luck, like everywhere else in Holland, the drop zone was soggy from never-ending rain. Frank took me to the exact field where Gavin landed, on the site of a former German airstrip. Across from the field was a large house that had concrete dummy bombs that the Germans used for target practice as part of their fencing. I would have loved to walk the fields, but on that day, a stroll would have meant seeing how wet I could get my socks.

On September 17, 1944, 10 units of the 82nd flew aboard 482 C-47s and 50 gliders that left from airfields in the area of

Grantham, UK between 0950 and 1040. Aboard those transports were the HQ and HQ Company of the 82nd, the HQ and HQ Battery of the Division artillery, the Signal Company, Battery A of the 80th AA Battalion, the 307th Engineers, the 504th PIR, the 505th PIR, the 508th PIR, the 325th Glider Infantry and the 376th Parachute Field Artillery Battalion.

To see the drop zone in Groesbeek, drive to the north-northeast on the Wylerbaan. Approximately a mile-and-a-half north of town, the Wylerbaan is intersected by an east-west road called Derdebaan. At that intersection is a memorial to the 508th PIR landings. The fields and farmland just east of the Wylerbaan are where the 508th landed by parachute and glider. To the south of the drop zone is where the 505th was supposed to land (across from the National Liberation Museum).

The 82nd Moves Out

A Division report called the parachute drop into Holland the best in its history. The jump went smoothly, thanks to the work of Pathfinders who arrived ten minutes before the air fleet, as well as clear weather and only mild German flak. All of the units landed between 1250 and 1400, and generally came down where they expected to, except for two battalions of the 505th, which because of a mix-up in the marshalling area, ended up about a mile off target. A big difference compared to the chaos of D-Day. Men gathered in full-strength units very quickly and moved out to their objectives.

The HQ units established a division CP about 1000 yards west of Groesbeek by 1700. The 505th seized the town itself, linked up with the 504th at the Maas-Waal Canal Bridge in Heumen and had all 11 of its' objectives accomplished by 2000. The 504th landed on three drop zones around the Maas River near the Maas-Waal Canal. A battalion landed northeast of the town of Overasselt and encountered strong enemy resistance, which it ultimately overcame, and captured the Maas-Waal

Canal Bridge at Heumen intact. By 1930, all of the initial objectives of the 504th were achieved. The 508th landed successfully north of Groesbeek and met up with the Dutch Resistance shortly afterwards. A textbook operation until that point.

The 508th was told by the Underground that Nijmegen was lightly defended, so the Regiment moved out to seize the Waal River bridges there. Several books I read complimented the Dutch Underground for providing critical intelligence to the Allies upon their arrival. In the case of Nijmegen though, the intelligence couldn't have been more wrong. Just south of the Nijmegen bridge, the Germans had an 88-millimeter artillery piece on a 360-degree swivel that could fire straight down every street. Near the gun, at least one tank provided supporting fire and the Germans also had machine gun nests throughout the area.

The 508th Regiment advanced from the east, and as it neared the south ramp of the Bridge, resistance increased. By 2000, the Americans were engaged in house-to-house fighting in the adjacent neighborhood. Sniper and machine gun fire held up the Americans, the 88 fired down each street and the tank blasted away. Securing the Nijmegen Highway Bridge couldn't be accomplished quickly. The Underground had not gotten this one right. And in Arnhem, the British paratroopers waited for help.

I found an official report that suggests that September 18, 1944 was generally a quiet day for the 82nd Division. The 504th and 505th largely held their positions and conducted patrols. The 508th redeployed a battalion from Nijmegen to clear glider landing zones northeast and east of Groesbeek, and captured a large number of Germans, as well as 16 antiaircraft guns. In mid-morning, 450 gliders landed, bringing anti-tank and additional airborne artillery units, and shortly after that, 135 B-24s dropped supplies down to the men, who recovered approximately 80% of the materiel.

On September 19, 1944, British armored units finally linked with the 82nd allowing for offensive operations towards Arnhem. The 2nd Battalion of the 505th was attached to the Guards Armored Division and the combined force moved into Nijmegen to try to seize the highway and railroad bridges across the Waal. The fight wouldn't be easy for this very experienced Battalion, which had already made three combat drops (Sicily, Italy and Normandy) before Operation Market Garden.

The 505th launched a two-pronged attack. After moving from their positions near the Sionhof Hotel in Nijmegen, the companies of the 505th split into two forces (western and eastern). The western force included several British tanks and moved towards the Nijmegen Railway Bridge. As that group neared the railroad yards, a Dutch civilian caught the attention of a British officer with an incredible surprise: a British airman who was shot down near Nijmegen and who lived in a hidden room under a floor in her home.

On September 19, 1944, Easy Company of Band of Brothers fame was in a defensive position near Eindhoven before it moved towards the town of Nuenen. A vicious German counterattack pushed Easy back in a fight that was captured in the miniseries vividly (including Denver "Bull" Randleman getting trapped behind enemy lines).

But that same day, well to the north of Nuenen, a different Easy Company was locked in its own savage fight against elite German infantry, snipers, tanks and artillery. E and F companies of the 505th Regiment of the 82nd Airborne were pushing their way into Nijmegen to take the Highway Bridge. The two companies were joined by three tanks of the 2nd Guards and three platoons of tanks from the 1st Guards. This task force comprised the eastern force in the Regiment's attack through Nijmegen.

The column moved out at about 1345, heading towards the Bridge from the area of the present-day Hotel Belvoir Best

Western on Graadt van Roggenstraat, which is where I stayed. Some of the brick townhouses in the area still bear the signs of combat. As E Company moved up the street, the German 88 swiveled around and fired into the first British tank, setting it on fire. Within moments, a second British tank was destroyed, and shortly after that, a third tank was in full retreat after taking a round through the turret that miraculously did not kill anyone inside. Three hours into the attack on Nijmegen, Easy Company of the 505th Regiment was fighting for its' life.

The 1st platoon of E Company cleared the remaining houses at the end of Graadt von Roggenstraat in order to get a clear shot at the Germans manning the 88. From one of the windows, the paratroopers saw Germans setting up another anti-tank gun and more enemy soldiers came across the Bridge on foot and on bicycles. The Germans knew Allied units were in the area because they knocked out the British tanks. However, the Germans didn't know Americans infiltrated the houses in the area.

The plan of the 505th was to get into position undetected and to then spring an ambush. Dozens of German soldiers moved back and forth in full view of American machine guns and rifles, and it was difficult for the non-coms to keep their squads from opening fire before the trap could be set.

As one story goes, a British artillery spotter moved up to join the Americans and when he saw the Germans in the open he panicked and opened fire with his rifle. The element of surprise gone, all hell broke loose as American and Germans poured everything they had into each other from point-blank range. The Americans knocked out one antitank gun, but a second hit the building at the end of Graadt Von Roggenstraat, killing one man and wounding another. Two British tanks rushed forward but they were knocked out instantly. The situation went from bad to worse in a hurry.

The 2nd Battalion commander, Lieutenant Colonel Benjamin Vandervoort, devised a new plan. Vandervoort had a unique distinction among all paratroopers: he was portrayed by John Wayne in the movie, "The Longest Day." Without a doubt, the Duke doesn't play you unless you were one hell of a soldier.

What earns a soldier the honor of being portrayed by John Wayne? I had this image that it would basically take landing single-handedly on Omaha Beach with just a combat knife and killing a battalion of German defenders, or parachuting into Berlin and strangling Hitler in his bed, or shooting down half the Luftwaffe with one plane. But surprisingly, Vandervoort wasn't Superman.

Benjamin Hayes Vandervoort was born in Gasport, NY, not far from Lake Erie, on March 3, 1917. If you look closely at his birth date, it will seem kind of strange that John Wayne portrayed "Vandy" Vandervoort. Wayne was 10 years older than was Vandy, and "The Longest Day" was filmed in 1962, when The Duke was 55 years old. Personally, I don't care!

Vandervoort served in the infantry and was an original member of the 505th Regiment when the 82nd Airborne Division was created. He was the S-3 of the Regiment when it dropped into Sicily during Operation Husky, and was promoted to Lieutenant Colonel and given command of the 2nd Battalion on June 2, 1944.

On D-Day, Vandervoort famously broke his ankle when he dropped near Ste. Mere Eglise but despite the injury, he still led the Regiment. He was admired by his men and had a reputation for getting difficult missions done with a minimum of casualties. General Matt Ridgway described Vandervoort as one of the bravest and toughest battle commanders he ever knew and those sentiments are backed up by the fact that Vandervoort won two Distinguished Service Crosses. In late 1944, Vandervoort was injured by German mortar fire and his wounds required a long time to heal. In 1946, he left the military and shortly thereafter went to work for the CIA. He was married and had a son and a daughter. On November 22, 1990, Benjamin Vandervoort died after falling in the nursing home where he lived.

Vandervoort's new plan in Nijmegen was to send F Company plus several British tanks to flank the Bridge from the southwest. The task force sprinted across the main street, which is known today as the N326 or the Sint Canisiussingel. The allied force continued one to two blocks west, turned to the north and worked its way towards the Bridge via two streets, the Gerard Noodstraat and the Derde Walstraat. German small arms fire was heavy enough to cause the tanks to pause, but they proceeded forward and successfully cleared out the Germans.

As September 19, 1944 neared a close, the Highway Bridge was still in German hands, and the beleaguered paratroopers in Arnhem were in even more desperate shape. But there was nothing more that could be done in Nijmegen that day. Soldiers on both sides fortified their positions for the night, and patrols sensed each other's lines. It was a stalemate, and the commanding officer of the 82nd Airborne, General Jim Gavin, knew something bold was needed or the British and Polish paratroopers in Arnhem were doomed.

The Waal River Crossing

Gavin devised a two-pronged attack to get control of the Nijmegen Highway Bridge. One prong was comprised of the 505th Regiment and the British tanks, and the mission was brutally simple and simply brutal: a full-on charge across open ground towards fortifications held by a full battalion of SS troops with machine guns, mortars and artillery support.

You could not imagine many scenarios worse than what the 505th would have to face, but if you did, you probably could not come close to conjuring up what the 504th Regiment was about to experience. Perhaps making the story even worse was that the 504th Regiment had to sit out Normandy because it had been so badly mauled in Sicily and Italy. Without a doubt, the 504th, known as the Devils in the Baggy Pants, was accustomed to tough fights, but this one would be remarkable.

General Gavin chose the 504th Regiment to cross the Waal River in boats and knock out the Germans on the opposite bank because it was experienced in amphibious operations. During the American invasion of Anzio, the Regiment was attached to the amphibious landing forces. Plus, Gavin knew that the Regimental commander, Colonel Reuben Henry Tucker, was one of the best men in the Army. I would have loved to have had a drink with him and Colonel Sink and just sat back and listened to them share stories.

Reuben Henry Tucker III was born on January 29, 1911 in Ansonia, CT, which is about 90 minutes northeast of New York City. Tucker already was a hero by the time he entered West Point, having saved his brother and a friend from drowning in a freezing pond when he was only a teenager. Tucker's family had a proud tradition of military service and it was no surprise that Reuben wanted to attend West Point. However, he was not a top-notch student and it took him five years to secure entry into the Academy. Even then, he failed mathematics and was only able to stay at West Point by re-testing and restoring his academic standing.

During World War II, Tucker volunteered for the paratroops and was assigned to the 504th Regiment in May 1942 as the Executive Officer. In December 1942, Tucker was selected as commander of the entire Regiment, an amazing accomplishment for an officer who was only 31 years old.

The 504th first saw combat during the invasion of Sicily, and it was harrowing. On July 11, 1943, as the air armada carried the 82nd to their drop zones, American ground forces and ships mistook the troop transport planes of the 504th for enemy aircraft and opened fire. 23 STICs were shot down and men aboard many other planes were wounded.

Tucker was known as a tough combat leader and became one of the most decorated commanders in the Army during World War II. He received two Distinguished Service Crosses, one of which was personally awarded to him by President Franklin Roosevelt. After a variety of different assignments after the War, Tucker retired from the Army in 1963 and became commandant of the Citadel. On January 6, 1970, Major General Reuben Tucker was found on the campus of the Citadel, dead from an apparent heart attack. He was buried in the National Cemetery in Beaufort, SC, near his oldest son, who was killed in combat in Vietnam.

On September 19, 1944, Tucker knew what he was getting into at the Waal River. If the amphibious operation wasn't dangerous enough, time was making things worse. The British and Polish paratroopers around Arnhem were being annihilated by the Germans. The paratroopers in Arnhem desperately needed British armor to link with them before the Germans wiped out the Red Devils.

Gavin wanted the 504th to cross under the cover of darkness early on the 20th, but the boats they were to use did not arrive in time. Crossing in daylight meant a suicide mission, but Gavin couldn't hold up the British armored heading for Arnhem by another day. The Waal had to be crossed in full view of the Germans.

About 1,000 yards west of the Waal River bridge in Nijmegen, right near a power plant, is the stretch of river that on September 20, 1944, was the site of some of the most brutal fighting endured by any American paratrooper unit in the course of the war. It was there that the 504th and Company C of the 307th Airborne Engineer Battalion crossed.

The assault force was provided with 26 thin-sided canvas boats to cross the 100- to 200-yard-wide river. After reaching the shore on the north side, the paratroopers had to run across a low-lying flood plain that stretches several hundred yards until it meets a dike with a road on top. After discharging each wave, the engineers manning the boats had to turn around under fire, and head back to the other side, returning the wounded and picking up more men.

As men made preparations for the amphibious assault, fighting broke out in the area from where the boats would launch. Some snipers were killed, and a few dozen prisoners were taken. The launching site was not secure. A bad omen.

The original attack time was scheduled for 1330, but the late arrival of the boats pushed H-Hour back to 1500. A smoke screen would be laid down five minutes before the attack started, and the men would head to the water at 1457. The assault teams reached the water approximately 20 minutes prior to the scheduled attack. Paratroopers in the first wave got a good look at their task. Many of these veterans of Sicily and Anzio handed watches, wallets and other possessions to their friends on shore, with the grim belief that they wouldn't come back.

At 1500, under the cover of smoke, 260 men headed for the water but had difficulty getting the boats underway. The boats supplied were heavier than expected and the men got bogged down in the mud on the south bank. By the time the last boat got into the water, the smoke cleared, and when the assault force was about half-way across the river, the Germans opened up. One estimate is that half of the men in the first wave of boats were killed or wounded.

Germans on the north side of the Nijmegen Highway Bridge fired machine guns and artillery, while from northwest of the memorial, in a patch of woods that will be cleared to construct the new bridge, mortar and artillery fire rained on the Americans on the beachhead and in the water.

The planners expected that the boats would return to pick up more men to ferry into the fight but everything went to hell quickly. Heavy fire tore apart the men and the boats. Some boats were sunk and some were waterlogged. Only 10 of the original 26 boats made it back. And on those 10 boats, six of the engineers who piloted them were injured severely. Plus, the men in the second wave had the shockingly demoralizing sight of seeing the boats return full of wounded, including 34 casualties from Company C alone.

But the 504th pressed the fight, and German fire eased by the time the second wave of men crossed in the 10 remaining boats. By the time of the fifth and final crossing, the only German fire came from snipers.

On the 60th anniversary of the Waal River Crossing, six 504th veterans returned to cross the Waal River again. Among them was Lt. Colonel (Ret.) James "Maggie" Megellas, who is said to be the most highly-decorated 82nd Airborne World War II veteran.

Shortly before the 1944 crossing of the Waal, Megellas and some of his men nervously watched a pre-attack strafing run made by British Typhoon fighters against the German positions. They were horrified by the amount of German anti-aircraft fire blasting at the British planes and knew the crossing would be bloody. Their fears were realized halfway across the River, as the German 20-millimeter guns, artillery and mortars found their range. Megellas and the men in the first assault wave experienced hell as bullets whipped through the air, men were hit, water splashed and a direct hit sank a nearby boat in the middle of the river.

After finally reaching the other side, Megellas and his men rested for a second on the bank, then made a 500-yard charge across the flood plain until they reached the dike. Revenge was the only thing on their mind as they silenced some of the antiaircraft guns, which were positioned in a small fort. Megellas went on to be awarded the Distinguished Service Cross in Holland for his attack against a German fortification while carrying a wounded soldier on his back.

During the Battle of the Bulge, Megellas won the Silver Star for a daring action near the town of Herresbach. Megellas led a column of 27 men, including replacements who had never seen combat. He and his platoon, plus two tank destroyers, ran straight into a German battalion walking towards them on the road with the support of a Panther tank.

Megellas opened fire immediately and charged the German tank, which fired at him with its' machine gun. Divine intervention must have caused the tank to miss. Megellas disabled the tank with a Gammon grenade and then threw a hand grenade through the hatch that killed the crew. When the fighting ended, there wasn't a single American casualty. Between 135 and 250 Germans were killed and at least 200 were taken prisoner. James Megellas killed an estimated 25 Germans and knocked out a tank by himself. Now that is John Wayne-worthy.

In 2004, Megellas returned to Holland to cross the Waal River again but not in a canvas boat. This time, the veterans would travel in World War II-era DUKW landing craft. This time, Megellas wouldn't have to worry about bailing out his boat as he crossed or about artillery, mortar or machine gun fire.

However, Megellas almost didn't make it. Shortly after attending a memorial service a few days earlier, he fell sick and was hospitalized in the Netherlands in near-critical condition for three days. Although unable to eat solid food, Megellas was granted permission to leave the hospital and celebrate the anniversary of the heroic crossing. One of the original river boats used in the crossing by the 504th is on display at the National Liberation Museum in Groesbeek.

The 505th Takes the Bridge

The amphibious assault by the 504th was only one part of Gavin's plan to take the Nijmegen Highway Bridge. The actual taking of the Bridge was up to the 505th and the British Guards Armored, who both spent the previous day locked in a vicious stalemate with a full battalion of German SS soldiers who had no plans to retreat or surrender.

Throughout the night of the 19th and the day of the 20th, the 505th repelled a number of strong enemy attacks, including one that penetrated the American perimeter by nearly 1000 yards deep by about 1000 yards wide. Much of the fighting was hand-to-hand and casualties for the 505th were high, but the Germans were pushed back. Outside of Nijmegen, the Germans were hitting the rest of the 82nd in full force.

Although the soldiers of the 505th knew they were going to try to take the Bridge, they almost didn't have time to think when the order finally came down. At 1600 the men were told to move out in 20 minutes. The attack by the 505th was in a tightly confined area around the south side of the Nijmegen Highway Bridge. The Americans already held the area around the current Hotel Belvoir, as well as some blocks to the west and south. But an SS battalion had defensive positions in a castle-like structure on the site of the modern-day Valkhof museum (in the Hunnerpark), which is adjacent to the bridge.

Much of the German-held area around the Bridge was reduced to rubble and SS troops fought from small strongpoints, behind walls and even in pockets among the wreckage. Despite intense fire from the paratroopers and near point-blank blasts from the British armor, the Germans refused to run. These fanatics were determined to make a last stand.

To get to the Bridge, the Americans had to cross an open plaza. The Germans held their fire until the paratroopers were out in the open and then let loose. Crossfire ripped across the open areas and enfilading fire hit the paratroopers. The British tank commanders were reluctant to help the paratroopers out of fear of German anti-tank weapons. Here the Americans were fighting under the command of a British general with a half-assed plan that could get them all killed and the Guards Armored didn't want to risk their American-built tanks? Were the British out of their minds? Eventually, though, the British tanks joined the attack.

E and F companies advanced slowly, losing men by the minute, especially officers. The paratroopers fired from the hip as they advanced. Machine guns fired at each other from only a few hundred feet apart. Americans tossed grenades into German holes or silenced the occupants with bayonets. The fighting was savage and few Germans surrendered and fewer Americans were in the mood to take prisoners. As the paratroopers fought to within yards of the Bridge, the noise reached a crescendo. A group of 60 Germans broke across the Bridge and made it safely to the north side. Another group of 30 tried to do the same. None made it. Of the 600 German defenders, only about 100 survived.

As dusk approached, four British tanks headed across the Bridge, expecting it to be blown out from underneath them. But the explosive charges that were set underneath the Bridge never went off. After a brutal day of fighting, the Nijmegen Highway Bridge was taken intact.

Visiting the site of the German's defense of the Highway Bridge, it is odd to see crosswalks and pedestrian traffic where the 88 stood, and a concession stand where the tank was located. Nijmegen is a small city where life goes on today. Where cars line up at red lights, and people hurry across the streets, walk their dogs, live in garden apartments and eat at small restaurants. A small city that became the site of a pitched battle is long back to being a small city again. It all seems so normal and quiet. The most dangerous part of it all seemed to be the whizzing cars and the confusing traffic circles, and the possibility of getting hit by a scooter while trying to take a picture.

During the first month in Holland, the 82nd Airborne suffered 469 men killed, 1,933 wounded and 640 missing. They killed 2,490 Germans and took nearly 3,000 prisoners. They crossed the Waal, seized the Nijmegen Highway Bridge, and fought their way through Nijmegen and the surrounding areas. But unfortunately for the British paratroopers in Arnhem, neither the 82nd nor the Guards Armored could get to them before the Germans did.

• • •

Son and the Island

Easy Company Lands in Son

The First and Second Battalions of the 506th boarded their aircraft bound for Holland at Membury Airfield in England on September 17, 1944. The planning for Operation Market-Garden was done hastily, and the great detail that characterized Operation Overlord was not possible, meaning that not all of the kinks could be worked out.

The 101st Division had many objectives, especially securing scores of bridges that were vital to the rapid movement of British Armor from the front to Arnhem. When General Taylor saw the overall plan he felt that the 101st Airborne couldn't afford to drop in small scattered units as it did in Normandy because he needed brute force. That meant having an entire regiment land on the same drop zone and move as fast as it could to key objectives. Actually, in the case of the 502nd and 506th, the only area large enough to drop a whole regiment was a set of fields outside Son that could accommodate both of them side-by-side. The operation in broad daylight was almost like a demonstration jump.

The upside of this strategy was that each Regiment was able to form up in mere minutes: there was no time-consuming search for other soldiers of one's unit. But the downside was serious. The only landing zone that could accommodate such a large drop was not close to the critical objectives that needed to be taken. The regiments had to cover a lot of ground very quickly once they landed.

The flight to Holland was largely uneventful for most of the 506th until about five minutes from the drop zone when the air armada ran through a thick flak belt. Most of the planes made it through fine except for Colonel Sink's STIC. After hearing a number of bangs, Sink looked out the window of his plane and announced to his men something to the effect of "there goes the wing." None of the men on his STIC panicked and everyone jumped and landed safely.

Other than Sink's experience, the parachute drop went extremely well for the 101st. Of the 428 planes carrying the Division, only three failed to find their Drop Zone. Between 1300 and 1330, nearly 6,800 men landed with a casualty rate of under two percent.

However, the following glider landing did not go smoothly even though it took place in broad daylight. Only 53 of the 70 gliders landed safely, and seven actually touched down behind enemy lines. In one glider, a flak burst wounded the pilot and co-pilot. One of the infantrymen saw both flyers knocked out as the glider hurtled towards the ground, and he crawled into the cockpit and without any prior flying experience landed the aircraft safely, saving his life as well as those of the other men on board.

Drop Zone C and the Canal Bridge

The expanse of fields that encompassed Drop Zone B of the 502nd and Drop Zone C of the 506th was in an area northwest of Son. Drop Zone C was easy to find for the pilots carrying Easy Company and the rest of the 506th. The site was a wide area of farmland next to the Paulushoef Farm at the present-day Sonniuswijk 42, on the northern/northwestern side of the town. The farm was chosen because the Paulushoef name was spelled in tile on the roof of the barn, making it easy to spot by the C-47 pilots.

Today, the Sonniuswijk area is still level, green farmland, and it is not hard to imagine the fields in mid-September 1944, buzzing with the activity of a division landing by parachute and glider. Dick Winters wrote that while the plane ride was relatively calm for him, the landing was treacherous. As men got out of their parachutes, loose equipment – helmets, bags, rifles – rained onto the ground all around them.

I imagine that for years, the owners of the farm must have turned up all kinds of gear every time they plowed their fields.

While you can drive and park in front of the Paulushoef farm, it is private property today.

After landing on Drop Zone C, the 1st and 2nd Battalions of the 506th split up and headed by different routes to their common objective: the Wilhelmina Canal Bridge. Once the bridge was captured, the 506th would reform and move as rapidly as was possible southward to Eindhoven to secure four bridges over the Dommel River and to link up with British armor. Speed was essential.

The 1st Battalion cut through a forest known as the Zonsche, and German 88 fire hit a number of the squads. Don Burgett wrote of the heavy fire A Company received and of the deaths and wounding of several of his comrades. First Battalion fought its way through, headed directly south to the Wilhelmina Canal, and turned east towards the bridge, which was about 1,000 yards away.

As 1st Battalion headed east, it encountered another German 88 a few hundred yards west of the Wilhelmina Canal Bridge at the approximate intersection of two streets, Ranonkelstraat and Begoniastraat. Don and A Company knocked out the gun and proceeded east towards the bridge.

The other route, taken by Dick Winters, Lewis Nixon and Second Battalion, was along a road called the Rooijesweg, which eventually leads to the bridge. Heading east on Sonniuswijk you come to a T-intersection with Rooijesweg and if you turn south, the road becomes the Niewstraat, which takes you directly to the Wilhelmina Canal Bridge. As you head south on Niewstraat, at #70, there is a health care facility called the Zonhove. On D-Day, there was fighting in this area and the Americans set up an aid station in what was then a sanitarium, and a monument commemorates the action there.

Winters wrote that he felt it was a mistake by Taylor to have the men drop so far from the Bridge because in the time it took to reach the canal, the Germans could set explosives. I doubt Taylor had much of a choice in the matter because of the hasty planning for Market-Garden. However, Winters' critique was correct, and as he and his group came within 25-35 yards of the bridge, the Germans detonated explosives they had a chance to prepare as 2nd Battalion marched. The bridge exploded right in front of Winters and Nixon, nearly killing them with a shower of wood and stone chunks. Had the 506th landed near the bridge, it might have been taken intact.

Within moments of the bridge explosion, Winters looked up to see the commander of the 1st Battalion, Major James LaPrade, along with Lt. Milford Weller and Sergeant Donald Dunning, run up to the smoldering ruins. Some reports say LaPrade swam across the canal, but Winters wrote he saw the Major tiptoe across the debris, pistol in hand, trying to keep from getting wet. Three months later, LaPrade was killed in the snowy town of Noville, Belgium, on the first day his battalion fought in the siege of Bastogne.

A Lieutenant Colonel when he was killed by a piece of shrapnel in Noville, James LaPrade was born in Kenedy, TX on May 4, 1914. Kenedy is a small town in southeastern Texas, about halfway between Corpus Christi and San Antonio, and during the war, it was the site of a prisoner camp that housed Germans, Italians, Japanese and South Americans.

LaPrade entered the US Military Academy at West Point in July 1935, and graduated in 1939 with several men who became airborne legends, including Robert Cole, Julian Ewell and Henry Kinnard. Initially, LaPrade served in the 29th Infantry Division, which would later be decimated at Omaha Beach on D-Day, but he volunteered for the paratroops. When the battalion's first combat commander, Colonel Turner, was killed in Normandy on June 7, LaPrade was chosen to lead the unit. James LaPrade won the Silver Star with Oak Leaf Cluster and was buried in the cemetery at West Point in 1949. Sadly, his brother, Lieutenant Robert LaPrade, was killed on Guadalcanal. Robert was as brave as his brother, earning a Navy Cross for taking out a machine gun despite mortal wounds.

On the night of September 17, 1944, Easy Company crossed the remains of the bridge over the Wilhelmina Canal in Son, and a steady rain began to fall.

Easy Company on The Island

After securing Eindhoven, Easy Company spent several days fighting in an area with a radius of approximately 20 miles. Much of that area is unrecognizable today due to extensive development, including the replacement of sections of Hell's Highway with a modern super highway. Visiting the area was for me a demoralizing experience, witnessing the permanent loss of battlefields where young Americans died far from home.

Easy Company ran into ferocious German counterattacks in Nuenen and Veghel. David Kenyon Webster, in his book, "Parachute Infantry" gave a chilling account of enduring what some Easy men called the worst shelling of the War, which occurred in Veghel on September 23. Webster's description of the desperation of the men to dig foxholes under fire made me break into a cold sweat, and is worth the cost of the book. No book about Easy Company has such a vivid account of combat, and only Don Burgett's books compare in terms of describing being on the receiving end of German fire.

On October 2nd, the 506th was ordered to a ten mile-long expanse of land between the Waal and Neder Rhein rivers known simply as, "The Island." Hell's Highway ran through the Island from the north at the Bridge Too Far in Arnhem to the Nijmegen Highway Bridge in the south.

The Island itself is completely flat, and only a series of dikes prevent it from being flooded completely. To the north (across the Neder Rhein), is a rarity in Holland: high ground. And it was there that German artillery sat, with a clear view of anything trying to move across The Island. The Americans limited their movements to nights, as any daytime activity was certain to draw German artillery fire.

During its' stay on the Island, the 506th got a taste of two new Nazi weapons. For the first time, the men experienced being hit by Screaming Meemie rockets, and they got their first look at V-2 rockets heading for England. They struggled through foul weather and even worse British rations.

The Island: Schoonderlogt

Many fans of Band of Brothers know the arch as soon as they see it. The one behind Dick Winters in the photo taken while he was billeted at the Schoonderlogt Estate. It's almost iconic. And it is hard to find unless you have a guide, a really good map and/or a GPS unit!

The Schoonderlogt Estate became the headquarters of the 2nd Battalion. The present-day estate is ringed by fields and drainage ditches, and I imagine it looks much like it did during the War, although it was recently renovated. To reach Schoonderlogt, go to the town of Valburg, and take the Stationstraat to the northeast, crossing the railroad tracks. Stationstraat bends to the left and then around to the right and takes you to a T-intersection. Make a left turn onto Logtsestraat, go about 100-200 feet, and the estate is on your right.

When I visited Schoonderlogt, there was no one around except for a horse who watched me from a nearby corral. I felt like telling him that I was there because of Band of Brothers, but I was pretty sure he knew. Just then, a Dalmatian trotted out to the point underneath the arch where Dick Winters posed for the famous wartime photograph. The dog barked with confidence, stared at me and then went back into a farmhouse. I think either he told me that I was in the right place or he thanked me for coming, but I wasn't sure. The dog was born in the Netherlands, and I don't speak Dutch.

Happy that I was seeing a part of Holland that actually looked like I imagined it did in 1944, I headed off to see the site of what I consider the most incredible combat feat of Dick Winters' career: the Crossroads.

Crossroads

Dick Winters wrote that he thought Easy Company's actions at the Crossroads were the highlight of the unit's combat career – a case where superior training, discipline, courage and tactics led to the defeat of a disorganized enemy force ten times larger. I think Winters is entirely right, but I would take that sentiment one step further, in a direction he would certainly not welcome. I think that the Crossroads bayonet charge was the single smartest, bravest and fearless act Winters ever undertook and that the success of the attack was largely due to him.

Some people feel Winters should have won a Congressional Medal of Honor for leading the attack at Brecourt Manor. That may be warranted based on the lives saved on Utah Beach and the textbook execution. However, it always seemed to me that the assault on Brecourt was a typical problem that the paratroopers were trained to solve, and that while Winters was present in a lot of the fighting, a lot of other soldiers were equally, if not more, involved.

I have no similar hesitations about the Crossroads. There, faced with the realization that the Germans could outflank him and his men and catch them exposed in a field, Winters made the daring and brilliant tactical decision to attack, and put himself in the most vulnerable position of any of his men – yards out in front, firing by himself from an exposed position on the dike road into at least two companies of German troops. How he survived astounds me.

The Crossroads area – for now – is much like it was back in October 1944: empty and green, with ditches criss-crossing the field. The dike road was improved after the war and paved, but otherwise looks almost exactly as it did in the miniseries. The road from where Winters fired into the Germans is exactly as I imagined. Even the drain under the road from where the Germans fired the rifle grenade that killed William Dukeman is there. It's virtually pristine and I hope it stays that way, but I fear development will claim the Crossroads too some day.

The Crossroads is kind of unusual because it is one of the few battlefields where you can stand in one place and see where everything happened. From where the German machine gun was on the dike road, you can see from horizon to horizon and find where Winters led the reconnaissance, the field across which they attacked, the dike road and the field where the Germans were.

To get to the Crossroads, follow the dike road west of Heteren. The dike road parallels the Rhine River and is simply the last east-west road on The Island. About a mile west of Heteren, you will reach an intersection with a road leading to the left, and a smaller one running down to the right. A small star is visible off the road to the right. That simple star lets you know that you have reached the Crossroads.

The Crossroads is actually a pretty simple four-way intersection. To the north, a road leads down to the river and ends near a ferry dock that the Germans used to infiltrate the island. To the south a couple of miles is the town of Hemmen, where Colonel Strayer had his headquarters. The east-west road runs along the top of the dike. In a way, the Crossroads intersection looks completely unremarkable. It's knowing what happened there that makes it a thrilling place to see.

When the Second Battalion deployed to the sector of the Island near the dike, it was spread out dangerously thin. Listening and observation posts were established near the dike road, but they were so far apart that it was possible for entire German companies to ferry across the Neder Rhein and sneak through the American lines undetected. One of the counter-tactics the

Americans employed was to send patrols out periodically to detect any German movement.

On October 5, 1944, at about 0400, a patrol that included Sgt. Art Youman, Rod Strohl, Moe Alley and Joe Lesniewski, stumbled upon Germans near the dike road. The outcome is depicted in the miniseries in the scene where Floyd Talbert's peaceful playing with a German Shepherd was disrupted by the patrol roaring into the farmhouse carrying Alley who had taken 32 grenade fragments.

Winters mustered a rifle squad and moved along the south shoulder of the dike. They crossed the dike and went down into a drainage ditch that paralleled the dike on the north side. You can still see that ditch today. Winters halted the patrol about 250 yards from the Crossroads, confused by the sight of German machine gun fire toward Hemmen, several miles away, which gave away the position.

Winters moved by himself to a position about 25 yards from the Crossroads, surveyed the situation and went back to assemble a small team of riflemen. The little group took firing positions about 40 yards away from the German machine gun emplacement and on Winters' signal, dropped seven Germans. As Easy's machine gun roared covering fire, Winters pulled the men back to another drainage ditch that ran perpendicular to the dike road about 200 yards from the Crossroads.

Winters got on the radio and ordered Lt. Welsh to send up the rest of Easy's 1st Platoon, and he also requested the light machine gun teams commanded by Lt. Reis of the Battalion HQ Company. As the men waited in the field for reinforcements to arrive, German soldiers reorganized and fired rifle grenades, killing Corporal William Dukeman, an original Toccoa man.

William Heister Dukeman, Jr., serial number 19087501, was born on September 3, 1921 in Strasburg, CO to Gertrude and

William, Sr. In 1929, the Dukeman family moved to Keenesburg, CO and he graduated from high school there in 1939. After graduation, Bill Dukeman left home with a few friends and traveled to Albuquerque, NM, where he found odd jobs to get by through the Depression.

Dukeman enlisted in San Francisco, CA on August 22, 1942 and volunteered for the Airborne, in part because of the higher pay. "Duke" made it all the way through Toccoa and jumped into Normandy on D-Day. During the campaign there, Dukeman suffered a bullet wound through his jaw, but recovered in time to jump into Holland. Dukeman was injured a short time later, but stayed on the line, and when Bull Randleman went missing in Nuenen, Dukeman filled in.

And on a cold, windy rainy day, I looked at the spot where Bill Dukeman died. An empty, soggy field, with no one in sight, lonely and sad in the raw weather. I thought about what David Webster wrote of Dukeman's death: "he was far away from Colorado and its high and beautiful mountains."

As dawn rose on the field where Bill Dukeman died, Lt. Reis and the balance of the men and machine guns arrived. Dick Winters knew he was in a terrible position. Easy Company was lying completely exposed in a field. All the Germans had to do was figure out the Americans were in the field and they could have deployed along the dike road and had a turkey shoot. But for some incredible reason, the Germans, supposedly a disciplined, experienced group of soldiers, did nothing.

I think that one thing that the miniseries missed was a chance to show a camera angle that would have been chilling: a view from the dike down into the ditch where Winters had his men. As I stood on the dike in the rain, I had a perfect view directly into the ditch where Easy Company was lined up. One machine gun in the spot where I stood could have killed every single man.

Winters knew that the Germans would eventually figure it out, and he decided that retreat was not an option. The only choice was to attack. He gave the order to fix bayonets and prepared the men for a charge into the German lines.

The attack was three-pronged. Sergeant Floyd Talbert deployed to the right flank with 3rd squad, Lieutenant Thomas Peacock to the left with 1st squad. Winters would lead 2nd squad straight up the middle. Reis' machine guns opened up to force the Germans to keep their heads down and Winters told his men to follow him when they saw him deploy a smoke grenade. Winters rose, tossed the smoke canister and sprinted towards the German lines alone. Several seconds later, the smoke finally discharged and the men ran towards the German lines. Winters was in front of his men by at least 20 yards, all alone.

As Winters raced the 200 yards across the field, he tripped on strings of barbed wire, but kept moving. He leaped forward onto the road leading from the Crossroads to the river.

In a windy rain, I stood on the spot where Dick Winters reached the road, about 150 feet north of the memorial. I shivered, not from the weather, but from knowing the history of the spot where I was. In front of me, about ten feet away in the next field, was where a lone German sentry crouched and looked up to see Winters. Winters jumped back to the American side of the road and threw a grenade, but he forgot to remove the pin. Seconds later a potato masher grenade came over from the German side and failed to detonate, so Winters jumped back on the road and shot the sentry point-blank.

To my right, I looked at where the road met the dike. Back in 1944, Winters stood on the same spot and saw at least a full platoon of SS troops hugging the ground, trying to avoid the covering fire from Lt. Reis' machine guns. Winters aimed and fired point blank into the Germans. The Nazis reacted in slow motion, not shooting at Winters until he had emptied two clips and was onto a third. By that time, Easy Company arrived and immediately opened fire, ripping into the Germans, who were sitting ducks.

As the bloodbath raged, another German company appeared over the dike heading back to the ferry. Those German soldiers were part of the 363rd Volksgrenadiers, who had just attacked the Third Battalion of the 506th in a fight during which Major Ollie Horton was killed. Winters saw the Volksgrenadiers and called in an artillery strike, decimating the fleeing Germans, and he also called up Fox Company for reinforcement.

The attack did not end at the Crossroads. Winters turned his men to the north and advanced with the hope of capturing the ferry and trapping the enemy. Easy Company got within 200 yards of the river when a second group of 363rd Volksgrenadiers came over the dike and attacked from the right rear flank. Winters saw his flank was vulnerable, stopped the attack towards the river and pulled his men back. But by that point, Easy was in full view of the German artillery on the hills to the north and shelling erupted and wounded nearly two dozen men.

I think that if the weather was dry I would have walked on the field where the charge took place. Instead, in the drizzle, I squinted and tried to picture Winters running across the field, in front by himself, totally exposed and with his bayoneted Garand in hand. When you see the field, you will shudder at how exposed was Winters. He might as well have been screaming at the Germans, "Hit me!"

I flashed back to Ephrata and Lancaster. I thought about the Winters family asleep in their Lancaster home in the middle of the night, unaware of what their son was doing at that exact moment. How terrified they would have been to know he chose to lead a bayonet charge. How relieved they would have been to know he wasn't killed and how proud they certainly would have felt about the victory.

Lancaster Hospital, Ephrata, Lancaster, Toccoa, England, Normandy and now the charge in Holland. Who among the medical staff that delivered Dick Winters could imagine what that baby was going to accomplish and where he would go. And there was much greater drama to come.

The Crossroads, ironically, ended Winters' career as a company commander. On October 9, he was promoted to battalion XO, a position that was normally held by a major. Winters was followed as commanding officer of Easy Company by a lieutenant well-known to fans of Band of Brothers, Fred "Moose" Heyliger.

Approximately six weeks later, Easy Company was relieved and pulled off the line. On September 17, Easy dropped into Holland with 154 officers and men. On November 25, only 98 men sat in the trucks that drove down Hell's Highway to a new base in France. Several officers, including Buck Compton, had been wounded, along with 45 men. And their commander, Moose Heyliger, was knocked out of the war due to friendly fire, and was replaced by a new officer: Norman Dike.

The men who arrived into Camp Mourmelon had not showered for nearly ten weeks. They expected to heal, recover and refit and prepare for a spring jump into Germany. Men took raucous leaves into Paris, or at least made plans to raise hell there. There were even plans for a Christmas football game. They earned a long rest and needed the time to recover from a miserable experience in Holland that failed to achieve a breakthrough into Germany.

But the Germans had other plans.

• • •

IV
Bastogne

Bastogne: the First Visit

From the first time I saw Band of Brothers, the story of Bastogne stood out among everything else. It wasn't first among equals. It wasn't one of several awing Easy Company combat experiences. To me, Bastogne always felt like the most serious, the most brutal, the most gripping chapter of the Easy Company story.

Bastogne has an intense gravity. It almost feels like how they describe a black hole as so dense that light particles cannot escape the gravitational pull. It's no accident that I've been to Bastogne more times than any other place where Easy Company served. I've found myself pulled by an emotional gravity to Bastogne. For me, every place where the men of the Airborne served is important, but when I stand in the woods of the Bois Jacques near Foy, surrounded by old foxholes, I am chilled, humbled and haunted in a way that no other place can come close to so doing.

Even on the sunniest, warmest day, I feel cold chills when I stand in the woods where men endured artillery, mortar, infantry and tank attacks, or on the fields where small units of infantry and tankers scraped together the narrowest of victories against a ruthless, well-armed enemy. I feel haunted by thoughts of men, starving, freezing and seeking cover from shell bursts and explosions. When I am in the Bois Jacques, I usually have the feeling of being watched. I often turn around half-expecting to see a gaunt, unshaven soldier looking for his foxhole and trying to keep warm.

In Noville, I shudder thinking about how in just over 24 hours, the 1st Battalion of the 506th suffered 212 officers and men killed or wounded. How the men were rushed from a march straight into fighting in the fields around the town, and how many of them were gunned down as they neared the German lines. They never had a chance. My mind wanders to thinking about how many men died slowly and alone, and whose bodies were encased in snow until the spring thaw.

Some Basic Advice

I've visited Bastogne several times, learning more on each trip. From a practical perspective, it's valuable to give yourself plenty of time – there is much more to see than you will expect, and you'll find yourself taking longer at any given stop than you planned. Read a number of books about the Battle of the Bulge, but remember that you don't have to take all of those books with you (they're heavy). Book your hotel in advance and expect that most of the lodging in the area is bare bones, with internet connections or television with English-language stations as surprising rarities. The local residents largely speak French, and in the off-season it can be a little difficult to find a fluent English speaker.

Another important thing is to prepare for the possibility of bad weather, especially in the late fall and spring, when there can be either bright sun or heavy rain, or both. You'll spend a lot of time walking around in woods and in fields, so having the wrong shoes or not having outerwear can make your life miserable.

Finally, and I can't stress this enough. Go on the internet and look up tourguide Reg Jans. He will give you the tour of a lifetime, and you'll make a good friend.

Those are my suggestions for a good trip, and so I look back and laugh and know that with the exception of reading Band of Brothers, I violated every piece of that advice on my first visit to the area!

Seeing Bastogne for the First Time

My first trip to Bastogne was at the tail end of a business trip in late October 2006. I made about every mistake that I could, but in the end, it worked out incredibly well. I stood in the empty Bois Jacques among Easy Company's foxholes as winds swept through the trees creating noises that sounded like people murmuring. Completely eerie. Sometimes, even if you do things wrong, you still can get rewarded for your efforts!

That first visit was a single-day round-trip that started and ended in Frankfurt, Germany, which is about four hours away by car. I spent the previous night at the airport Sheraton so that I could pick up my rental car the first thing in the morning and drive through western Germany and eastern Belgium into Bastogne. Perhaps it was anxiety about renting a car in a foreign country by myself for the first time, or looking at the complexity of the directions according to what I downloaded from Mapquest Europe, or that the forecast was quite bad, or that I did not have a map of Bastogne with me, or that I had a very tough business trip at a job that I hated, or the sense that I was going someplace monumental, but I barely slept the night before my visit.

Waking up full of nervous energy, and with some slight agitation from not being well-rested, I arrived at the rental car agency at 7 AM: opening time according to the company's web site. Naturally, I was greeted by a sign that stated the desk would not open until 8, so I went and got a cup of coffee. Then a second. Then a third. When they finally did open, the young woman at the desk told me she didn't think they had a car with an automatic transmission. I waved my confirmation for a sedan with an automatic, and after a 40-minute delay, I finally got underway with a car I could drive.

Overcoming nervousness about getting on the right highway, I found driving in Germany very easy. The road signs are all well-marked and I was able to figure things out with little difficulty. I reached the Autobahn, and like most Americans given their first chance on that road, I decided to hit the gas and see what it was all about. Cruising along at 200 km/hour (about 120 MPH), I was pretty impressed until I heard a roar on my left and after lifting my head from ducking, I saw the back of a Ferrari disappear into the horizon ahead of me. I never even saw the car in my rearview mirror. Quickly, I moved over to the right lane.

Getting off the E42 highway, I drove near Saint Vith, Belgium and then cut west on the 827, a small two-lane road that goes through the towns of Beho, Sterpigny and Sommerain. Had I actually taken the time to do research, I would have learned that I was driving through some of the most hotly-contested towns during the Battle of the Bulge. I might have also learned that I was just south of the town of Vielsalm, where the survivors of brutal fighting in Saint Vith and the surrounding areas regrouped before moving on the offensive. The road I was on was actually part of the American line. It took the Americans Army a month to clear the road I crossed in probably 45 minutes, but I drove along unaware and with just Bastogne on my mind.

The 827 takes you to an intersection where you have a choice to get to Bastogne: drive the N30, a small, local road through Noville and Foy, or get onto the A26, a highway that shaves off half the time. Even after three-and-a-half hours of driving, the last hour of which was in heavy rain, it was not even a question: the local road. Not only do I favor taking local roads over highways, but I knew that down the N30 was one of the most important towns where Easy Company ever fought: Foy.

I entered the town of Houffalize, Belgium by descending a hill that gives a spectacular view of the town and the Ourthe, one of the key rivers that the Germans wanted to capture. The town itself is charming, with small shops, bakeries, butcheries and restaurants, and shows little sign of the fighting that raged there 60 years ago. Well, so I thought. Heading uphill, a Panther tank suddenly loomed in a small park on the west side of the road. My first sign of the Battle of the Bulge.

Although my heart raced from knowing I was approaching Foy and Bastogne, I stopped nonetheless just to stare at this massive tank. I wondered about the story of this tank. Was it destroyed by the Americans? Captured intact? Was it part of the Battle of the Bulge or did it come from another theater?

Back home, when I had a chance to research, I learned that this tank was indeed knocked out by American troops during the Battle of the Bulge and was found upside down in the Ourthe River. One note I saw said that the German crew was found dead inside the tank, drowned, but like many things on the internet, it's just a story. I also found an article dated 2004 about American veterans visiting Houffalize on the 60th anniversary of the battle and celebrating with local residents, who also remembered the 200 civilians killed in the near-flattening of the town.

After a brief look at the tank, my last bit of patience was spent and I jumped in my car, my heart pounding, and raced up the hill. Reaching what seemed like a plain, I headed south, the rain pelting the window, and passed through an intersection. Out of the corner of my eye, I saw a sign pointing to the left that said "Rachamps." My first sighting of a town I recognized from Band of Brothers: Rachamps is the town where the choir sang for Easy Company in a convent at the end of the miniseries episode, "The Breaking Point."

Then I came to Noville. I knew Easy Company attacked Noville, but even if I read more about the fighting in and around the town before my trip– which I hadn't, foolishly – I was so anxious to go into the Bois Jacques and see Bastogne that I just slowed down a little and kept going south. In the distance I saw the outline of a church steeple, and I knew, instantly, that I was looking at Foy.

When I arrived at Foy, I noticed that the present town did not look like how it was portrayed in the miniseries, but I did not care. I knew that this is from where German artillery, tanks and mortars pounded the paratroopers in the woods of the Bois Jacques.

And if I found the Bois Jacques, I knew that in those woods I would find the foxholes Easy Company dug that still dot the forest floor. Since I was in Foy, I knew that the woods to the south had to be the Bois Jacques, and Easy Company's foxholes had to be in there. I drove south on the N30 through the single light in Foy and after passing a few houses, I saw a wide open field to the left of the road and behind the field, there they were: the Bois Jacques. I parked my car on the shoulder of the road, got out and debated myself in the middle of a downpour. I thought long and hard about leaving my car on the side of the N30, hopping the barbed wire fence and running out to the woods. Chills ran down my spine, and not because of the cold rain.

I was seeing the spot where Easy dug in. Where Guarnere and Toye lost their legs. Where the men froze, fought, endured.

My challenges at the time were insignificant compared to those of Easy Company, but I found myself with a few problems. First, it was pouring cold rain and I had no protection, no jacket, no umbrella – just a pair of water-resistant hiking boots that would do me little good in shin-high wet grass. Second, from the N30, I saw barbed wire on all sides of the field leading to the Bois Jacques. I saw no clear way to get to the woods without trespassing, something I feel you should never do, especially on someone's farm. Third, while I knew I was looking at the Bois Jacques, I wasn't 100% sure where each American unit was positioned, even though I had a good idea.

I went back to the car, realized my clothes were soaked through and turned on the heat. I had to try to get some protection and an idea of how the hell to get into the woods, so I drove into Bastogne. If I only had this book back then!

I passed the hamlet of Luzery on my left, not realizing that was where 2nd Battalion and Easy went into regimental reserve on the first day of the battle. I drove past the hospital not knowing that was the area where Red Falvey's bazooka platoon was photographed heading up towards Foy on December 19, 1944. I entered Bastogne itself and came to a traffic circle, unaware that I had just passed the Rue de la Roche, the road by which the 506th walked into combat.

From the traffic circle, I did know one thing. The massive church that was in front of me looked exactly like the one depicted in Band of Brothers as the aid station where Eugene Roe fictitiously met Nurse Renee Lamaire.

Turning right onto the street in front of the church, I immediately realized that during the middle of the day, Bastogne is busy and finding a parking spot is challenging. A slow line of cars crawls through town, interrupted by pedestrians at crosswalks, jaywalkers, and vehicles parking or pulling out of very tight spots. About 60 years earlier, this street was jammed with trucks, tanks, half-tracks, jeeps and other vehicles, soldiers, civilians and anti-aircraft guns. This day, it was shoppers dodging rain and small European cars.

After finding a spot and figuring out how to buy a parking ticket from one of the many machines in town (put it on your dashboard), I went out in search of a jacket or an umbrella. I found no clothing stores and no department stores and the only protection that I could spot was a small pink umbrella. Out of desperation, I paid five euros for the cheap girls' umbrella and went outside, no longer the only person in Bastogne without some cover in the middle of a rainstorm, but hardly looking like someone fascinated by military history.

I passed by the town square, not noticing the bust of General Tony McAuliffe, commander of the 101st during the siege of Bastogne, and walked a block further down the Rue Neufchatel, where I spotted a small military museum. Crossing the street, I didn't notice the plaque in front of the "Baby City" store that was built on the site of the aid station where the real Nurse Renee Lamaire was killed.

Thinking that I could get some good practical advice on going into the Bois Jacques and finding the foxholes, I went into the museum, paid my admission fee and tried to start a conversation with an older woman working there. Unsurprisingly, given my luck with the weather, she did not speak a word of English. So I stood there poorer by the admission fee, without any advice on where the foxholes were or how to get there.

I was disappointed but undeterred. I didn't come this far not to see the Bois Jacques and the foxholes. Channeling my inner soldier, or at least conjuring up a line from Clint Eastwood's movie, "Heartbreak Ridge," I figured that I was going to adapt, overcome and improvise. I went out in the rain and opened my pink girl's umbrella ready to complete my mission.

I got back into my car, turned around and headed back to the Bois Jacques and Foy. Within minutes, I was back in Foy, and it dawned on me how close the Germans got to the center of Bastogne. Foy was held by the Germans and the Americans were in the woods to the south. It took just a few minutes to get to the center of Bastogne by car. The Bastogne perimeter seemed so damn small.

Up until this point, I felt like I had a lot of bad luck with the weather, and it also became clear to me that I didn't quite know where I was going because I was still looking at the open fields with the barbed wire fence. But I was committed to adapting, overcoming and improvising, and soon things fell into place. As I returned to Foy, I sensed that the weather eased up, or at least it felt that way.

Making a right at the light in Foy, I went east a few hundred feet and found myself at a Y-intersection and parked in an area on the right. I saw an open field and again looked at the Bois Jacques. And I found myself looking at a road that clearly ran right along the edge of the woods.

Pausing for a moment, I knew I was looking at the part of the Bois Jacques where Easy Company dug in. I had the proof in the small map in my copy of Band of Brothers. I was right. (Mistakenly, I trusted the map in the book and thought that the field in front of me was the one across which Easy attacked Foy on January 13, 1945. It was a while before I learned the charge actually happened on the other side of the Bastogne-Foy road).

Everything seemed humbling and awesome, in the true sense of that latter word. I was dumbstruck and chilled, and I stood engrossed. I realized that the outer perimeter of Easy's lines were visible clearly to artillery spotters in Foy. I could see the lines perfectly and I didn't have an 88. Just a pink umbrella. It became completely obvious why a fire to warm your hands would have been out of the question. And I wondered how many times Americans in those woods looked down on where I was standing.

Things slowed for me. I was not impatient, I didn't race to get to the woods. I took my time trying to soak in the significance of where I was and made a promise to remember that moment for the rest of my life. I can still picture the distant woods in the mist and rain perfectly.

I drove down the road, toward the town of Bizory, and came upon the woods in only a few hundred yards. There was literally no traffic; everyone else had the common sense to stay indoors in that weather. But the cold rain was of no consequence. I was prepared to adapt, overcome and improvise, and I had a little girl's umbrella to help. I pulled off the side of the road by the first group of trees on the right and parked on the shoulder, locked the car and climbed up an embankment of about three feet. I ducked under the branches of a pine tree and upon straightening up, noticed the foxholes. Everywhere. Some shallow, some deep. Many were asymmetrical. The lack of uniformity among the foxholes made me think about how many of these were probably dug very quickly and with purpose by men under fire. Some of the holes had me wondering if they were dug by men or gouged by German artillery.

These foxholes were on the edge of the woods by the road. I guessed they were the outer perimeter of the line overlooking the Germans in the woods on the opposite side of the road. I decided to go deeper and stand on the treeline overlooking Foy and look at the town that stared at Easy Company for a month.

I walked west through the trees until I came to a clearing that had some short trees on the other side. I didn't know if the field was there back in 1944, but I knew those short trees looked a lot like regrowth. My heart sank when I realized that there probably used to be forest where those short trees stood. And if the forest was harvested, then it probably meant that some foxholes disappeared in the process. This was bitter for me. The residents of the area are hardly rich. They are farmers and ranchers and logging is part of their way to make a living, as has probably been the case for generations. But this was different to me. These were Easy Company's foxholes.

I cut around the field to the next section of forest and my mind eased. I stood at the edge of the trees looking across the field at Foy and was among the foxholes of the outer perimeter. The OP was the outermost ring of foxholes on the line, and perhaps the most dangerous place to be because you were the first line of defense and in the most exposed position. I tried to find the spot where I had looked towards the woods a few minutes earlier when I parked in Foy. The tops of the buildings and the church steeple were visible, but not where I parked and stood.

I walked through the woods, but took care not to step into a foxhole. I have always treated the foxholes as places where men suffered and where some died, so I leave them alone out of respect. I found myself alone, among the thousands of trees of the Bois Jacques, which swayed and creaked in the wind, and the forest was filled with eerie groans. If you believe in ghosts, you would have been certain that you were not alone. I found myself looking over my shoulder, half expecting to see a glimpse of Doc Roe, Don Hoobler or Carwood Lipton. Deep in the Bois Jacques, you feel surrounded by the stories, and you wonder what this area looked like in winter, covered in snow, and you wonder what you would have done had you fought there.

An hour spent in the woods felt like mere minutes and I did a double-take when I looked at my watch, stunned at how much time had passed. Silently, I walked out of the woods and got back into my car and headed back to Frankfurt. That night, in the restaurant of the ultra-modern Frankfurt Airport Sheraton, with a wine steward, warm meal and my journal, I reflected by myself on the day, which began with nervousness and agitation and ended with serenity and solemnity, and the absolute certainty that I would return, which I did several more times, including once with very special friends.

• • •

Bastogne: the Big Picture

The Write Stuff?

When I first contemplated this book, I had a harder time with one topic than everything else combined: Bastogne. The story of Bastogne is very well-known, and I think that was the big problem for me. If you go to Amazon's book listings and type in "Bastogne," you will get nearly 3,000 hits. I wanted my book to have something fresh and innovative, and I was fairly intimidated by the body of literature out there. What could I add given the number of books by veterans who fought there and by well-recognized scholars? There is even a book by William Cavanagh called, "A Tour of the Bulge Battlefield," that gives directions to many spots in the Ardennes, although the section on Bastogne is small.

Eventually, I settled on the question, "What do I wish I had that I hadn't seen in any of the books on Bastogne?" And that led to a number of ideas. First, I never saw a map of how Easy Company attacked Foy or a layout of the company foxhole positions in the Bois Jacques and I could provide that. Second, I never heard much about the rest of the 101st in the Bastogne perimeter and I knew some interesting stories.

The third idea was based on the kind of slap in the face that I took in Holland when I realized that there were a lot of other units that I never thought much about when I focused on just Easy Company. The Battle of the Bulge was Holland multiplied by five. It took a fair amount of reading, especially of books by Toland, MacDonald, Koskimaki and Marshall, to understand that Easy Company did not endure the worst or contribute the most in the Battle of the Bulge or in Bastogne as the book or miniseries might lead you to believe. And something that I thought would be important to provide the fan of Band of Brothers is a sense of what other American divisions were doing, in addition to writing about Easy Company in and around Bastogne.

I think describing the role of other units is important because of the way the miniseries presented things. The episode on Bastogne was graphic: panicked soldiers retreating in chaos while Easy Company calmly and professionally walked into combat knowing it might be surrounded. And it wasn't just the miniseries: even Dick Winters wrote that he was ashamed of the men they passed.

Winters was entitled to his feelings at the time because he had no idea what was going on. However, what I learned about the first few days of the Battle of the Bulge changed my mind completely about the image of Easy Company saving the day and about the other units running from the fight. I understand why Ambrose as an author focused on Easy Company. The unit and the men are very compelling and worth getting to know, plus Ambrose had to focus on one company, not 30, in order to tell the story with flow. Otherwise the book would have mushroomed to 800 pages, as is the case with "Rendezvous with Destiny."

But Ambrose as a historian committed a grave mistake in not recognizing units other than Easy Company, especially during the Battle of the Bulge. Although it may sound heretical to fans of Band of Brothers, it's important to pull back and say that other units endured even worse than did Easy Company and that other soldiers were just as brave. We have to recognize those other men: it's our duty to do so.

Ambrose and the producers of the miniseries do not tell you anything about the retreating soldiers who filled Winters with shame. Some of those men were panicked mobs, to be sure. However, some were the shattered remains of the 4th and 28th infantry divisions, both of whom spent the previous few months being ripped apart in a largely-unknown offensive in the Huertgen Forest. The Huertgen cost 31,000 Americans killed, wounded or missing, and the 4th and 28th were down to under 50% strength. They were sent to the Ardennes to recover in a quiet part of the line when they were hit by the Germans on December 16, 1944. Rather than turn tail and run, the two divisions fought like hell and in some spots were ordered to hold their positions and fought to the last. These men delayed the Germans for three full days before they finally pulled back through Bastogne.

Ambrose and the miniseries producers even left out big sacrifices by other parts of the 506th Regiment. Easy Company, which was part of the 2nd Battalion, lost 14 men killed in over a month of fighting around Bastogne. By comparison the Regiment's 1st Battalion had 212 casualties *in the first 24 hours* of combat during the Battle of the Bulge.

Nor does Band of Brothers mention that the first part of the 101st to go into combat was actually the 501st Regiment, which ran head-first into a strong German force east of Bastogne. The tough fighting by the 501st gave the rest of the Division time to dig in. And it may be a surprise to some Band of Brothers fans to learn that the 101st Airborne was not the only unit in Bastogne. Combat Command B of the 10th Armored Infantry Division, plus tankers from the 705th and 609th Tank Destroyer Battalions fought side by side with the encircled paratroopers and provided firepower that kept the Germans from overwhelming the lightly-armed 101st Airborne.

Plus, there were a number of artillery units in Bastogne, including the 420th, 755th, 463rd, 477th and 969th. The story of the 969th is one that deserves its' own book as it was a segregated unit. I am not sure how many people know that some of the heaviest artillery in Bastogne was manned by an all-black unit that was subjected to racism within the U.S. Army. Yet the 969th and its' massive guns made the Germans pay dearly and saved the lives of a lot of white soldiers in Bastogne.

So my third idea was to try to incorporate as much information, albeit in an abbreviated fashion, about other units that fought in Bastogne or in the Ardennes, to help put Easy Company's fighting into context. And if you are planning on going to Bastogne, this information might help you plan your trip.

And one of the first things I could have used on my initial trip was a primer on the Battle of the Bulge.

Wacht um Rhine

The Battle of the Bulge was fought in the hilly, wooded Ardennes region where the borders of Luxembourg, Germany and Belgium meet. In some respects, parts of the area look a lot like the Dells of Wisconsin, the Catskill Mountains of Pennsylvania or the Black Hills of South Dakota and Wyoming. Other parts are rolling farmland with pine forests. I find that kind of terrain beautiful, and the setting enhances my love of the Ardennes.

Hitler devised the plan, which was codenamed "Wacht um Rhine" or "Watch on the Rhine." He knew that the Ardennes area was lightly defended by recovering or brand-new American units, and that Allied planners did not expect an assault through the region as evidenced by the low manpower and significant geographical gaps between some units.

Hitler felt that a German offensive could smash through the unprepared Americans, cross the Meuse River and seize the port of Antwerp. This audacious plan had the objective of either defeating the American and British armies, or creating such devastation as to force the Allies to negotiate peace with the Germans. At a minimum, Hitler expected the attack to cause great friction between the British and Americans.

Most of Hitler's senior military staff thought the offensive was too risky and would use up all of Germany's available reserves. They saw the terrain as difficult to navigate with tanks and they were nervous about a fuel shortage that was so bad that the plan would work only if the Germans could capture American gasoline dumps intact. But no objection could change the Fuhrer's mind and the reluctant commanders went along.

The American Situation Before the Battle

The American front in the Ardennes was approximately 65 miles long, and stretched from the northeastern corner of Belgium near the border with the Netherlands down to the tip of Luxembourg. Along this border, in towns, forests and hillsides, four divisions were dug in and parts of their positions extended in a bulge shape into the German front.

The 99th Infantry Division was the northernmost unit, and was positioned near the towns of Losheimergraben and Bucholz, areas that were hit on the first day of the battle. Shortly before the Germans attacked, the 99th Division moved from static defensive positions to allow the 2nd Infantry Division to pass through its' lines. The 2nd Infantry was launching a bitter offensive against the German defensive positions of the Siegfried line in order to take German dams along the Roer River. When the Germans attacked through the Ardennes, Allied planners actually thought the whole situation was a ruse to lessen the pressure caused by the 2nd Division.

The Americans were so unprepared for an attack that at the southern end of the 99th Division's line, the key crossroads town of Lanzerath was held by only about 20 men of the 394th Regiment's I&R Platoon.

Just south of the 99th Division's position was a large valley among the Schnee Eiffel mountains called the Losheim Gap. Border towns in this large natural geographic funnel between Belgium and Germany were guarded by only a few small units of the lightly-armed 14th and 18th Cavalry squadrons. The cavalry units were assigned temporarily to the 106th Division, a brand-new unit called the Golden Lions that was under the command of General Alan Jones, Sr. In parts of the Losheim Gap, there were no American units at all and German soldiers sometimes walked through the front lines to visit family in the area.

The 99th Division guarded the north, the brand new and untested 106th Division protected the center, and in the south were the bloodied 28th and 4th Divisions, trying to recover from their decimation in the Huertgen Forest. The 28th licked its' wounds in the hilly areas in southeastern Luxembourg, and the 4th was anchored to the south. You could call it four divisions, but in reality, it was probably more like two-and-a-half.

A few miles away, on the other side of the Schnee Eiffel, obscured by fog that prevented aerial reconnaissance, were four German armies comprised of 30 infantry and armored divisions ready for a three-pronged attack. To the north, the infamous Sepp Dietrich, one of the most fanatical Nazis, commanded the Sixth Panzer Army. One of Dietrich's officers was Colonel Joachim Pieper, a brutal Panzer commander and a favorite of Hitler.

In the middle, Hasso von Manteuffel prepared his Fifth Panzer Army to capture the crossroads town of Bastogne and then move west towards Brussels. The German Seventh Army under the command of Erich Brandenberger would attack to the south and a small contingent of German paratroopers would drop behind American lines.

The Battle Opens

The Battle of the Bulge began at 0530 on December 16, 1944 with a furious artillery bombardment of the forward American positions followed shortly by infantry and armored attacks along the entire frontier.

Just as I was fascinated about Dick Winters' origins and about the landings of the men in Normandy on D-Day, I wanted to see where the Battle of the Bulge began. On my second trip to Bastogne, I drove about an hour to the German border to visit some of the towns that were among the first hit. By driving what is known as the "Ourtal Route" which includes roads such as the N874 from Bastogne, the E421/N62 in Luxembourg and then up to Losheimergraben from Saint Vith, you will see gorgeous European farmland and you will pass through many of the key battle sites although in kind of a reverse chronological order of the battle.

My destinations were the small towns of Krewinkel and Lanzerath, which may have been the first two places attacked by the Germans on the first day of the offensive. If not, it would have been close. The paradox is that one of the most massive combat operations of all time was launched through some of the smallest, sleepiest towns you could possibly imagine.

Krewinkel is one of my favorite towns for a couple of reasons. First, the fight there is well-documented. John Toland, in his book "Battle" wrote of the experiences of Sergeant John Banister of the 14th Cavalry Squadron, who was on the receiving end of the initial German attack. Plus, Cavanagh's book has hand-drawn maps of the American positions and the fighting.

Second, Krewinkel is tiny, which creates its' own charm. It would be a nice place to get snowed in on Christmas morning. The town is nestled in a tight little valley with steep hills to the east towards Germany. There is one road that runs sort of north to south with a couple of side streets, an old church, a new church and pretty much nothing else. There is one really interesting thing though: in this part of Belgium, many of the residents speak German, not French. In Lanzerath, the German-speaking Belgians acted differently just before the invasion, according to several American soldiers. They seemed to know what was coming and were in a good mood.

The initial German artillery barrage jarred awake the cavalrymen in Krewinkel. The Americans rushed to their positions and witnessed the eerie sight of artificial moonlight the

Germans created by reflecting searchlights off the low clouds. An attack wasn't a surprise to the men in Krewinkel. They noticed an increase in German activity in the area and heard what sounded like armor on the other side of the hills east of town over the previous few days.

Nonetheless, when German soldiers began to appear out of the distance, the American platoon had to scramble into action. The Germans hit the town in two spots and were able to get towards the church in the center, but the cavalry fought back hard and retook Krewinkel. As the Germans retreated, one of them yelled in perfect English for the Americans to "Take a ten minute break, we'll be back." One of the American sergeants returned the verbal fire and said, "Fuck you, we'll still be here."

The Germans were as good to their words as were the Americans. In the second assault, dozens of Germans were killed by machine gun, rifle and mortar fire, and the small group of American soldiers held out for over six hours before pulling back to the nearby town of Manderfeld. The fight in Krewinkel was similar to many others that day: small groups of men recovering from the surprise of the initial attack, holding their ground against superior numbers, figuring out what was going on and buying time. It wasn't the mass panic you might think if you relied only on Band of Brothers.

On one of my trips, I spent time in the field with a guide named Hans Wijers, a military historian who leads the cadets from West Point on tours of the Ardennes. Hans and I parked near the new town church, and found buildings that were used by the Cavalry in December 1944. We strolled through the sleepy town and noticed some buildings still had bullet holes in their thick walls.

Diagonally to the northeast from the new church is a road that dips before it climbs a hill and disappears towards Germany. Hans and I walked along on the sunny day, and as we descended into the dip, we passed through what used to be a minefield. The trail we took to the east, towards Germany, was well-worn: the Germans came down that road during their attack. At the top of the hill, we turned around and had a view of Krewinkel and Manderfeld, and then we cut across a pasture. First, we looked for bulls to make sure we wouldn't get gored. Then we looked down to make sure we didn't step in any of the hundreds of cow pies that served as a modern-day minefield.

There is a cluster of bushes at the top of the hill and we looked around until we found a barely-visible depression in the ground. Hans told me that after the War, he met a German soldier who said that two days prior to the offensive, he dug that depression, covered it with snow and then spied on the Americans. He had a telephone with him to report troop strength and movement, and also to identify key positions. Apparently, the German veteran liked the view a lot: he moved to Krewinkel when he retired.

Not far from Krewinkel is the town of Lanzerath, where another small group of soldiers made a heroic last stand. The I&R Platoon of the 394th Infantry Regiment and a few artillery spotters put up a fierce defense against a battalion of German paratroopers, although some say it was more like a regiment. The defense of Lanzerath was the subject of a book called "The Longest Winter" and was also featured in The History Channel's series, "Shootout."

Lanzerath was hit early on the 16th and the two dozen men there fought off the Germans with machine guns, BARs and rifles. Several times they contacted their HQ and were ordered to hold to the last man, so they stayed in place and fired into the Germans, who charged across open, snow-covered fields. The Americans fired until their machine gun barrels warped from heat and until ammunition ran critically low, but they refused to retreat even after losing contact with their headquarters. They hoped to withdraw under the cover of darkness, which was around 1630 in that area.

Unfortunately, just before dark, the Germans launched flanking attacks and captured all of the Americans. Miraculously, the men weren't massacred as was happening to prisoners all over the Ardennes, and they were marched off towards Germany. One part of the German offensive was stalled for an entire day by the bravery of a squad-sized group of Americans.

There is a monument to the I&R Platoon in Lanzerath on a dirt road that parallels the main road leading to Losheimergraben. One of the best ways to orient yourself requires a little backtracking. If you drive north from Lanzerath towards Losheimergraben, you will come to a junction with a left turn for Buchholz. Before the turn-off, on the left, is a broad hill with a small forest in the distance. Those woods are where you will find some of the foxholes of the I&R Platoon, and a road that runs along the field in front of the trees is where the monument is located.

While the I&R Platoon held to the last, the rest of the 99th Division was engaged in violent combat to the north, particularly around Losheimergraben. Driving from Lanzerath to Losheimergraben, you cross a bridge over a railroad cut. On December 16th, surprised American sentries saw a large column of German troops marching towards Buchholz along the railroad tracks. The 99th got men in position and surprised and slaughtered the Germans in the deep ravine.

In Losheimergraben itself, a small group of soldiers held off an intense German armored attack for hours before finally surrendering. The 99th Division fought so well and so stubbornly, that the 2nd Division was able to withdraw from its' advance through towards the Roer dams. The two divisions then pulled off a miraculous maneuver. While both were engaged in combat, they repositioned themselves in an orderly fashion, forming a new defensive line in the nearby hills known as Elsenborn Ridge. Had any of the regiments broken, the Germans would have routed the retreating Americans, but that never happened. What was all the more remarkable is that the 99th Division was new to combat but fought like a veteran unit.

The fighting in Krewinkel, Lanzerath, Losheimergraben and the Elsenborn Ridge was a far cry from what you might have thought from Band of Brothers alone.

While the 99th Division performed brilliantly in its' first real action, the newly-formed 106th Division simply fell apart. The small cavalry units in Krewinkel, Afst and other small towns in the Schnee Eiffel area had to pull back after sustained attacks by the heavy armor and infantry divisions of the German Army. The Germans descended on the Golden Lions and quickly outflanked the 422nd and 423rd regiments and cut them off from their headquarters in Saint Vith.

The two regiments had trouble staying in touch with headquarters but they reestablished contact with General Jones, and he promised reinforcements. Those reinforcements never made it out of Saint Vith. The few American armored units who arrived there were attacked almost immediately by German tanks and infantry who reached the headquarters town.

Jones also told the 422nd and 423rd to fight their way west towards Saint Vith. The two regiments attacked the Germans near the town of Schonberg, but point-blank tank and heavy artillery fire shredded the Americans. Unable to punch through, the Americans surrendered on December 19, the day Easy Company arrived in Bastogne. Some of the Golden Lions wanted to fight further, but some saw surrender as the only option. If the Americans didn't surrender, it is likely they would have been slaughtered. Completely encircled, with no reinforcement, little heavy weaponry and facing a tough, well-armed enemy with artillery, the Americans had no chance. Soon the survivors of the 106th were marching towards prison camps in Germany along with the 99th Division men from Lanzerath and Losheimergraben.

For the poor soldiers of the 28th Division, who were recovering from the Huertgen, the fighting was sudden and brutal as the Germans stormed the Our River at the border town of Dasburg. The 28th was under the command of one of the heroes of D-Day, General Norman "Dutch" Cota, who was portrayed in the movie, "The Longest Day," by Robert Mitchum. On D-Day, Cota led one of the critical breakthroughs off Omaha Beach east of Vierville-sur-Mer, and was repeatedly exposed to enemy fire. Cota was a tough SOB.

According to the website of the 28th Infantry Division Association, "The Keystone Division" (it was comprised largely of men from Pennsylvania, the Keystone State) suffered 15,000 casualties during the Battle of the Bulge after being hit by a total of nine German divisions. Half a division versus nine German divisions.

The 28th Division saw fierce combat on all parts of the line, but things got especially hairy around the town of Clervaux, from which roads led to Bastogne and Saint Vith. The Germans wanted both of those other towns, so they gave maximum effort to capturing Clervaux (also called Clerf in some books). The American commander there, Colonel Hurley Fuller, requested reinforcements several times, and other than a few tanks, nothing could be spared to save the town. He requested to withdraw but Cota told him to fight to the last. Fuller was reduced to using cooks and clerks against German armor. After fighting for hours, German tanks overran the Americans and took the town. Toland tells the story of the men incredibly well and I recommend his book highly.

Many men of the 28th Division, including Colonel Fuller, were captured. However, some of the men of the 28th made it west, where on December 19 they trudged past a new group of soldiers who were getting off trucks near the town of Bastogne. These new soldiers had Screaming Eagle patches on their shoulders.

The Battle Continues

It took the Allied commanders a full day to realize that the German assault was not a diversionary tactic to relieve pressure from the attack of the 2nd Infantry Division. Once Eisenhower understood the extent of the German offensive, all available units, including the 82nd and 101st Airborne Divisions, were rushed into combat.

Also entering the fight in the early stages were the 7th and 9th Armored Divisions, which joined the defense of Saint Vith under the command of General Bruce Clarke. Toland describes an unusual situation in that General Clarke was less senior than was General Jones of the 106th Division. However, Jones, for a number of reasons, including health and exhaustion, ceded command to Clarke. After several days of bitter fighting, including another dramatic defense by cooks and clerks, the Americans had to give up Saint Vith and retreat to the town of Vielsalm.

In the northern sector, the advance of Joachim Pieper sped along rapidly after getting through Lanzerath. Town after town fell and soon the column headed towards a dot on the map called Baugnez. Pieper was well-known prior to the Battle of the Bulge as a fanatical Nazi who committed atrocities against civilians and prisoners. On December 17, east of the town of Malmedy, his lead tank reached the Baugnez crossroads at the precise moment an American unit, Battery B of the 285th Artillery Division, showed up. The Americans should never have been there. MPs in Malmedy warned units not to go in that direction, but the 285th got lost and passed through an MP post that was unmanned because no vehicle traffic was anticipated.

The Germans captured the 150 men of Battery B, led them into a field adjacent to the road and ordered them to stand in formation. At least one German officer fired his pistol at the prisoners but American officers ordered their men to hold ranks, fearing all would be shot in the back if they tried to run. Other German soldiers, including some passing by on vehicles, opened fire on the Americans as well, leading to a killing spree known later as "The Malmedy Massacre." Germans walked among the wounded and shot survivors, but some Americans returned to safety by playing dead or by fleeing during the firing. Word of the massacre spread among the Americans very quickly. Historians noted that the news of the massacre may have made some American troops fight tougher either for revenge or because they thought they would be killed if captured.

The site of the Malmedy Massacre is in the town of Baugnez at the intersection of the N62 and the N632 roads. A new museum stands adjacent to the field where the massacre occurred. To the east of the intersection is a memorial to the more than 80 victims.

Less well-known than the Malmedy Massacre is the killing of eight American prisoners in the town of Ligneuville, several miles south of Baugnez. SS officers executed the men by the side of the road near the Hotel De Moulin and among the victims was Staff Sergeant Abraham Lincoln, a descendant of the legendary president. Pieper's unit committed other massacres in other towns as well.

After cutting through the American lines with little resistance, Pieper's column ground to a halt around the town of La Glieze. Small groups of American soldiers with anti-tank guns and explosives kept knocking out Pieper's tanks and the bridges they needed to get through hills, narrow canyons and river crossings. At a critical area called Trois Points, after watching another vital bridge blow up before him, Pieper muttered, "those damn engineers." With American soldiers pouring in on him, no fuel and no room to maneuver, Pieper ordered his men to abandon their vehicles and march back to Germany. A massive Tiger Royal tank from the battle is on display in La Glieze.

Forming the Bastogne Perimeter

Once Manteuffel's center attack broke through the 28th and 106th Divisions, his army targeted the next strategic objective: Bastogne. This key town had seven roads leading in and out and was a vital transportation hub. All the Americans could muster west of Clervaux were small roadblocks that were knocked aside by the Germans. American units fled towards Bastogne with the Germans only minutes behind.

No one in either the 82nd or 101st Airborne Divisions had a clear idea of what was going on as they headed into combat. The men left their camps in France on the night of December 17 in bad shape. They had little equipment, especially winter gear. Some soldiers sent their weapons in for repair after pulling out of Holland, so they went into Bastogne unarmed. Ammunition of all types was in low supply and there were barely any rations. Some paratroopers were still on leave, and that included General Taylor, who was in Washington, DC to testify before Congress. That is how the 101st came to be commanded by General McAuliffe during the siege.

The actual deployment of the Airborne divisions was not settled when they left France. While en route, a decision was made to send the 82nd north to the towns of Sprimont and Werbomont while the 101st would head to Bastogne. It is just as likely that the 82nd could have been sent to Bastogne, and history may have ended up treating the two divisions very differently if that happened.

The 101st reached Bastogne some time after the arrival of Combat Command B of the 10th Armored Division, under the command of Colonel William Roberts. The 705th Tank Destroyer Battalion, which was attached to CCB, also arrived well before the 101st got into Bastogne. The men of the 10th Armored and the Tank Destroyers would go on to provide critical heavy firepower throughout the campaign, and were involved in ferocious fighting on December 19th that allowed the 101st to form their defensive perimeter around Bastogne. Simply put, without the contribution of the Armored, the defense of Bastogne would have been impossible, though they are rarely mentioned.

Among the units that were part of Combat Command B were, the 609th Tank Destroyer battalion, the 3rd and 21st Tank battalions, the 90th Cavalry Squadron, the 755th, 969th and 420th Field Artillery battalions, the 79th Anti-aircraft Battalion, the 20th and 54th Armored Infantry battalions and the 9th and 55th Engineer battalions.

Colonel Roberts was ordered over his objections to break his force into three combat teams that deployed to defend roads to the east and north of town. The first team to reach Bastogne was commanded by Lieutenant Colonel Henry Cherry and was eponymously named, "Team Cherry." Cherry's forces deployed east towards the town of Longvilly, which is about 10 kilometers from Bastogne along the N874 road.

A second combat team, commanded by Lieutenant Colonel James O'Hara, deployed southeast of Bastogne, in a town about five miles away called Wardin. The third combat team was commanded by Major William Desobry and deployed north of Bastogne to Noville.

The bulk of the 101st Airborne arrived after dark on December 18th after a tortuous ride that was accomplished with the help of another group of soldiers not often noted for their contribution or place in history. The trucks that carried the 101st were driven by African-American truck drivers who were known as the Red Ball Express, and due to segregation in the military were forced into a support role. Without sleep for nearly 24 hours, these men drove the paratroopers into combat with so much emphasis on speed that they took the incredible risk of using their headlights. Normally, light discipline would have been mandatory because of risk of air attack, but the situation was dire enough for an exception.

In the middle of the night on December 18, 1944 the men of the 101st hopped out of their trucks into a freezing countryside unsure of where they were. Some saw a sign for the town of Champs, and almost none had ever heard of the town of Bastogne.

. . .

Entering Combat

The Three-foot Jump and the March through Champs and Hemroulle

The tiny village of Champs still looks much like it did on the night of December 18, 1944, when a long line of trucks broke through a crowd of retreating soldiers and parked in the surrounding fields. Unlike the other soldiers going through Champs who were retreating to the west, the men in these trucks were heading into the fight. These were soldiers of the 101st Airborne.

Since I'm fascinated by beginnings, Champs is special to me. It was the place where the legend of Bastogne started. The trucks parking in the fields near Champs was Act I, Scene I in the legendary defense. And it all started with the men making what they called a "Three Foot Jump," a term to describe getting out of a truck instead of a plane.

I enjoy visiting Champs at different times of the day. Daylight allows you to see the area clearly and pinpoint the flow of the battle and specific landmarks. But visiting at night is different and in a way, more moving. Standing on the road, with no traffic and nearly no sound, it is easy to picture Don Burgett and Don Brininstool of A Company and Dick Winters, Carwood Lipton, Bill Guarnere and the rest of Easy Company, and hundreds of other men, passing through in the dark the way they did in 1944. It doesn't matter that today you will not actually see soldiers and equipment retreating from, or heading to, the battlefront. And it doesn't matter there are no distant sounds of fighting near Magaret or Longvilly. There is still the palpable sense of danger and foreboding of December 18.

The fields where the trucks parked are around Champs and towards the hamlet of Rouette. Once the 506th got out of the trucks, it was all by foot for the next month. It's amazing to me to think what I know took place in and around Bastogne. For those men who were getting off the trucks, it was all in the future for them. None of them had a clue about what was happening or what would happen.

While you may not be in danger of an artillery strike while visiting Champs, you are not completely safe. Belgian drivers make New York taxis seem safe. They drive recklessly and speed like madmen. It is easy to be lulled into thinking that you are in quiet farm country. There may not be a lot of people around, but I cannot overemphasize the need to take care when you make U-turns, and when you're – inevitably – driving slowly looking off to the side of the road for certain landmarks. And always remember that if you stop in the area of a blind curve, some of those speeders will never have a chance to react. You could end up looking like you got hit by an 88.

Getting to Champs was difficult for the drivers of the Red Ball Express as the road was jammed with men and equipment heading in the opposite direction. One of the more incredible incidents of that night involved a headstrong lieutenant who was part of the column retreating to the west. This lieutenant commanded several trucks parked across the road in both directions so that the 101st could not get through.

The lieutenant stated that he had orders to hold his vehicles in that location and he would not move until he received a new order. The irate soldiers in the 101st thought about shooting him and when I read that story for the first time, all I could think of was that the lieutenant was unbelievably lucky that Ron Speirs was not in the lead vehicles. Otherwise, the lieutenant would have been the first kill of the Battle of the Bulge by the 101st Airborne! Eventually, the lieutenant, confronted by a senior officer of the 101st, pulled some of his vehicles out of the way.

Champs

The church in Champs makes a convenient place to park. Look at the road and think of the men with Screaming Eagle patches on their jackets heading down this hill and off towards Bastogne into the direction of the fight.

Downhill from the church you will find one of the many symbols of the defense of Bastogne, a Sherman tank turret. Next to the turret you will find a board that describes the fighting in and around Champs. Also, you will see information about a tour route that you can follow, and at each stop, you'll see a tank turret and a sign post.

The miniseries has a short scene in which shortly after detrucking, the men are supplied with ammunition by Lt. George Rice. This incident was absolutely true, and Lt. Rice of the 10th Armored provided men of the 506th with vital ammunition. However, this did not happen after the men got out of the trucks. Lt. Rice actually met the men north of Bastogne on a stretch of the N30 road between Luzery and Foy. You will pass this area on your way to Foy and Noville, although it is unmarked.

Hemroulle

East of Champs is the hamlet of Hemroulle, which is one of my favorite spots in the Bastogne perimeter. That's because it is one of those tiny places that you might ordinarily miss as you're driving to a more well-known spot, such as the Bois Jacques. Spend 15 to 30 minutes in Hemroulle, and I think you'll be happy that you did so.

The Hemroulle church is part of a touching story that began during the siege when the town was defended by men of the 502nd Regiment and the 463rd Parachute Field Artillery. The 502nd was desperately short of winter camouflage, so the commander of the Regiment, Lt. Colonel John Hanlon, rang the bell of the church in Hemroulle and asked the assembled villagers for any white sheets that they could spare, which in a town so small, amounted to only 48 sets.

After the war, Hanlon, back home in Winchester, MA, organized a drive to collect sheets and bed linens for the people of Hemroulle as thanks for their generosity. According to the website for the St. Mary's Parish Family Church of Winchester, a "Sheets for Hemroulle" day was held on November 23, 1947 and raised 740 sets of sheets. Hanlon returned to Hemroulle on February 21, 1948 and presented his gift. Quoting the St. Mary's website,

> ""Jack" Hanlon returned to Hemroulle with the hundreds of donated sheets. Once again, as he had on that December day in 1944, Hanlon rang the chapel bell and the villagers gathered, waving small American flags in celebration of "Winchester Day." He then handed each family several sets of sheets as a smiling Mayor Gaspard looked on."

The church website goes on to say that the residents of Hemroulle were so touched by the gesture, that they donated several treasured paintings from the church to a number of churches in the Winchester area.

By the church is a weatherbeaten signboard that describes some of the fighting in the area, which included a fierce tank battle on Christmas Day. Band of Brothers left out the 502nd Regiment of the 101st, and it also never mentioned the 463rd Parachute Field Artillery Battalion, which is honored simply with a display case on the right side of the church. The first time I learned of the 463rd Parachute Field Artillery Battalion was in George Koskimaki's book, "The Battered Bastards of Bastogne," but it took further research to find out more about this unit, which I had mistakenly assumed was part of the 101st Division.

The 463rd was a battle-hardened unit waiting to be assigned to the 17th Airborne Corps when the breakthrough in the Ardennes occurred. Recognizing the seriousness of the situation, the commanding officer of the 463rd, Lt. Colonel John Cooper, offered his unit's services to General McAuliffe, himself an artillery officer. Even though the 463rd was not part of the 101st Airborne, McAuliffe realized more artillery could be useful. Cooper was directed to Colonel Joseph H. Harper of the 327th Regiment, and asked if his artillery was needed, to which Harper replied, "You're goddamn right."

The Christmas Day Tank Battle at Hemroulle

On the morning of Christmas Day, 1944, the Germans launched an attack with 18 Mark IV tanks of the 115th Panzergrenadier Regiment of the 15th Panzer Division, as well as two battalions of the 77th Panzergrenadier Regiment. The destination of the attack was Bastogne, but the German commander got confused, perhaps because it was dark when he moved out, and he headed in the wrong direction, towards Hemroulle.

Past the ridgeline overlooking Hemroulle, towards the hamlet of Mande St. Etienne, were men of the 401st Glider Infantry and Companies A and B of the 327th Glider Infantry Regiment. The German armor broke through the lightly-armed infantry in their foxholes, and the only option for the Americans was to duck, let the tanks pass and then engage the infantry following behind. SLA Marshall wrote that the Americans suffered four dead and five wounded, but the 68 men left in these positions fought hard and inflicted many casualties and even captured 92 Germans.

Somewhat oblivious to the problems of the German infantry behind them, the tanks kept moving ahead after breaking through the foxholes of the glider infantry. The German tank commander split his armor into two forces: one group headed forward towards Hemroulle, while the other turned to the northwest in the direction of Champs and the nearby hamlet of Rolle.

I suppose it might have been easy to get confused in the dark and mistake the church steeple of Hemroulle for Bastogne, but it seems to me that it should have occurred to the German commander that the resistance he faced was too light. If he was in Bastogne overlooking a church, it stands to reason that the Americans would hit his tanks with everything they had. And I'm happy he didn't figure out his mistake until it was too late.

I'm also happy that the German commander did something simply amazing. After pulling to the crest of the hill overlooking Hemroulle, the tanks stopped in the dark and their crews got out and prepared breakfast. American observers spotted the outlines of the tanks, but because of communication difficulties, did not know if it was German or US armor.

As the Germans relaxed, Lt. Colonel Cooper ordered the antitank and artillery gunners of the 463rd to aim at the tanks and prepare to fire as soon as the signal was given. Cooper told his men to be as quiet as they could to avoid alerting the Germans. Suddenly, American observers noted that the gun barrels had the distinctive muzzle features of only German tanks. The order was given to "let the shit hit the fan." The tanks were blasted apart by antitank guns, artillery and bazookas. As their tanks burst into flames, the Germans regrouped and tried to move forward towards "Bastogne." By 0830 the German infantrymen advanced along the western ridge to within 200 yards of the church in Hemroulle. But the soldiers of the 502nd, 327th, 401st and 463rd Artillery repulsed the German attack.

Drive towards Bastogne from Hemroulle and just a few feet past the church, is a road leading to the right. Go up that hill, past several farmhouses until you come to a ridgeline that gives you a sweeping view of farmlands. If you miss that turn, then you can also get to this area by making the left turn off the road as you drive from the Hemroulle church towards Champs. There you can stand on the fields where the German attack was repulsed, among cows who now graze where tanks once parked. Breezes blow down the long grass, creating an illusion of invisible armies walking through. From there you can see Bastogne. You can see where the 327th and 401st soldiers were. You can see Hemroulle. You can see Champs. A sweeping 360 degree view of the battlefield.

The German tanks and infantry that headed for Champs fared no better than those that attacked Hemroulle. Several companies of the 502nd Regiment were alerted to the Germans and prepared for the assault. Near Champs were two tank destroyers of Company B of the 705th Battalion that engaged the German tanks as they moved diagonally over the hills towards the Hemroulle-Champs road. The tank destroyers knocked out two German tanks but were quickly disabled themselves. The Americans were not in a position where they could trade the Germans in a tank-for-tank exchange.

After dispatching the two Company B tank destroyers, the German armor reached the Hemroulle-Champs road and turned north towards Champs. This turn to the north exposed the flanks of the German tanks to two more TDs hidden in the woods to the east of the road. With the sides of the German tanks in view, the TDs opened fire, knocking out several. 502nd bazookamen destroyed two more tanks and rifle and machine gun fire decimated the German infantry riding on the panzers. One tank managed to break into Champs, but it was destroyed, probably by a bazooka. A fantastic description of the fighting in and around Champs is in George Koskimaki's book.

You can see the spot where the German tanks were caught broadside by the American tank destroyers if you head back towards Champs from Hemroulle, and look for a long stand of trees on the left side of the road (in perpendicular fashion). There are not many trees on the road, so this spot is distinctive. As you face the trees on your left, look to the fields and woods to your right and you will see the area where the TDs and infantry opened fire on the Germans.

By 0900, the Christmas Day attack on Hemroulle and Champs was over. The Germans lost 18 heavy tanks and hundreds of infantrymen. The Americans lost two desperately needed tank destroyers and took several casualties, but unknowingly, they had just survived the last day of the siege: on

December 26th, advanced units of Patton's force broke through the German encirclement of Bastogne.

But for the men who got out of the trucks on December 18th and then walked through Hemroulle into fighting positions around Bastogne, it would be a week of hellacious combat, frostbite, hunger and supply shortages until the siege was broken.

• • •

On to Bastogne

Bivouac and Resupply

As you drive from Hemroulle to Bastogne you pass underneath a highway overpass and come upon fields on both sides of the road, with a few houses off to the left. There are no markers of any sort to indicate that this area was the site of a few memorable stories during the Battle of the Bulge. To me, perhaps every place around Bastogne is part of the story of the siege, and you simply can't mark everything as notable: you'd never be able to finish touring the area.

The field on the left was the site where a C-47 named "Ain't Missbehavin" ended up after a crash landing on December 27, 1944 during an aerial resupply mission. The pilot, Captain Ernest Turner, realized he lost both engines to anti-aircraft fire and that he was too low to try to bail out. He crash landed on the snowy, icy field to the right of the road and skidded across into ditch in the field on the left. In George Koskimaki's book, "The Battered Bastards of Bastogne" there is a picture of the plane in the field with its' crew posed by the nose and several first-hand accounts, including that of Captain Turner.

Where Ain't Missbehavin' began its' crash landing on the right side of the road is a large field that was part of the area where the 506th, 327th, 502nd and 501st regiments of the 101st Airborne bivouacked after arriving in Bastogne. I can only imagine what the men thought as they rested in the bitter cold, not knowing what the situation was but being keenly aware of not having the right equipment.

Later, this field was the site of another important part of the Bastogne story: this was where the first aerial resupply of the siege occurred on December 23, 1944. You can imagine how uplifting it must have been for the men all around this area to look up and see supplies being parachuted onto this spot.

Entering Bastogne

The roads from Champs to Bastogne have been reconstructed and are slightly different than they were back in 1944, but not that much. From Hemroulle you will come to an intersection with a light and make the right turn there to follow the road that the 501st and 506th regiments followed into Bastogne, the Rue de La Roche. The 501st was in the lead and it arrived in Bastogne around daylight. Since the 501st was in front, it got the first assignment of any of the Division's regiments: travel east of Bastogne towards Longvilly to "clear up the situation." Just as if the 82nd, not the 101st, was sent to Bastogne, if the 506th had been ahead of the 501st, the story of Band of Brothers would have been very different.

As you head towards Bastogne along the Rue de la Roche, you will see a military installation on the left, and a cemetery to the right. This military base is known as the Heintz Barracks, and it is where General McAuliffe kept his headquarters for a few days. McAuliffe's headquarters is still devotedly maintained by a small group of Belgian soldiers stationed at the base.

In October 2008, I had the chance of a lifetime: to visit the Barracks with Red Falvey, who saw Bastogne for the first time in 1944 as his bazooka platoon marched towards the Bois Jacques. I was joined by my friend Reg Jans, a great local tourguide, his friend Roby (a very well-known tourguide in the area), and several soldiers who were stationed at the base. Red was treated like royalty and presented with a special plaque thanking him for his service during World War II, and we were given a personal tour of McAuliffe's headquarters and the base itself.

However, my first visit did not go quite so auspiciously. The first time I was there, I was by myself, in front of what is an active military base, with my camera, taking pictures. It all seemed like nothing special to me but that wasn't the case with the MPs who were in the guardhouse by the gate. Despite having a number of books on the Battle of the Bulge in my hand,

I was approached by an MP. At 6 feet 1 inch tall, I'm not normally accustomed to looking a man straight in the sternum. As I tilted my head back, I remembered the scene in the movie, "Raiders of the Lost Ark," where Indiana Jones is confronted by the shirtless German soldier at the airplane, and how Indy just slumped when he saw the size difference.

The guard started talking to me in French, and I responded with a poorly pronounced "Parlez-vous Anglais?" I didn't need any translation to know that he wasn't happy. He responded in very broken English, "No pictures, not allowed." A second MP came out of the guardhouse and I started to get concerned that my camera was about to be confiscated. Thinking that I was already in a little bit of a bad way, I decided that the best defense would be a good offense, so, I looked them in the eyes, interrupted their questioning of me and asked in my bad impression of French if McAuliffe's headquarters was on the base. Seemingly confused, they pointed to a building towards the rear of the base and said that the HQ was there, but that entry was forbidden. My strategy worked because I put my camera away, said "Merci, au revoir" and waved as I got back in the car. Seemingly mollified, the MPs watched me drive away and went back into the guardhouse. A close call.

The cemetery across from the barracks played an important role on December 23, 1944 as a landmark for the C-47 pilots of the first aerial resupply of the 101st during the siege of Bastogne. The Germans placed intense flak belts to the west of Bastogne, so the C-47 crews approached Bastogne from the east. The first plane carried Pathfinders Jack Agnew and Jake McNiece. Landing near the cemetery, the Pathfinders dodged German fire and ran towards the Barracks for cover.

After arriving, the Pathfinders set up their radio equipment to guide the C-47 fleet heading for Bastogne. One of the most famous pictures taken during the siege is that of a soldier on top of a pile of bricks setting up an antenna for a radio transmitter. That soldier was later identified as Jack Agnew, and he was guarded by men of the 327th Glider Infantry. As you look at the cemetery, past the far left corner is an area where there used to be a brick kiln, and behind it was the pile of bricks on which Agnew perched.

About 100 yards towards Bastogne, on the left side of the road, is the convent where Nurse Renee Lemaire lived.

The 101st Enters Combat

The 501st led the way through Bastogne, down the Rue De La Roche. Today, as you follow this road, it will lead you to a traffic circle. The 501st would bear right and head towards the town of Neffe to the east of Bastogne.

One of the small stories that I did not know until I read a few books about the Battle of the Bulge was the amazing luck in having the 501st regiment first in line. By a stunning coincidence, the regimental commander, Colonel Julian Ewell, spent a few days on leave in Bastogne only a month earlier. The 101st had nearly no maps, the soldiers were walking into fog, no one knew what was going on, and here, commanding the lead regiment was the only person in the Division who knew the area intimately.

Ewell knew little about what was ahead of him, where were the Germans and where he should go. General McAuliffe was known for his terseness and his orders to Ewell were simply to "clear up the situation." Ewell was informed of the presence of Team Cherry, the 10th Armored combat team and he sent the 501st east with the expectation of a link-up.

As Ewell's men moved out, the lead jeeps got lost in the fog and headed south towards the town of Marvie instead of towards Neffe. That amazing luck of having Ewell's unit in the lead paid off. He realized they were in the wrong place and put them back in the right direction just in time to run head-first into a German infantry and armor reconnaissance in force. Had the

501st not been first into Bastogne, the war in Europe might have gone in a totally different direction. Some other unit might have arrived first and gotten completely lost in the fog. The Germans could have slipped behind the other unit and that would have allowed the back door to Bastogne to be open and the battle might have been lost before it even got started.

As the 501st entered combat, the 506th marched along the Rue de la Roche. A block above the present-day traffic circle is a small, unmarked street that leads from the Rue de la Roche to the N30. The 506th followed that road and turned to the left and marched to their positions in the northern perimeter with 1st Battalion in the lead, followed by 3rd Battalion, the Headquarters unit and then 2nd Battalion. Since 1st Battalion was in front, it was deployed to Noville to support the men of the armored infantry's Team Desobry, who were already engaged in a pitched battle with dozens of German heavy tanks and infantry. The assignment of securing Foy was given to 3rd Battalion and Easy Company and the 2nd Battalion were sent to regimental reserve in the hamlet of Luzery.

Follow the N30 north in the direction of Noville and Foy and Luzery, and you will pass a number of modern buildings, including the new hospital. There is a famous picture on page 445 of "Rendezvous with Destiny" showing a bazooka team trudging by that spot. The picture is mislabeled as it is actually a shot of Red Falvey's bazooka platoon heading north towards Foy. The area looked much different then, and the hospital did not exist. Ironically, part of the growth of the Bastogne area can be attributed to German retirees, who take advantage of the lower Belgian taxes.

Just past the hospital by a few hundred yards is a small turn-off to the right to the hamlet of Luzery. There is little to see in Luzery today: it is just some old houses and many more new ones. I am certain that some of the old houses have significance, but I did not see any memorials or other descriptions of what took place there during the siege.

Heading north towards Foy, the woods on the right are the Bois Jacques and that is where Easy Company and 2nd Battalion spent nearly a month. In the area of the last few buildings on the right before you see Foy is the unmarked spot where Lt. Rice delivered ammunition to the men of the 506th as they marched.

When Lieutenant Rice was distributing ammunition to the men, the sounds of battle in Noville would have been loud, close roars, and the men who grabbed bullets, grenades and other ammunition must have known that they were about to be put to good use. The first to get a chance would be Don Burgett and the men of 1st Battalion.

• • •

Noville

Noville was arguably the most brutal single battle fought by any part of the 506th during World War II, but in the book Band of Brothers, the only description of the combat there is part of one paragraph on the first page of Chapter 11, "Bastogne." Hardly any recognition that in about 24 hours, 1st Battalion suffered 212 casualties, and Don Burgett's A Company was reduced from 200 men to fewer than 60.

The historian SLA Marshall wrote in, "Bastogne: The First Eight Days:"

> "The contemporary accounts which attempted to apportion the credit for the saving of Bastogne had much to say about the 101st Airborne Division and relatively little about any other units."

I think Marshall was right, but I would extend his generalization to say that many of the recent accounts of Bastogne don't focus on the Division, but on Easy Company specifically.

There is virtually nothing in most of the books about Easy Company or its' men to tell that Team Desobry of Combat Command B and a few tanks and tank destroyers held off a three-pronged attack by Tiger and Panther tanks for several hours until 1st Battalion arrived in Noville. Or that the collective American force in Noville, despite being outnumbered and outgunned, fought so ferociously that the Germans pulled back, unsure of who or what was in front of them. That delay by the Germans in Noville was one of many that allowed the American defensive perimeter to be formed in the nick of time.

And it's not part of the well-known history of Bastogne that when the defenders of Noville were ordered to withdraw towards Bastogne, they found that they were cut off from the American lines by German armor that swept to their south. It was a siege within the siege of Bastogne. Many men who survived Noville were killed or wounded as they fought their way through the Germans back to the American lines.

For the story of Noville, I recommend several books. Marshall and Toland both give good scholarly accounts of what happened there, along with a sense of what the fighting in Noville achieved for the Americans. Personal accounts of fighting can be found in Don Burgett's book, "Seven Roads to Hell," which I reread so many times that I had to order a new copy. I also recommend Don Addor's, "Noville Outpost of Bastogne: My last Battle." Addor was one of the soldiers in Team Desobry.

The Battle of Noville

Noville is situated at the center of a gently-sloping bowl, with high ground to the east, north and west in almost a U-shape. The highest elevation is immediately to the southwest of Noville where a recently-forested hill stands. That hill is where Dick Winters and Easy Company froze the night before attacking the town in January 1945.

Several roads converge in Noville, with one leading south to Bastogne and another to the north to Houffalize.

When the Germans attacked the Ardennes, units of Combat Command B, which included men of the 20th Armored Infantry Battalion of the 10th Armored Division, were scrambled from locations around the area and ordered to Bastogne by the overall sector commander, General Troy Middleton. Middleton was in Bastogne on December 18th and at around 1600, was met at his headquarters by Colonel William Roberts, commander of Combat Command B. Middleton didn't have time to give Roberts a full briefing, and even if he did, his intelligence was far from perfect. The Germans were coming and there was a lot of activity to the east. Beyond that, nothing else was certain.

I've wondered a lot about what it must have felt like for Middleton and Roberts. They didn't know where the Germans were or what was the size of the force. They knew the American infantry divisions in the east were hit hard, and they could see men retreating through Bastogne. And it was getting dark. It must have been chilling and I think that if I were there, I would look over my shoulder towards the horizon constantly. Where were the Germans? Would they hit Bastogne? When? Where?

Middleton told Roberts that Bastogne was the primary strategic objective in the region and that other American units were coming, but the chaos was so great that nothing could be assumed. Roberts was ordered to split his command into three combat teams, each of which would set up a roadblock on a road leading into Bastogne. Roberts was reluctant to break up his command because if the Germans were coming in such force, he wanted to have his whole unit together. But he nonetheless sent task forces into position as they rolled into town.

The first of Roberts' units to arrive was under the command of Lt. Colonel James O'Hara. Team O'Hara, with 500 men and 30 tanks of various sizes, was sent to the southeast about five miles outside of Bastogne along the road to Wiltz. Team O'Hara had few men and mostly light tanks: no wonder Roberts didn't want to break up his unit.

Colonel Henry Cherry's unit was the second to arrive and it was ordered east towards the town of Longvilly along the present-day N874. Cherry was told to expect to meet units of the Combat Command Reserve, which he encountered west of Longvilly. The men of the Reserve were retreating in panic, and Cherry halted his column in order not to get mixed up with the fleeing soldiers. As a result, Cherry's column stretched from Longvilly back to the town of Neffe. Arriving at Roberts' headquarters at 2000 on December 18th, Cherry reported his problematic deployment and the panic.

About a mile or two south of Longvilly, on the other side of a set of short hills, heading right into the flank of the unsuspecting Americans were the lead companies of the Panzer

Lehr's 902nd Panzergrenadier Regiment, two regiments of the 26th Volksgrenadiers and 15 tanks. The Americans wouldn't learn of the German presence until they saw the muzzle flashes from the panzers.

Roberts' third combat team was under the command of one of his youngest officers, Major William Desobry. Desobry saw Roberts as a father figure, and Roberts thought equally highly of his protégé. Before sending Team Desobry north to Noville, Roberts gave some fatherly advice: "You are young and by tomorrow morning you will probably want to pull out. Remember, I am telling you not to pull out until I give the order."

Team Desobry reached Noville on December 18th at about 2300 in complete darkness. Desobry, who did not know the area or have good maps, did not see that the town was in a slight depression surrounded by higher ground. Had he known the terrain, he probably would not have set up headquarters in town or ceded the high ground to the Germans. Desobry deployed men and light tanks to form three roadblocks, each about half a mile outside of town on the Houffalize, Bourcy and Vaux roads.

Retreating soldiers, some from the 28th Infantry Division, streamed by Desobry's men, making it difficult to form a roadblock. Team Desobry tried to get some of the soldiers to stay and fight, especially those who were infantrymen or engineers, but there was little success in recruiting a reserve, and many of the men who did pass through had no weapons or equipment anyway. SLA Marshall wrote that one unit did join Team Desobry, but I never found another reference to who were those men.

One of the eeriest moments to me would have been the deathly quiet that fell over Noville after the last stragglers moved through town at about 0430 on December 19. Don Addor wrote that there was silent darkness and fog, and that the men on the line knew that anyone or anything that came along next was likely to be German. Over on the other side of Bastogne, near Champs, men of Don Burgett's 1st Battalion were on the march towards Noville, but at that moment, no one in Team Desobry knew when reinforcements would arrive. And until then, it was their job to hold the town.

The painful silence lasted one hour until 0530, when several halftracks approached from the east along the Bourcy road. The roadblock opened fire and the halftracks retreated. About 20 minutes later, the northern roadblock was attacked by Germans cleverly riding in captured American Sherman tanks. The roadblock crew thought it was American armor because the sound was distinctly that of a Sherman. They were right about the equipment, but when the tanks opened fire, the Americans realized what had happened, and a shooting match ensued.

Around sunrise at 0830, two Tiger tanks attacked from the north. Thick fog blanketed Noville, and the American defenders heard the roar of German tanks, but couldn't see anything. Both sides fired blindly into the fog, and eventually one of the tanks was destroyed and the other was damaged.

It was a long, tense night and agonizing early morning for Team Desobry. They knew the Germans were in the area in force, and they knew from the stragglers of the 28th Division that the situation was very serious. But because of darkness and fog, no one knew exactly what was going on. When the fog finally lifted at about 1030, Team Desobry was stunned by the sight of hillsides bristling with German tanks. The defenders counted between 30 and 40 tanks, with 14 on the hill to the north alone. That was when the Americans realized that they were in a depression and the Germans had the high ground all around them.

Quickly the American tankers of Team Desobry opened fire, and, luckily, a few minutes later, they were joined by four or five Tank Destroyers from the 705th and 609th TD Battalions. Among the tank destroyers were a couple of M-18 Achilles, which had 90-millimeter guns that could knock out the big German Panthers and Tigers. American armor knocked out 11 German tanks in quick order. However, the Germans stubbornly charged into town and two tanks made it to within 75 yards of Desobry's headquarters before being destroyed.

The close call plus an emerging ammunition shortage, led Desobry to request a pullout from Noville, but Colonel Roberts reminded him of his admonition at the time of deployment, and said that 1st Battalion was on the way. Desobry promised an attack, and the aggressiveness pleased Roberts. The commander of 1st Battalion, Colonel LaPrade, the man who crossed the Wilhelmina Canal in Son, arrived in Noville before the bulk of his men did, and he drew up a battle plan with Major Desobry. Desobry and LaPrade were fighters and for them it was time to go on the offensive. Burgett's A Company, arriving in Noville around 1330, would attack to the northeast, B Company to the northwest and C Company to the east.

Burgett's battalion arrived in Noville at 1330 and the men were told to be prepared to go right on the offensive. These men spent a freezing night driving in open trailers to Bastogne, marched to Noville with only a short rest and were not only short on sleep, but they also lacked warm clothing, supplies and, in some cases, weapons.

Don Burgett's account of the battle is haunting and tense. In a real-time narrative, he describes the march into combat, the cold weather, the uneasy feeling in his stomach, the sounds of heavy fighting in the distance getting louder as they neared town and the confusion from lack of information. Burgett wrote about fog circling the town, and smoke from burning vehicles and buildings, screams of pain from unseen soldiers, and mortar, artillery and tank fire.

For Burgett and many of the men marching into Noville, the battle plan was communicated by people in the front of the column yelling for those behind them to move forward. Simply following the men in front, the troopers of 1st Battalion rushed forward without any idea of where the Germans were or in what strength. They just charged ahead into the fields.

Few men of 1st Battalion reached the trees on the high grounds around the town. Many were riddled with gunfire from tanks and infantry and died in the fields. The soldiers whose bodies were not recovered were blanketed by snow over the coming days and weeks. Many took what cover they could and many others pulled back towards town. The attack was a horrible failure.

Squad leader Sergeant Don Brininstool made Burgett and his buddy, Harold Phillips, scouts. As Burgett and Phillips moved through a cluster of homes in the northeastern part of town, they counted 16 German tanks on the fields in front of them. Fighting those 16 German tanks were two American Shermans, which used the houses of Noville for cover. The Shermans blew up two tanks and the remaining German armor and infantry pulled back to the hillside. Dodging artillery fire, Burgett and Phillips moved far out from the cluster of burning buildings that was Noville and reached a number of haystacks at the base of a hill where they knew the Germans were waiting.

If you visit Noville and head towards Bourcy, before the last house on the left you will see an unmarked dirt road. Follow that road until you come over a hill. At the base of the hill, you will reach a T-intersection. That field in front of you is where the haystacks stood. Turning around towards Noville, I saw the church steeple way in the distance and knew I didn't want to be where I was standing back on December 19, 1944.

As Burgett's squad arrived, the bow of a German Tiger tank appeared, terrifying the men hidden behind the haystack armed with just rifles, no bazookas or any defensive weapons. Brininstool knew the men were completely vulnerable and ordered Burgett to run back to town and get permission for the squad to withdraw. Judging the risk from his tough-as-nails squad leader greater than that from the Tiger, Burgett not only ran to town, dodging machine gun fire, but he ran back with orders not to retreat. By the time of his return, the haystacks were completely engulfed in flame, lit by the tracers of the tank's machine gun. To hell with the orders: the squad broke for Noville, the Tiger lurching into a hot pursuit after Burgett.

The crew of the Tiger could have killed Burgett if they wanted to, but they must have thought he would lead them to a command post. Burgett raced down the road and ducked into a house with a couple of A Company men. They bolted out through the back door just as a point-blank blast from the Tiger obliterated the front room, vaporizing the body of an old man lying in the bed there.

Burgett and his squad regrouped that afternoon and moved back out into the fields just in time for a combined German armor and infantry attack. Without even a bazooka, the paratroopers hid in their foxholes and allowed the German tanks to pass through their positions, rose and cut down the infantry. In town, the American tankers blasted many of the German tanks and the surviving ones pulled back, opening fire on the paratroopers, who then were targeted by an artillery barrage.

Nightfall comes early to Noville in December. Normally a mid-December sunset is before 4:30 PM, but on that day fog and smoke must have made it darker earlier. In Noville Colonel LaPrade and Major Desobry were in a home being used as a headquarters. According to a story I heard, Lt. Rice, the hero who provided ammunition to the men of the 506th south of Foy, drove up in front of the headquarters and parked his jeep, a move that the observant Germans interpreted as an indication of a CP. German artillery and tank fire targeted the building, spraying the interior of the room with shrapnel, killing LaPrade instantly and wounding Major Desobry.

Desobry was taken by ambulance to the Division field hospital west of Bastogne, but the driver did not know that the Germans captured the medical facility. Some wounded American soldiers were murdered by the Germans, but Desobry and the medical staff were taken to Germany. Desobry not only survived the war, but he rose to the rank of General, commanded the Military Assistance Command in Vietnam from 1966 to 1968 and later commanded Fort Knox.

Parking at the Noville church on a spectacularly sunny, warm April day, I spotted the house that served as the headquarters across the street and about 100 yards south of the intersection with the Bourcy road. Freshly-painted in a pleasant, welcoming, warm yellow, the house had two numbers, 448 and 15A. I stood in front of the house, probably near where the artillery shell that killed Colonel LaPrade landed. I wonder if it is difficult to live in a place where something famous happened because of gawking tourists like me, or if it is an honor.

I didn't know at the time, but there is an irony about that house and its' history. Desobry originally had his headquarters at the intersection by the light in the town schoolhouse. However, when LaPrade arrived, he recommended to Desobry that they move just south. Ironically, LaPrade chose to the move into the building where he was killed.

Noville reminded me a little of being in one of the many tiny towns that I have visited in Nebraska, South Dakota and Montana. Just one sleepy street passing among a few buildings with a single streetlight. No stores, no restaurants. Just you, the street, the buildings and the weather. It was peaceful on the verge of being delicate, with a warm breeze, sun, quiet. The contrast to the night of December 19th was incomprehensible.

Noville is today what it was then, a small town with just a few residents, surrounded by farmland, ranches and harvestable forests. The people who lived there were simply unlucky to be caught in the middle of the fight. And being caught on a battlefield between two fighting armies meant terror for the townspeople who couldn't get out of the way. Don Burgett and Don Addor wrote how they sought shelter in basements along with young children, their parents and the elderly.

The tragedy continued for the townspeople of Noville even after the battle. The Gestapo entered the town at 0800 on December 21st and gathered eight civilians, including Father Louis Delvaux (the priest of Noville and Bourcy) and the schoolteacher, accused them of being part of the resistance and executed them one by one in a small courtyard behind the present-day church.

The yard where the civilians were killed is on the southeast corner of the church. I walked there through a parking lot that is adjacent to the signboard in town that describes the battle. There I saw the iron gate with "1944" on its' face, and a monument with eight names. I wonder if the people who were executed thought – before the Gestapo came – that they were lucky to survive a ferocious battle that killed many of their neighbors.

I walked back to the headquarters building and reflected solemnly on the bloody, confusing, terrifying, and what must have been lonely night of the December 19, 1944. That night, with LaPrade dead and Desobry wounded, Colonel Sink visited Noville to assess the situation and would have found burning buildings, wrecked and flaming equipment, thick clouds of smoke, gasoline and oil, shattered bodies of dead and wounded troopers strewn among the town, the clatter of small arms fire, explosions from incoming and outgoing tank and mortar fire, blasts from German artillery, screaming and yelling, shadows of men moving through the confusion. It must have been like seeing hell. Sink placed 1st Battalion under the command of Major Robert Harwick, who was later wounded himself, and Major Charles Hustead took charge of Team Desobry.

The night of December 19th was captured well by Don Burgett in his book. Cut off from each other by darkness, smoke and fog, hearing the battle all around them, the men faced the night individually or with another man in hastily dug foxholes in the fields to the northeast of Noville. To the north and west of town, the American lines pulled back much closer to the center of Noville, as close as just past the cemetery on the Houffalize road. Don Addor in his book describes the night chillingly as well, and the only thing that I can imagine is that the men knew, without saying anything to each other, that they were going to die. Neither side would give or request quarter.

Alone in his foxhole in the field, Burgett heard an order to pull back, and he ran to the center of town. Somehow, in the chaos, someone heard an order that was never given. The bewildered men gathered in shattered homes, their faces lit by flames, and were told to return to their positions.

Burgett and his friend Siber Speer headed back out to a foxhole, but German artillery pounded their area so hard, they had to return to town. The German infantry would not attack as long as their artillery hammered away because of the risk of friendly fire. Entering a cellar, Burgett and Speer waited for the artillery fire to end and for the ground attack to begin. They saw the faces of several of the men of their platoon, and learned about the deaths of a number of soldiers during the battle.

As dawn approached, the artillery fire lessened and the men reentered their foxholes. There is a controversial story that was supposed to have happened before dawn. The story goes that in the darkness and fog, platoon leader Sergeant Ted Vetland borrowed a bazooka and three rockets and knocked out three tanks. He was supposed to have crawled up to each in the fog, felt for the side of the tank, backed away with his bazooka and fired, killing the crew. Vetland apparently stated that things didn't happen that way. One thing is not unclear: Vetland was awarded a Purple Heart, a Bronze Star and a Silver Star during World War II.

The Germans launched several tank and infantry attacks towards Noville through the lines of A Company. Burgett wrote that their positions were along a ridge about 200 feet from a road. The ground was level from the road to their positions, but there was then a bank of about four feet dropping to the fields that stretched to the German positions up on the hilltops and trees.

About 20 tanks were in front of A Company, and one came so close to Burgett and Speer, that dirt and snow crumbled into their foxhole. They stayed perfectly still, knowing that any move or sound could get them machine gunned or crushed. In some cases, German tanks straddled foxholes and asphyxiated the men with carbon monoxide from the exhaust.

After the tanks passed through the foxholes, A Company knew what was next: an infantry charge. The paratroopers, who were deadly marksmen, emerged and ripped the German infantry to shreds. Back towards Noville, the German tanks were blasted by American tank fire and retreated. At one point during the retreat, a German Panther tank drove up to where the Americans dug in. Systematically, it fired point-blank into the bank below each foxhole, killing the men inside before retreating.

As Noville was reduced to rubble, the 101st got organized throughout the Bastogne perimeter. In Foy, the 3rd Battalion took up positions and 2nd Battalion moved into the Bois Jacques. The 501st Regiment, which had been fighting for a day, dug in to the south of the 506th, from Bizory down to Neffe. Artillery was in place near the present-day Mardisson memorial, and the 502nd, 401st and 327th were in position elsewhere.

Thanks to the fighting of the 501st to the east and the forces in Noville to the north, the American lines were established, and it was time to withdraw the survivors of 1st Battalion and Team Desobry. At 1200 on December 20, the order was given to withdraw from Noville via Foy, about a mile to the south.

Foy is so close to Noville that you can imagine standing in one town and hearing a car alarm go off in the other. It doesn't take five minutes to drive from one town to the other. Maybe only two minutes. But on December 20th, 1944, it was as if Foy was a million miles from Noville. Despite the proximity of the towns, the defenders of Noville were unaware of what was happening to their south, and into what they were heading.

Unable to take Noville, the Germans skirted around the town in a classic Blitzkrieg move and turned back to the east and hit Foy through the towns of Cobru and Recogne. Another German force launched a simultaneous offensive against Foy from the northeast. Foy was occupied by 3rd Battalion, which faced German armor and heavy artillery on two fronts. A violent firefight began around 0800, and by noon, it was impossible for 3rd Battalion to hold position any longer. It moved from Foy into the Bois Jacques, just to the south, from where the men saw German infantry and tanks take the town.

The Noville survivors were unaware that they had been cut off and withdrew in a long column formed by the few working jeeps, half-tracks, trucks and tanks left. Men rode on top of, or inside, the vehicles. The 1st Battalion deployed with B Company in the lead, followed by Company C. Don Burgett and the men of A Company were the rearguard and had the additional job of making sure the church steeple was destroyed.

Both sides tended to destroy church steeples out of fear that the other side would use them to direct artillery fire and to hide snipers. In my travels, I was told that many steeples in Europe today do not match the architectural style of their churches because they were replacements of originals destroyed during the War. The soldiers in Noville packed the church steeple with explosives and a timer, and in case they did not detonate, A Company had to finish the job.

A Company left town with many of its dead in the fields, and watched as the charges blew the steeple. They reflected on their hasty drive from France, the march into combat, 24 hours of brutal fighting and the fact that so many of them were gone. The column headed towards Foy along the N30, which is paralleled by a creek on the west side. Beyond the creek are fields that stretch towards a ridgeline near the hamlets of Recogne and Cobru. To the east are fields that stretch to a high, forested ridgeline.

Fire poured into the lead vehicles as a German ambush was sprung from both sides of the road. About a quarter mile north of Foy, you can get a good view of the German ambush positions on the hill to the west, facing the road. The Germans were also positioned in the town, with tanks among the buildings to the east and northeast of the streetlight. The Americans were hit up and down the column, and the shock of the ambush quickly gave way to a mad scramble for protection. The situation dissolved into chaos, with no organized defense, only men who fought in small groups with little coordination.

Burgett and several men from A Company jumped into the creek running to the west of the road, and went on the offensive, determined to clear out the Germans, or at least take out some of the enemy before being killed. This aggressive attack was typical of the paratrooper mentality: they never retreated. The tactic worked, and despite taking some casualties, the accurate fire of the Americans drove the Germans back across the fields and up to the ridge.

Further up the column, four of the five American tank destroyers roared forward and encountered the German armor at near point-blank range. The lead TD knocked out a Panzer, which sent the remaining German armor fleeing out of town to the east. Like Burgett and his squad, the TDs instinctively went on the offensive: retreat was never an option. I imagine that no one on that column was going to put up with this bullshit from the Germans after surviving Noville.

Other men in the column blazed away at the Germans from whatever little protection they could find. Some fought back from the American vehicles, which were raked by all kinds of fire. Many of the men of the column made their own individual decisions to break for the safety of American lines. Some, like Don Addor, were wounded and needed the help of their comrades to reach vehicles, while others jumped on whatever could move and some simply ran.

The escape route for the survivors of the ambush was not straight down the N30 towards Bastogne. There may have been a roadblock or a burning vehicle that forced the men to swerve about 50 to 150 feet to the west of the current streetlight. They darted around the intersection, crossed over the road to Recogne and either went straight into the woods, or cut back towards the N30 and sprinted south. Burgett described being in a truck and firing a .50 caliber machine gun as the vehicle hit the bank of the Recogne road, then skidded across a snowy, icy field before rejoining the road to Bastogne.

At the intersection in Foy, I wondered about how many American men died or were wounded during the ambush. I have never seen a casualty count. Did they feel like the civilians of Noville who were executed: thankful and thinking they were safe after surviving the battle only to be killed a short time later?

When the ambush erupted, 3rd Battalion, which had been pushed out of Foy into the Bois Jacques, surged forward. The attack relieved some pressure on the column, and some 3rd Battalion men served as spotters, pointing out the German armor to the American tankers.

I have seen different estimates of the length of fighting during the ambush. One person wrote that it was three hours, another indicated a shorter battle. Whatever the length, on December 19, 1944, 1st Battalion of the 506th went into battle with about 600 to 700 men. A day later, it pulled out with casualties of 13 officers and 199 men killed, wounded or missing.

The survivors fought through the hell of Noville and then the shock of Foy. The armored infantry and tanks were redeployed in other parts of the perimeter. Some of those men would be wounded or die later in the siege. Don Burgett and the other men of 1st Battalion who were still alive were sent to recover in Luzery a tiny town adjacent to the woods just south of Foy: the Bois Jacques.

• • •

The Bois Jacques

The first time I visited the Bois Jacques, I had a lump in my throat. I was visiting ground that was sacred to me. The second time I went, the lump came back. And the third and the fourth times. Every visit that I've made to the small forest that is known as Jack's Woods was preceded by a period of unease and tension thinking about the tragedy, endurance and triumph that the forest represents.

The Bois Jacques are always on my mind when I visit Bastogne, even if I am on a battlefield on the other side of the perimeter. Wherever I am in the area, I find myself turning around to see if I can spot the woods. If I am over in Hemroulle standing on the site where the German tanks got blasted by the 463rd on Christmas Day, I subconsciously turn around and try to find the Bois Jacques.

The excitement and unease and emotion are all present until I finally get to the woods, at which point things get eerie and distorted. Things slow down, I lose track of time, and except for the occasional sound of an airplane engine, I feel totally cut off from the outside world. I emerge from the woods hours after I go in, usually thinking I was in them for only 45 minutes.

The trees of the Bois Jacques are mostly firs, and the forest is shaped in an arc that stretches from the south to east of Foy (almost like 3 to 7 on the face of a watch). Amazing to me is that they are fairly small. Maybe given the history, I expected them to be intimidating and dark, deep and thick with towering trees that have trunks as wide as a man's armspan. But in reality, the area where Easy Company spent most of its time is not much more than about a mile wide (if that) and only about half a mile deep.

Parts of the woods changed substantially since 1945 due to logging and farming. Large sections of woods are now open fields and the railroad line that ran through is gone as are some foxholes. But despite the changes to the woods and the surrounding area, the Bois Jacques have a very familiar feel and are instantly recognizable. They look as you imagine they would from reading "Band of Brothers" or seeing the miniseries. Once you are in the forest and after have walked among the rows of pine trees, the Bois Jacques become comfortable in a way. You have this feeling of certainty: you are in the exact place where Easy dug in.

The easiest part of visiting the Bois Jacques is finding them. The real challenge, at least for me, is how to spend under about three or four hours in them. I find myself walking around looking at where Easy Company was dug in, where Toye and Guarnere lost their legs, where Red Falvey of Headquarters Company dug in with his bazooka platoon, where Private John Julian was killed on patrol, where the "Thousand Yard Attack" took place and where Don Burgett and A Company cleared a section of the woods.

I recommend leaving yourself extra time when you visit the Bois Jacques. They are a place where you can walk around and I think that if you are like me, you will find yourself wanting to see things for a second or third time to absorb and to reflect. This is a place where you will appreciate not being in a position where you have to rush.

It was an amazing coincidence that my first visit to the Bois Jacques began by going through Foy. Foy and the Bois Jacques are inextricably linked to me because of the miniseries episode, "The Breaking Point." So, it's fitting that your visit to the woods should start in Foy. And if you think you want to go to Foy later to stay in chronological order (Easy didn't clear Foy until January), you can take comfort in the fact that 1st Battalion went through Foy on the first day the 506th was deployed in Bastogne.

Head east from the one street light in Foy, drive past the church, and at the T-intersection, bear right and park in the little lot right there. From that parking lot, you are looking at the bulk of the Bois Jacques. To the right of the road towards Bizory, past the field, is where Easy Company spent nearly a month, and where Toye and Guarnere lost their legs, and where a young lieutenant named Thirlkeld was killed in the same artillery attack. The treeline facing Foy is dotted with the foxholes of Easy Company's outer perimeter (OP).

The road is a vital landmark of the battle. For the first two weeks of the siege, that was No Man's Land, with the Americans on the west and the Germans on the east. Foxholes of each side's outer perimeter (OP) positions are located immediately in the woods on either side of the road. Early in January, Easy and 2nd Battalion cleared the woods on the left side of the road, and in there is the place where Don Hoobler shot a German officer who was riding a horse.

Behind the woods on the left, further down the road about half a mile, is the section of forest where Private John Julian was killed during a January patrol that was depicted in the miniseries. And on the right side of the road, in the rear, is the area where companies D and F of the 2nd Battalion dug in, where Dick Winters saw a German looking for the latrine and where A Company was involved in a fierce fight on December 21st.

Some people who ask me about the Bois Jacques want to see where Easy Company attacked Foy, but that happened on the other side of the Foy-Bastogne road. And some people ask where Skip Muck and Alex Penkala were killed. Their deaths occurred in the forest south of the town of Recogne, in what are called the Fazone Woods, not in the Bois Jacques.

Many people have specific things they want to see in the Bois Jacques, based on some of the events that happened there, so a useful planning tool is a primer on the fighting in Jack's Woods.

The Bois Jacques: December 19 and 20, 1944

Most of us associate the Bois Jacques with Easy Company and 2nd Battalion, but from a factual perspective, 3rd Battalion was there first, and also last. On the first day of deployment in Bastogne, it was 3rd Battalion that moved into the Bois Jacques, staying there on the night of December 19th until it moved into Foy around 1000 the next morning. In January, 3rd Battalion attacked Foy from the Bois Jacques a week after Easy moved out.

After 3rd Battalion moved into Foy on December 20th, Regiment ordered 2nd Battalion to enter the woods and "to take that portion of the 3rd Battalion's line east of the highway and inclusive of Halt Station," (according to the after-action report). The second part of the order required the 2nd Battalion to link up with the 501st Regiment, which was positioned south of the railroad line towards Bizory.

At about 1100, 2nd Battalion moved into the Bois Jacques, and the three rifle companies dug in along an L-shaped position. One leg of the L faced Foy, and covered about 500-750 yards between the Bastogne-Foy and Foy-Bizory roads. The other leg of the L ran about 1000 yards along the Foy-Bizory road to the train station known as Halt. Halt actually wasn't the name of the station: there was a sign that said "Halt," the word for stop, and since then it has always been known as Halt Station.

Easy's position was along the entire northern front facing Foy, and a few yards to the south on the Foy-Bizory road. Below Easy was Fox Company, which completely faced the Foy-Bizory road, and on the southern flank was Dog Company, which was positioned – ironically – behind the spot where the Easy Company memorial is today.

The 2nd Battalion completed the digging in part of the orders with little difficulty. However, completing the order to link with the 501st Regiment and form one, continuous American line did not happen smoothly. The miniseries briefly mentions this event, in a fictional scene where General McAuliffe comes up to the line along with Colonel Sink. In the scene, Nixon emerges from his foxhole and complains about not being able to find the 501st. I dislike this scene because it makes

McAuliffe seem like a stuffed shirt, it overlooks what 1st Battalion went through in Noville and it also makes it seem like the 501st messed up.

My original impression from the miniseries and from the book was that 2nd Battalion must have been in the right place and that the 501st was confused. Well, the reality is a lot different from what makes good television drama. The area where the two regiments were to link up is behind the present Easy Company memorial about fifty yards west of the road. In 1944, the area looked a lot different than it does now. Rather than today's large open field behind the Easy memorial that stretches to the horizon, the woods extended all the way down to the railroad tracks and behind the present memorial was a much smaller field.

Dog Company did not dig in the length of the woods to the railroad track which created a gap of 100 to 200 yards. Patrols were sent out to the south to establish contact with the 501st Regiment, which itself was sending out its own patrols to try to find the 506th. Communications problems were made worse by poor weather, including thick fog and dropping temperatures. Compounding the situation was that while the 2nd Battalion of the 506th had not been in combat, the regiment of the 501st it was supposed to meet (also the 2nd Battalion) spent the previous 24 hours fighting and was not just exhausted but also keeping an eye on the Germans to the east.

The 2nd Battalion of the 501st passed through the hamlet of Bizory at 1200 on December 19th (about the time Easy Company went into reserve in Luzery) as it deployed east towards Magaret to try to help Team Cherry. Bill Sefton was an officer in the 2nd Battalion of the 501st and he wrote a war memoir entitled, "It was My War: I'll Remember it the Way I Want To." His men relieved a group of engineers in Bizory and sent a rifle company eastward. As the company came to the crest of Hill 510, it ran into the lead elements of a Germany column and a fierce firefight broke out. Hill 510 can be seen from the Easy

Memorial as the high ground to the southeast. The 2nd Battalion spent much of the remainder of the 19th engaged in battle with the Germans and that evening, pulled back into a series of defensive positions that ran from the south to the north in the direction of Halt Station.

Contact between the two American regiments was not completed until about 0700 on December 21st, and the Germans exploited the problem with the link-up. About 250 Germans from the 77th Regiment, 26th Volksgrenadier Division, snuck out of the woods on the east side of the Foy-Bizory road, opposite the site of the Easy Memorial and successfully moved undetected between the American regiments and behind Dog and Fox companies of the 506th.

The group of Germans that snuck through the gap behind the American lines was the one that was involved in two incidents depicted in the miniseries. The first one involved Dick Winters spotting a German who got turned around in the forest and ended up walking through the American lines to relieve himself in the CP slit trench. Winters remarked later about how confused the German must have been and how bad the American security was for the enemy to get all the way to the command post.

The "Hinckle" incident was the second depiction in Band of Brothers of the Germans behind the American lines. Late in the day on the 20th, as darkness fell, Medic Ralph Spina and Babe Heffron, trying to find their way back to Easy Company from an aid station, stumbled into a German foxhole that had been covered in snow. The occupant asked in German if it was his comrade only to come up shooting when Heffron yelled back in English as he and Spina bolted for their positions.

The fighting in Noville, Neffe and Bizory slowed the Germans long enough to allow the 501st and 506th to set their lines and link up and prepare for the German onslaught, but one immediate threat existed: the Volksgrenadiers behind D and

F Companies. Those Germans behind the 2nd Battalion lines soon became the problem of Don Burgett and 1st Battalion, which had just been chewed up in Noville. After fighting through the ambush in Foy, Burgett rejoined the 58 survivors of A Company and sat in a farmhouse in Luzery by a fire, where he ate a small tin of cheese. The respite was short as he and his buddies, Phillips and Speer had to pull guard duty at a machine gun post along the railroad line.

Burgett got back to Luzery the next morning to be rousted for another mission: to clear the Germans in the Bois Jacques. On December 21st, 2nd Battalion deployed to keep the Germans from escaping. At 1100, 1st Battalion marched up the Bastogne-Foy road, and approximately halfway between Luzery and Foy, formed skirmish lines and plunged into the woods, moving south of 2nd Battalion's positions. Don Burgett's book is the authoritative work on this fight.

Burgett and 1st Battalion spent three hours clearing out the Germans from the woods. Siber Speer, who spent the previous night freezing next to Don Burgett on guard duty, was shot in the face and was dead before he hit the ground. Seven other A Company men were killed, reducing the strength to 51 out of an original 200. This put A Company in a killing mood and hand-to-hand fighting broke out. The Germans who weren't killed fled right into the positions of the 501st near the railroad tracks, where they were cut down. The Germans suffered at least 65 men dead and had many wounded and at least 85 taken prisoner. By 1730 on December 21, the Americans were in firm control of the area.

December 22 and 23, 1944

The 22nd and 23rd were an endurance test for 2nd Battalion, as the men were pounded by German artillery. The paratroopers experienced tree bursts – the explosion of artillery shells in the pine trees – which caused a shower of shrapnel, tree limbs and wood splinters. Men did their best to form foxhole covers, and a couple even used German bodies for protection. But although the artillery pounding was bad, 2nd Battalion had not yet faced the type of intense combat that had already involved most of the other units in Bastogne.

On the morning of December 23rd, nearly a week after the 101st left France for Belgium, the skies cleared enough for the first aerial resupply of the men trapped in Bastogne: 241 transports delivered nearly 150 tons of supplies, most of which was recovered by the Americans thanks to the Pathfinders. Accompanying the transports was a squadron of P-47s, who hammered German positions, including tanks that were sitting ducks. The tanks showed up clearly in the snow, and tracks gave away any that tried to hide in the woods or among buildings.

December 24, 1944: NUTS!

At 0830, 2nd Battalion saw its' first major combat in Bastogne when Germans attacked along the Foy-Bizory road. The Germans emerged from their main lines a few hundred yards back from the road and surged ahead in a reconnaissance in force. This attack was portrayed in the miniseries as the one in which Walter Gordon was scalded with his own cup of coffee in his foxhole after being wounded in the spine by a sniper's bullet. Shifty Powers then killed the sniper who shot Gordon, and by 1100, 2nd Battalion repelled the Germans, killing 37 and taking three prisoners.

That afternoon, the American soldiers in Bastogne received a legendary message from General McAuliffe:

> Headquarters 101st Airborne Division
> Office of the Division Commander
> 24 December 1944
>
> What's Merry about all this, you ask? We're fighting - it's cold - we aren't home. All true but what has the proud Eagle Division accomplished with its worthy comrades

of the 10th Armored Division, the 705th Tank Destroyer Battalion and all the rest? just this: We have stopped cold everything that has been thrown at us from the North, East, South and West.

We have identifications from four German Panzer Divisions, two German Infantry Divisions and one German Parachute Division. These units, spearheading the last desperate German lunge, were headed straight west for key points when the Eagle Division was hurriedly ordered to stem the advance. How effectively this was done will be written in history; not alone in our Division's glorious history but in World history. The Germans actually did surround us. their radios blared our doom. Their Commander demanded our surrender in the following impudent arrogance.

December 22nd 1944

To the U. S. A. Commander of the encircled town of Bastogne.

The fortune of war is changing. This time the U. S. A. forces in and near Bastogne have been encircled by strong German armored units. More German armored units have crossed the river Ourthe near Ortheuville, have taken Marche and reached St. Hubert by passing through Hombres Sibret-Tillet. Libramont is in German hands.

There is only one possibility to save the encircled U. S. A. Troops from total annihilation: that is the honorable surrender of the encircled town. In order to think it over a term of two hours will be granted beginning with the presentation of this note.

If this proposal should be rejected one German Artillery Corps and six heavy A. A. Battalions are ready to annihilate the U. S. A. Troops in and near Bastogne. The order for firing will be given immediately after this two hours term.

All the serious civilian losses caused by this Artillery fire would not correspond with the well known American humanity.

The German Commander

The German Commander received the following reply:

22 December 1944
To the German Commander:
NUTS!

The American Commander

Allied Troops are counterattacking in force. We continue to hold Bastogne. By holding Bastogne we assure the success of the Allied Armies. We know that our Division Commander, General Taylor, will say: Well Done!
We are giving our country and our loved ones at home a worthy Christmas present and being privileged to take part in this gallant feat of arms are truly making for ourselves a Merry Christmas.
A. C. McAuliffe

The End of the Siege

For the next several days, the Germans abandoned ground attacks against 2nd Battalion in favor of artillery strikes. In the frozen ground, you had to chip through cement-like dirt coursed with tree roots. Getting four feet deep required a tremendous amount of work that left a man sweaty and hot. Sweat would lead to hypothermia as you cooled down in the extremely cold temperatures and high winds. But with artillery shells landing on the ground or causing tree bursts, mortars and Screaming Meemies, the deeper you could dig your foxhole, the better.

Despite the artillery strikes, the absence of ground attacks made Colonel Sink feel comfortable enough to redeploy 1st Battalion to the western perimeter in the area of Savy. Easy and 2nd Battalion stayed in their foxholes overlooking Foy and Sink moved his command post from Bastogne to Luzery at 1530 on December 25.

The next day, a small group of armored infantry belonging to Patton's Army fought its way towards Bastogne from the south. Near sunset, Lt. Charles Boggess' tank, Cobra King, punched through the German lines and linked with the 326th Engineer Battalion near the town of Assenois. The siege was broken, but the American force coming up from the south had a lot of fighting to do before reinforcements and supplies could be delivered to the 101st Airborne.

Importantly, the breaking of the siege did not mean the 101st was relieved. It was now time to go on the offensive which meant many more casualties than does digging in tight and defending. A lot of Americans were about to die.

Easy Company Goes on the Offensive

As the New Year dawned, Easy Company sat in the foxholes they occupied since December 20. Easy experienced some fierce artillery poundings and also a couple of German assaults from the east, but until that point, its' casualties were among the lowest of any rifle company in the 506th.

That changed in January, when Easy was involved in an offensive action on the northern perimeter that had the goal of taking Houffalize. The whole offensive was like a series of dominoes. Houffalize could only be targeted after first controlling Noville, but that required taking Recogne and Cobru and then Rachamps. But you could not make those attacks without first seizing Foy. A successful attack on Foy could be made only if the Americans cleared out the Germans from the woods surrounding the town.

The first stage of the clearing of the Bois Jacques involved having the paratroopers cross the Foy-Bizory road, and press east half a mile in what was called "The 1000 Yard Advance." On New Year's Day, a patrol was sent to find the German outer perimeter positions east of the Foy-Bizory road. Lieutenant Thomas Peacock was chosen to lead the patrol, which caused nervousness among his men. Peacock was seen as the type of officer who could get a lot of his men killed because of his lack of caution, poor planning and nervousness.

The miniseries captured this patrol and the unease the men, especially the NCOs, had about following Lt. Peacock into German lines. At 1200, the men moved back from their line and took communion with Father Maloney. At 1300, the patrol moved to the extreme right flank of the Battalion, marched through D Company's position near the railroad tracks, and then advanced across the Foy-Bizory road towards the Germans, with the railroad tracks on their right, and the woods on their left.

As feared, Peacock did not have a real plan and gave the men few details. About 200 yards past the road, Peacock ordered the men to form a column of twos. The formations plunged northwards into the woods with orders to advance until contact was made with the enemy outer perimeter. Among the snow-covered trees, the two columns quickly lost contact with each other, and the scouts got separated from their squads. Ambrose wrote that the snow was very soft and there was almost silence in the woods.

You might wonder how men could lose each other so quickly, but in the thick, snowy pine forests, I know I probably would be distracted by ducking below the branches of pine trees and would spend a lot of time looking where I stepped. I am not surprised by the confusion in the Bois Jacques now that I have seen them.

As the men moved deep into the woods, machine gun fire erupted catching Private Julian in the throat. The American patrol walked right through the German OP and hit the Main Line of Resistance instead. Julian, who was the scout for his squad, went down as did the other scout, Private James Welling. The men got to Welling and pulled him back but intense fire made any attempt to reach Julian impossible. John Julian died slowly and alone in the frozen Bois Jacques, 4,000 miles from home. Confused, and unsure what happened, the patrol, which included Bull Randleman, John Martin, Skip Muck, Burr Smith and Pat Christenson, ran back to the railroad tracks. The men returned to their foxholes to spend a freezing, demoralizing night thinking about the man they had to leave behind near the German lines.

With a clear picture of the German lines thanks to the patrol, the offensive could be launched the next day. The 2nd Battalion formed a long skirmish line and at 0930 plunged into the woods towards the Foy-Magaret road, 1,400 yards to the north and east. On the right flank of 2nd Battalion was a battalion of the 501st Regiment. Sporadic artillery and machine gun fire was received, and some casualties were sustained among the 506th, but the fighting was minor. Again, Easy dodged a bullet so to speak. On the right flank, the Germans attacked the 501st in force with infantry and armor, and there were a lot of casualties.

After staying overnight in the eastern Bois Jacques, most of 2nd Battalion returned to its' old positions overlooking Foy at 1500 on January 3rd. Seeking to get back to their old positions before dark, some of the men of Easy Company took a shortcut across an open field, an unwise move that was observed by the Germans, who waited for the men to reoccupy their foxholes.

As Easy Company moved into its' old positions, the men noticed that the area had been ravaged by heavy artillery and tree bursts. The paratroopers hastily tried to strengthen their foxholes just as the Germans unleashed the furious artillery barrage that cost Joe Toye and Bill Guarnere a leg. Also killed in the attack was Lieutenant Charles Marion Thirlkeld of HQ Company, who went up to the front in order to hear about Easy Company's advance through the woods.

The next day, Easy Company and the 2nd Battalion were relieved and their ordeal in the Bois Jacques ended. They entered the Bois Jacques on December 19th and marched to regimental reserve northwest of Luzery on January 4th. After a short rest, they cleared the woods west of Foy and dug in there. On January 9th, while in a section of forest south of Recogne called the Fazone Woods, Easy Company was shelled and two Toccoa men, Skip Muck and Alex Penkala, were killed.

Visiting the Bois Jacques

Back in Foy, standing in the parking lot, looking down the Foy-Bizory road, the Bois Jacques on either side, I was having one of my best visits to Bastogne ever. Ironically, my trip started off poorly. I began the day in Denmark, and my plan was to fly into Amsterdam, and then drive a couple of hours into Belgium. Well, my late morning flight out of Copenhagen was cancelled, and I got into Amsterdam on the first Friday afternoon in September at about 1500. Anyone who knows anything about Netherlands traffic will cringe hearing that I finally got on the highway towards Eindhoven at 1600.

The traffic in the Netherlands is shocking. It's like driving in Los Angeles rush hour traffic for the entire length of the country. I crawled along for hours, stopping occasionally at rest areas to use coin-operated toilets and to get fast food hamburgers and coffee. Four-and-a-half hours later, I drove through Eindhoven, which is only 75 miles from Amsterdam. Another two hours later, I was in Liege, finally ready to cross the Meuse River, the target of the Nazi armies during the Battle of the Bulge. It was 2230, it was totally dark, I was tired and I wanted to get to my hotel. Nearly seven hours to go 150 miles. I think the Germans made better progress on December 16, 1944.

Then I got into Belgium and it all changed. I hit the E25, the highway running from Liege down to Bastogne. There was no traffic and I drove for at least 20 minutes without seeing another car as I sped along under the orange sodium highway lights. Every road sign told a story of the Battle of the Bulge. I passed Werbomont, where the 504th Regiment – the survivors of the Waal River – fought. Malmedy, the massacre site. Trois Ponts, where Pieper was stopped. Manhay, the site of a brutal Christmas Day panzer attack. Fraiture, near the Alamo-like defense of Parker's Crossroads. Then Bastogne. I pulled off the highway and even though it was pitch dark and I was dead tired, I had to drive to Champs to imagine the 506th walking through on December 18, 1944.

Finally, I got into the Best Western Melba hotel, and woke the proprietor, who looked at the clock and saw it was near midnight. My quick trip from Amsterdam turned out to be a nine-hour ordeal. But it felt great to be in Bastogne. I got my room key, went back to the car to grab my bag and I stood in the cold, clear September night. I walked from the parking lot to the street and looked down towards the town square named after General McAuliffe. I stood on a spot that was right in the middle of the siege years earlier. A few hundred feet away was the site of the aid station destroyed in the Christmas Day bombing. I breathed deeply, smelling the clean, crisp air, and headed back inside. I would have loved a beer, but Bastogne is a small town that closes early, so I prepared to get a good night's sleep and be rested for a great day out in the field in the Bois Jacques.

I woke up around 0700 and headed downstairs into the open breakfast area and plopped my books and maps down on an empty table as I searched desperately for coffee, which was mercifully brought to me. After securing caffeine, I headed to the breakfast buffet, which is a typical feature of European hotels and rolled into your room charge. I knew that since the staff spoke French, they were sure to have one of my favorite breakfast staples: pain chocolate. In a pinch, I will take a plain croissant with Nutella, a chocolate-flavored hazelnut spread, but there is nothing like the taste of a fresh chocolate pastry.

Fully-caffeinated, fresh batteries in camera, sunglasses on, I stepped out into a glorious, cloudless morning, nearly knocked to the ground by the sharpest azure sky I had ever seen. An incredible harvest season morning. If I were back in the States, I would have found a convenience store and bought a thermos and filled it up with coffee for my day out in the field. However, I didn't quite find that option in Bastogne. There wasn't a 7-11 in sight, so I opted for a couple of Diet Cokes. That would sustain me for a long while. My lunch was as simple as you could get: some protein bars I brought from the US that were packed right next to some very important American flags.

All set, I drove to Foy and went down the street to the east of the church, pulled into the parking lot and stared at the Bois Jacques. The bad travel experience was the last thing on my mind.

If you want immediate gratification, you can drive from the little parking lot and just pull over by the first stand of trees on the right. All you have to do is walk up the bank and look down. All around you are Easy's OP foxholes. I have to admit, for a first time visitor, you might as well just see the foxholes right away and satisfy the urge.

But if you have more patience than I do, drive about half a mile until you come to a field on your right. At the end of the field on the right, by what looks like a hedgerow is the Easy Company memorial, which is dedicated to the Band of Brothers and their experience in the Bois Jacques.

The Easy Memorial

Ironically, the Easy Company monument is located in front of an area that was in actuality held by Dog Company of the 2nd Battalion, and is close to where the 501st Regiment eventually held the line.

The memorial itself was dedicated on June 10, 2005, and is very simple, with one panel listing the names of the 14 Easy Company men killed in that area in December 1944 and January 1945. A simple description of the story of Easy Company in the woods entitled, "May the World Never Forget," summarizes the combat experience, and an etching of a helmet hanging atop the butt of a rifle symbolizes the men lost in the fighting. Flowers are often present at the base of the memorial.

Oddly, there are several factual errors on the monument. The ticking on the helmet indicates a different unit, for example. But that doesn't bother me much given that the important thing is the overall intent. My own personal wish is that it was a memorial to the 101st Airborne and the men of Combat Command B, but I have to say that because of Band of Brothers, I think many more people are interested in the history of the Airborne than before the miniseries and book.

Breaking Down the Bois Jacques

There is a lot to see in the Bois Jacques, and segmenting the woods into distinct zones can make it easier to visit. Like a Chinese menu, you can take what you want from any column and create your own itinerary, whether it is seeing the entire woods, which can be done in three to five hours if you are like me, or you can see one part in under 30 minutes, which would mean you rushed.

My mental map of the Bois Jacques is broken up into five segments, three on the west side of the Foy-Bizory road and two on the east. On the western side, the three parts are: where

Don Burgett and A cleared the Bois Jacques, Fox Company's foxholes and Easy Company's foxholes. On the eastern side of the line, across from the memorial is the area where the January 1st patrol went, and above that is Easy's path during the 1,000 Yard Advance. Out of some habit, I often find myself first going to the area of the patrol.

From the Easy Memorial Walking Eastward: the January 1 Patrol

I like to explore the eastern woods by parking across from the Easy Company memorial in a dirt clearing where there is plenty of room for cars. Nearby is a path running east-west across the road and down to either horizon. That is what remains of the old train line that ran through the area during the Battle of the Bulge. The stone farmhouse on the other side of the path from the Easy memorial is Halt station itself.

The woods east of the Foy-Bizory road have always felt uncomfortable and strange to me. I guess that is because I know that is where the Germans were. That is where you see foxholes of the men who were trying to kill the Americans. I've always felt anger towards the Germans: they were responsible for the murders of millions and were ruthless and savage. Perhaps my unease is from knowing that young American men died thousands of miles from home trying to defend democracy in this small patch of woods. Perhaps it is from knowing that I was walking in the steps that young Private John Julian took when he was killed on New Year's Day, 1945.

The January 1st patrol was a prerequisite to an operation the next day in the Bois Jacques east of the Foy-Bizory road. The American commanders needed to get a sense of where were the German positions, so they ordered a patrol to find the enemy's outer perimeter.

January 1, 1945 was snowy and bitterly cold as the patrol crossed the road near the Easy Memorial and walked down the railroad line about 200 meters to a point where they entered the woods in a column of twos.

I followed the trail of the patrol and walked along the railroad track about 200 meters where I encountered an area that was logged and overgrown with extremely dense, absolutely impenetrable, bushes and short trees. So impenetrable that the bushes and trees were impossibly tangled and intertwined and I could not have taken one step.

I decided to approach the route of the patrol from another direction. I walked back to my car and saw a spot, literally on the point of the southwest corner of the woods where I could duck under some branches and in between the trees. I found a map in George Koskimaki's book that indicates that what I used to get into the woods was part of an old logging road, though I found the space between the trees not much wider than my chest.

Once I got in among the pine trees, it was easy to walk, although it was very dark, despite it being mid-day. The forest is so thick that light does not penetrate in many spots and you get a phenomenon of occasional beams of light shining through the canopy, illuminating patches of ground. If you have ever been in St. Peter's at the Vatican, and seen the way beams of light illuminate some of the chapels, the effect is similar.

In the woods, I tried to walk as far to the east as I could before hitting the thick brush I saw from the old railroad track bed. I made it only about 100 elongated steps before I encountered the impenetrable bushes and trees. I couldn't go the route that Julian took, but I thought I could try to find the area where he was killed near the German MLR.

I knew I had to move about 100 more steps to the east to be parallel to the spot where they entered the woods. I had another issue: the thicket of brush extended 200 paces to the north. That wasn't so bad, because I knew the patrol got about that far into the woods when it hit the MLR. Doing the math, I figured if I got to the point where the bushes ended to the north, and went 100 yards east, that would be about where Julian was killed.

At the northern edge of the new growth, I came to an old logging road that was barely visible. The logging road allowed me to move eastward about another 100 yards. I kept looking at the logged area and had this sick feeling that the German MLR must have been destroyed by logging and the spot where John Julian was killed by a machine gun burst that hit him in the throat was gone forever.

But to my surprise, when I walked another 100 yards and turned to the north, right away I saw several enormous foxholes. For certain, those were not OP positions. These were very well-prepared MLR foxholes. I felt very sad because if that is where Private John Julian was killed, it couldn't have been a lonelier, more isolated place. Even in the summer, on a cloudless day, there was little direct sunlight. The trees isolate you even when they aren't covered in snow. What a terrible place to die alone.

From the Easy Memorial Walking Westward: Don Burgett and A Company

The area west of the Easy Memorial is beautiful and pastoral and was a perfect place to walk in the sun under the blue sky as I tried to shake off the sadness of John Julian's lonely death.

I headed down the old railroad track bed, which is now a very nicely-maintained trail, and I looked to the right at the long open field that stretched nearly all the way to the Foy-Bastogne road. The setting is beautiful, but the open field means that much of the area where Don Burgett and A Company fought to clear the Bois Jacques, and the spot where the German soldier stumbled into Dick Winters' battalion slit trench are long gone.

Heading down the path about 50 yards past the train station, I walked through the area where the Germans who fled Burgett and his buddies were killed or captured by the 501st Regiment. This is about the same area where the two regiments linked up on December 21, 1944 at 0700. About another 100 yards further, I turned to the north looking at what used to be woods, and where the German got captured at the latrine.

The railroad track bed, after running straight west for several hundred yards from Halt Station, bends to the left towards the town of Luzery. I tried to find any sort of landmark that indicated that it was the site where Burgett pulled guard duty, but nothing stood out. I knew I was close to Luzery, so I had to settle for knowing that I was in the approximate area.

Company F's Foxholes

As you head towards Foy from the Easy Company memorial, the first section of forest on the left has a few foxholes in it, including ones from the 501st Regiment, not just D Company of the 506th. But just above that area of woods is an eerie dead zone of what at first looks like pristine forest. But when you get in there you see that there are no foxholes whatsoever due to a large post-war logging of the woods.

Coming to a section of logged forest is always depressing to me. For the veterans of D Company of the 506th, I can only imagine what it must feel like to see a wiping clean of the area where you lived for a month during one of the most famous battles in modern history. I wonder if it is even more bitter that there are German foxholes that remain on the other side of the road while yours are gone.

I get unnerved by that empty section of forest, and I usually do not spend much time there. The forest seems lifeless. The trees seem thinner. I just don't like being there. Instead, I usually head towards Foy until I reach a logging road that meets with the Foy-Bizory road. That logging road makes a very convenient place to park, although if you go there after heavy rains, you may find it almost impossible to get your car out of the thick mud!

Reliable maps of the logging roads from 1944 are impossible to come by, but I believe that this logging road was one that led from the front line positions back towards Luzery. When I saw it the first time, immediately I thought of jeeps bringing men back to the aid station in Bastogne. The episode of the miniseries that focused on Doc Roe was running through my head as I stood looking at the dirt path that wasn't much wider than a car.

Just north of the logging road is another section of thick, dense forest and is where you will find the foxholes of F Company of the 506th. Fox Company held most of the center section of the line facing the Foy-Bizory road, and like other units, is barely even mentioned in Band of Brothers.

I usually walk into the Fox Company positions from the asphalt road not the logging trail and I go up the embankment and down into the OP foxholes. Walking through the quiet woods you notice a wide variety of foxholes. Some are wide and deep, perhaps for two men. Others are smaller, perhaps for one man. There are trench-type positions, which I know some men preferred to foxholes, but it occurred to me that some of them may have been used for latrines. Deep into the line, about 50 to 150 feet from the road (and farther) are large foxholes that were probably manned by officers, and perhaps were the company CP or a makeshift aid station.

Fox Company's foxholes make a very interesting statement about the different tastes of the men as evidenced by types of fighting positions. And they also testify about the difference between being out on the OP, being in the MLR and being back in a company position. You can easily see that some men were right on the line and others were a lot further back. Rank had its privileges.

About 200 to 300 feet into Fox Company's positions, there is a logging road that runs from the south to the north ending at Easy's positions overlooking Foy. That would make that road the one on which Easy Company men were evacuated from the line, including Bill Guarnere, Joe Toye and Walter Gordon.

I hoped that I would bring insight into the unheralded story of Fox Company, which is overlooked in Band of Brothers, but I was unable to find very much about its' experience in Bastogne. As far as I could tell, only one book was written on the unit, *"Fighting Fox Company of the 506th,"* but it is long out of print and I could not find a copy anywhere.

The book was written by Bill Brown, who went to school with the younger brother of an F Company trooper named Orel Lev. Brown met Lev on his last leave before leaving for England in 1943. Lev jumped into Normandy and won the Distinguished Service Cross for his actions in Holland before he was killed on October 8, 1944.

George Koskimaki collected some brief accounts of the F Company experience in the Bois Jacques from Tom Alley, Leonard Hicks and E.B. Wallace. The food situation was so bleak, that Private Wallace went searching in the snow for a can of K-ration cheese he had casually thrown out earlier, and Wallace and Alley had a meal of soup made from old beans found in a storehouse near the train station. Not only were they short on food, but like many of the airborne soldiers, the men of F Company were poorly-prepared for the extreme cold and snow. Private Hicks hit a home run when scrounging in Bastogne, as he found an old warehouse with two to three thousand burlap sacks that the men could use to protect their feet.

Another resource is a website dedicated to one of the soldiers of F Company called "The Letters of Andrew E. Tuck," that contains excerpts of many of the letters he sent back to the States during the War. Lieutenant Tuck died at the age of 22 in an accident in Austria after the Germans surrendered.

Perhaps the most important thing I found in my research was the names of five Fox Company men who were killed in Belgium: Salvador G. Ceniceros, George E. Lovell, Carl B. MacDowell, Willie A. Morris and Earnest O. Payne.

Easy Company's Foxholes

As much as I've said I wanted to know more about other units than just Easy Company, and as much as I've pointed out the unavoidable bias of Band of Brothers, I find it hard not to be honest about something. When I am among the foxholes of F Company, I find myself looking to the north a lot. I keep looking in the direction of Easy's foxholes. No disrespect is meant to Fox Company; it's just that the miniseries episodes on Easy Company in Bastogne were what really drew me into all of this history, and I feel this pull to Easy's spot on the line. The gravity I mentioned is certainly real to me.

Walking through the woods to Easy's positions is simple and, in an odd way, peaceful. On a summer day, there is the smell of the pine and surprisingly little noise. No snow, tree bursts, Screaming Meemies or Germans.

There is no clear visual cue to tell you when you've moved from Fox's position to Easy's. The foxholes look very similar in terms of alignment (with an OP and an MLR) and a variety of types and sizes. I know for sure that when I overlook the field towards Foy that I am in Easy's position. But on the Foy-Bizory road, I pretty much use an unscientific method and just guess that the last 150-200 feet of trees was Easy's sector.

The closer I get to the field overlooking Foy, the more I notice a difference in how I feel. The foxholes and trees look pretty much the same as they do in other parts of the Bois Jacques, but things for me take on a feeling of reverence. The feeling is like walking into a centuries-old European cathedral only to discover services are underway. You become quiet, respectful and reflective.

I spend a lot of time in that part of the Bois Jacques not thinking about the unit, Easy Company, but rather about many of the individuals to whom Band of Brothers introduced us. There's a picture in the book of Carwood Lipton in his foxhole in the Bois Jacques. I'm not standing where Easy was dug in. I'm standing where Carwood Lipton was dug in. And where Bill Guarnere, Joe Toye, Don Malarkey, Bob Rader, Don Hoobler, Buck Compton and all the men in the book and in the miniseries were dug in. The book and miniseries allowed us to connect with specific soldiers, and in the Bois Jacques, I've found myself reflecting on standing near foxholes where I might have found Hoobler or Muck or Penkala, only a few days before they died. It's a very humanizing experience.

Just across the narrow, two-lane road from Easy's foxholes is the forest that was held by the Germans for several weeks. In the dark of night, men were probably within mere yards of each other on opposite sides of the road, trying to stay warm and keep very quiet. The forest along the road directly opposite Easy's positions was logged after the War, and the bushes and short trees have no foxholes among them. But it's not hard to imagine how incredibly exposed you were on the OP along the road.

The main body of Easy's foxholes was in the trees overlooking the field between the Bois Jacques and Foy. Today, the woods overlooking Foy have two rectangular areas that were cleared by logging, with a third, thinner area towards the Foy-Bastogne road. Were it not for the third clearing, from the air the woods, with the two rectangular areas logged would make that part of the Bois Jacques look like an "E" lying on its side, which would be an incredible coincidence. Unfortunately, the loss of so many foxholes from the logging makes any such phenomenon hardly worth it.

From the Easy outer perimeter positions facing the Foy-Bizory road, there are a few options for reaching the foxholes overlooking Foy. The field itself is fenced private property, and while there is an access to the field, you'll need to climb over a short barbed wire fence to get into the foxholes. Much easier, and without the risk of trespassing, is a walk you can take through the woods westward until you reach the first clearing where you will see a barbed wire fence. You simply walk back through F Company's positions, passing by many foxholes and modern-day recreations of foxhole covers, and cut through the woods on the southern end of the clearing. Then you can walk back through the forest to the outer perimeter overlooking Foy. It's like walking along a U.

The woods overlooking Foy bristle with foxholes. Some are right on the edge of the treeline and you get a chilling feeling of what it meant to have OP duty. Every two hours, the sergeants went among the foxholes and brought men out to the OP for a shift. On Christmas Eve, Sergeant Bob Rader felt so bad about sending men to OP duty that he went out there instead along with his childhood friend, Corporal Don Hoobler. Today, trees grow out of some of the OP foxholes. Some foxholes seem deep. Some seem shallow. Some seem crater-like, almost smooth and circular. Those were carved by German artillery.

Back several yards from the OP are the MLR foxholes. While the MLR was close to the OP, they weren't so exposed that any movement could be detected by the Germans in Foy. That said, lighting a match would have been suicidal. To the rear of the MLR holes, much further back, are additional foxholes that I presume belonged to a platoon or company command post or were an aid station. I always wondered if those foxholes were where Norman Dike hid when not walking away from his command.

To the west, towards the Foy-Bastogne road, is another clearing and then another thick section of woods, and you have the same choice of walking around through the woods or climbing fences. In that second section of woods is another north-south logging road. Towards the line overlooking Foy are the typical formations of foxholes: OP on the edge with MLR slightly behind it. But well back from the line, about 150-200 paces, is a set of massive foxholes near a recently-logged patch of woods. I was told that Dick Winters' battalion CP was to the southeast of that spot so it isn't the home run I thought it was when I found it. But when you see a set of foxholes that large so far from the line, you get the feeling that someone important was there.

Each trip I take to the Bois Jacques involves one special ritual. When I go, I stop by the small hardware store in my town that sells American flags that were made in the United States. For this job, no made in China flags can do. I bring about 12 to 15 flags in my bag and I place them in foxholes throughout the Bois Jacques as a tribute to the men who served there. Ordinarily I never enter foxholes out of respect knowing that someone might have died in there. But I do step into the foxholes to place the flags that came from America, just like the men of the 506th who dug those holes. Bringing the flags from home for me is very emotional and quite private. When I am there with friends, I usually like to place the flags by myself. I feel so proud of the men and so grateful to them, but also so sad that many of these young men never came back alive from a confusing, frozen forest 4,000 miles from home.

These are the foxholes where Easy lived for two weeks, before going on the offensive and pushing the Germans out of the eastern part of the Bois Jacques.

The 1,000 Yard Advance

John Julian's patrol gathered intelligence for the offensive to clear the Bois Jacques on January 2, 1945. The name, "The Thousand Yard Advance" came from the approximate distance the Battalion had to advance. There are a number of ways you can follow the path of 2nd Battalion during the operation, and I tend to move east straight out from the position of either Easy or Fox Company. I usually park by the logging road that cuts through Fox's position, and simply cross the road and walk eastward.

My most scientific approach to retracing the offensive is to take 1,000 large steps, which, given that I am just above six feet tall, is about 1,000 yards. Here and there I've had to move around bushes, but usually my main obstacle in warm weather is mosquitoes. In the summer, the woods teem with them, and, sometimes, when some careless pig dumps garbage in the Bois Jacques (sometimes right into the foxholes), you also have to contend with large, biting flies.

Heading directly east from Easy's position on a gorgeous September day, I quickly came across the German OP, and a few very large foxholes some distance behind them that were in the German MLR. Easy had to clear the occupants of these holes, which sends a chill down my spine every time I pass through.

Several hundred yards into the woods, I encountered a north-south logging road, which is the only one of its kind in that whole area of the Bois Jacques. I believe this has to be the road where Don Hoobler and a small patrol encountered a German officer riding on horseback. The officer spun the horse around and tried to take off, but Hoobler shot him, killing him instantly. Hoobler found a pistol on the German officer and kept it as a war prize. Unfortunately, the gun had no safety and it discharged accidentally, severing Hoobler's femoral artery. Don Hoobler bled to death among his comrades who couldn't save him.

As Hoobler encountered the officer on horseback, nearby, another dramatic event was unfolding. As described in Band of Brothers, Private Ralph Trapazano yelled to Sergeant Christenson, "Hey, Chris, I've got a Kraut." Sergeant Christenson found Trapazano face-to-face with a German SS trooper holding a submachine gun. Christenson noted the SS trooper had no fear on his face, so "Chris," as he was known, raised his rifle and took up the slack on the trigger causing the German to think twice and drop his weapon. Christenson advised Trapazano to shoot the next time he was in such a situation.

Not mentioned in Band of Brothers is that the offensive also involved the 2nd and 3rd Battalions of the 501st Regiment, which entered the woods from the south, along the railroad tracks. I never found any mention of whether they found Julian, and I wonder how long the private's frozen body remained in the woods.

On January 3rd, the 501st reached its objective, a logging road several hundred yards into the Bois Jacques, by about 1530. As the battalions reached the road, they were hit by a violent attack on their right flank by the 26th SS Panzergrenadier Regiment, 12th Division. The 12th was known as the Hitlerjugend (Hitler Youth) Division because most of its members were drawn from the Hitler Youth program in the 1930s. The division was infamous for committing war crimes, including the massacre of Canadian prisoners in Normandy in June 1944. They attacked the 501st with infantry, tanks and half-tracks. Despite suffering terrible casualties, the men of the 501st fought back, knocking out some of the tanks and half-tracks with bazookas and anti-tank guns.

The 1st Platoon of E Company of 2nd Battalion of the 501st was commended for knocking out one tank and two half-tracks with the only three bazooka rockets they had, then knocking out three more tanks and two more half tracks with an anti-tank gun. The men overran the German positions and turned the enemy's guns on them, completing the rout of the Hitlerjugend.

On January 13th, the Germans were finally cleared out of the area to the east by two battalions of the 502nd Regiment and a makeshift unit of the 327th Glider Infantry Regiment called Ace Company that consisted largely of cooks and clerks and the few troopers who hadn't been wounded. It was during this attack that Colonel Stopka, the leader of the paratrooper attack on Marmion's Farm in Normandy, was killed by American P-47s even though Stopka's soldiers placed identification markers around them.

January 13, 1945 was notable for something else in addition to the friendly fire tragedy: it was the day Easy Company attacked Foy.

• • •

Foy

Just mention Foy to any fan of Band of Brothers and they'll think immediately about the miniseries episode, "The Breaking Point." The stoic heroism of Carwood Lipton, the breakdown of Lieutenant Dike and the fearless leadership of Ron Speirs all come to mind. I think that most Band of Brothers fans would say that after the Bois Jacques, the place near Bastogne they would most want to see is from where Easy Company attacked Foy on January 13, 1945.

Foy has a gloomy importance and seriousness that seem disproportionate to the size of the town. There is just one streetlight in Foy and I doubt that it is really necessary. The town itself is just an intersection, a church, and a few buildings on two or three streets. There are no stores or cafes, no tank turret with descriptive sign. By car, you'd drive through the town itself in fewer than 30 seconds if you were moving at any speed.

What Foy feels like and means to me is difficult to describe but the one word that comes to mind is ominous. Easy looked at Foy for nearly a month knowing it would have to attack at some point, and the town stared back and let them know full well of the casualties that would occur there. No matter from where you started, an attack on Foy meant a charge across an open, snow-covered field against buildings with thick stone walls that could shield men with machine guns, mortars and rifles.

After clearing out the eastern part of the Bois Jacques, Easy Company went into reserve and then pushed the Germans out of the woods to the west of Foy. In the Fazone Woods, named after a lake in the area, on January 9, 1945, Easy experienced one of its worst shellings of the war, and Alex Penkala and Skip Muck were killed by a direct hit to their foxhole.

Then the word came down. The woods around Foy were secured and the town would be attacked on January 13, 1945. Easy Company was selected to lead the assault.

The Attack on January 13ᵗʰ and the Counter-attack on January 14ᵗʰ

The tactical plan was for Easy Company to attack from the southwest under the cover of machine gun fire at 0900. Dick Winters wanted an attack at first light so that the men could be concealed, but the request was denied. In the event that Easy got bogged down, I Company of 3rd Battalion was readied to attack on Easy's right flank (just to the west of the Foy-Bastogne road). By the end of the day, it took five rifle companies and tanks and tank destroyers from the 11th Armored Division to capture Foy.

When I stand on the treeline overlooking the field across which Easy attacked, it occurs to me that several natural features may have had an impact on the battle. The attack started from a tree-lined east-west road to the southwest of Foy. The ground from the road slopes up towards town, so from the treeline, you only see the outerbuildings and the tops of the structures in Foy. I wonder if that slope meant that Winters could not see Easy Company once it got into town.

The sloping ground might have also had an impact on the attack time to my untrained eye. Darkness or low light might have made it near impossible for Winters to see the progress of the attack. Also, when I stood on the spot from where I Company attacked Foy, I think it would have been very difficult to see Easy Company unless it was daylight. Could Colonel Sink have thought that daylight was an important factor given the terrain?

Winters placed two machine guns that gave covering fire as the men advanced the 200-250 yards towards town. Just like January 1945, the field across which Easy Company attacked still has very few trees for cover, although there were some haystacks the men used for protection. The fire probably hit the church steeple and a number of rooftops, but it would not have been very effective beyond that.

As the machine guns fired, Easy Company advanced in a skirmish line moving as best as it could in the deep snow. On the left flank, the 22 men of 1st Platoon reached some shacks and cattle pens where they saw three Germans run into a little building. Lt. Jack Foley threw a fragmentation grenade into the shack and a lieutenant and two sergeants stumbled out. Two of the men reached for concealed pistols leaving the third one enough time to scream "dummkopf" before they were cut down.

The other platoons made steady progress as Foley's hit the edge of town. They got within 75 yards of Foy without any casualties and that is where everything fell apart. For Dike, to get Easy within 75 yards and then freeze up seems fairly shocking, especially since there was only sporadic fire until that point. He made it two-thirds of the way across the field only to panic.

Dike's meltdown started when he lost sight of 1st Platoon. Rather than going straight into Foy, he halted the attack and hid behind a haystack while 2nd and 3rd platoons were exposed in the field. At that close range, the Germans saw Easy Company and put down increasingly heavy fire. Foley realized something was wrong and he circled back to Dike. Foley yelled for Dike to move, but got no response. Finally, Dike gave an order to encircle the town from the west, so Foley and Sergeant John Martin came up with an attack plan in a few seconds. They had very few trees for cover, so it meant running in view of German snipers who quickly took out five Easy Company troopers, including Frank Perconte, who got hit squarely in the ass. Unable to locate the sniper picking them off, Foley radioed back to the Company CP and was advised that a haystack to their right was the possible location, and the men raked it with gunfire. The sniper fire stopped.

Dike then froze completely: he stopped giving orders and would not talk to battalion over the radio. That led to one of the most interesting parts of the Easy Company story: the emergence of Ronald Speirs. Speirs was not even a part of E Company: he was a D Company officer who happened to be near Winters in the treeline overlooking Foy. When Winters needed a man who could take the Company into Foy he turned and there was Speirs. Winters ordered him in and Speirs charged ahead about to become the longest-serving combat commander of Easy Company in the War.

The miniseries takes some liberties with the situation. Dick Winters did not start charging into the fight only to be yelled back by Colonel Sink. Winters realized that as the commanding officer, he could not go in and take over. But it is absolutely true that Speirs happened to be right by his side, and it is absolutely true that Speirs ran full speed and was targeted by a German 88, which somehow missed him. Ron Speirs versus an 88? I'd say that the odds were in his favor. He reached the haystacks, got the situation from Sergeant Lipton, shouted out orders for the machine guns and mortars to fire and told the men to head straight into town, which is what Dike should have done.

Without waiting to see if anyone followed him, Ron Speirs took off into Foy. When he reached the outer buildings of the town, Speirs could not see I Company and, just as the miniseries depicted, he ran right through the German lines to try to link up. Even crazier, after finding the I Company CO, Speirs ran back through the German lines to where Lipton and the men were clearing out houses. Ron Speirs was a born leader and one tough SOB.

Easy Company surged through Foy, and house to house fighting turned into a savage brawl and privates Kenneth Webb and AP Herron were killed. Some of the Germans hid in buildings and sniped at Easy Company from behind. Frank Mellett was shot through the heart by a sniper. Burr Smith was shot in the leg by a sniper hidden in the church steeple as he ran east down the road from the intersection. Shifty Powers spotted the sniper and killed him with a rifle shot in the forehead. Popeye Wynn made the legendary observation, "It just doesn't pay to be shootin' at Shifty when he's got a rifle."

Third Battalion Attacks Foy

When Easy Company got hung up, Regiment ordered I Company to attack along the left of the road to Bastogne. I Company was barely a shell of the unit that arrived in Bastogne a few weeks earlier. On January 9th, the 3rd Battalion took 156 casualties in an offensive to clear the Germans out of the Fazone Woods. Near Cobru, the Battalion was hit by German artillery, Panther and Tiger tanks and infantry. If the annihilation of 1st Battalion in Noville was barely mentioned in Band of Brothers, the decimation of 3rd Battalion near Recogne and Cobru was not described at all.

One of my favorite stories of the attack on Foy involved some quick thinking during I Company's attack. The 3rd Battalion set up 81mm mortar positions under the command of Lieutenant Peter Madden of the regimental HQ Company. The mortar squad took over 20 casualties in the Fazone Woods and the shorthanded team was told there were three German machine guns spotted in Foy. As I Company attacked, Lt. Madden waited and waited for an order to fire the mortars. The silence was incomprehensible, so Madden tried to contact Colonel Patch of 3rd Battalion on the telephone for permission to open up. A voice at the other end of the line ordered Madden to hold his fire, which made no sense. Madden asked for the identity of the person on the phone and realized that Germans had tapped into the line and he immediately gave the order to blast away. Madden's decisiveness was, literally, a life-saver, as the men in town were being hit hard by machine gun fire.

Like Easy Company, I Company had a hard time attacking Foy. The road was mined by the Germans, which meant American vehicles, including armor and ambulances, could not come up from the south. So I Company had to stick to the fields and back yards of houses and by the time it reached Foy, it suffered several casualties, thinning the already depleted ranks. The Germans had several tanks, including two Tigers, in Foy. Company I bazooka man Private Albert Cappelli ignored the pain of bleeding wounds in both legs, moved into position and drilled one of the Tigers, causing it to lose power. After knocking out the tank, Cappelli was hit in the legs again.

The 3rd Battalion surgeon, Captain Bernard Ryan, accompanied the men during the attack. Ryan was in Noville on December 19th, where he arrived to find 50 casualties in the aid station. During 3rd Battalion's clearing actions around Cobru, Ryan treated many of the wounded who managed to bring themselves to the aid station. The next morning, Ryan noticed many men frozen to death in the fields who couldn't drag themselves all the way to medical attention. The dead were trailed by long streaks of blood in the snow.

Doc Ryan and Sergeant Joe Madona of I Company were standing in the doorway of a house in Foy that was turned into an aid station. Suddenly several shots ricocheted into them or hit them directly. Ryan was thrown to the floor with two rounds in his lungs, and Madona, standing nearby, was killed by a shot to the head. As Ryan lay on the floor being treated by a medic, the men in the house heard noises from the cellar, and realized that it was full of Germans. Many of the surviving I Company men wanted to shoot the Germans on sight, but calmer heads prevailed and four Germans were immediately pressed into service carrying the wounded back to safety. By 1100, I Company, with only 11 riflemen left, set up a position on the north side of Foy to prepare for a counterattack.

Regiment realized I Company was in trouble so it sent H Company into Foy on the east side of the Foy-Bastogne road. H Company received a few incoming rounds from tanks but took no casualties and made its way through deep snow into town, where it took 20-30 prisoners. That afternoon, F Company of the 506th and B Company of the 401st moved into Foy as well. B Company was in the Bois Jacques and moved in along the left side of the Foy-Bizory road.

Things quieted down near sunset at around 1630 and various positions were set up. F Company's CP was in the second house on the southeast corner of the intersection. But evening brought a shocking surprise to B Company on the outskirts of Foy to the northeast. The Americans had been told to expect a counterattack, and were inside a house warming themselves when they heard a vehicle pull up. A B Company trooper walked outside and saw a German half-track filled with troops. He ran back inside, calmly told the men in the house who was there, and B Company surrounded the vehicle. Some of the paratroopers did not even have time to get weapons. Perhaps the Germans intended to surrender or perhaps they were equally shocked, but they gave up without so much as a single shot.

The counterattack came during the night when German artillery hit Foy. At 0415 six German tanks and 75 infantrymen attacked Foy from the north and the east. The attack was repulsed, but the Germans came back a short time later with 14 tanks and a battalion of infantrymen. This time, after house-to-house fighting, the Americans withdrew from Foy and reorganized west of town. With a barrage of artillery and tank fire, the Americans retook Foy by about 0930 on January 14.

Visiting Foy

Easy Company's jump-off point is reachable from two directions, and the easiest one to find is on The Foy-Bastogne road. Drive about 1500-2000 feet towards Bastogne and look for the first right turn you can make. There is a dirt road that runs among the first significant treeline that runs to the west.

As you drive down the dirt road, you will see a house that as of 2008 had a large children's playset in the yard. That is the approximate area from which I Company attacked Foy. In the yard, covered by vines and bushes is an old pillbox that I believe was built by the Belgians before the start of the War.

Further to the west is an entrance to a field on the right and it is between there and a second dirt road ahead from where Easy launched its attack on Foy. On my last visit there, I saw a rain-beaten paperback copy of Band of Brothers in the tall grass by the side of the road.

At the jump-off point, I breathed in deeply and enjoyed the sweet smell of the surrounding forest and farms and looked down at Foy, thinking to myself that Dick Winters was doing the same thing from that spot back on January 13, 1945. At the time of my visit, I was probably old enough to be his grandson, but I was still about 10 years older than was Winters the day of the attack. Amazing to think.

When you get into Foy, it will be hard to comprehend that so much happened there. The town is so small that it is hard to understand how it could have taken hours to clear the Germans. Plus it is so quiet that if you stand by the church, the sound you are most likely to hear is that of animals in the barn across the street.

The church steeple is from where the sniper shot Burr Smith and was killed by Shifty Powers. Across the street from the church is a long farm building and on the eastern side are dozens of bulletholes that remain from the fighting nearly 65 years ago. The adjacent stone building is riddled with holes as well.

After the attack on Foy there was little time for Easy Company to rest: Recogne, Cobru, Noville and Rachamps awaited.

• • •

The Last Chapter in Bastogne

The Last Phase of Combat for Easy Company

Clearing Foy did not earn a rest for Easy Company: the next day it attacked the town of Recogne and the nearby village of Cobru. Securing those two towns was necessary in order to take Noville to the northeast. Then, after Noville, the hamlet of Rachamps needed to be secured. The post-Foy combat was not portrayed in the miniseries, although the famous scene of a girl's choir singing to the men was an actual event that took place in the convent in Rachamps.

The chapter of the book that deals with the attack on Noville starts off in a very interesting and unusual fashion – Ambrose disagreeing with Winters' assessment of the situation. Clearly, Ambrose was a fan of Winters, and the historian wrote the book with a tone of admiration. But the exchange at the beginning of the Noville chapter was remarkable because Ambrose dismissed Winters' criticisms of the attack as being off-target.

Winters complained about Easy Company being used to attack Noville by saying that the unit was hit hard by casualties and that the offensive was General Taylor's way of trying to curry favor with Eisenhower. Ambrose countered the latter by noting that the 101st was under orders to attack and that Taylor had no choice. At the time of my first reading I remember thinking that Ambrose had some nerve. But the more I learned about what happened, the more I think that Ambrose was absolutely right.

After seeing that I Company was reduced to 11 men in Foy, and knowing that Easy had not sustained nearly that level of casualties, I don't know who Winters expected to attack Noville. Perhaps he felt that another Army unit should have attacked, but there were no others in the area. Ambrose, for all of his disagreement, never challenged Winters on this point in the book, though.

I had a lot of mixed feelings when I saw this difference of opinions between Ambrose and Winters after I learned a lot more about the Battle of the Bulge. I really admired Winters a lot, but I learned that he had his point of view, and that perspective wasn't fair in this case. It is difficult to learn one of your heroes can be biased.

Recogne and Cobru

Just a few minutes west of Foy is the hamlet of Recogne, which 2nd Battalion attacked at 1200 on January 14th. Recogne today is even sleepier than is Foy because it is off the main road. To get there, you drive west from the light in Foy. A few hundred yards west of Foy, look for a dirt road on the left. That will take you back to the treeline from where Easy attacked Foy.

But on the right side, you will see a dirt road that runs to the north, and it is worth following it to something that most people miss when they visit the area. You will know you are in the right spot when you see a small monument with American and Belgian flags a few hundred yards to the north on the left hand side of the road.

That monument is on the site from where one group of Germans ambushed the survivors of Noville on December 20, 1944, but it commemorates something even more important. From 1945 to 1948, this was the site of a temporary cemetery for the Americans killed during the Battle of the Bulge. 2,701 American soldiers were buried there until their bodies were moved elsewhere. On the site of the cemetery is a marker with an inscription, the first two lines of which state: "We have only died in vain if you believe so; You have to decide the wisdom of our choice." That quote was featured in the Currahee scrapbook in 1945.

This is where men like John Julian, Skip Muck, Alex Penkala, Siber Speer and all of the others would probably have been buried, if their remains not been evacuated earlier. There were men from dozens of different battalions and parts of the United States. Some of them were found right away and others were covered in snow until spring, or discovered weeks, months or years after the fighting.

On a windy day, the flags of the monument snap loudly in the wind, but lay limply when the breeze dies. The field itself is simply an empty, nondescript pasture. It makes you appreciate the dignity and majesty of the immaculate, tended American Military Cemetery in Luxembourg, where most of those men who were killed in the Battle of the Bulge and not returned to the US were reburied.

Recogne is not much more than a handful of largely post-War houses. What is most notable about Recogne is the ominous-looking German cemetery, which holds the remains of 6,807 soldiers killed during the Battle of the Bulge. The cemetery is located on the left side of the road as you enter town from Foy and it is easy to park immediately in front.

The cemetery has an eerie feel, despite being well-kept. There are a number of thick, menacing trees, some of which are merely trunks with many arms sawed off. In the autumn, when the leaves fall off the trees and the rains come, there is a feeling of desolation and abandonment.

The German soldiers were buried three to a grave with one tombstone for six men (three on either side of the marker). The cemetery walls were built with pink sandstone from the Eiffel Mountains, just over the Belgian border in Germany, the place from which the Germans launched one of the prongs of Watch on the Rhine. The stones from Germany, from home, are a nice touch, but with weathering over the years, they have taken on a dark, stained coloring. Even the chapel has a gloomy feel.

I have been told a number of things anecdotally about the cemetery, but it is hard to separate fact from fiction. I heard that many of the Germans were buried face-down, a final act of revenge by the Belgians. I wondered why the men were not reburied in Germany, and was told that Recogne is so close to the German border that it could be visited easily, plus there was little money after the war to reinter the soldiers back home. However, those answers do not make much sense if the men were from central or eastern Germany and since the German government had the money to bring them back at some point.

Another thing that I was told was the presence of ghosts in the cemetery. Ah yes, the local-tells-out-of-towner ghost story. If you find the website for the Ardennes Ghost Project, you will find a story about strange whispering noises and about a ball of energy being observed moving in front of the chapel.

To the south of the cemetery are the Fazone Woods, the place where Muck and Penkala were killed. Immediately in front of the woods is a dirt road that is a continuation of the one from which Easy attacked Foy. On that road you will find a monument to the Native American troopers of the 101st. The location was chosen because it is near a ranch where they raise buffalo, a significant symbol to the plains tribes.

Easy Company attacked Recogne from those woods at noon on the 14th after a brutal cold front blew through the area. In some respects, the men were worse off than they were when they first got to Bastogne. Because of the weather, resupply had been difficult over the previous few days and they were suffering from a lack of everything. Winters was also concerned about something else. He had to get his men from the woods south of Recogne all the way up to Noville in one day, in deep snow, in broad daylight and with the Germans able to see much of the landscape. Winters spotted a natural ridge on the right side of the road from Recogne to Cobru and up to Noville. He realized that if his men were close enough to the shoulder of the ridge, they would be hard to spot from Noville.

The 1st Battalion of the 506th wasn't so lucky. It was put into the operation as well and was positioned on the left of 2nd Battalion at the western end of a long field. The Germans saw 1st Battalion perfectly and called in a tank and artillery bombardment. Winters described seeing men and body parts thrown in the air like in the movie Dr. Zhivago.

Winters and Easy Company moved straight up from Recogne to Cobru, which they reached by 1530. They had difficulty crossing a stream due to harassing German machine gun fire, but they eventually got into position to the southwest of Noville. Winters described spending that extremely cold night hugging a hillside that had a natural depression where men could hide. Until recently, that hillside had been tree-covered, but it was logged in the fall of 2008, much to my horror.

The logging revealed a deep, long trough in the hill that in some places seemed almost 15 feet deep. That is probably where Easy Company froze; the bone-chilling temperature felt even worse after the men worked up a sweat all day moving up from Recogne. Winters stated that the cold was so bad that he thought about a night attack.

During the night, Lipton decided to conduct a reconnaissance of Noville and crept into town with a radioman. When he got there, he spotted a number of Sherman tanks and thought American armor beat Easy Company to Noville. Then he realized that the tanks had shell holes through them and that there were dead Americans on the road. These were the remains of the men left behind in Noville a month earlier. Today, at the hilltop, there is a dirt road that leads to a paved road that takes you to the center of Noville. I believe that is the road that Lipton crept up on his night patrol.

The attack launched the next morning, and while Easy Company had some difficulty with German tanks, it was apparent the enemy pulled out during the night. By 1200, Noville was secure.

Rachamps

Shortly after seizing Noville, the 506th took the town of Rachamps to the northeast. Although they didn't know it at the time, Easy Company had just seen its' last combat in the Bastogne area. And they had no way of knowing that from that point on, combat would get lighter for them and things would start looking up. There was the patrol in Haguenau to come, but there would be no more all-out battles. Easy Company knew nothing about its' future when the cold, miserable men were treated to what must have seemed surreal: a performance by the girls' choir at the Rachamps convent. The convent is just up the street from the town church, and has a Jupiler beer sign hanging from the front that says underneath, "Cercle Paroissial."

When I saw the old convent, I immediately thought of the miniseries and the fadeouts of the men who were gone.

• • •

The 501st on the Southeast Perimeter

Finishing the Tour of the Bastogne Perimeter

After seeing the Bois Jacques, Foy and Noville, you might feel fulfilled: you came and saw where Easy Company served. That's pretty much what I did on my first visit: I saw only Easy's foxholes and left feeling like I had accomplished something. I made my connection with the Band of Brothers.

Now when I go, I like to travel all over the Bastogne perimeter because of what I've learned about other regiments. After all, it was the siege of Bastogne, not just one rifle company. I often start my visits on the western perimeter, in Champs and Hemroulle, the area controlled by the 502nd and the glider infantry, because that is where the 506th detrucked. That was the beginning of Bastogne for Easy Company. But I also like going to the southeastern perimeter because that is where the 501st became the first regiment of the Division to see combat. And the pièces de résistance are the farm where the German surrender demand was received and Assenois, where the siege of Bastogne was broken.

Delivered by Luck: The 501st Airborne and the Fight for Bastogne

SLA Marshall pointed out the luck of the 101st Airborne to have Ewell's 501st regiment at the head of the Division's column towards Bastogne. The luck was twofold: Ewell was a talented and fearless combat leader, and he spent several days on leave in the Bastogne area one month earlier. I heard a story that he was in Bastogne to see a nurse he met in Holland. If that story is true, that nurse saved the 101st and changed the course of the War whether she ever realized it or not.

The 501st detrucked near Mande-St. Etienne shortly before midnight on December 18, 1944. Ewell arrived at Division headquarters and received the famous order to "clear up the situation" in the area of Longvilly. About the only thing the Americans knew was that the Germans were coming in from the east, overran two hastily-prepared roadblocks and were on their way to Bastogne. The 501st, McAuliffe's first unit on hand, would go in that direction and reinforce Team Cherry.

Marshall wrote that McAuliffe later remarked about Ewell:

> "Ewell didn't ask a question. He said: "Yes, Sir," saluted and went on his way." Recalling that scene some days afterward, General McAuliffe was to remark: "There were many men and commanders in my operation who did outstanding things. But Ewell's was the greatest gamble of all. It was dark. He had no knowledge of the enemy. I could not tell him what he was likely to meet. But he has a fine eye for ground and no man has more courage. He was the right man for the spot I put him in."

Ewell's knowledge of the ground allowed him to spot that his men were going in the wrong direction and he personally got them back on track heading east on the current N874. His 1st Battalion walked past where the Mardisson Memorial is located, and his 2nd Battalion went up the hill towards where the monument stands. The actual road 2nd Battalion took was a dirt trail that parallels part of the current road leading up to the Mardisson. At the kilometer marker near the memorial, it stayed left and headed towards Bizory.

On the road to Bizory, in the field to the right where the Peace Woods are located, the 907th Glider Field Artillery Battalion set up shop. The commander of the artillery, Lt. Colonel Clarence F. Nelson, arrived in Bastogne and was given an imprecise map to use to establish firing data. And, of course, there wasn't enough M3 ammunition for his specially-designed glider 105-millimeter howitzers.

Regular 105s took M2 rounds, which had seven charges, but the snub-nosed glider howitzers fired rounds with only four charges. On December 20th, the 907th was running dangerously low on ammo when one of their men found a depot with M2 rounds. There was one problem: it was miles away from Bastogne and the Germans were quickly encircling the town. Despite the risk, he dashed out and grabbed as much ammunition as he could and made it back to his position just before the 101st was cut off. The gun crews cleverly removed three charges from each round and created a whole new supply of ammo just as their original shells were used up.

Where the 907th dug in near the Peace Woods is on the back side of a slope facing Bastogne. The Germans to the east, south and northeast only saw the front of the hill and never spotted the American artillery. The 907th did such a good job of positioning that it could fire on any enemy position without being spotted and was so well-hidden that it did not receive a single round of incoming fire during the whole siege. The timing of the 907th coming on line couldn't have been better. As the guns became ready to fire, word came in that the 1st Battalion of the 501st was hit hard by German tanks near Neffe. The 907th let it rip.

Major Raymond Bottomly's 1st Battalion headed east on the road from Bastogne to Neffe and due to the fog, visibility was only a few hundred yards. When the lead scouts of Company B reached the western outskirts of Neffe at about 0800 they received German machine gun fire. Company B fought back from an area where the road bends just west of the intersection by the church in Neffe.

This bend is also the site of the deepest tank penetration by the Germans during the siege. Next to a small house on the north side of the road, number 93, a German Panther of the 2nd Panzer Division designated #533 broke through 1st Battalion and Team Cherry. The tank was on its way to Bastogne when it hit a mine in front of the house, which is believed to have served as Ewell's CP for some time.

Much of the fighting in Neffe took place around the church, and you can find an information board by the small parking lot there. Two things struck me each of the times I visited the church in 2007. First, there is never anyone there: an area bitterly contested at the time is routinely deserted today. Second, be very careful when taking pictures from the road. The N874 in this spot is a pure straightaway. Cars roar through here at breakneck speed, and you have to watch carefully.

Colonel Cherry and his men occupied a chateau just south of the church, and on the night of December 18th, houses changed hands between the two sides on several occasions. On the morning of the 19th, Team Cherry's roadblock detachment knocked out a tank near the church, but had to pull back under a withering assault. As the roadblock team pulled back from the intersection, it was joined by 1st Battalion of the 501st. Yards south of the intersection, Colonel Cherry and his men defended Neffe from their chateau CP. That evening Cherry's chateau command post caught fire. He sent back to Colonel Roberts a simple message: "we're not withdrawing, we are moving."

Bizory and Magaret

When 1st Battalion got locked up, Ewell sent Major Sam Homan's 2nd Battalion to Bizory to flank the Germans and to link up with the men of Team Cherry in the town of Magaret. If you drive from Foy, past Halt Station and go down the hill, you come to the small town of Bizory and a T-intersection. If you turn left towards Magaret and pull over, you are on the site of a big fight on December 19th, and the bullet holes in the buildings in that area attest to the intensity of the combat.

Northeast of Bizory is an elevation known as Hill 510, and on the northern side of it, Fox Company established positions facing south. Dog Company was positioned in Bizory itself, while Easy Company moved eastward along the road towards Magaret to try to link up with remnants of Team Cherry there. As Easy moved out, the 26th Volksgrenadier Division (which attacked the 506th a few days later) moved towards Bizory. The

Germans were between Easy and Fox companies and were spotted immediately. Homan's Battalion opened up with mortars and called in a round of artillery. The Germans were cut to pieces and the survivors took off, but they regrouped and attacked again. Homan assigned one of his companies to take Hill 510, but the Germans were too strong and he informed Ewell that he could not reach Magaret.

Had the Battalion been able to reach Magaret, they would have accomplished little. Company C of the 20th Armored Infantry Battalion under the command of Captain William Ryerson was in Magaret and was decimated quickly by a German armored attack from the south. Ironically, this German force was heading for Bastogne and took a wrong turn, putting it right on top of Ryerson's small unit instead. Holding onto a small portion of town, Ryerson got the order to retreat shortly after midnight on December 20th. If you continue along the road from Bizory, past Hill 510, you will come down a hill, bearing to the right into Magaret. On your left, shortly before the intersection with the Bastogne-Longvilly road, you will see a Sherman tank turret and a display that has pictures of the wrecked remains of Captain Ryerson's tanks.

East of Magaret on the N874 is the town of Longvilly and on the right side of the road is the Grotto of Notre Dame de Lourdes. Up and down the road in this area, American tanks, trucks, jeeps, tank destroyers – vehicles of all kind – were stuck bumper-to-bumper when the Germans arrived. American vehicles burst into flame as they were hit by artillery, tank and anti-tank gun fire.

While surveying the scene of total destruction, I looked across the street at a house near where a wrecked Tank Destroyer stood after the battle. In the corner of an upstairs window, I saw that I was being watched. A sleepy cat did a turn and sat down and looked at me. I said hello to him and went on my way. Looking at my pictures when I got home, I wondered how the cat was doing.

Wardin

The 3rd Battalion was the last unit of the 501st to face the Germans and it suffered a largely unknown tragedy: the slaughter of I Company in the town of Wardin. Ewell tried to outflank the Germans in Neffe by sending Lieutenant Colonel George M. Griswold's 3rd Battalion to take the small town of Mont, which is about a kilometer southwest of Neffe. Most of 3rd Battalion marched from Bastogne along the Rue de Hetres towards Mont, though Company L went down the Rue de Wiltz (and the current N84) towards the town of Marvie to protect the right flank. When Griswold reached Mont, he met a group of engineers who manned a roadblock they created by felling trees on the road from Wardin.

If you go to Mont today and look towards Neffe, you will see immediately the problem that faced Griswold. The ground between Neffe and Mont is open fields, and the German tanks in Neffe would have a field day against any infantry on the march. There was no way to send 3rd Battalion against Neffe.

Ewell decided instead to send I Company to the town of Wardin to try to link up with Team O'Hara. The CCB combat team was in Wardin at one point, but unknown to Ewell, fighting on the 19th was so heavy that the armored infantry moved into positions on hills south of the town. I Company arrived in Wardin after clearing out some woods north and west of the town and 3rd Platoon saw Team O'Hara on the hillside but no effort was made to link up with the armored infantry.

The lack of coordination with Team O'Hara was noticed by the men of 3rd Platoon, who wondered why their commander, Captain Wallace, did not meet up with the tanks only 600 yards to the south. A physical link-up was critical because radio contact had been impossible to establish. However, this breakdown was just the latest in a string of bad luck for I Company, which entered Bastogne with leadership issues. In Holland, three of its senior officers were killed, and just a few days before deployment to Bastogne, the first sergeant and all three platoon leaders were busted and sent to other units.

O'Hara and his men saw I Company enter the southwest side of Wardin and what they detected next must have horrified them: a strong column of German armor and infantry coming in from the east. Team O'Hara could not train their guns on the Germans, who cut through a shielding valley. No men could be sent to warn I Company because Team O'Hara was suddenly hit hard itself. Artillery was unavailable because it was firing away into Hill 510 and in Noville. Amidst the chaos, I Company entered Wardin, unaware of the strong German force heading for them and that they would not get any help.

A CP was set up in a stone house near the town square, scouts were sent out and men from 1st Platoon began to take up positions near the church when all hell broke loose. The scouts were spotted immediately by German tanks that fired into the CP point-blank, killing one sergeant and wounding several others. The men at the church were sent scattering by one tank, and soon came across two others. A trooper with a bazooka blasted one of the tanks at close range, destroying it and causing the driver of the other tank to pull out in a hurry. Although other tanks were arriving with infantry support, the men of I Company didn't run. They took cover and fought with rifles, bazookas and machine guns. A second German tank was knocked out then a third and a fourth.

The platoons of I Company heard each other fighting, but were not in contact. Germans swarmed into all parts of Wardin and soon the platoons and squads were outflanked. Captain Wallace ordered every man for himself. Sergeant Richard Ketsdever left the CP, closely trailing Executive Officer 2nd Lieutenant William Schumaker, and ahead of Captain Wallace. Ketsdever went flying over Lt. Schumaker, whom he thought tripped, and then Captain Wallace landed on top of the sergeant. Getting up, Ketsdever saw both of the officers were killed by rifle or machine gun fire, and he crawled through a creek bed up towards Bastogne. Many of the men of I Company who survived crawled through this creek to evade the Germans.

Of the 140 men in Company I who went into Wardin, only 83 made it back to the Regimental CP in Bastogne. George Koskimaki wrote that had the tanks of Team O'Hara coordinated with the infantry of I Company, the outcome in Wardin could have been decidedly different.

By the evening of December 19th, the men of Team O'Hara and the 501st pulled back and tightened their lines. Due to the decimation of Company I, General McAuliffe attached the 1st Battalion of the 327th Regiment to the 3rd Battalion of the 501st.

Marvie and the Glider Infantry

The hamlet of Marvie south of Neffe has always charmed me because it is one of several small, nearly unknown towns, like Hemroulle, that saw the Americans prevail barely, saving the entire perimeter from a potentially fatal breach. Each time I visited, the town was completely deserted and to stand there alone, no tourists around, looking at the fields of battle is special and, at least in my case, bonds me to the town.

I usually park by the tank turret in the center of town. If you look closely, you will see the turret has two holes in it, one that looks like it was from entry and the other that looks like that is where a round exited. I wondered if there was anyone in the turret when that round hit. On my last trip, a small dog barked at me as I took pictures of the field, church and the tank turret. I turned to him, wondering if I should say something in French, perhaps about the battles that took place 63 years (360 in dog years) earlier, but he lost interest in me, turned and went back to his yard.

On the morning of December 20th, the Germans tried to break the defensive perimeter around Bastogne in the area of the Wiltz-Bastogne road to the southwest of Wardin. Engineers built a makeshift roadblock with fallen trees, and the Germans tried to remove the barrier. Team O'Hara, which was in Mont, observed the Germans and ordered in an artillery strike by the 420th Armored Artillery Battalion. Team O'Hara then opened up with mortars and other weapons and the Germans altered their course of attack – right in the direction of Marvie.

In the wee hours of the morning, Marvie was being held by a small, undermanned unit of the 326th Engineering Battalion that was hardly able to hold off a strong armor and infantry attack. At 0400, 2nd Battalion of the 327th Glider Infantry Regiment was ordered to Marvie and was told that it was moving into a reserve position and that the Germans were 40 miles away. I have come to figure that any time anyone in the military tells you that you are in a safe position, you better start to worry.

By a stroke of luck, the 2nd Battalion arrived in town a few minutes before the Germans did. The 2nd Battalion had only a short time to dig in before reports of German armor and infantry in the fields to the east began to filter by around 1130. Company E of 2nd Battalion dug in on the eastern edge of town in the area around the church, and Company G set up on the southern edge of town. As G Company began to occupy positions, the Germans attacked. The morale of the paratroopers was boosted by the appearance of four American light tanks that sped into Marvie. Although the light tanks didn't have much stopping power with their smaller guns, the additional support was welcomed. At least it was something, and the men of the 327th thought they had some good fortune. They thought wrong: the light tanks sped to the north and straight out of Marvie, leaving the horrified paratroopers on their own.

The Germans appeared on a hill to the east and to the southeast of Marvie and opened up with heavy tank fire.

Tigers, with their 88-millimeter guns, fired away and one of the early blasts wounded Captain Hugh Evans of G Company in the head. The commanding officer of the battalion, Lt. Colonel Roy Inman was also wounded in the fighting, which pushed into individual houses in the southern end of Marvie. After a series of house-to-house fights, tank fire from Team O'Hara drove off the Germans.

Marvie was also the site of a German attack on December 23rd that came perilously close to breaching the defenses. That day, the 327th was reinforced by engineers of the 326th Regiment, whose contribution would be vital that night. After sunset, the Germans launched a tank and infantry attack that was spotted only after they tripped flares close to the American lines. One soldier estimated that a German tank was not visible until it set off a flare only 135 yards from his position. The tanks tried to cross a deep culvert via a single bridge, which opened to a road that led to Bastogne. However, an engineer knocked out the lead tank on the bridge, completely blocking the German armor.

One of the other reasons that I like Marvie is that it is the town where 1st Lieutenant Thomas Niland of the 327th won his Silver Star for organizing a defense on the 23rd. Niland may not be familiar to many readers, but his family story sure is – Tom was a first cousin of the Niland Brothers, the inspiration for the movie, "Saving Private Ryan."

Edward, Preston, Robert and Frederick were the sons of Michael and Augusta Niland of Tonawanda, New York, a small town north of Buffalo. Tonawanda happened to be the birthplace of Warren "Skip" Muck of the Band of Brothers. On May 16th, 1944, the Nilands received word that their son, Edward, was shot down over Burma. On D-Day, Robert, a paratrooper in the 82nd Airborne, was killed and Preston died the next day near Utah Beach. When the Army learned of the tragedy that befell the Niland family, Fritz was sent home.

Somehow it makes sense that Tom Niland won a Silver Star in Marvie. His family's story would inspire Spielberg and Hanks to make "Saving Private Ryan," which then led to "Band of Brothers" which inspired me to go to Europe to see the places where Easy Company served. Then I would learn about other units such as the 327th and visit places like Marvie. A perfect circle.

Having seen most of the perimeter, there were two other critical places left to visit: Assenois, where the German siege of Bastogne was broken and the Kessler farmhouse, where the Germans made their surrender demand.

• • •

Reflections

A late September evening in Bastogne and I am sitting in La Cappadoce restaurant, which is around the corner from the town square. I walked there from my hotel down a long, lonely, empty street called Avenue Mathieu in the deep darkness of a gorgeous, cloudless, star-filled, early September night, a touch of autumn chill and a planet shining bright in the sky. I passed the back side of what was the 10th Armored aid station that was obliterated in the Christmas night bombing attack. The site is a half-block west of the town square on the Rue Neufchatel and is now a Baby City store. There is a plaque that honors Nurse Renee Lemaire and all of the other victims on the wall outside the store.

As I reached the square, the loneliness of the street gave way to a plaza full of life, energy and activity. A carnival is in town that night, and screaming, laughing children are lining up to go on the Ferris wheel. I sat in the restaurant with a bottle of Leffe brune, a dark Belgian trappist-style beer, and looked down the street in the direction of the church. Cars crowded the street, people walked their dogs and couples window shopped. A teenage girl showed her friends dance moves. They're all laughing. They are enjoying freedom.

The energy of the evening made it seem fitting that my last stop of the day was an unassuming pillbox near the Bois Hazy, at the southern end of Bastogne in the direction of Assenois. On that spot, a Sherman tank under the command of 1st Lieutenant Charles P. Boggess of C Company, 37th Tank Battalion, 4th Armored Division punched its way through the German lines and encountered men of C Company of the 326th Engineers: the siege of Bastogne was broken.

To reach the pillbox, start at the Place McAuliffe and go south on the Rue Joseph-Renquin, and make the first right onto Rue d'Assenois, bearing left onto Rue de la Wachenaule. You will come to the N4 highway. Keep straight over the bridge until you see a small sign for a right turn towards Assenois, past some industrial facilities, including a big one on the left.

As you pass that last industrial facility on the left, look for a stand of trees on the left and slow down, and you will see what looks like a concrete slab with a dirt pull-out in front and, across the street, a dirt road leading to the west. That slab is the pillbox where Boggess met Lt. Duane Webster of the 326th Engineers on December 26th at 1640. As Boggess wrote, "the siege of Bastogne was over, although the fighting wasn't."

But that fighting made it possible for the Belgians to enjoy a wonderful autumn evening 63 years later, and for me to observe it all over a good dark Belgian beer.

NUTS!

A spot that every visitor to Bastogne should see is only about five minutes from the pillbox. Heading back towards Bastogne, make the first right turn onto the N4 heading in the direction of Arlon. Keep a sharp eye for a light yellow farmhouse on the right about 1,000 yards from the spot where the ramp meets the highway.

At 1130 on December 22nd, four German soldiers approached the American lines along the road near the hamlet of Remoifosse, which is just up the hill from the farmhouse. They were met by soldiers of F Company of the 327th Glider Infantry and one of the Germans asked to speak to the commanding general. Blindfolded, the four men were brought to this building, the home of Jean Kessler, which served as a platoon CP. The two officers among the four were brought further back behind the lines to a Company CP. The Germans carried a letter from their commanding general demanding the surrender of the Americans to which they got the following reply: NUTS!

The Next Phase

Easy Company pulled out from Bastogne a month after arriving in the middle of the night, freezing, poorly-supplied and unsure what was going on. The Company suffered at least 45 men killed, wounded or missing, and to their shock, they weren't sent to recover. German activity elsewhere along the front resulted in Easy Company being sent to the southeast. A few weeks later, they were in Haguenau, France, where "The Last Patrol" was made.

I elected not to go to Haguenau after learning that the town was badly flattened during the war and basically there was little to see. Haguenau is several hours by car from Bastogne or Munich, and it seemed to me that a long drive with little to see was not exactly how I wanted to use my limited time and resources.

I also had a lack of interest in Haguenau because of the creative liberties the producers of the miniseries took when they used David Kenyon Webster as an angle for the episode that took place there. I am sure the producers found it intriguing to use Webster, a Harvard student, as a vehicle to tell a story about a man returning to Easy Company.

Unfortunately, the story itself had little to do with the truth and Webster probably would have vomited or sued if he was alive to see the episode. Webster was described by many as a pain-in-the-ass private who liked the men with whom he served, but didn't respect his officers, especially Lt. Peacock. Anecdotes abound how he complained all the time and refused to do anything beyond the absolute minimum of what was required. He himself wrote that he never volunteered, and he always tried to get out of extra assignments. But Webster was not shunned upon his return to Easy Company and he did not ignorantly ask about men who turned out to have been killed or wounded. Also, he did not get Sergeant John Martin stuck on the dangerous patrol across the river: Sergeant Ken Mercier, who was never mentioned in the miniseries, actually led the patrol.

Webster was a pain to be sure and I can understand in a way why Don Malarkey, in his book, disliked that the miniseries made Webster a key character. But as much of a pain as Webster was to people around him, his book, "Parachute Infantry" is a must-read for Easy Company fans. Webster gave the single best account of what it was like for Easy Company from February through the end of the war, and his observations about the soldiers and the experience are written with an eloquence and insight unequalled, even by Ambrose. He is a tremendous writer, and his account of the shelling in Veghel is terrifying.

So, I decided to pass on Haguenau if all I would see was post-war construction. Besides, I had one more extra-special trip to make: going to Germany and Austria with a man who saw them for the first time carrying a bazooka in 1945.

The house in Ephrata, PA where Dick Winters grew up

Mt. Currahee in Toccoa, GA on a sunny summer morning

The road the men ran to the top of Currahee is now the Robert Sink Memorial Trail and can be seen behind the sign

The field at Brecourt Manor. A machine gun was in the corner and the first cannon to the left. Cannon 4 was immediately in the foreground by the hedgerow with cannons 2 and 3 behind it

Memorial to the men of STIC-66 next to the church at Beauzeville-au-Plain

One of the "Bloody Pews" at the church in Angoville-au-Plain

The remains of the church in Graignes which was destroyed by the SS

The iconic arch at the Schoonderlogt Estate on The Island in Holland

Reflections 357

Crossroads. Winters and his men crossed the dike around this spot down to the field on the left. The German machine gun position was far right on the elevation. The men charged across that field

A picture of the Bois Jacques taken in Foy on my first trip

Eerie foxhole in the empty Bois Jacques on my first trip

The Easy Company Memorial near Halt Station in the Bois Jacques

The former convent in Rachamps where a girl's choir sang to Easy Company

Red Falvey at the grave of Lt. Charles Marion Thirlkeld

Red Falvey returns to Hitler's Eagle's Nest

The field where the last official picture of Easy Company was taken in Kaprun, Austria

V
Richard "Red" Falvey

Red Falvey, Reg Jans and I walked up the road from the Easy Memorial near Halt Station towards Foy. We passed the big open field on the left and entered the first patch of woods looking for a very important spot in the Bois Jacques: the foxhole where a then-23-year-old Sergeant Richard Falvey of the Headquarters Company of the 2nd Battalion of the 506th Regiment spent a very difficult Christmas in 1944.

We searched the woods until Red realized that we were too far north of the train station to be near his foxhole. It had to be in the area that was now a field overgrown with weeds and low bushes. Red walked out into the field and realized that there were no foxholes. The site of a most desperate Christmas spent watching for Germans in the Bois Jacques was destroyed when the area was logged.

I was crushed and wondered if Red would be upset that it was gone. A historic spot permanently erased by someone who probably didn't think twice. Saddened by the destruction, I still stood there in amazement at where I had come from watching that first episode of Band of Brothers. Here I was in the Bois Jacques with an original Toccoa man looking for his foxhole. And that it was Red Falvey made it extra special.

The First Meeting

Every June, a World War II history event is held at the Reading, PA airport. They fly in old planes, veterans come and sign autographs and there are talks, original equipment and lots of reenactors. My first visit was in 2007, and when I went, I never knew about Red Falvey. He was never mentioned in Band of Brothers or any of the other books that I read.

I actually went to Reading to see several Easy Company men who were being featured as guests: Bill Guarnere, Don Malarkey, Forrest Guth and Buck Compton. The organizers never even mentioned that Red would be there.

So, I arrived with my copy of Band of Brothers, stood in a long line in the hot sun (that year was a scorcher) paid my $20 and got my book signed by the Easy Company veterans. The whole operation was rushed. You got to the table, went down the line getting signatures and were pretty much told to move along so everyone else could get through. I hoped to talk to the veterans, but had no real chance because of the crowd. Nonetheless, I was pretty satisfied because I got my book signed.

Instead of going home, I decided to walk over to the other side of the airfield, where a group of 506th reenactors were dressed in full jump gear with all of the heavy equipment in brutal heat about a day shy of the 63rd anniversary of D-Day. Standing among the reenactors was an older man in a jump suit wearing a Screaming Eagles cap. I asked one of the reenactors if the gentleman was a veteran. Sergeant Richard Falvey, an original member of the 2nd Battalion's Headquarters Company, was about to become part of my life.

I introduced myself to Red who was as friendly as anyone I've ever met. He told me to go with him into one of the tents (something like, "good heavens, let's get out of this sun"). He told me about being in Headquarters Company, jumping into Normandy from the C-47 that is now in the museum in Ste. Mere-Eglise and about some of the men he knew. Then I got him to sign my copy of Band of Brothers, and he wrote in the inside cover, "never give up." I went home pleased with my day and my autograph and thought, "Boy, Red Falvey is a nice guy."

Lt. Charles Marion Thirlkeld, Jr. Brings us Together

Our lives really became connected with a phone call six months later. We hadn't talked since Reading and I started to introduce myself. He seemed to know who I was right away and asked me with astonishment in his voice, "How in the world did you know about Thirlkeld?"

I didn't know anything about Charles Marion Thirlkeld, Jr. until I met Buck Compton for lunch near his home about two hours north of Seattle about a month earlier. Buck told me some of his war stories and I mentioned I was writing a book and shared some of the things I had found. He seemed to be impressed by my research skills and asked if I could find anything about a replacement officer, a Lt. Thirlkeld (or something like it), who served with the 2nd Battalion for only a few weeks before he was killed in Bastogne during an artillery attack.

At the time, I was motivated to find out what I could for Buck, given that he is a hero of mine, and that he took time to meet me. I was able to find some information about Thirlkeld on the internet, including that he was in the Headquarters Company, but little else. Then it occurred to me that if he was in the HQ Company, there was someone who might be able to help: Red Falvey.

I wrote a letter to Red telling him we met the previous summer and asked him if he knew anything about Thirlkeld. (When Buck Compton published his own book in 2008, he discussed Thirlkeld). The letter I sent showed up at the house of Red's son in upstate New York. I forgot to include my phone number, but I did put in my e-mail address and shortly I got a note from Red's son, asking me to call his father.

I sat in my kitchen in New Jersey, dialed, and got a greeting with which I'm so familiar, "good evening." I started to introduce myself by saying I was the one who sent the letter about Thirlkeld and found Red had been ready for this call. He said he hadn't heard anyone mention Thirlkeld for decades. After asking how I knew about Thirlkeld, I told him about the meeting with Buck Compton. Red replied, "He was the lieutenant of our bazooka platoon in Bastogne and I spent the past 60 years wondering what happened to him. No one even remembered anything about him. I just heard he had been killed and we didn't know what happened. He was lost to history."

I was in a state of astonishment. Here I was about to bring closure to Red about a man he served with and who died 23 years before I was born. A man he wondered about for 60 years. A man who was unknown even to the most ardent Band of Brothers fan.

Charles Marion Thirlkeld, Jr.

Charles Marion Thirlkeld, Jr. was born in Maryland on July 17, 1921, the son of Colonel Charles Marion Thirlkeld, an artilleryman. The elder Thirlkeld served at Fort Sam Houston with the 12th Field Artillery Regiment during the 1920s, and I found two potential coincidences that I could never confirm, but had me thinking about how small a world it can be.

First, I found a reference to the senior Thirlkeld in a document in the Patton Library's Camp Hood Collection, but I couldn't find out if the Colonel ever served with Patton or if they attended school together. The coincidence would be amazing if they did: it would have meant Colonel Thirlkeld knew the General whose tanks broke the siege of Bastogne, where his son was dug in with the 506th. Second, when I read the artillery regiment rosters, I spotted another potential amazing coincidence. I saw a Captain Anthony McAuliffe of the 11th Regiment. I wondered if The Colonel was friends with McAuliffe, who commanded his son's division in Bastogne.

In September 1940, Charles M. Thirlkeld, Jr. enrolled in the Citadel, which with the exception of the service academies had the highest percentage of its students enter World War II of any school in the country. During the War 280 former Citadel students were killed, and on that list of young men is Thirlkeld.

Thirlkeld did not graduate from the Citadel because his entire class was called for service. In January 1942, he transferred to Louisiana State University. In June 1943, he completed Officer Candidate School and was commissioned as a 2nd

Lieutenant at Camp Hood, TX. Thirlkeld volunteered for the paratroopers and received ID number 01825509.

When Thirlkeld arrived in Europe, he spent a brief time on Eisenhower's staff at Supreme Headquarters of the Allied Expeditionary Force (SHAEF). After Operation Market-Garden, Thirlkeld joined the 2nd Battalion of the 506th as a replacement officer, and was assigned to the HQ Company while the Regiment was in Mourmelon, France. Thirlkeld became the leader of the Company's bazooka platoon, which included Red Falvey. Red said that the bazooka guys were a "bastard platoon" and that Thirlkeld tried to teach the men, some of whom had trained for communications and other areas, a number of new things.

The veteran platoon leader in Easy Company, Compton, took an immediate liking to Thirlkeld. Compton enjoyed seeing an original map of D-Day that Thirlkeld picked up at SHAEF headquarters and also was interested in Thirlkeld's family (by then his father was an officer somewhere in the Pacific). And no sooner had they become friends than did the 101st get sent to Bastogne.

On January 3, 1945, the bulk of the 2nd Battalion of the 506th returned to its foxholes overlooking Foy after completing the Thousand Yard Advance. Thirlkeld's bazooka platoon was in a position near the current Easy Company memorial on the south side of the Bois Jacques when he apparently got word that Compton and the other men returned from the clearing operation. Thirlkeld may have wanted to hear what happened in the clearing maneuvers, but for whatever reason he headed up to the northern Bois Jacques, to the section of woods overlooking Foy, where he met up with Compton.

Compton, Thirlkeld and a few other men were talking when artillery shells exploded among their positions with no warning. (This was probably the barrage that cost Bill Guarnere and Joe Toye their legs). Compton dove into a nearby foxhole, and when the shelling was over moments later, he emerged to find Thirlkeld dead, with a huge wound through his chest, caused most likely by a large piece of shrapnel.

1st Lt. Charles Marion Thirlkeld, Jr. was killed by enemy artillery in the Bois Jacques south of Foy on Wednesday, January 3, 1945 at the age of 23. His body remains in Europe today, not far from where he was killed, at the Luxembourg American Cemetery, Plot D, Row 5, Grave 7. His name is on a bronze plaque at the Citadel commemorating the men of the University who died during World War II that is located at the entrance to The Summerall Chapel. His photograph, name, class and date of death are in the University's World War II War Memorial album in The Citadel Museum.

Compton told me he brought up Thirlkeld with several of the Easy Company veterans, but none could recall the young officer. It seemed that his short service, the reluctance of the veterans to get to know replacements and over 60 years of time had made Thirlkeld a forgotten man to everyone except Buck Compton.

And to Red Falvey.

Red's voice was full of excitement, and those decades disappeared as he finally learned how Thirlkeld died. On January 3rd, Red was in his position in the southern Bois Jacques when word came down that Thirlkeld was killed. No one had any information about what actually happened to him. Decades after the war, Red still wondered what happened to Thirlkeld, and here I was telling him.

Amazingly, there were other men Red Falvey served with about whom I'd bring closure all these years later as well.

Christmas Day, 1944

Christmas Day 1944 was extremely violent in Bastogne. The Luftwaffe bombed Bastogne and the Germans launched a savage armor and infantry attack near Hemroulle.

But at the southern edge of the Bois Jacques, in the corner of the woods about 20 yards back from the Foy-Bizory road and not far from Halt Station, Red Falvey was spending a quiet Christmas. He sat in his frozen foxhole engrossed in his bible, which was given to him by his mother, who had underlined passages for him. Among the sounds of combat and shivering, starving men, that bible must have been a small reminder of what it meant to be human. And it must have been a comforting reminder of home and his mother. He once told me that someone said to him that it must have been difficult for him to leave home for the War and he replied, "Difficult for me? Can you imagine how difficult it was for my mother to see me go off to war?"

Red was so involved in his bible that he didn't notice that he had company. Captain Dick Winters had come up to the line with a couple of other officers and Red never heard them tramp through the snow. Red realized that had they been Germans, he would have been a goner. Winters looked at him and said something like, "how are you doing Falvey." Red responded with a short "Fine, sir." Winters saw the bible, nodded and left. I imagine that a serious and religious man like Winters appreciated the importance of the bible on that frozen Christmas Day, spent in the hardened, snow-covered Bois Jacques.

That day, Red Falvey had the most modest of Christmas dinners. While back at regimental headquarters, which had just moved up from Bastogne to Luzery, Falvey got two pieces of thick bread. He placed them between his shirt and jacket to keep them warm and trudged back to his position on the line, his feet covered in burlap sacks that were found in a warehouse in Bastogne (and were a godsend to the men on the line). Despite being extremely hungry, Red Falvey took the bread back to the men of his bazooka squad and split it among them. Two slices of bread served as Christmas dinner for four men. Red has said that since then, he has never had a huge appetite, and always eaten quite modestly.

Unknown to him at the time, Red Falvey had received a much bigger gift, though it wouldn't warm him up or fill his stomach. Being a bazooka man during the encirclement of Bastogne could be a risky proposition given that with only limited armored support, nearly no air cover and low stocks of artillery ammunition, it was often the paratrooper on the ground who had to fight it out with German tanks.

Red was lucky in that the Germans never seriously challenged the line where he was dug in near Foy. However, Private Norman Osterberg, a bazookaman in the HQ Company of the 327th Glider Infantry had a much different experience. On December 23, 1944 Osterberg found himself in the middle of the German tank assault against Marvie. The Germans threw 15 tanks and an infantry battalion against an undermanned E Company of the 327th, along with a half-strength company of Engineers and the survivors of Team O'Hara. In a fight that lasted for three hours, Osterberg repeatedly exposed himself to enemy fire, and knocked out tanks that came as close as ten yards from his position. Wounded in the attack, he held his ground nonetheless, and kept blasting at the Germans who eventually retreated. For his valor, Osterberg was awarded the Distinguished Service Cross.

And on Christmas Day near Hemroulle, bazookamen were heard from profoundly. After the riflemen of the 502nd picked off the German soldiers riding on a group of 18 tanks, bazookamen came forward and knocked out two Mark IV tanks bearing down on Champs.

Although he was spared a tank attack, one thing was for sure: Richard "Red" Falvey was a long way from Yonkers, NY.

Red Falvey

Red grew up in Yonkers, which is part of the greater New York City area, and only a few miles north of the George Washington Bridge. I know it well because my grandparents lived there for many years. My grandfather used to take me for walks over to the sheer rock cliffs known locally as the Palisades, where we'd look down on the Hudson River and on the trains that ran along at the base of the of the cliffs. Little did I know as a kid that Richard "Red" Falvey was a conductor on freight trains that ran through that area.

The Falvey's big frame home at 309 St. John's Avenue was the local gathering place for the kids in the neighborhood, part gym, part clubhouse and all cigarette butts. Red's father purchased the house with his salary as a surveyor, a job that saw him work on the construction of the Holland Tunnel.

Red went by a different nickname then. He was a tough kid who proved himself in his basement boxing ring, and he was known as Muggsy. Hard to imagine when you're talking to the nicest guy you'll ever want to meet! I wasn't surprised though to learn that young Richard Falvey had a sensitive side. He was born with a birthmark on his left cheek and other kids in the neighborhood teased him when he was young. His mother would tell him that he had been kissed by an angel, though I have to think that the teasing and the boxing success had to have been somewhat related.

Muggsy had a number of good friends in the neighborhood, but Hugh Francis Redmond stood out. Redmond was one of the toughest kids around and went by the nickname of Coxey. Hugh Redmond would go on to lead one of the most interesting and tragic lives of all of the young men in the neighborhood.

Red Falvey credited Hughie Redmond with teaching him how to drink beer and how to smoke. In a book written about Redmond, one of the stories Red recalled fondly was of the time when Hughie went to purchase a couple of loosies (a loosie is a term for a single cigarettes) from the store of Mr. Miller, an elderly Jewish gentleman with a thick accent. Hughie negotiated the purchase in a fake, thick accent, keeping a straight face the whole time, much to Red's delight outside, and the two of them laughed as they walked down the street with their Camels.

Falvey attended Roosevelt High School, and along with Redmond, was an athlete (they were on the varsity track team in 1936). In 1935, Muggsy and Coxey got the idea to train for the Olympics – if not the 1936 games in Berlin, then the 1940 games. One day in the late winter of 1935, they agreed to run every morning before school. Sure enough, at 5:30 the next morning, with the temperature at 18 degrees, Redmond showed up at Falvey's house and tapped on the window. The training for the Olympic career of Richard Falvey was over before it started as he went back to bed.

Redmond always seemed to have new and different ideas. He spotted an ad for a Charles Atlas course in a magazine and worked odd jobs to save up the money to afford the materials and equipment. Since it was the Great Depression, he couldn't tell his mother he spent money on exercise equipment, so when it finally arrived, he dumped the pile of books and equipment in the basement of the Falvey home. Neighborhood kids worked out on the weights and played with the bats, balls and pool table, and, of course, smoked, leaving behind piles of cigarette butts.

With the attack on Pearl Harbor, all of the young men in Yonkers knew that their turn to go into the armed forces was coming up. In August 1942, Red and Hughie were sitting in Bebe's pool hall in Yonkers when Falvey said that he was going to join the paratroopers. True to his word, Richard W. Falvey of Westchester County, NY, enlisted on August 27, 1942 at the Main Post Office in Yonkers, NY. He received Army serial number 12128145 and was designated a private in the infantry. The term of his service: "Enlistment for the duration of the War or other emergency, plus six months, subject to the discretion of the President or otherwise according to law."

His records stated that he was born in 1921, that his highest completed education was four years of high school, and that his occupation was code number 538, "Skilled brakemen, railroad." Richard Falvey was listed as "Single, without dependents." His records didn't show it, but back home, there was a sweetheart who was getting regular letters from him. He'd see those letters again – when he married her after the war. Three weeks after he enlisted, Richard Falvey was in Camp Toccoa, GA, a long way from home.

Unknown to Red, the day he arrived at Toccoa, Hugh Redmond was busy back in Yonkers. Hugh enlisted in the paratroopers himself, and on a rainy day while running to the latrine, Red Falvey looked up to see his friend. Incredibly, Hughie had been assigned to the HQ Company of the 3rd Battalion; Red was in the same unit of the 2nd Battalion.

Hugh Redmond jumped into Normandy on D-Day and also dropped into Holland. He was wounded severely in Holland and it took a while to recover from his leg wounds, but eventually he returned to Yonkers. Needing a job, Redmond chose a post-war profession that not unique among former paratroopers: he joined the CIA (although he simply stated that he was a businessman working for an import-export company). He was sent to China, where he worked to get Chinese officials who were enemies of the Maoists out of the country.

As the situation in China deteriorated and the communists swept across the country, it was clear that it was time for Redmond to leave. He packed quickly and headed for the docks with his wife, a Chinese national. As High Redmond boarded an ocean liner, he was pulled to the side and detained. The speculation was that his wife was an agent for the Communists and that she ratted him out. He spent the next 19 years in captivity in China, never admitting any connection to the US government. Redmond's mother, the US government and others worked feverishly to get him home. China never released him and in 1970, Hugh Redmond died in prison. Ashes were returned to the US and on August 3rd, the remains of Hugh Redmond were buried in Oakland Cemetery in Yonkers.

In Toccoa, while the two old friends trained in separate battalions, Red Falvey made a whole new group of buddies who were from all around the country. His pals included Gordon King, who led an attack on a German 88 in Normandy. King ordered his squad to shoot high on a hedgerow to pin down the Germans, while another member of Headquarters company, Virgil Kimberling, ran up and knocked out the crew with grenades.

Then there was Leland "Pete" Peterson. Red Falvey excelled at the physical training in Toccoa, despite having broken his arm as a child while pretending to be Tarzan. That break almost cost him his opportunity to be a paratrooper. After failing his first physical, Red tried a second doctor and simply didn't tell him about the break. The doctor didn't ask and Red was taken into the paratroops.

Falvey and Peterson were two of the best athletes into the entire Regiment. On one occasion, all of the men of the 506th were entered into a physical fitness competition that included running, climbing and all of the other exercises that were depicted in Band of Brothers. Out of the entire Regiment, Pete finished first, Red came in second! For finishing at the top, the two of them won three-day passes.

Staff Sergeant Leland Peterson was born in Columbia County, OR in 1920, and enlisted in Portland, OR on August 3, 1942, about the same time that Red Falvey was filling out his papers in Yonkers. Pete Peterson was well-liked by all of the men who served with him. On January 2, 1945, Pete drove a jeep loaded with food back to the men on the line in the Bois Jacques and struck a mine, killing him. His death resonated deeply among his friends.

There was cross-eyed 1ˢᵗ Lieutenant Patrick J. Sweeney. How he made the paratroopers is pretty amazing given all of the ways they screened out men with physical issues. Red said that there were times when Sweeney would dress down the squad and he'd look at one guy while his cross-eye focused on someone else, and neither man could figure who was in trouble.

Easy Company fans all know about 1ˢᵗ Lieutenant Frederick "Moose" Heyliger, who actually was at first a member of the Headquarters Company's mortar squad. Moose was one of the most-respected men in the 2ⁿᵈ Battalion and to the men in his unit, he was one of the most enjoyable to train with. Moose, apparently, never ran quickly and just sort of shuffled his feet or trotted, so when his squad went running, they never had to go too fast and never got tired out.

Joe Witzerman (Tech. 5) designed the unit patch for the 506ᵗʰ Regiment. Not only did he survive the war, but he went to work for Disney as an animator. Privates Nicholas Panagulis and Marino Narducci were also in the communications barracks. Private William Wingett was in the company and he later on ended up in Easy Company.

Red also knew David Kenyon Webster, another man who later joined Easy Company. Webster drove officers crazy with his nonchalant attitude towards his superiors, and he made the censors who had to monitor letters home even madder. He was a prolific writer and included so much information in his letters home that the officers who censored mail simply had to tear them up. Red had only one letter censored, and that was for mentioning that they had completed a night jump.

Private William E. Ash, a Southerner, was, in Red's words, "a short little guy that would imitate a preacher in the hills" and make everyone laugh, and the men loved him. He often sang, "Galway Bay," a song written in 1850 with the lyrics:

'Tis far away I am today from scenes I roamed a boy,
And long ago the hour I know I first saw Illinois;
But time nor tide nor waters wide can wean my heart away,
For ever true it flies to you, my dear old Galway Bay.

My chosen bride is by my side, her brown hair silver-grey,
Her daughter Rose as like her grows as April dawn today.
Our only boy, his mother's joy, his father's pride and stay;
With gifts like these I'd live at ease, were I near Galway Bay.

O! Grey and bleak, by shore and creek, the rugged rocks abound,
But sweet and green the grass between, as grows on Irish ground,
So friendship fond, all wealth beyond, and love that lives alway,
Bless each poor home beside your foam, my dear old Galway Bay.

Had I youth's blood and hopeful mood and heart of fire once more,
For all the gold the world might hold I'd never quit your shore,
I'd live content whate'er God sent with neighbours old and gray,
And lay my bones, 'neath churchyard stones, beside you, Galway Bay.

The blessing of a poor old man be with you night and day,
The blessing of a lonely man whose heart will soon be clay;
'Tis all the Heaven I'll ask of God upon my dying day,

My soul to soar for ever more above you, Galway Bay.

William Ash was prescient. David Kenyon Webster wrote in his book, "Parachute Infantry," that Ash would often say "we's goin' tuh coombat and we ain't never comin' back." Ash told Red just before D-Day that in his family, every male from earlier generations who went to war never made it home and that would include him. William Ash was right: he died on D-Day.

Red never knew what happened to Ash, only that he was killed. But David Kenyon Webster did, and wrote about it in his book. 64 years later, I read Webster's account of Ash on D-Day to Red over the phone. Again, I experienced bringing closure to Red more than six decades later. Webster was wading through a flooded field on D-Day when he heard someone call his name. It was Ash, lying on the ground with a badly injured ankle. Webster said the two had to move to higher ground but Ash replied that he was done for. He refused Webster's help and simply said that he knew it was going to be his last jump. Webster followed Ash's wishes and moved on to his objective by himself. Ash apparently reconsidered things and dragged himself to a farmhouse that was being used as a makeshift aid station. A short time later, a German unit captured the farmhouse and killed everyone there. William Ash's prophecy was fulfilled.

There was 2nd Lieutenant Russell Hall, whom the men called Squeaky because of his voice. Lieutenant Hall died in Veghel on September 23rd. Private William Broadhead would die near Hall that day.

And then there were Earl Hale, Charlie Rhinehart and Edward Eidemiller. Red's bunkmates.

As young men do, the four of them developed nicknames for each other. Basically kids at the time, they used the Dick Tracy comic strip for their inspiration, passing out names such as "The Mole" and "Piggy." And Red Falvey, since he was the youngest, was "Junior." Not so bad, when he could have been BD Eyes, BO Plenty, The Brow, Faceless Redrum or The Claw.

Hale was fortunate to survive World War II. He made it through D-Day, Market Garden and Bastogne, and participated in the January offensive operations in the Bois Jacques, Foy, Recogne and Noville. In Rachamps, Hale and Joe Liebgott captured six SS officers and were holding them prisoner in a house when artillery shells began exploding nearby. One of the officers took advantage of the distraction caused by the shelling, reached in his boot, pulled out a dagger and stabbed Hale in the throat, slashing his esophagus, but missing his arteries. Liebgott immediately shot all of the Germans and Hale miraculously recovered.

On Christmas Day, 1942, Richard Falvey received his jump wings after completing his fifth training jump at Fort Benning. That night, Red Falvey and the men of the 506th enjoyed their last Christmas dinner in the US for three years.

Red was at Toccoa in the beginning and served with the 2nd Battalion all the way through to Austria. From the humidity of Toccoa to the flooded, muddy fields of Holland to the frozen woods of Bastogne and the idyllic Alpine valleys of Austria. But there is a touch of irony in Red's journeys. Before he was sent to Europe – aboard the British ocean liner *Samaria* – he and the 506th were sent to Camp Shanks in New York, just about 10 miles from 309 St. John's Avenue, Yonkers, NY.

The 506th was under tight security at Camp Shanks, and was watched by armed guards in a compound ringed with barbed wire. Apparently, the military leadership was paranoid about German spies finding out about troop movements. Red told me he always felt guilty about a question he asked: would the men get leave? He was told no, and soon an announcement was made saying that no one was allowed out of the compound, let alone off the base. Red thought that his question may have jeopardized leave for everyone. I think given the mentality of the military commanders at the time, he didn't have to worry about being the cause of no one getting leave.

Red spent his last several days in the US before shipping out only about 30 minutes away from his family. From the Tappan Zee Bridge, you can see the general area of Camp Shanks, the skyscrapers of New York City and Yonkers without even turning your head. They're all that close. But for the Falveys in Yonkers and their son on the military reservation in Orange County, NY, it might as well have been a thousand miles.

D-Day

On D-Day, Red was a communications man in the Headquarters Company. Looking back, certain things seem funny about his jump into Normandy. He probably was not the only one in his unit to jump with pockets full of candy, but it's likely that there aren't a lot of other men who did that.

Also, as a communications man, it seems unusual that one of the first things that he did in Normandy was to rip up his radio code books and bury them. Red was concerned about the codes falling into German hands, so he destroyed and hid them.

Other things about the jump weren't so funny. During the 11-minute or so flying time over Normandy, the planes were hit hard. Red, in his STIC with Captain Stephen Hester and his friend, Otto Sykes, waited for the green light, and as he did, he saw one plane go down in flames and another explode in mid-air. Red's STIC is the C-47 that is currently on display at the Airborne museum in Ste. Mere Eglise, the *Argonia*.

Red landed in an apple orchard in Normandy near Audoville-au-Hebert, and Sykes quickly found him and helped him get out of his harness. Otto and Red searched around and within a short while, joined up with many other men of the 2nd Battalion, including Colonel Strayer and Captain Hester, who had gathered many of the men by placing torches in the trees as a guiding signal. Among the troopers they saw was Joe Slosarczyk, a fellow trooper from the Headquarters Company of the 2nd Battalion.

Red was safe, but he didn't know at the time that other men of the Headquarters Company weren't as fortunate. Unknown to Red, William Ash would die soon. Private Don Eckels would also die on D-Day. Red eulogized Eckels simply: "a great kid. A wonderful kid." Later that day, John D. Halls of the Headquarters Company of the 2nd Battalion, would die at Brecourt Manor. Band of Brothers inaccurately portrayed the young man who died in the fighting there as John Hall of A Company, but he was actually from Red's unit.

One of the biggest blows came a day later when his friend Ben Stoney was killed as the Company moved through Vierville towards Ste. Come DuMont. As fighting raged around the church in Vierville, Stoney was killed by a sniper's bullet to the head and his body lied in the church entrance near the cemetery. Stoney was from California and was one of the few men in the 506th who had four full years of college education. He enlisted on August 4th, 1942 and was about 23 when he was killed. The Germans pulled back but found they were surrounded by a swamp. A number of American tanks joined the fray, and white flags popped up. About 125 German Fallschirmjager, paratroopers, surrendered and another 125 were dead or wounded and Vierville was taken.

Headquarters Company went into reserve in Angoville-au-Plain before moving out with the rest of the regiment towards Carentan. June 13, 1944 – Bloody Gulch – was a tough day. Red was with the Battalion HQ unit about 100 yards behind the main line when an artillery barrage caught him and the other men out in the open. He was lifted off his feet and thrown across the road and into a ditch by an explosion. He had been talking to another man from the Headquarters unit. Now that man lay dying near a hedgerow calling for his mother. There was little time to mourn as the fighting intensified. Red called it the only day he could remember when the unit went backwards – about 40 to 50 yards and behind a bend.

That day also saw the death of Joe Slosarczyk, the only man of the communications unit killed during the War. Joe had a unique assignment on D-Day. As a back-up in case the radios malfunctioned, Slosarczyk jumped with a number of homing pigeons who could carry messages to England. Sadly, Joe landed in water and all of the pigeons drowned. As Red would comment, it was amazing to think that with all of the technology that the paratroopers had available to them, they still used pigeons.

Holland

Red Falvey and the rest of the Headquarters Company went into action next in Holland during Operation Market-Garden. I read somewhere that for a number of men in the Second Battalion, September 23, 1944 was the worst day of the war for them. For Red Falvey, it would be one of those days where being in the right place at the right time was the difference between life and death.

On September 23rd, the 506th was heading up Hell's Highway, with men stretched out from the town of Veghel to Uden to the northeast when a fierce German armor, artillery and air attack split the column. The majority of the Regiment was pinned in Veghel, but a few small groups were part of scouting parties sent ahead to Uden.

Dick Winters, Lewis Nixon, Harry Welsh and some men of Easy Company were in one of those groups in Uden, and watched the attack on Veghel from the church tower. Red Falvey was in another group on the other side of Uden, and neither unit knew the other was there. Winters wrote that the Germans could have wiped out the badly-outnumbered

Americans, but save for a minor probe, no attack came. Red was in Uden for three days without hearing from anyone else or seeing any action.

Red Falvey was in the right place at the right time. But back in Veghel, John Broadhead, Robert Rogers, George Siegwarth and Lt. Russell Hall were dead. George Siegwarth was born in 1921. He had a grammar school education and enlisted on August 26, 1942 in Milwaukee, WI, not far from his birthplace in Marathon County. Like Siegwarth, John Broadhead was born in 1921 and had only a grammar school education. He was born in Alabama, but enlisted in Tacoma, WA on August 18, 1942. From other units, Wilson Doyle, Harold Brucker, Donald Harms, Jack Mattz, Carl Pein, Louis Rigsby, Charles Rogers, Joseph Trpelka, Joseph Watkins, Anthony Yodis, Bruno Rybinski and Lt. Harold Watkins were also killed. In all, at least 15 506th men were killed on September 23, 1944. Many more were wounded, and survivors, such as Webster, never forgot the terror.

Overall, Holland did not leave a big impression of Red who says that even though the 506th spent more time there than in any other campaign, when he thinks of the War he thinks mostly of Normandy and Bastogne.

Bastogne

Like all of the other men in the 506th, Red Falvey was shocked by the German breakthrough that came in the Ardennes. After driving a long time to get to Bastogne, he and the bazooka platoon detrucked and got in the long line of paratroopers heading east into the fight. As they marched towards the sounds of the fighting, men streamed by in the opposite direction, yelling things like, "Fellas, turn back, you'll get killed. Don't go."

Red's bazooka platoon deployed with the 2nd Battalion, and found himself in his foxhole on Christmas, cold and starving.

When we visited Bastogne, Red pointed out that he never really knew what was going on elsewhere on the perimeter and in the Ardennes. He didn't ever know what the other divisions were up against. He just knew that he was cold and hungry, and he was told that German armor could break through his position at any time.

Red spent a lot of the war being at the right place at the right time, but on January 13, 1945, his luck ran out. Headquarters Company was moving up from the Fazone Woods to support Easy Company's attack on Foy. The column must have been spotted because the Germans fired Screaming Meemies from Recogne that hit many of the men, including Red. He was sent to the aid station and was awarded the Purple Heart.

After recovering, he returned to his unit and stayed with it until the end of the War, spending the last several weeks in Kaprun, Austria, in the middle of the Alps.

After the War

Richard Falvey had always thought to himself that he wanted to live outside New York City, and during World War II, that thought became a promise to himself. It wasn't just Dick Winters who swore that if he made it home alive that he would find a place to live out the rest of his life in peace and quiet.

Red Falvey returned home to Yonkers and married his sweetheart, Lee, and went to work as a railroad conductor, mostly on freight trains, but occasionally on a passenger line. Red and his wife had three children, and in the early 1970s, he kept his promise to find a peaceful place to live. The Falveys moved to Hammondsport, a small town in upstate New York, about an hour and a half from Rochester, and about five hours from New York City. Red would work a few days on the trains and stay in Yonkers, and then drive back home to Hammondsport, far from the city.

Red has a large, wooded lot, set back off a dirt road, and he happens to have a pretty good next door neighbor: his son, Rich. Red's wife passed a few years ago, but he has company at home: his dog and the squadron of hummingbirds that has taken up residence in the woods on his property. Red told me the birds hum because they can't remember the words.

He keeps himself busy with a lot of projects, from building a new garage at his son's place to helping his son plant an apple orchard to chopping a lot of wood. Red also has another big interest: keeping the memory of the Screaming Eagles alive. In 1994, Red was part of a group of 38 veterans, aged 68 to 83, who participated in the celebration of the 50th anniversary of D-Day by parachuting into Ste. Mere Eglise (this time without machine gun, rifle and anti-aircraft fire). Despite objections from the Pentagon, which feared the public relations consequence of an accident, the veterans "requalified" by making three training jumps and got the green light to jump into Normandy.

Ten years later, a group of veterans, including Red, wanted to reenact their jump on the 60th anniversary. Red was 83 at the time and had recently recovered from hip surgery, but for him, the jump was special and he didn't think twice. The mayor of Ste. Mere Eglise was concerned about the nightmare that would ensue if one of the men were hurt, and he insisted that the veterans complete a number of certification jumps. Red was game and agreed to get recertified. His first jump went fine, but on the second, Red dislocated his shoulder, which kept him from making the jump. He hoped to jump anyway, but somewhere, some higher-up decided to cancel the jump altogether.

Red also had a chance to celebrate the 50th anniversary of the end of World War II in Moscow. He and six other paratrooper veterans were invited to attend the ceremonies by the Moscow Parachute Club. Unfortunately, the fear of the officials in Ste. Mere Eglise in 1994 and 2004 weren't without justification. In 1995, as the veterans were making a practice jump in Moscow, 82nd Airborne veteran Rollie Duff had a parachute malfunction and was killed. Apparently, he was working on the problem all the way to the ground. President Bill Clinton was in Russia at the time for the celebration and when Red and the other veterans met him, he promised to take Duff home on Air Force One.

He has spoken of his experiences to a wide variety of audiences, including the cadets at the Air Force Academy, students at Gettysburg College, and at the war college in Carlisle, PA as well as to the parishioners at a local United Methodist Church. One of the things that he likes to do in his talks is recite the prayer Bob Wolverton made just before the D-Day jump. We both share our fascination with that prayer led by a man who died much too young.

Red also participates in re-enactor activities and other historical gatherings, including the one in Reading in 2007 where we met. Then it all came together with the story of a young man who died in the Bois Jacques in January 1945: Lt. Charles Marion Thirlkeld.

Since then, I've enjoyed talking to Red regularly, and rattling through a variety of subjects, from the New York Yankees to raising children to trains. And of course, there is the war to talk about and the men of the 506th, including Colonel Sink, Major Strayer, Clarence Hester, Charlie McAllister and Otto Sykes.

The one person we didn't talk about was Charlie Rhinehart.

One day, while searching the internet, I came across the obituary of a Charles Edward Rhinehart of Arizona, and I saw that he was in Easy Company. I sent a letter to Red and asked if he knew him. Before long, we were on the phone again, and as was the case with Thirlkeld, I knew I stumbled onto something big. Red filled me in on how Charlie Rhinehart was a very good friend during the War and for years after they got home, the men in his unit tried in vain to track him down. They always wondered what happened to Charlie.

I read the details of the obituary to Red. That Charlie passed away on March 31, 2008. That he was born in Colbart, OK on November 30, 1919 and was a miner before the War. That he returned home and married his girlfriend, Louise, and spent 62 years with her, and that he worked for Mountain Bell Telephone until he retired in 1983. Charlie and Louise raised two daughters, Cindy and Donna, and had eight grandchildren.

And Charlie was buried in the National Memorial Cemetery of Arizona at a ceremony on April 11, 2008.

Red asked me if there was any contact information for Louise, because he really wanted to hear about Charlie's life after the War and to share his memories, but neither Red's son or I could find a phone number.

Being naturally nosy, and really hoping to hit a home run for Red, I found a phone listing that I thought might have been for Charlie's daughter Cindy, and I called. Within a few seconds, I learned that I indeed was talking to Charlie's daughter, and what I thought would be a five minute call to put her in touch with Red turned into an hour conversation during which I learned what an amazing guy Charlie was, and that he simply wanted to put the War behind him and move ahead with his life, so he didn't stay in touch with his Army buddies.

Within a day, Cindy and Red were on the phone, sharing stories, and he told her about a period of Charlie's life that he didn't talk much about with his family. I spent a lot of time wondering what that must have been like – to hear about your father from someone who spent years with him before he met your mother and decades before you were born. The day after he talked to Cindy Case for the first time, I heard from Red who told me "young man, you lit a fire under two families. You are something else."

Charlie Rhinehart seemed a John Wayne-type: bigger-than-life with the experiences of a man who enjoyed every day and had no regrets. He was born in Oklahoma and had a couple of different jobs before the War, including being a cowboy and working in the mines of Arizona.

Red gave me a picture of Charlie in uniform on his final leave to Arizona before heading to Europe. Scrawled on the back of the picture is a description that states, "Corporal C.E. Rhinehart home on furlough [February] 1943. A good pal. Nickname "Mole."" Mole was his Dick Tracy nickname.

On that furlough, Charlie Rhinehart lost a horse but found a wife. Knowing that he was going off to war in Europe, Charlie released a wild horse he broke back to the free herds in Arizona. On the train back to rejoin his unit, he met Louise.

Charlie had a hard time getting all the way back east from the back country of Arizona, and was actually three days overdue before reporting. His lieutenant didn't want to mark Charlie down as AWOL, probably because he knew it was a long way back from Arizona. Either that or he just figured he'd need Charlie's skill as a radioman and as an explosives expert (he had a lot of experience while working in an open pit copper mine back home).

A couple of other paratroopers were displeased by the way the lieutenant let Charlie off the hook without discipline, so the two decided to administer their own punishment with their fists. The two really didn't appreciate that it wasn't a good idea to pick a fight with a guy who worked in the Arizona mines and was a cowboy.

Charlie settled it the old-fashioned way by knocking them both out and that was that. Apparently, Charlie had a little bit of a reputation and his daughter suspects he lost his stripes from time to time. So knowing that, one of my favorite stories is about Charlie receiving a Good Conduct Medal pinned to his chest by Colonel Sink personally. Colonel Bob said to Rhinehart, that it gave him "great pleasure to finally be pinning a Good Conduct medal on you, Charlie."

Colonel Sink knew Charlie not just as a tough character, but also as an excellent radioman in the HQ Company, which put the two in proximity to each other from time to time. Charlie told his family that he admired Sink, because the Colonel was always on the front lines with his men. In the meantime, he felt the barracks for the HQ men were nicer than those of E Company – the showers were better and it smelled nicer.

Charlie returned to Arizona after the War, and he didn't look back. He didn't keep in touch with the men with whom he served and he didn't go to any of the reunions. Cindy said, "My Dad never had any desire to be at these reunions, would have shunned any attention or publicity. He always felt he was doing his duty for his country and all glory should be given to God."

Cindy has a lot of records and pictures that her father kept from his days in the Army, and she's been going through them, and been learning more about her father from others, including some of the veterans with whom he served. And she corrected an error on the official Easy Company website, which mistakenly omitted Charlie.

And she also helped us celebrate the birth of our twins, and provided a bunch of advice on taking care of newborns, especially on when it's okay to start on solid food.

The Trip

Technically, I didn't lie to Red about the real purpose of the trip. It was more that I just didn't tell him everything.

As 2008 progressed and I completed a large part of the outline of my book, I stared at one gaping hole: I had never been to Hitler's Eagle's Nest or to Kaprun, Austria, where Easy Company spent its' last few weeks as a formal unit. How could I complete this book without seeing where the war ended for Easy Company? Even without writing a book, I needed to see some of the places portrayed in the last couple of episodes of Band of Brothers. I had already been to the Dachau concentration camp in Germany (the camp Easy liberated was actually a sub-camp of the Dachau system).

But I hadn't seen the parts that had a more peaceful side, as paradoxical as that may seem as they occurred in Hitler's playground in the German and Austrian Alps. I always found the scene in the miniseries during which Winters swims in Zell Um See while soft piano music plays behind the narration to be very touching. After everything the men had been through, it seemed that it was a warm, peaceful, fitting way to end the war.

So, I told Red that I wanted to see Hitler's Eagle's Nest near Berchtesgaden, the Austrian Alp lake town of Zell Um See and Kaprun, Austria. Easy went to Berchtesgaden and then moved to Zell um See, which is about an hour drive, even though the two towns are not that far as the bird flies. Kaprun is just a few miles from Zell um See, and that is the town where the last formal picture of Easy Company as an entire unit was taken. If Toccoa was the beginning, Kaprun was the end of the Easy Company journey for the men, and for me.

I told Red that it would be an honor and a delight to have him come with me to visit these places, and also told him that we could make a quick trip to Bastogne to try to find his old foxhole and to visit McAuliffe's headquarters. It didn't take him much time to agree to accompany me.

What I didn't bring up is the idea that was planted during our first long telephone conversation. I didn't tell Red that I was going to take him to the grave of Lt. Thirlkeld in the American Cemetery in Luxembourg for a reunion. And I didn't mention that one of the flags I had in my bag on this trip was for Red to put on Thirlkeld's grave.

Reunion with Lt. Thirlkeld

Red and I flew into Frankfurt from Munich and walked through the bowels of the airport until we found the National car rental office so we could get our car and drive the few hours to Luxembourg, where we would spend the night. I talked briefly with the man behind the counter and asked him to make sure our car had an automatic transmission. I saw him grit his teeth so before he said a word, I pulled out my reservation confirmation and pointed to the word "automatik" next to the description of my car – a medium-sized vehicle similar to an Audi or Volkswagen. This is like a habit for me I suppose.

He nodded silently and I knew what that meant: there was not a car with an automatic transmission left. I started to sweat and began to wonder if Red knew how to drive a manual transmission, and if he could do it for several hours, at night, in Germany. Then I saw the man lift his head up with a smile, and he said, "I think you will like this car." I responded, "Automatic?" He just smiled and said, "Yes."

Red and I headed off to the garage to get the car and we walked down the concourse. And walked. And walked. I guess we walked a full one mile underground and here I was thinking that Red wasn't going to make it home because of me. It was coming up close on a death march. We got lost several times before we finally realized we had to go upstairs one level to find the parking space. Finally, we got to the right place, but we were leaving Frankfurt an hour later than I had hoped, it was getting dark, I was worried about getting to Luxembourg and I didn't want Red to see me agitated. I thought he might get nervous.

Well, whatever agitation I had disappeared completely when I saw our car: a brand new BMW 3-series. When I opened the door, it had new car smell, there was a GPS system, I knew I'd get a chance to open it up on the autobahn and everything was okay. Red and I climbed in and I turned on the satellite navigation system. The display came up, I set the language for English and we were on our way. Within moments, we heard a woman's voice telling us, "turn right in 25 meters."

Red laughed at the system and said that something popped into his head. When he was in Europe, the Americans listened to a German radio personality named Mildred Gillars, who was better known as "Axis Sally." Gillars was actually an American, and she peppered her broadcasts of music and news with references to cheating wives and girlfriends back in the States and other inflammatory remarks. The voice coming over the car's navigation system was, by contrast, completely helpful. But in the end, we called the system Axis Sally, and every time we heard directions, we responded, "thanks Sally."

As we headed west from Frankfurt, the system told us we had about 275 kilometers to go and that we'd be in Luxembourg City in under three hours. Just in time for dinner! The BMW raced without any engine noise so I continuously checked the speedometer to see how fast we were going. Axis Sally was right on target, and we pulled into Luxembourg City in time for dinner. Red didn't seem to notice the sign for the American Cemetery, which relieved me, and we found our hotel, which was right across from the airport.

Red was true to his word about not being very hungry since experiencing starvation in Bastogne. While he had just a bowl of soup, I had a big dinner. Next to us, a group of young businessmen tried to impress each other with their business acumen as they dined at a long table. That was one of those experiences that teaches you that regardless of nationality, people really are the same all over the world. Each guy tried to outdo the other. That's what young men do. We finished dinner and I went off to bed, telling Red we had to be out of the hotel the next morning because we had some place to be at 9AM. I told him it was a surprise. He laughed and told me "you're something else young man."

Right on schedule, we left the hotel at 8:45 and we were at the cemetery within ten minutes. Red was impressed by the site yet he still didn't realize what was to come. The morning was gorgeous, with brilliant sunlight, no clouds and damp dew on every blade of grass and flower.

The cemetery is 50.5 acres and is home to 5,076 Americans who died during World War II, most during the Battle of the Bulge. A large cathedral is near the entrance and steps lead down to the graves, which are arranged in nine sections. Among the dead are 22 sets of brothers who lie side by side. The cemetery is also the place where General George Patton is buried. Patton could wait.

I told Red, "We're looking for section D," and walked ahead of him. He trailed me a bit and I got to Row 5, Grave 7 first. I pointed to it and called to Red, "here it is." He walked over and I said, "this is really why I wanted you to come to Europe with me. Here's Thirlkeld."

I stepped away and let Red take it in with privacy. I gave Red one of the flags I brought from the US and he planted it in front of Thirlkeld's grave. I felt terribly sad, but at the same time was just stunned at what was happening in front of me. Here we were not even ten months after that phone call.

We talked a bit but mostly I let him alone. What we both wondered was if Thirlkeld's grave had been visited and, if so, when? Had we been the first people to visit him in decades? We were both in a deep, emotional state as the sun rose over backs, and the shadows of the trees over the graves pulled back. When the sun was high enough so that there was no shadow, I took several pictures of Red standing next to Thirlkeld's grave. That moment of reuniting Red with Lt. Thirlkeld after 63 years, was truly a gift for me. But we had a lot more to do that day, and even I didn't know how the rest would turn out. Before we headed for Bastogne, though, I had something personal that I had to do.

Several flags remained in my bag as I found four of the five Easy Company men buried in the cemetery. Kenneth Webb, killed in the attack on Foy. John Julian, killed in the Bois Jacques. For some reason, I was drawn in particular to the graves of Warren "Skip" Muck and Alex Penkala.

I think it might have been because I read Don Malarkey's book and he described Muck in great detail. Malarkey's deep love for his friend was beautiful but also tragic given the violent death of Muck, who was a well-liked soldier. I walked over to the southeast corner of the cemetery and found Penkala's grave and placed an American flag in front of the cross. For some reason, I expected to find Muck next to Penkala. I looked around, even though I knew from the plot number that Muck could not have been nearby. After walking about 100 feet, there was Skip Muck.

I reflected at the graves of Muck and Penkala and found Red and we got back in the car. We had something remarkable ahead of us in Bastogne.

A Bazookaman Returns to Bastogne

How does someone born in 1968 show Bastogne to a man who fought there during World War II? I didn't worry too much about the issue, but it was on my mind a little bit as Red and I sped past Arlon towards Bastogne. Early on, I figured he knew everything about what happened there and I'd just be repetitive and boring. Red reminded me that during the War, he was just focused on his duties and had little idea what was going on elsewhere. Decades later, he revisited the area with several of his comrades but he said they didn't know exactly what they were seeing.

We came up the highway into Bastogne and I realized that we didn't have a lot of time before we needed to meet my buddy, Reg Jans, at the Heintz Barracks so I headed for Assenois and we retraced the path of Boggess' tank until it reached Company A of the 326th Engineers at the pillbox, officially breaking the siege of Bastogne. Then we headed to the Kessler farmhouse where the surrender demand was received. Red had not seen the farmhouse before so it felt good to show him something new.

We got back on the highway and got off in Hemroulle and drove to Champs to see the road that Red marched along into Bastogne on the night of December 18, 1944. I also took him up the hill outside of Hemroulle and showed him how the December 25th German tank and infantry attack played out. But we ran out of time. We had to get to the Heintz Barracks.

Right on time, there was Reg, who is not only a good friend, but one of the best tour guides I know because he is passionate about the whole history of the Airborne, not just what happened in one particular spot involving a single unit. He can tell you the combat histories of men from different companies and regiments from Normandy to Holland to Bastogne. He also has a lot of energy, which you want in a tour guide. Having someone who likes to be out in the field and can go for a long time is a joy, and he is also flexible enough to create an itinerary based on whatever your interests.

I imagine though that Reg is a little more tired than the last time I saw him because he and his wife adopted an adorable boy from Africa. Someday, Mathieu and my kids will accompany Reg and me as we, older and slightly less spry, walk through the Bois Jacques and try to pass on what we have learned. By that time, there will be no World War II veterans alive and it will be up to us to share the legacy to the next generation.

Reg greeted us and we talked a little bit about the cemetery across the street from the Barracks and how the Pathfinders landed near there on December 23, 1944. He pointed out the area past the southeast corner of the cemetery where the famous picture was taken of Jack Agnew setting up his radio beacon on top of a pile of bricks. To the southwest was the drop zone for the first aerial resupply, as the planes flew in from the east.

I told Red that we were going to get to go inside the Barracks to see what is known as the McAuliffe Cave, the bunker where the General had his headquarters for the first part of the campaign. But I didn't really have any idea of how it would happen or what it would look like inside. Reg knows everyone, so I figured he somehow would wave to a guard, we'd go in, and see this little cave or something like that. I had never even seen a picture of the bunker so I had no idea what to expect.

Reg made a phone call and we were soon met at the gate by his good friend, Roby Clam, a well-known tour guide in the area. Roby waved at the guards and the gate opened up. Unlike the time I was in trouble for taking pictures at the Heintz Barracks gate, this time I was going inside in style.

Shortly, a car pulled up, and out stepped three Belgian Army Soldiers, Adjudant Lemoine, 1st Chief Corporal Marecaux and Adjudant Passelecq. Admirably, Lemoine and Marecaux are not just active soldiers, but they are dedicated volunteers who, with friends, tirelessly find new World War II artifacts to add to the collection of materials on the base, and who maintain several historical displays. Their devotion is tremendous, and enabled me to see a lot more than just a room.

The three of them wanted to meet Red, who was somewhat astonished by the attention. The three young Belgian soldiers looked at Red with a sense of pride, gratitude and awe. They asked Red to pose with them for pictures, which he did with great happiness. In a touch of contrast and reality, Marecaux and Lemoine had to leave us to attend a military funeral, and later they were sent to Afghanistan.

Adjudant Passelecq stayed and took us on a tour of the base, which is home to the 1st Field Artillery Regiment. We walked from the gate towards the right where there are two long barracks buildings, one of which still has faded German words on it, a sign of the Nazi occupation of the base for four years after the defeat of Belgium. In the middle of the second building was a set of stairs leading down to the basement bunker of General McAuliffe. I found it surreal. Here I was visiting the bunker with a veteran of the battle guided by a Belgian Army soldier.

Passelecq showed us the room in the bunker that McAuliffe used as his headquarters, and then around to some of the other rooms in the basement, including the one where the famous Christmas dinner picture of McAuliffe and his command was taken. The story goes that the men were told to look gloomy so as not to make it seem like they were enjoying a warm dinner while the men froze on the line.

When I was in the bunker, it wasn't hard to imagine myself there in 1944. Whether it's the exhibit they have there or the aura of the room, I felt a palpable sense of the desperate defense, and also felt a rush of adrenaline thinking about the response when all agreed the surrender demand would be met with "NUTS!" I also had a little flashback to my earlier, unsuccessful visit to the Barracks, although I didn't share the story with the group. I had a wonderful time taking pictures, listening to the conversation and looking at the historical artifacts and displays there. At that point, the tour really got dramatic.

Roby gathered us together and made a short speech in Red's honor, thanking him for being there in 1944 and again, among friends, in 2008. Then he gave Red a special medal that was made for the 60th anniversary celebration that was attended by several veterans, and Red signed a document that every returning veteran is asked to sign. It's a Who's Who of the men who were in Bastogne.

Then, Adjudant Passelecq presented Red with a plaque thanking him and all of the soldiers who fought in Bastogne. I could tell that Red was delighted but he was also filled with emotion and thanked them seriously. Quickly though, the room filled with smiles and laughter as Red told stories, and Reg and I asked questions about the different men in the 506th. The whole experience was a delight and became one of many once-in-a-lifetime aspects of the trip.

After the tour, Reg, Red and I drove to the Bois Jacques to see if we could find Red's old foxhole. I was so looking forward to finding the place where Red sat with his bible on that cold Christmas Day in 1944. But it wasn't to be, when we figured out the foxhole was long gone, replaced by flat ground and weeds.

I felt bitter about losing an important part of history and I hoped he wasn't disappointed, but what happened next lifted my spirits a bit. The three of us were spotted from the road by a man named Joel Robert, who was born in Foy and still lives there. Joel is also fascinated with the wartime history, talked to Reg in French and guessed correctly that Red was a veteran. Joel scrambled from his car with an autograph book, and then produced a piece of shrapnel he found in the area and handed it to Red.

I stepped away for a few minutes to allow Joel to ask as many questions of Red that he wanted to, while I went to find a creek mentioned in one of the books that described fighting in the Bois Jacques. After walking about 50 yards, I turned and saw Joel and Reg there with Red, deep in conversation, and I had a comforting thought. Here are three young(ish) men, all committed to learning the history so we can pass it on, in the Bois Jacques with a man who fought there. Although the foxhole was gone, knowing that there are people who won't forget the stories and will tell them accurately made me feel good.

Reg, Red and I then walked up to the position where Easy Company looked across the field at Foy, and we wandered from point to point talking about the battle and the men. Not to be repetitive, but going for a walk in the Bois Jacques with a Toccoa man was just inconceivable months earlier.

Afterwards, we drove towards the Fazone Woods and saw the approximate area where Red was hit by shrapnel from a Screaming Meemie on January 13, 1945. In that one day, I saw where Red detrucked on the December 18th, where he was dug in on Christmas and where he got hit and sent back to the aid station in Bastogne in January. The best way to end the day was for the three of us to have a nice dinner in Bastogne.

Red and I stayed in a hotel in Houffalize and the next morning, drove through Parker's Crossroads to La Glieze and saw the Tiger Royal tank and the area around Trois Ponts where the engineers and the 82nd Airborne stopped Pieper, the Malmedy massacre site, Lanzerath and Krewinkel.

Then we got back in the car and sped along the Autobahn back to Frankfurt Airport to drop off the car and then go to our hotel, the ultra modern Sheraton where I stayed after my first visit to Bastogne. The walk from our rental car to the hotel was even longer then when we picked up the car, and I thought again that I was going to kill this poor man by making him go further and further. Finally, we found the entrance to the hotel and dropped off our bags and settled in for dinner at the restaurant where I had a chance to reflect after that first trip to see the Bois Jacques. I looked across the table at my company and thought about then and now and how lucky I was to be there with Red.

A Friend to Man

The trip started with a visit to the Eagle's Nest and Kaprun, Austria and ended with a visit to Bastogne. It was beyond describable. Not just because Red is a war veteran who was willing to indulge me in coming along, but also because he is such a nice person, and anyone who gets to spend time with him is fortunate.

Red probably would tell you that you were being too kind if you thanked him for his friendship. He's a very modest and welcoming person, and it is in his nature to be kind. He mentioned that he was particularly inspired by a poem written in the 19th Century by Sam Walter Foss called, "The House by the Side of the Road," which goes:

> There are hermit souls that live withdrawn
> In the place of their self-content;
> There are souls like stars, that dwell apart,
> In a fellowless firmament;
> There are pioneer souls that blaze their paths
> Where highways never ran-
> But let me live by the side of the road
> And be a friend to man.
>
> Let me live in a house by the side of the road,
> Where the race of men go by-
> The men who are good and the men who are bad,
> As good and as bad as I.
> I would not sit in the scorner's seat,
> Or hurl the cynic's ban-

Let me live in a house by the side of the road
And be a friend to man.

I see from my house by the side of the road,
By the side of the highway of life,
The men who press with the ardor of hope,
The men who are faint with the strife.
But I turn not away from their smiles nor their tears,
Both parts of an infinite plan-
Let me live in a house by the side of the road
And be a friend to man.

I know there are brook-gladdened meadows ahead
And mountains of wearisome height;
That the road passes on through the long afternoon
And stretches away to the night.
But still I rejoice when the travelers rejoice.
And weep with the strangers that moan,
Nor live in my house by the side of the road
Like a man who dwells alone.

Let me live in my house by the side of the road-
It's here the race of men go by.
They are good, they are bad, they are weak, they are strong,
Wise, foolish- so am I;
Then why should I sit in the scorner's seat,
Or hurl the cynic's ban?
Let me live in my house by the side of the road
And be a friend to man.

Red has been a friend to me and to many others. He told me that his house in Hammondsport isn't by the side of the road, though I imagine that he would certainly be happy helping anyone who came by.

The next day, Red and I boarded the flight from Frankfurt to Newark and there on the entertainment system was Band of Brothers. I set him up to watch the miniseries and saw him get extremely choked up, especially after the first episode. Another chill ran down my back.

As he watched another episode, I downloaded the pictures from the trip onto my computer and began to go through them one by one, and there on my screen were the shots of Hitler's Eagle's Nest and Kaprun, Austria, where Easy Company spent its last several weeks as an official unit before being disbanded forever.

. . .

VI
Germany and Austria

The End of the War and the End of Easy Company

I stood beside an idyllic hillside pasture in the Austrian Alps town of Kaprun on a stunning Indian Summer afternoon. The azure sky fought with the golden sun to see who was the brightest. Tree leaves seemed almost radioactive yellow and gold at the peak of their fall colors. The barest and warmest of breezes occasionally teased me, rustling a few leaves here and there causing me to look around, and when I did, the only person I saw was Red Falvey.

He had been to Kaprun before: his first visit was in 1945, when he and the men of the 506th waited with uncertainty about when they could finally go home. And here he was with me on the first step of our October 2008 trip to Kaprun, Zell Um See, the Eagle's Nest and Bastogne.

I turned back and looked at a large pasture with a warm smile on my face. This field was just like many in the area, but it had a unique symbolism: it was the place where the last official picture of Easy Company as an active unit was taken. To me, this was the symbolic end of Easy Company in World War II.

I stood near the pasture, across from an old castle, and waves of thought struck me.

One set of thoughts flowed around this Eden. The men who survived the War made it to an Alpine heaven, where they spent a summer among lakes, forests, valleys, hills and mountains. Many of the young men who made it to this field survived a brutal year in Europe that included three major deployments (Normandy, Holland, Belgium) and other combat that killed or maimed many of their comrades. They witnessed the brutality of the concentration camps. They volunteered for a combat experiment, the paratroops, and defeated the Nazis.

These men spent the last part of the War in an area of stunning beauty, peace and safety. They were in a place where men prematurely aged by combat could become young again, playing sports, getting drunk, causing mischief and doing all of those things that you do when you are in your teens and early twenties. I thought about David Webster's description of swimming and drinking by the lake. Dick Winters wrote that he nearly got killed while hunting a mountain goat in the area. And Red told me that he tried to ride a horse and was thrown and was lucky not to break his neck.

It seemed that the men deserved to end the War in Austria during the summer, although I've wrestled whether deserve is a strong enough word. It was something more than deserved. I thought about tree bursts in the Bois Jacques in the freezing cold. About Bob Wolverton killed while still in his parachute. About paratroopers executed in Graignes. About Tom Meehan's widow receiving the telegram. About Bill Guarnere losing his leg while trying to save Joe Toye. About Skip Muck and Alex Penkala taking a direct hit in their foxhole. About the shelling in Veghel on September 23rd. About all of the men of the 101st and 82nd. About the men gunned down on Omaha Beach and the other men of the infantry. Definitely, deserved isn't enough.

There is a well-known picture of Don Malarkey and Burr Smith taken on a balcony in the lake town of Zell um See, just a few minutes northeast of Kaprun. The War was over and the two good friends survived and were together. They were safe and in an Alpine lake resort town. But if you look closely at the picture, you will see that while Malarkey is looking towards the camera with a slight smile, Smith is looking to the left of the photographer. His eyes are burning in intensity. They aren't the eyes of a young man. They're striking, deep, serious and wary. He was probably about 20 at that time. Those eyes said that deserve is not enough.

But while deserve may not be enough, it is comforting nonetheless to know that the men of the 506th (and other units) had a chance to recover as best they could physically and mentally (although many would wrestle their demons for years) and get the time to celebrate survival before they shipped out.

One of the nicer, overlooked parts of Band of Brothers is Michael Kaman's soundtrack. There is a scene in the last episode in which Dick Winters swims by himself in Zell um See. During the scene, actor Damian Lewis narrates a reflection, while soft, warm piano music plays in the background. I was at that very lake, looking at the still, cool waters, the crisp evening air in my nostrils, the hills and pastures on the eastern side of the lake lit up by the setting sun, the hills behind me on the west side dark in shade. The music played through my mind, and I felt glad that the men got this. I was glad that they weren't deactivated immediately and sent back to the States. I think that it would have been traumatic to be split up quickly and to have to say goodbye so abruptly.

And while I was caught up in the satisfaction of knowing that the War ended in such a nice place, I thought about something else. Being in Kaprun meant that this was pretty much the last of my first visits to places where Easy Company served. While I would not technically complete the whole tour until the next day when I made it to the Eagle's Nest, it still felt like I had traveled the arc of the story.

If we're going to get technical, it's true that I have not been to every place through which Easy passed. I have not yet gone to Fort Benning, Camp Mackall, Haguenau, Mourmelon or Aldbourne and I suppose I could go visit them in the future. Haguenau was rebuilt completely after the War, but I still could have seen the river the patrol crossed. And I suppose I could have a pint in the Aldbourne pub where some of the men drank. But I had essentially seen all of the major places in the story of Easy Company. From the bus and train stations in Toccoa through Normandy, Holland, Belgium and Germany to this field in Kaprun, and I felt like I had seen where the story formed and where the legacy was forged.

Interestingly, none of the individual trips I took seemed remarkable. Going to Normandy is not that hard. Holland?

Torture in the sense of crowding, but generally a piece of cake. Toccoa? Come on that's just a few hours from New York. But it dawned on me at the pasture that I went from knowing nothing when I watched the miniseries air in 2001 to seven years later being in Austria with Red Falvey, a D-Day veteran who started in Toccoa and made it all the way through to Kaprun. I had hundreds of comments on my pictures posted on Flickr, and over 70,000 views through the site and about another 600,000 from internet searches. And importantly, I made many new friends. I was somewhat knowledgeable, and absolutely thrilled that I had the chance to see these places for myself, truly appreciating that not many people could do what I did.

As it washed over me how much I'd accomplished, I felt a little melancholy about reaching the end of the line. I spent seven years with places to see for the first time and now it was turning into places I would revisit. But I realized too that I barely knew a fraction of the whole story so there would always be something new to learn. Plus, if I was going to do this right, I would have to start from the beginning with the 82nd Division, because I had just scratched the surface. So, I smiled from knowing I had a lot more work to do and got back to enjoying where I was.

I looked around at the verdant hills and the changing leaves and then back at the field. I wished I could have gone back in time and bought the guys posing for the photograph a beer, even if that might have bankrupted me. I wished I could have gone back and shook every hand and said thank you. That would certainly have been a lot of fun.

And my mind drifted again, and I realized something that I had missed completely. For all of the warmth of the moment and the beauty of the area, I wasn't standing at a place that was just the symbolic end of the Easy Company. This was also the symbolic center of the Third Reich. I was in Bavaria, where the Nazi party had its' roots. Berchtesgaden, where Hitler maintained his mountain home, the Berghof, and where his Nazi henchmen had their dachas, was only an hour away. You had to be a Nazi to live there. And just a few hours earlier, on the highway outside of Munich, I saw the exit for the Dachau Concentration Camp.

• • •

Dachau Concentration Camp

Rage

When I was getting ready to go to the Dachau concentration camp for the first time, I was filled with pure rage. I had a hatred of all Germans. I was blaming all Germans for the Holocaust, not just the Nazis. I knew it was illogical and raw and misplaced. But that's how I felt.

I was going to the place that the Germans used to perfect the concentration camp concept. Dachau was ground zero: that was the first camp the Germans ever built and what came afterwards originated from there. The death machinery and methodology of the Holocaust were perfected there. I thought about the people who never had a chance once the Germans got them. I wanted payback. And there was no way to get it other than to be angry as hell.

I saw the Band of Brothers episode, "Why we Fight," and my stomach turned. Easy Company liberated the Buchloe concentration camp near the town of Landsberg, which is about 20 miles west of Dachau. Buchloe was a subcamp of Dachau, which operated dozens of satellite sites. Dachau also rented prisoners as slave labor to local businesses, such as BMW, many of whom had their own prison facilities on site. The camp received compensation for the laborers, who were often abused horribly by their employers. The death of a laborer required a minor compensation to Dachau.

That Dachau was so spread out and that there was slave labor at factories alongside German workers meant one obvious thing: the German populace knew what was going on. This wasn't just some hidden atrocity of the Nazis. The German people knew of the anti-Semitism and supported it, and many participated in acts. No one knew about Kristallnacht in 1938? Come on. As the German armies swept through Poland, executions were carried out by thugs and paramilitary groups, not just the SS. The more I learned before my trip, the more

I seethed. I had no doubt that were I an American soldier in World War II, I would have shot German prisoners, and probably civilians.

In 1998, I went to the synagogue on Oranienstrasse in Berlin, and saw an exhibit about the destruction of the City's Jewish population. There were pictures of people who were sent to camps and died. The people in the pictures looked like members of my family. I saw the graveyard, which the Nazis thought would be an ironic place to use for the deportation of Jews to the camps and learned that the Germans knocked down the tombstones to insult the dead. I wanted to kill every German in Berlin.

I saw the documentary, "The Ritchie Boys," about a group of American soldiers who fled Nazi Germany. These men were recruited for their ability to speak German and for their knowledge of the country and returned to Germany to fight the Nazis knowing that they would be executed if they were captured. My blood boiled.

And my anger was fed by the reality that the Holocaust was not some isolated event in the middle of the 20th Century and that World War II solved everything. The president of Iran hosted the International Conference to Review the Global Vision of the Holocaust, a denial symposium, in December 2006 and routinely makes claims that the systematic destruction never happened. In June 2009, African-American security guard Stephen Tyrone Johns was killed by an anti-Semitic racist at the Holocaust Museum in Washington, D.C. The vermin who shot him was an American veteran of World War II. And in New Jersey, not far from where I lived, a couple named their son, Adolf Hitler. They had the gall to be upset when a bakery refused to put his name on a cake. One of their other children has the middle name, Aryan Nation. Anti-Semitism and hatred are alive and well in the 21st Century.

So, the last thing I wanted to do was visit Dachau for the first time with a German.

I am so thankful that I did.

A German Humbles Me

I had to go to Munich for a meeting at my company's office there, so I decided to arrive a day early in order to visit Dachau. I planned to go on my own because I knew it would be emotional and it never occurred to me to go with someone else. But the gods of fate had an alternate plan in the works.

I mentioned my itinerary to my colleagues and they immediately took charge of my visit to Dachau. They would not hear of my going there without being guided by a co-worker, Bernd, whom I met once a year earlier. They told me he was an expert on the camp and had a lifelong interest in the history of what happened there. I tried to explain about wanting to see it by myself because of the emotionality, but none of my efforts worked. With typical German efficiency, they arranged a tour guide. I was reluctant and disgruntled.

Then I got an email from Bernd eagerly agreeing to give up his Sunday and volunteering to pick me up at my hotel and drive me to Dachau. He explained that he was a lifelong historian of the camp and spent years chronicling the atrocities there. He was part of a group that sued the Bavarian government to preserve Dachau and he interviewed former prisoners to make sure there was a full first-hand account of what happened there.

I felt horrendously embarrassed for my rage at all Germans. What was going on? I was ranting about hating any German, and here was this man who barely knew me, giving up part of his weekend and telling me in animated tones about the horrors of the camp and his efforts to preserve it and make sure all of the secrets there were exposed. Here I was with an expert who was not only furious about the atrocities at Dachau, but who had actually spent a large part of his life uncovering the history of the camp. I was outraged as a Jew. He was outraged as a German.

Dachau

A typical gray winter day set the tone for the visit to Dachau, making things even more ominous and depressing. As we drove, Bernd explained to me that as a young man in high school he was bothered by the issue of what did the average German know about the Holocaust and why didn't those who were aware do anything. He wrote a thesis and got special access to restricted Nazi records, and what he found shocked him. He concluded that the average German knew about the Holocaust and that many people in the country were supporters to some degree. He asked his mother why she didn't do anything, and she replied that she didn't know for sure what was going on and that it was dangerous for an average person to say something. You could get a midnight visit from the Gestapo and disappear. His research as a young man led him to become part of a historical society. When the Bavarian government tried tearing down parts of the camp, he and others sued to keep it all as intact as was possible. Here was a true activist and historian.

The inconceivable thing about Dachau is that it's tucked into a neighborhood. We drove past some strip malls, a train station, by some houses and reached the parking lot. I couldn't believe it. This wasn't set out of sight in some rural area or in a forest as Buchloe was depicted in Band of Brothers. It was right in town. In the U.S., it would almost be like driving through a town and finding a large high school campus amid the homes. The feel is almost the same, and it's sickening how common and matter-of-fact it all is.

Dachau Concentration Camp

The camp wall abuts houses on one side, and their windows look right onto the guard towers and SS barracks not even 75 feet away. I have been told that there always were people living or working near the camp, and it wasn't just post-War construction that resulted in homes and schools and stores being within throwing distance. The camp itself is only 10 miles northwest of Munich and is close enough for many people to have known not only of its existence but also its purpose.

When you arrive at Dachau today, you walk through an entry house with a heavy swinging iron door with words in block letters, "Arbeit Macht free." Roughly translated, it means, "Work brings freedom." The same words were at the gate in Auschwitz. For the women, children, elderly and sick who passed by those words at Auschwitz-Birkenau, there was only death. Perhaps the Germans felt that somehow, their grotesque attempt at public relations might convince some people that Dachau was a rehabilitation and work camp for political prisoners.

Dachau was the first concentration camp, and is located on the site of a former munitions factory in a medieval town from which the camp took its name. All of the concentration camp horrors originated from the ideas tested and perfected at Dachau, whether it was the gas chambers or the ovens. And the camp was used to train the Nazi guards who stayed at Dachau or who went to perform atrocities at other places.

The camp opened on March 22, 1933 and the Kommandant, Theodor Eicke, established a basic layout that was used as the prototype for all other camps. By the time Eicke died from a Soviet bullet near Kharkov in 1943, he was the chief inspector for all camps and made sure they met his gruesome standards. I would love to have bought the Russian who shot Eicke a round of vodkas.

Compared to Auschwitz, Dachau is small and is distinctly different from the larger camp in Poland. At Dachau, there is only one small gas chamber and only two sets of ovens. In

Auschwitz-Birkenau, 1,100,000 people were killed, about 90% of whom were Jews poisoned to death with gas. Over 200,000 prisoners passed through Dachau, and only about one-third of them were Jews. Although many prisoners died after being transferred from Dachau to other camps, it is estimated that about 40,000 died there, often of disease and malnutrition. Some were victims of horrific medical experiments that were conducted in a special set of barracks. But Dachau was not a death camp, per se.

The camp layout was a series of long, wooden barracks that were separated from a main building by a large courtyard where the prisoners were often tortured in full view of others. Behind the main buildings in the camp was a set of SS barracks, where political and religious prisoners were held (at least 3,000 religious, deacons, priests, and bishops were imprisoned in Dachau, and many who ended up in the SS barracks were tortured and then executed).

Surrounding the camp were barbed wire fences, ditches and guard towers. Administration and training buildings were adjacent to the entrance to the camp. In the rear, separated from the main camp, was an area that contained gas chambers, crematoria and execution ranges, and on the opposite side was an area where female prisoners were forced into sexual slavery. Nearly one mile from the camp site is the place where several hundred Soviet soldiers were executed.

Dachau was liberated by two American infantry divisions that arrived from opposite directions, leading to some controversy as to which actually arrived first. On April 29, 1945, soldiers from the 442nd and 45th infantry divisions arrived at opposite ends of the camp and both units are credited with the liberation. When the Americans reached Dachau, they found 32,000 prisoners. Barracks that were designed to hold 250 prisoners were stuffed with 1,500 each and train cars were found stuffed with corpses.

Walking through the steel gate under that gloomy winter sky made me feel heavy and slow. We joined up with a tour, but the guide knew nothing compared to Bernd. As we walked around, Bernd pointed out the courtyard and explained how prisoners were forced to stand endlessly. Any prisoner who was sick and could not make it out of the barracks was killed, in most cases. The prisoners stood for hour after hour and any man who collapsed was beaten, tortured or killed. Some prisoners were forced to put their hands behind their backs and were hoisted in the air by their wrists, dislocating both shoulders. There were many other tortures in which the guards not only excelled, but delighted. I remember hearing of one record at the camp containing the diary of a Romanian guard who wrote with glee about beating a Jewish prisoner to death with a pipe.

Disease was rampant in the camp as each barrack swelled in numbers. Reconstructed barracks demonstrate the various phases of prisoner accommodations during the camp's history. In the beginning, there were 250 men per barracks and there was enough room for a small bunk for each prisoner. By the end of the war, each barrack was stuffed with six times as many prisoners. The prisoners slept on long, multi-tier wooden planks and if one man rolled over, everyone else had to as well. When prisoners in the upper bunks were struck with dysentery and had diarrhea or vomited, it seeped through down onto those who were in the lower bunks.

The worst part to me was the medical experiments. The tour guide knew about some of them, but Bernd filled me in on everything that happened. He brought me to the exhibit in the former administrative building that showed before and after pictures of the prisoners, many of whom died during the experiments. Seeing the pictures of skeletal men who went through excruciating pain and then died is incomprehensible.

Bernd and I stepped away from the tour and stood on the spot of the medical barracks and he told about the experiments performed by a doctor in the Luftwaffe named Sigmund Rascher. Bernd was bewildered by Rascher and said that he was a medical doctor who swore to the Hippocratic Oath. He looked at me with pleading eyes and asked, "How could a doctor do this to human beings?" I had no answer.

Rascher conducted experiments for the Luftwaffe under the justification that they could potentially save the lives of German pilots. The experiments were documented with typical German efficiency and accuracy, and notes, photos and movies provide the evidence (which the deniers overlook), much of which was presented, along with witness testimony, at a special Doctors Trial in Nuremberg.

Medical experiments were conducted on many prisoners, and at least 180 to 200 prisoners were selected for the ones for the Luftwaffe, and one witness stated that 70 to 80 died. Many of the subjects were previously sentenced to death by the Nazis, and included 40 Russian soldiers. Rascher sent a note to Heinrich Himmler describing the autopsy results on a Jewish man who was sent to Dachau to be executed for being with a non-Jewish woman and breaking a German law against race-mixing.

One set of experiments involved the effects of high altitude and were perversely done with prisoners who were dressed in Luftwaffe uniforms. Prisoners were put in a compression chamber to see at what altitudes flight crews could survive without oxygen. The simulated altitude was raised up to as high as 68,000 feet. Many of the prisoners died; one well-known photograph shows a dead prisoner hanging from a harness in a Luftwaffe uniform.

Cold water experiments were done to explore the effect of ditching on a plane's crew. These experiments began in August 1942, and the prisoners' deaths were long and agonizing. Two Russian officers were thrown naked into a tank of freezing water without anesthesia. It took 20 minutes for those two men to die, according to records. For the prisoners in flight equipment, it took longer to die, sometimes up to an hour and a half. The Germans concluded that death occurred only among those who were wearing life jackets that allowed the back of the neck to be immersed in the water. Other experiments were done to try to warm men who were frozen to a state of near death. Some men were warmed by body contact with women (an odd request by Himmler himself), while others were warmed using blankets or submersion in hot baths.

Rascher had a fitting, albeit bizarre, end to his life. Himmler somehow learned that Dr. Rascher and his wife had young children. This became a mystery because the doctor's wife was well beyond child-bearing years. An investigation discovered that the children were actually adopted orphans and Rascher and his wife were executed in April 1945 just before the end of the War.

Other horrors were carried out at Dachau, including exposing prisoners to malaria and inflicting severely painful wounds with mustard gas in order to test the effectiveness of experimental drugs. The Nazis had no limits to their savagery. In testing the effectiveness of sulfanilamide on battlefield wound infections, victims were exposed to various bacteria, and had their circulation damaged by the tying off of blood vessels. The German "doctors" worsened the infections by grinding wood shavings and broken glass into the wounds. At a different camp, prisoners had sections of bone, muscle and nerve fibers removed. I cannot imagine the agony of the victims.

Numbed to a point where I could no longer feel, we walked to the far left portion of the camp, past rows of empty spots where barracks once stood. We passed through another gate, and what I saw on the left was immediately recognizable: it was a crematorium. So many people were dying in Dachau that the Nazis needed to burn the bodies because carting them through town to a cemetery might have raised objections.

Next to the small building that was the old crematorium was a larger one, and I could easily see the ovens through the open doors. We walked into the room and I looked up at large rafters. Bernd pointed to them and said that some prisoners were hung from the beams and then cut down and thrown into the ovens.

On the other part of the building was a changing room and, next to it, a gas chamber. Here is where the guards at Auschwitz and elsewhere learned how to use Zyklon B. I was almost afraid to go into the room, even though I knew nothing would happen. I saw what the gas chamber looked like from the inside, knowing that for millions, their last steps would have been into a room like that one.

When some people see these sights they cry or even weep audibly. I just went dead inside. I couldn't take anymore. But Bernd made sure I saw it all. I wanted to flinch, but here was this German historian making sure that I saw everything that happened there. He took me to the firing range in the adjacent garden to show me the execution area and the blood ditch. And the area where human ashes were dumped. I had no rage. I had no anger. I felt like I weighed one ton. I wanted to go to sleep.

But he took me across the compound past a memorial sculpture in the front of the administration building. Inside the large structure, we stopped to look at dozens of pictures and artifacts, and walked out the back. There was the long SS barracks for special political and religious prisoners. One of the distinctions of Dachau compared to other camps is the diversity of political prisoners, many of whom were not Jewish. Approximately 2,720 priests were prisoners in Dachau, and at least 1,034 of them died there. One cell housed a miniature shrine that still exists.

Many political prisoners died in Dachau. Georg Elser, who tried to assassinate Hitler in 1939, was executed on April

9, 1945. Charles Deletraint, a leader of the French Resistance, was executed in 1945 as well. Politicans from Austria, Germany, Poland and elsewhere died in the camp at the hands of the guards or the Gestapo or from illness and malnutrition.

The barracks are long and dark, with peeling paint and empty cells. It is utterly depressing. You could literally not imagine hope there.

And that is how I walked out of Dachau at first, hopeless. Empty. But almost immediately, it began to hit me. The rage wasn't directed at Germans. I still hated the Nazis, but I wasn't blaming all Germans. And it was thanks to going to Dachau with a German.

The Rage Returns

Shortly after returning home and posting my pictures of Dachau on Flickr, some anti-Semite left comments that the Holocaust was a hoax and never happened. I tried to find out who it was but the coward had no profile information so I simply deleted the comments while wishing I could teach him a lesson with a baseball bat.

That was nothing compared to what I saw a year later when I returned with a friend of mine. As we walked near the building that housed the gas chamber, I spotted two men who were laughing, which caught my attention and spiked my anger right away. I saw that they were going to urinate on the ground near one of the crematoria, not 15 feet from a bathroom. I immediately rushed at them and yelled that I was going to kick their ass. They started to move pretty quickly and I cursed at them as they ran. I turned to my friend with my blood boiling and tried to calm down. And then we walked into the gas chamber.

• • •

In the Heart of the Reich

The Last Visit

It was the most momentous of trips, and yet I went into it concerned about the small, insignificant logistical details of a whirlwind visit rather than the fact that I was going to Europe with Red Falvey and that I'd get to see Austria and the Eagle's Nest for the first time. Anyone who knows me will tell that you I'm neurotic, and even I know that I tend to worry a lot about preparation and details, but from my perspective there was a reason this time.

The itinerary was somewhat less complicated than was the invasion of Normandy: meet Red in Newark Airport for an overnight flight to Frankfurt. Connect to Munich, get our car (hoping it was automatic), drive a few hours to Austria, see the sights and then try to find our hotel in Berchtesgaden at night. Visit the Eagle's Nest the next morning, fly back to Frankfurt that afternoon and then drive several hours to Luxembourg. Wake up, visit the cemetery, head to Bastogne, meet Reg, stay overnight in Houffalize, wake up, tour the northern Bulge battlefields and head back to Frankfurt to stay overnight and return to Newark the next day and then get Red on his flight back to upstate New York. I worried about delays, weather, finding locations and being able to get sleep on the overnight flight so I could have energy to drive us around in Austria.

I don't know why but I always overthink things before they happen. When I used to play ice hockey, I always hated the warm-ups and the national anthem. I just wanted the puck to drop and get the game going, and once it did, I was fine. When it comes to trips, the upside is usually that I overplan and am very well prepared. The downside is that my mind races. At least as is the case with playing hockey, I tend to relax once a trip is underway.

I got to Newark Airport in a bit of an agitated state, and for reasons beyond logistics. This was my first extended trip away from my five-month old twins, and I was worried about them and missed them before I even walked out the door. On top of that, a few days after my return, my family was going to move cross-country so that I could start a new job. We were trying to clean out our house, arrange a move, take care of the kids and do just too much stuff to allow a trip to Europe, but this was the only time that I could do this.

My edginess worsened when it took me 45 minutes to find Red in the lounge at Newark Airport. He was sleeping peacefully when I finally spotted his Screaming Eagle hat and sat down next to him. He greeted me warmly and I calmed as it neared time for boarding. I was further relaxed by having used frequent flier miles to get us in business class. The bigger seats gave me a chance to try to get rested for a big next day. I didn't want to get us lost and I sure didn't want to fall asleep behind the wheel, taking Red out with me.

Relaxing completely was impossible due to my insane, neurotic quirks. I'm a creature of habit, and I always prefer to fly in a window seat on the north side of an aircraft. The bizarre reason: on my first ever trip to Europe, I sat in business class on the left side of a Lufthansa jet to Germany, and stared at Polaris, the North Star and caught a magnificent view of sunrise breaking over the North Atlantic. Flying back, I sat on the north side of the plane and looked out at Greenland. I was astounded by the views and always liked sitting on the north side of planes from then on. Sitting on the south side just didn't seem right. The extra bonus is that when you sit on the north side of a plane, it's always a little cooler because you are rarely in the sun.

On this flight, we had to sit on the south side of the aircraft so I dwelled on that issue. While I'm sure many readers would enjoy grabbing a beer with me, I am certain they'd hate flying with me. And it gets worse, I like to have the window, which means that if I need to go the bathroom, I'd crawl over you and probably wake you up.

But once we boarded, the business class seats were incredibly roomy, and I had a nice quick dinner, followed by a melatonin tablet, a Tylenol PM and a beer, and I was asleep before I knew it. About four or five hours later, I woke up feeling great. I got just enough sleep to make sure that I'd be fine driving. I saw the in-flight map and realized I had time to do four things: go to the bathroom, brush my teeth, get a cup of coffee and get my iPOD set up for another of my rituals.

I got back to my seat with my coffee and was the only person awake in business class. The first rays of sunrise were turning the horizon to a salmon-pink arc, which grew to a slight dull orange. There were no clouds and I saw the Atlantic Ocean. Stars and planets were still visible to the south. And I was the only passenger awake to enjoy this view.

As the plane neared the Irish coast, I set up my iPOD to play Respighi's symphonic poem, "The Fountains of Rome." Another of my superstitions on an international flight is that when the plane makes landfall after crossing an ocean, I play the movement, "The Trevi Fountain at Noon." The first time I did the overnight flight to Europe, I had a portable CD player with me and the Trevi Fountain played just as the plane broke over the Irish coast. Another instantly-formed habit.

We crossed over a coastline and I got my first glimpse of a verdant Ireland, deep green in the pre-dawn bluish light, with the lights of the town of Goleen below. The notes of "The Trevi Fountain" played through my headset. Next to me, Red slept soundly all the way to the English Channel, which we crossed opposite Dunkirk, the site of the disastrous British invasion attempt. I felt great as he woke up. All of the worries about logistics were gone. The trip was underway, and we were going to arrive a few minutes early. We touched down and had an easy time getting through passport control, although we had a lot of walking to do, passing countless smoking areas that gave the air in the Frankfurt airport a stale, dirty quality.

The flight to Munich was simple and quick, and since I knew the airport very well, I found the rental car agency right away. A charming young woman took care of our check-in and when I asked if the car had automatic transmission, she looked at me, smiled and said, "I am sure you will like this car." As with every place on the trip, there was a lot of walking in the airport, but when I got to the spot where the car was parked, the agent's words rang in my ears. This couldn't be our car. It was a massive Mercedes sedan. In the States it would have cost $60,000 or maybe even $80,000. The weather was spectacular, I felt rested and I was going to be on the autobahn in a car that I knew could do 140 miles per hour without any engine noise.

We took off through Munich and I pointed out the sign for Dachau. A chill ran down my spine. Red and I talked about the beer halls of Munich and the rise of the Nazis, as well as our families, the New York Yankees and his last trip to the area in 1986. The highways were easy to find: the 9, the 99, the 8 eastbound towards Berchtesgaden. I had all of the directions with me, and was confident that I could find our first stop, Kaprun, to see the where the last picture of Easy Company was taken, and then find our way to Zell um See and up to Berchtesgaden for the night.

However, Red had other plans. He grabbed a map and came up with a new route that he thought would be quicker: the E60 south to Kufstein, the 173 to the 178, head south at St. Johann in Tirol down on the 161 and straight east on the 168 to Kaprun. Five new roads I knew nothing about and some of them ran through the mountains, which probably meant slow speeds and lots of turns. But he was the adventurer and my navigator so away we went. The road gods were with us. Nearly every mile of highway in the other direction had construction or accidents and long lines of traffic. However, we shared the road with hardly anyone no matter what road we picked. And we only made two wrong turns that we fixed in mere minutes.

The Austrian Alps are absolutely stunning, and the snow-covered peaks were bright white under an azure sky. Each turn revealed a new mountain or another wildflower-filled glacial valley, and we spent about an hour proclaiming each new area as the most beautiful place we had ever seen. We were about 100 miles away from where The Sound of Music was filmed, and I was thinking to myself that the producers should have just headed a bit west. We were both in a very relaxed mood, and we snacked on chocolate that we brought from the States for the ride.

The 161 dropped down the side of a valley giving us a beautiful view of the town of Mittersill. We had to pull over for a quick view of the stunning area, and we joked that the parking brake on the Mercedes better work otherwise it was going to roll away fast on the steep decline. We were about 10 miles west of Kaprun and Red said the area looked very familiar.

I didn't want to speed because I was concerned about getting a ticket in Austria. I can only imagine what that would turn into. Worst case, I'd be sent to Dachau, but even the best case of paying a fine in Euros would have been painful. Impatiently, I observed the speed limit as we drove east on the 168.

To get to Kaprun, you turn south from the 168 and go directly into the middle of town. There is a railroad track that Red remembered from the War, and we pulled over by the siding and looked at Kaprun. The town is at the base of a low mountain that is in front of a much higher, snow-peaked alp. A gorge cuts up towards the high mountain and leads up to a ski area and lakes. Forests cover some of the hillsides, and large meadows are perched around the outskirts of the town, like a green scarf.

It was easy to imagine the men of Easy Company enjoying the area during the summer of 1945. The hills where Dick Winters hunted for a mountain goat (and nearly got killed). The fields where men played sports. The lakes where they swam.

This was it. I was five minutes away from seeing the last stop. The field where the last official picture of Easy Company as a unit was taken. We drove into town on Landestrasse, and I headed towards the center of Kaprun by bearing left onto Sigmund Thunstrasse. There were many tourists walking around and I was a little concerned about hitting someone while trying to navigate, but the crowd opened up and there it was – the left turn onto Schlosstrasse.

I drove up the hill and just past the last houses on the right there was an open field. Across from the field was a castle. That was it. That field was where the last picture of Easy Company as a unit was taken (the picture can be found on the 506th Airborne Infantry Association website in the history section where you can find photographs of 2nd Battalion). There was plenty of room to park, so I pulled over, breathed in the clean air and got my camera out. I clicked away to document the ending place.

Easy Company was arranged on a set of bleachers, with the top of the castle in the background, and the photographer was in the middle of the field. Where I was standing on the road was behind the bleachers. I wanted to run out into the field for a picture, but I decided that where I stood was just fine.

If I had been there back in 1945, I would have seen a lot of familiar faces from Band of Brothers: Don Malarkey, Burr Smith, David Webster, Earl Hale, Floyd Talbert, Babe Heffron, Joe Liebgott, Rod Strohl, Paul Rogers, Bob Rader, Clancy Lyall, Carl Fenstermacher, Popeye Wynn, Skinny Sisk, Bull Randleman, Ronald Speirs, Jack Foley, Moe Alley, Brad Freeman, Pat Christenson, Walter Hendrix, Rod Bain and Ralph Trapuzzano. But I would also have seen a lot of replacements and wondered who the hell they were.

I think what would have struck me the most if I stood there in 1945 is who was absent. On the 506th Association website, there is a picture of Easy Company taken in 1943. Many of the men in that picture were gone two years later. Bill Evans was killed in STIC 66, along with Murray Roberts, Sergio Moya, Carl Riggs, Jerry Wentzel, Bill McGonigal, John Miller and Gerald Snider. Salty Harris, Everett Gray, Robert Bloser and Ben Stoney also died in Normandy. Jim Diel, Robert Van Klinken and Bill Dukeman died in Holland. Don Hoobler, Skip Muck, Alex Penkala and Frank Mellett were killed in Bastogne. Eugene Jackson died in Haguenau and Bill Kiehn was killed in Alsace.

Then there were the men recovering in hospitals such as Bill Guarnere, Joe Toye, Albert Blithe, Moose Heyliger and Shifty Powers. And there were other men who weren't in that picture in 1945. Dick Winters was on Battalion staff, and no longer part of Easy Company. Herbert Sobel was not in the 1943 picture (neither was Guarnere, actually), and he wasn't there in 1945.

The two pictures were almost like a time machine. The first one was taken at Fort Bragg. D-Day, Holland, Bastogne, Germany. None of that happened yet for Easy. The second picture was of a company with a storied unit history. For those who did make it to that field in Kaprun, could any have imagined that when they posed for the first picture in Fort Bragg?

I assumed it must have been a paradise for the soldiers in Kaprun – anyone visiting there today would probably fall in love with the region. After a hard-fought war, a couple of months in the Austrian Alps would be a nice vacation, right? That wasn't the case, however.

Red told me that when he was in Kaprun, he just wanted to go home. He had been away from his family for a long time and he couldn't wait to get back to Yonkers. But he was stuck there and he just waited. Red and I looked around and he pointed out the approximate area where the horse threw him. Imagine making it all the way to Kaprun only to be taken out by a horse.

David Webster wrote of the drinking and swimming and other activities the men pursued while in Austria, and I think that at first, it was an all-out, well-deserved party. But it quickly became frustrating to Webster. You could have too much time to relax in the Austrian Alps. Webster did a marvelous job describing the last few months and how he couldn't wait to get home. Band of Brothers also describes the tension of waiting, which was worsened by a lack of adequate food rations due to siphoning upstream.

Well, I didn't channel any of that frustration. I felt delighted. I had been to Toccoa and now to Kaprun: the start and the end. We spent about an hour there and when we left, I simply felt relaxed and satisfied. I wanted to yell, "Currahee!" at the top of my lungs. But I thought Red would think I had lost my mind. For someone who loves beginnings so much – Ephrata, the landing sites in Normandy, Champs – I was thrilled to see an end of sorts.

Red and I drove the few miles to Zell um See, where that picture of Smith and Malarkey was taken and where Winters swam as the Company and Regiment spent a little time in that town before riding out the rest of the War in Kaprun. We walked around the lake town as the sun began to set behind the western mountains, casting deep shadows across the valley. Zell um See is quite built up, which was a little disturbing. Kaprun seemed quite small and charming but Red pointed out that there was a lot of new construction there too. Despite the new hotels and restaurants, I had a chance to walk along the shore of the lake (the See) and thought of the episode of Band of Brothers during which Winters took his swim. The afternoon was silent except for the quacking of ducks and the hollow sound the wind makes when it passes through a valley. Now there was only one last place to see to complete my list of Band of Brothers sites: Hitler's Eagle's Nest.

Red and I headed towards Berchtesgaden as the sun set in the valley. Shadows enveloped the small town of Bruck, the site of an airfield during the War, and presumably the setting for the baseball game at the end of the miniseries. If we could fly, we'd only have to travel about 18 miles to Berchtesgaden, heading over the mountains and lakes. Instead, we drove a circuitous 60 miles by taking the 311, the A10/E55, and then getting off and cutting through the mountains until we reached the place where you had to be a Nazi to live: Berchtesgaden.

It gets dark quickly in the mountains and other than chocolates, we really hadn't eaten anything all day. I wanted to get to the hotel and figured we could grab dinner there and then rest up. When I planned the trip, someone recommended the Hotel Zum Tuerken to me and told me that it was the only hotel on the Obersalzburg (the mountain area that is home to the Eagle's Nest) and she said there was an incredible bunker complex underneath the hotel. Sounded convenient and pretty interesting. I went online, found the hotel's website and got a pleasant response back from Frau Scharfenberg and looked forward to the visit. If I had only taken a few minutes to learn more about the Hotel Zum Tuerken, I would have built in an extra half day. So much for being neurotic and an overplanner!

The Hotel Zum Tuerken has its roots dating back to the 17th Century, and the foundation for the current hotel was put down in 1911. In 1933, the Nazis seized all of the land in the Obersalzberg area, which overlooks Berchtesgaden. Hitler wrote part of Mein Kampf while vacationing in the area in the 1920s.

The Nazi leaders built homes for themselves there, and the most notable of them all was Hitler's dacha, the Berghof. The Nazis built the Berghof nearly adjacent to the Hotel Tuerken, which they turned into a headquarters for the SS and housing for Hitler's bodyguard. Over the next few years, the Nazis built an intricate network of bomb shelters and tunnels that lead from the Tuerken to the Berghof.

In 1945, Allied bombers remodeled the Berghof, installing natural air conditioning with some brilliantly-placed bombs. The Tuerken was damaged severely as well, and I can only imagine the reaction of the Scharfenberg family when they returned to their place in 1945. Not just the destruction, but the conversion into an SS barracks, with all kinds of tunnels and bomb shelters, plus the knowledge that Hitler lived next door. Frau Scharfenberg's mother petitioned the Bavarian government, regained control of the property and reopened the hotel in 1958. And I noticed none of that on the website because I'm an idiot.

Red and I arrived in Berchtesgaden after dark, and we looked for the sign for the Obersalzburg and headed up a mountain road with no streetlights. We thought that the hotel would appear shortly, but we kept snaking up the switchbacks, and soon we wondered if we missed a turnoff somewhere. As we went up another few hundred feet, Red pointed to the siderail and said, "This looks very familiar. It looks just like an area where Hitler's house was." At that moment, it occurred to me that I should have printed a map showing where the Nazi dachas were, but I was out of luck. Up and up we went, and I decided to turn around at the first pullout, but just as soon as I thought to do that, I saw a road off to the left and a sign for the Hotel Zum Tuerken.

We drove up in the dark completely unaware that the place we passed looked a lot different in 1933, when an SS guardhouse was built there. And we had no idea what else was around us. We were tired and hungry and relieved to arrive. Frau Scharfenberg threw a key down to us from an upstairs window and we entered inside. I looked around and thought the place was enormous and almost institutional-looking. It didn't seem quite like a hotel, but then again, I didn't pay attention when I made the reservation.

After dropping off our bags, we headed into Berchtesgaden for dinner, and the ride down seemed much shorter than was our first ride up. In the off-season, Berchtesgaden is very quiet, and many restaurants were closed. We found a traditional Bavarian restaurant, and after so many hours without a real meal, I gorged myself. True to his word, Red had only a small dinner. Inside, I laughed at the moment: I was an American Jew in Berchtesgaden with a Screaming Eagle veteran, drinking the best beer in the world and eating a typical Bavarian meal of sausage, sauerkraut and potatoes plus three pretzels. Stuffed and contented, as well as exhausted, it was back to the hotel for a well-deserved rest.

We woke early the next morning and I looked out our balcony window. I saw the road we took up to the hotel in front of me and bearing off to my left was what looked like a service road and a hillside. In the distance, Berchtesgaden was covered in a layer of fog. I inhaled the crisp mountain air and stared at the town below. It wasn't until Red and I were flying back to the US that I learned something stunning. The Berghof sat at the end of that little service road. From our balcony, I could see the exact place where Hitler's dacha was located; I just didn't know it.

When I got home and looked on the website, Third ReichRuins, I saw a picture from 1939 that must have been taken from my room. Now Red understood right away why the railing on the side of the road was so familiar. Back in 1945, he and a buddy were on that road when his friend fell off down into the woods. When Red and his friends rescued his buddy, they realized they were right next to Hitler's house.

We went downstairs for breakfast and were served by Frau Scharfenberg, who has the energy of a 25-year-old, even though she was over 80. We settled our room charge and went for a quick tour of the bunker complex, but our minds were on the Eagle's Nest. Had we known about the history of the hotel and how the tunnels led to Hitler's retreat, we would have stayed longer. However, we were focused: we wanted to get up the mountain. From the parking lot, we could see the Eagle's Nest several thousand feet above us, perched on the Kehlstein, a 6,017-foot mountain that looks out over Berchtesgaden

When you visit the Eagle's Nest, you cannot drive all the way up the mountain and you have to take a shuttle bus. As you drive up the Obersalzberg, you see clearly-marked signs for parking lots for the shuttles, so it is unlikely that you will get lost. The first shuttle leaves at about eight in the morning, and we probably caught the second bus of the day. We were able to park very close to the terminal, and I recommend going as early as you can. On our bus, the only other passengers were employees of the Eagle's Nest – no tourists. By the time of our return, the buses were crammed with tourists and the main parking lot was full.

We bought our tickets at a clearly-marked window and the driver of the bus pointed us to the shuttle and we headed up the mountain. The road to the Eagle's Nest is wide enough for one bus, and there are many hair-pin turns, so it's an exhilarating ride to the top. The bus let us out in a parking lot and Red recognized everything. A tunnel into the mountain led to the golden elevator that takes you to the Eagle's Nest, or the Kehlsteinhaus, as it is called.

Band of Brothers depicted Easy Company as the unit that got to the Eagle's Nest first, and by nearly every other account, including that of General Taylor, the truth is that the 7th Regiment of the 3rd Infantry Division took the Eagle's Nest. A short time afterwards, French soldiers arrived and it took about 16 hours for Easy Company to get to the Eagle's Nest.

The elevator that takes you to the Eagle's Nest today lets you out in a hallway with a door on the left that takes you right onto one of the outdoor terraces. When we got to the top, I couldn't wait to get out. It was the last place to visit and this was heavy-duty for symbolism: it was Hitler's place. If I had done things in proper order, I would have gone to the Eagle's Nest and then Kaprun. But it didn't matter: this was the last place I needed to go. The weather was spectacular, I was with Red, and I wanted to yell at the German workers, "We beat you. It took us one year from D-Day and we kicked your sorry asses!" But then again, I had learned a lesson about this generation of Germans versus those in 1930s and 1940s when I was at Dachau.

The Eagle's Nest is surprising in many ways. Hitler rarely used it: by some estimates he was there fewer than a dozen times, often for not much more than a few minutes. He preferred a teahouse that was within walking distance of the Berghof. Actually, many of the famous pictures and movies of Hitler were set at the Berghof. So I guess everyone who argues about who took the Eagle's Nest is kind of missing a point. They should worry about the Berghof, which was reached first by the 3rd Infantry Division, and by the French a short time later. The 101st arrived a few days later, by which time Hitler was a partially-charred corpse and the mighty German Army could be called defeated. Another surprise is the small size of the Kehlsteinhaus. I imagined a large mansion, but it is a few halls, some small rooms and a series of terraces. You could do a quick walking tour in fewer than five minutes.

I was delighted to find a hallway area that looked just like the one in Band of Brothers where Speirs, Nixon and Welsh were drinking themselves into oblivion as they received the word that the German Army surrendered. And I was even more delighted to walk around the side of the building and spot Red, in his camouflage shirt and wearing his Screaming Eagles hat, leaning on the terrace wall and looking out and enjoying the view. It had been 63 years since his first visit.

I walked up the mountain a few hundred feet to look down on the Eagle's Nest, and I got a couple of young hikers to take my picture. Walking around in the sun got me overheated, so I stopped at the concession stand there and got a soda, and stood and enjoyed the breeze. Red and I went for about a 20 minute walk and took in the view, trying to spot the Hotel

Tuerken and guessing where the Nazis had their villas down in the valley below. We saw an exhibit and then felt that we accomplished our mission. We saw Kaprun, Zell um See and the Eagle's Nest. We could now make our long way to Bastogne.

The elevator opened up and tons of loud tourists poured out, and it was like watching a gaggle of honking geese. Loud talking sounded like clucking and the horde couldn't quite figure out where to go as it slowly waddled out of our way. By the time we got back to the bus terminal at the parking lot, long lines of people were waiting to get to the top of the mountain. Our timing was perfect. I looked back up the mountain and felt satisfied that I came, I saw, I conquered. Or something like that. I ran through the checklist in my mind: Toccoa, Camp Shanks, Normandy, Holland, Bastogne, the Eagle's Nest, Zell Um See, Kaprun. Probably 50,000 miles of flying and at least eight trips. As we drove away from Hitler's playground, I felt like I earned a pair of jump wings.

• • •

VII
Legacies

Legacies

Red and I completed our whirlwind trip with a quick tour of the Ardennes and then flew home. We had a funny moment in the town of Honsfeld, where a famous picture was taken of German soldiers putting on the boots of dead Americans by a trough at an intersection. I wanted to show Red that spot and pulled in front of a house. Evidently, the home was for sale and we were approached by an elderly gentleman who spoke no English.

By some miracle, I was able to translate the gentleman's French for Red, and what transpired was an attempt to get us to buy the place. When I explained that we were just visiting and that Red was a veteran, the gentleman asked our ages. I said Red was 87 and the man said he was 88. Not once did the older gentleman stop to see if I understood what he was saying, and he merrily chatted away. It was one of those small moments that make trips so enjoyable.

Red wasn't the only 506th veteran I got to spend time with in 2008. There was my trip earlier in the year to meet Buck Compton that started the whole process of my becoming friends with Red. Also, I was invited to Michigan to Don Burgett's surprise 83rd birthday party, thanks to the persistence of Reg. I walked into the B Line Bar near Don's home in Howell, MI without having met any of the people there in person before then. It didn't take long for all of the guests to become one big group, sharing stories and learning about each other and, of course, celebrating the day with Don.

I hear a lot of people eulogize the passing of the generation that served in World War II, and many people talk with regret not just about losing those who served but about the fear that young people lack appreciation for the sacrifices made in Normandy, Bastogne, Iwo Jima, Okinawa and all of the other battlefields.

I've had some of those worries myself, but I generally maintain a sense of optimism. I think the next generations have been active in learning and passing on, with accuracy, passion and devotion, the stories and experiences of the men who served our country. There are so many signs that should make the veterans happy that no matter how crazy the world may seem, there are young people who care. At Don's birthday party, there was a large contingent of people half his age or younger who read all of his books and who traveled to Europe to see the battlefields for themselves. On Don's website, hundreds of people from all over the world post regularly on his forum, and over time, you can see how admirers who were inspired by Don's history are recommending travel destinations, books, tour guides and other resources to each other, and it's done with enthusiasm and camaraderie.

The 506th 2nd Battalion Headquarters Company reenactors with whom Red is affiliated give up large blocks of time to pay homage to the veterans, and their dedication and attention to detail is stunning. Visit them at the Reading World War 2 weekend and you'll think these guys just came from Fort Benning, circa 1943.

There are dozens of tour groups and hundreds of history books, with new ones coming out all the time. If you search Amazon for Band of Brothers or any of the other books about Easy Company or World War II, you will notice the sales rankings are very high.

Personally, I have seen my pictures about Band of Brothers and the War generate many views on Flickr, and they even come up in internet searches. And I've received hundreds of emails from people wanting to know more, or to say thanks or simply to say hello. I was contacted by the granddaughter of Archie Ponds, one of the scouts who disappeared ahead of Don Burgett on the road to Ravenoville. I heard from a relative of Leo Pichler, a 502nd trooper whose tombstone I photographed. And not long ago, I was contacted by a woman whose son was serving with the 506th in Afghanistan to let me know she sent him a link to my pictures. Many veterans from all kinds of branches of the military have contacted me as well.

And then there are the families themselves with whom I came into contact. Don Burgett's family at the B Line. Susan Smith Finn, Burr's daughter, shared so much about her father with me in response to an email I sent asking her about the picture of him with Don Malarkey in Zell Um See. Susan has become a trusted friend and I was delighted to help, albeit in very small way, in putting together her first trip to Europe, which included two days in the field with Reg, and a very special ceremony in Bastogne, where she accepted an honor on behalf of her father. I got to understand what a great man Charlie Rhinehart was through his daughter, Cindy. I also found a website maintained by the nephew of Colonel Robert Ballard, and I sent him and his family pictures of where he and the 501st served. They had never been to Europe and the pictures circulated among the family with great enthusiasm. And then I met people online such as Marion Chard, whose father was a combat engineer in the VI Corps and who is producing a wonderful documentary.

For the surviving veterans, I think they should feel hope that the stories of the men who never made it home and those who did are treasured and are being passed along by many grateful people. My hope is that this book will get even more people involved in preserving the legacies of all of the soldiers who fought and died to protect our country and our freedoms.

As for myself, I will continue my travels, although I think part of what interests me next is finding some of the burial sites of the veterans. I'd like to place flowers on the grave of Ben Stoney in Normandy, and also on Carwood Lipton's burial place. And when my children are old enough to understand, I will take them with me to Toccoa and Europe, so that they can see what thousands of young men did so that future generations could live freely.

The Last Chapter

Band of Brothers focused mostly on three years of the 20th Century, but the lives of the men who made it home did not end in 1945. I felt that any telling of the stories should include as much as I could find on those who returned home. I think it's just as fascinating to hear what happened to these men after World War II when the Band of Brothers became the Band of Grandfathers.

Band of Grandfathers

The combat scenes of Band of Brothers might be the most graphic and intense part of the miniseries. But in my mind, the best work done by the producers was to make sure that, like the book, the viewers were connected to the veterans themselves. The interviews with the veterans that preceded each episode allowed me to see that the real men of Easy Company looked just like the average person's grandfather, or the neighbor down the street. It was revealing to see that the men who I was guilty of misperceiving as supermen and John Wayne-types were really fairly common older gentlemen who had to serve, and who volunteered to do something incredible at a very young age.

Seeing the veterans, most in their 80s when interviewed, contrasted against the young actors was wonderful. The juxtapositions caused me to wonder about the decades between World War II and the making of the miniseries. When I thought about those older veterans, I hoped that they had the wonderful post-War lives that they deserved. There was the word deserved again.

Then came the last episode, which left me with a pleasant sense of closure. I didn't read "Band of Brothers" before seeing the miniseries, and so I was touched that the last episode concluded with a short narrative by actor Damian Lewis describing what happened to some of the men after the War. The narrative was followed by Carwood Lipton's quote of Shakespeare and Dick Winters discussing grandfather telling grandchild of not being a hero but serving among them.

When I read Band of Brothers, I found the book mentioned many men who were never introduced during the miniseries and the epilogue only had a description of the post-War lives of a handful of veterans. So many episodes' worth of men wrapped up so quickly. I felt that the book's description of what happened to only some of the men was only partially satisfying. I wanted to know more about the soldiers to whom I felt bonded.

Then, shortly after the miniseries aired, I found Carwood Lipton's obituary in *The New York Times*. The idea came to me to search through obituary websites to try to find out as much as I could about the men from Easy Company who survived the War. Based on newspaper obituaries and other sources I found, I pieced together information and found that many of the men returned home and some got married and had children, some stayed in the military and others sought careers in business and education. They retired, saw their families grow and welcomed grandchildren. Some stayed in very close contact with each other and attended reunions and saw each other when they could. They had hobbies, volunteered and did other things.

By the time I thought about writing this book, I was well-aware of the contribution of other units, not just Easy Company. So I decided to search for any man who served in the Division and provide all of that information in my final chapter. A rule that I had was that any paratrooper I found from another division would also be included. Somehow, it didn't seem right to me to omit a man who I knew served our country because he was not part of the 506th Regiment of the 101st. I tried where possible to find where each man was buried in case any reader happened to be near the cemetery and wanted to pay respects.

I read through the obituaries and was overwhelmed by the cross-section of America that constituted the paratroops. Stephen Ambrose wrote a book called, "Citizen Soldiers," that looked at how young men from many walks of life in democratic America defeated a Nazi army that was forged out of a militaristic, totalitarian society. Some Germans, including Hitler, thought democracy would make American a weak-willed foe. Yet in less than a year after D-Day, the war was over in Europe.

The obituaries confirm the diversity of the men who joined the fight. Some were West Point graduates while others had no military background. College graduates served alongside men who never made it out of high school. Every state was represented. And the men were all so young.

I felt that these obituaries were important, and I was glad that for a few hundred men, I could describe what happened to them after the War. Some of the men led truly remarkable lives, and I enjoyed getting to know about so many more soldiers. The generals down to the privates weren't finished doing amazing things once the Germans and Japanese surrendered, whether it was family, career, education or hobbies. And it appeared that many of them went on to live the happy lives they deserved.

The arrangement of the following sections is worth a few points. The first chapter is about Easy Company veterans, though I chose to put a few regimental officers, especially Colonel Sink, in the front. I cannot envision an Easy Company without Sink, and I believe that he deserved to be the first among equals.

The chapter after that is about the men who were in units other than Easy Company. The bulk of the chapter is in alphabetical order, though the first several pages are about some of the senior officers, as well as a few men I recognized from my reading. For example, Don Brininstool is someone I felt I knew very well from Don Burgett's books, and for that reason, I chose to have his obituary in the first part of the chapter.

The obituaries I found were all from secondary sources, and, therefore, I had to trust their content as accurate, although I had no way of verifying the information for so many men. I spotted errors from time to time and did the best I could to make corrections. For example, men of the 502nd Regiment were described as being one of the Band of Brothers. Given the limitations of the sources, I hope the following is acceptable to the surviving veterans and the friends and families of the deceased.

The Post-War Lives of Easy Company

General Robert F. Sink

"Colonel Bob" Sink, the feisty, quirky, fearless leader of the 506th regiment died on December 13, 1965 at the Womack Army hospital at Fort Bragg, NC following an illness that struck him at his home in Lexington, NC.

Sink's obituary described him as "colorful," an apt term for a man who demanded that his officers shave daily in combat, who was always at the front, who went off on a combat patrol on D-Day himself instead of sending men in his command, who was one of the four percent of the army's paratroopers qualified as a master parachutist and who celebrated his birthday every year by making a parachute jump.

Sink was born in Lexington, NC and went to school at Duke University before attending the U.S. Military Academy at West Point, from which he graduated in 1927. Fiercely loyal to his "Five-oh-Sinks," the colonel refused to accept an offer of promotion to general during World War II in order to stay with his unit until it was deactivated in 1945.

Following the war, Sink eventually became a general and commanded the U.S. Army Strategic Army Corps (STRAC), which was formed in 1958. This was a 125,000-man, four-division force that included the 82nd and 101st Airborne and the 1st and 4th Infantry. Later he was commander of Fort Bragg, the XVIII Airborne Corps and the U.S forces in Panama, the last of which was his final station before retiring from the Army in 1961.

Sink was married and had three children, including two step-children. His wife, Margaret, died on April 29, 1963. General Robert Sink is buried in Arlington National Cemetery, in Section 1, site 320-A.

Colonel Robert Strayer

Bob Strayer, the commander of 2nd Battalion, passed away in December 2002 at the age of 90. Strayer stayed in the Army after World War II and served in Korea and Vietnam, and was awarded with a Silver Star and a Purple Heart during his career. Robert Strayer was survived by his wife, Mildred, and was buried in Arlington National Cemetery with full military honors.

Major General Salve Matheson

Fans of Band of Brothers may not recognize the name Salve H. Matheson, but he was Major Strayer's Executive Officer and was, at one time, part of Easy Company. He went on to lead one of the most interesting post-War military careers of any of the men in the 506th, and also established a very large family. General Matheson died at the age of 84 on January 8, 2005 in Carmel, CA.

Matheson was born in Seattle, WA on August 11, 1920, and his family moved to Monterey, CA later that year. After attending school in Monterey and Pacific Grove, he graduated from UCLA, and then received a commission as a Second Lieutenant in the Army. He also attended the Naval War College in Rhode Island.

Following World War II, Matheson stayed in the Army and served in the 1st Infantry Division and the 82nd Airborne Division and commanded the 10th Special Forces Group in Europe. He saw combat in Korea, and participated in the amphibious operations at Inchon, Wonsan and Hungnam. Matheson served in Vietnam as the commander of the 101st Airborne's 1st Brigade, and among the battles in which he served was the American repulse of the Tet Offensive. In 1969, he returned to Korea, where he commanded the 2nd Infantry Division.

During his combat career, Matheson was awarded an incredible list of honors, including the Distinguished Service Medal with Oak Leaf Cluster, the Silver Star, the Legion of Merit, the Distinguished Flying Cross, four Bronze Stars, 12 Air Medals, the Army Commendation Medal, the Purple Heart, Master Parachutist Badge and Combat Infantry Badge.

He finally retired in 1975, and he returned home to Carmel, CA. He was survived by his wife, Patricia, three children, Catherine, Molly and Michael, and four grandchildren. Salve Matheson is buried in Section 31, Site 984 at the Arlington National Cemetery.

James "Moe" Alley

James H. "Moe" Alley, passed away on March 14, 2008 at the age of 85. Alley was born on July 20, 1922 in Mount Ida, AR to James and Grace. In 1942, he volunteered for the paratroops and was assigned to the Easy Company. During the War, he earned three Purple Hearts, including one for being peppered by a potato masher near the Crossroads in Holland.

Alley was discharged when the war ended and moved to Washington State in 1951 after being in California for a few years. In Washington, Alley was a general contractor, remodeling and building homes and commercial properties, mostly in the area of King County, which includes Seattle. In 1975, Alley married Elizabeth "Bettie" Riley in Seattle, and worked until he retired in 1987. In retirement, the Alleys stayed in Washington, although they traveled frequently, and finally moved to the town of Sedro-Woolley, WA. Bettie passed away in 2007 and Jim "Moe" Alley was survived by two sons, a daughter, three stepchildren, and many grandchildren and great-grandchildren.

Albert Blithe

While the miniseries took liberties with certain facts for the sake of the story, a most glaring error was that of the story of Albert Blithe, who did not die of the wounds he suffered in Normandy. Tragically, though, Blithe passed away on December 17, 1967 at the young age of 44.

Master Sergeant Albert Blithe was born on June 25, 1923, and enlisted in 1942. His enlistment records detail that he had three years of high school education, and his profession was listed in the category of "Skilled cranemen, derrickmen, hoistmen, and shovelmen."

Blithe's family contacted the producers of the miniseries and the veterans of the Company and reported that Albert did not die in 1948. While he was injured severely in the right shoulder in Normandy due to sniper fire, he made a full recovery and was released from an Army Hospital on October 8, 1945. He returned to Philadelphia and started a career with Westinghouse Electric, but he went back into the military, serving in the Korean War and later in Taiwan and Europe. During his military career, Blithe made over 600 parachute jumps and won a Silver Star, three Bronze Stars, three Purple Hearts, and an Army of Occupation Medal and earned his Combat Infantry Badge.

In December 1967, Blithe attended a ceremony commemorating the Battle of the Bulge and returned to his station at the Wiesbaden Air Force base. He felt nauseated upon his return and on December 11th, he was admitted to the emergency room with a perforated ulcer. Surgery was performed on December 12th, but his conditioned worsened and on December 16th, he developed peritonitis and renal failure. Despite intensive care, he died at 0055 on December 17, the anniversary of when the 101st was mobilized to go to Bastogne.

He was an operations sergeant in the 11th quartermaster company and was described by his commander as a well-liked, efficient and dedicated soldier. He was survived by his wife, Kaye, and a son, Gordon, who lived back in Fayetteville, NC. Albert Blithe was buried with full military honors in Arlington National Cemetery, where he rests in Section 31, Site 7672.

Maxwell Clark

One of the original members of Easy Company, Maxwell Clark passed away on March 14, 2008. Clark had a tough life evidently, as his mother passed away when he was 10 years old. After World War II, Clark lost contact with his friends from Easy Company, but was able to reconnect with them upon hearing about the Band of Brothers miniseries. HBO brought him to Normandy to attend the premiere of Band of Brothers and he was able to visit Europe again in 2005. He returned to Florida, where he lost his battle against Alzheimer's Disease, and was survived by his wife, Lucie.

Tony Garcia

Tony Garcia joined Easy Company after the Normandy campaign and viewers of Band of Brothers first got to know him in the episode, "Replacements." He passed away on August on August 18, 2005 following a stroke he suffered earlier that month.

Garcia entered the military in 1943, but the paratroops were not his first choice. He tried to enlist in the Marines, but the quota in his area was full and he ended up in the Army. After a short period of training as a radar operator, he realized he hated the assignment and volunteered for the airborne. I found a story that said that Garcia failed his original airborne physical because of a heart condition. However, he was able to get some pills to mask the condition and tried again. Not understanding that he should take only one pill, Garcia took several and his heart raced. The doctor mistakenly assumed that Garcia had been exercising outside and passed him, and, of course, Tony didn't correct the mistake.

After training at Fort Benning, Garcia arrived in England on June 3, 1944, too late to make the jump on D-Day. He joined Easy Company in time for the Holland jump and despite participating in every action the rest of the War, he was never wounded, a remarkable feat considering that the other two men of his mortar platoon, Skip Muck and Alex Penkala, were killed in the Fazone Woods and that his best friend, Lester Hashey, was severely wounded not far from him during a shelling of the Bois Jacques.

Following World War II, Garcia returned to Cheyenne, WY and finished high school, and after attending college in Iowa for a short time, moved back home and took a job with the Southern Pacific Railroad. Eventually, Garcia reenlisted and served in the Korean War for three years with the 11th Airborne Division's 187th Regimental Combat Team. Serving with him was his younger brother, Jay.

Back from combat for good, Tony Garcia settled in San Francisco in 1955 and took a job with Macy's working in one of their warehouses. While living at a guesthouse, he met his future wife, Nancy Robinson, who had recently arrived from DeValls Bluff, AR. Tony and Nancy married on December 13, 1958 and had four children. In 1972, they moved to a large home in San Bruno, CA, and Tony retired about 15 years later.

In 1984, he began returning to the Netherlands, to visit the places where he served during Operation Market Garden. He celebrated his visits with a flourish: he made parachute jumps. Tony Garcia made his last jump at the age of 74 in 1999.

Walter "Smokey" Gordon

Walter Gordon is remembered by viewers of Band of Brothers as the soldier who was paralyzed by a German shot while manning his machine gun in the Bois Jacques. The bullet that nicked Gordon's spine caused him to live the rest of his life with excruciating back pain. Readers of Band of Brothers may remember that an Army doctor refused to grant Gordon full disability, and intervention from his father, who threatened to get a local politician involved, finally allowed him to receive the benefits that he so clearly deserved.

Walter Gordon was born and raised in Jackson, MS, and had just completed his sophomore year at Millsaps College when he tried to enlist in 1942. Gordon was rejected by the Marines and the Navy because he was colorblind. He then managed, somehow, to avoid having his condition detected by an Army doctor and enlisted and volunteered in the paratroops, joining Easy Company in Toccoa. Gordon was wounded in Normandy and was pulled off the line, but rejoined the unit for the jump into Holland.

Gordon's wound in Bastogne was severe: a millimeter closer to the spine and he would have been paralyzed for life. After about six weeks of hospitalization in England, Gordon began to regain feeling in his legs, and by the next year, he was able to walk, although it was more of a shuffle, and he was transferred to the Lawson General Hospital in Alabama.

Gordon used his GI benefits to attend law school, but he ended up going into the oil industry. In 1951, he married Elizabeth Ball Ludeau of Ville Platte, with whom he had five children. Walter Gordon died on April 19, 1997

Forrest Guth

Forrest Leroy Guth passed away at the age of 88 on August 9, 2009, at Cokesbury Village, a retirement community in Delaware. Guth was born in 1921 in Lehigh County, PA, to John and Mayme, and after graduating from high school, went to work at Bethlehem Steel making armor plate for the Navy. He enlisted in the Army in July 1942 and volunteered for the paratroopers and became a part of Easy Company.

Guth was an interesting character and it is a shame he did not get featured in Band of Brothers. Guth was a tinkerer and he designed some of his own equipment and altered standard issue items. He sewed extra pockets on his uniform to carry more ammunition and supplies, and he even figured out a way to make his M-1 Garand shoot automatically. Some of his gear is on display at the Dead Man's Corner Museum in Normandy.

After returning home, Guth attended Millersville State Teachers College and became a teacher. He taught industrial arts at Granby High School in Norfolk, VA when he met and married Harriet Ann Amis. The two spent a year in New York City, where Forrest received a Masters Degree in Education. They then settled in Wilmington, DE where he taught high school for more than thirty years including two decades at Brandywine High School.

In his spare time, Guth was an accomplished carpenter and ran a specialty woodworking business for many years. He was active in the Westminster Presbyterian Church for nearly 60 years. In 1997, the Guths moved to Hockessin, DE. He traveled regularly speaking to American military forces around the world. He and his wife had two children, Nancy and John, and two granddaughters, including one who is a naval flight officer. Forrest Guth was buried at Arlington National Cemetery on October 30, 2009.

Lester Hashey

Lester Hashey was a replacement who arrived in England on June 6, 1944 but was unable to join Easy Company until July 12, when it returned to England. Hashey worked in the shipyards of South Portland, ME and on his 18th birthday quit and volunteered for the paratroops. Hashey served with Easy until he was wounded severely in the Bois Jacques, and remained in the hospital until after the war ended. Hashey stayed in the Army and retired in 1963 as a first sergeant.

Lester Hashey was survived by his wife of 46 years, Anna Perna Hashey. For 45 years, Hashey worked with the American Red Cross, teaching children how to swim, and adults skills such as CPR. He lived on Olde Mill Road in Scarborough, ME, and passed away at a local hospital.

Joe Liebgott

Joseph Liebgott was one of the older men in Easy Company, a 27-year-old private when he enlisted in September 1942 in

Alameda, CA. A native of Michigan, Liebgott lived in Oakland, CA at the time of his enlistment, and was working as a barber, just like his father. Apparently, Liebgott returned from the War and put his service behind him, choosing not to be involved in reunions and other activities. He lived in California, and may have moved from the Bay Area to Los Angeles, and had eight children and remained a barber, and passed away in 1992.

Carwood Lipton

During a visit to the museum in Toccoa, one of the staff members asked me who was my favorite person portrayed in Band of Brothers. The choice for me was clear: Carwood Lipton. Perhaps I liked Donnie Wahlberg's portrayal of him in the miniseries, but it struck me in all of the reading that I did that Lipton was one of the best leaders in Easy Company, and that his fearlessness in combat, his willingness to put his men before himself time and again and his vital role in the days leading up to the attack on Foy made him someone I wish I had the chance to meet. His post-War business success made him remarkable as well.

Clifford Carwood Lipton died at the age of 81 on Sunday, December 16, 2001, the 57th anniversary of the first day of the Battle of the Bulge, at FirstHealth Moore Regional Hospital in Pinehurst, NC, not far from his home in Southern Pines, NC. The cause was pulmonary fibrosis.

Lipton was born in Huntington, WV and from an early age, he had to look out for himself and others. His father died when he was young and as a child, Lipton helped his mother run a boarding house. In 1938, he graduated from Huntington High School, and he enlisted in the paratroops in August 1942. His leadership was recognized as he was promoted from sergeant to lieutenant on February 16, 1945.

Carwood Lipton led a remarkable life after the war, something that he seemed to deserve, given his childhood and service. He returned home and graduated from Marshall University in 1948 with a bachelor's degree in engineering science. He spent 36 years working for Owens-Illinois as a director of development international technical assistance and retired on Nov. 1, 1983. After retirement, he moved to Southern Pines, where he lived until his passing. "Lip" was survived by his wife, Marie, three sons, five grandchildren and a great grandchild. His first wife, Jo Anne, passed in 1975.

One of the little-known facts about Carwood Lipton is that it was he who suggested the book title of "Band of Brothers" to Stephen Ambrose. Lipton recalled the speech of Henry the Fifth in Shakespeare's eponymous work. Addressing his soldiers before the Battle of Agincourt in 1415, Henry said:

"We few, we happy few, we band of brothers;
For he today that sheds his blood with me
Shall be my brother."

Carwood Lipton spent years giving talks about his wartime experiences, and consistently described the strong ties among the men of Easy Company.

George Luz

One of the most memorable characters of Band of Brothers was George Luz, who was well-known for his sense of humor and ability to imitate people's voices. Luz was born on June 17, 1921 in Rhode Island and passed away at the age of 77 on October 15, 1998. Luz enlisted in 1941, and joined Easy Company in Toccoa and was a radioman on D-Day. Given all the equipment that he was carrying, Luz asked another Easy Company man, Roy Cobb, if they could switch places on their STIC, in order to be closer to the door. As the plane took fire over Normandy, a round struck Cobb, who stood in Luz's old spot.

Luz returned to Rhode Island after the war and lived in the town of West Warwick, with his wife, Del. The book Band of

Brothers stated that Luz was a handyman, but other accounts indicate that he was actually a maintenance consultant and he was killed in an industrial accident while working on a commercial clothes dryer. But Band of Brothers had one thing right: George Luz's funeral was a testament to how many people loved the man. A line stretched down the block outside the funeral home, and over 1,500 people attended his funeral after which he was buried in the Veterans Cemetery in Exeter, RI.

John Martin

John William Martin was one of the original NCOs from Toccoa and was part of the group of sergeants that was the backbone of Easy Company. He passed away on January 25, 2005 after battling with the effects of a number of strokes that forced him into a nursing home in 2004.

He was born on May 12, 1922, in Columbus, OH, and was the oldest son of William and Esther. While attending North High School, he held several jobs, and upon graduation, enlisted in the Army and volunteered for the paratroops. After the War, Martin returned to Columbus, OH and started a family with his wife, Pat. He worked for the C&O Railroad and also had a side business building homes.

In 1960, apparently over the objections of his family, he moved them to Phoenix, AZ, where he used his life savings to form his own construction company, and built custom homes in the Valley of the Sun area. Later he branched into commercial construction and managed projects in Arizona and Montana. In the 1970s, he decided to buy a house in Montana, along with three working ranches and he and Pat spent the better part of 30 years living between the Big Sky State and Arizona, all the while attending Easy Company reunions. John Martin was survived by his wife, Pat, a daughter and a son, as well as four grandchildren and seven great grandchildren.

Lewis Nixon

Lewis Nixon, a battalion operations officer and Dick Winters' best friend, was born on September 30, 1918 and died on January 11, 1995 at the age of 76. Born to a wealthy New York family, Nixon lived a life of luxury before the War. He traveled extensively, and attended Yale University for two years until he enlisted in the Army as a private. He enrolled in Officer Candidate School, and was commissioned as a Second Lieutenant, and ultimately volunteered for the paratroops. Nixon had a rare distinction for men of the 101st – he made three combat jumps. In March 1945, Nixon joined the 17th Airborne Division during Operation Varsity. Almost immediately after exiting his STIC, the airplane took a direct hit killing all of the remaining men on board.

When the war ended, Nixon returned home to work at the family company, Nixon Nitration Works in Nixon, NJ, which is now part of the town of Edison. Nixon divorced twice but in 1956, met his third wife, Grace, who stayed with him until he passed away from complication of diabetes. After meeting Grace, Nixon successfully dealt with his alcoholism.

Roy Pickel

Roy Pickel was one of the original men of Easy Company, joining the unit at Camp Mackall after previous training elsewhere. While on a training jump in England, Pickel injured his leg severely and was unable to stay in the paratroops. He was subsequently transferred to the 2nd Infantry Division's 9th Infantry Regiment. He passed away on January 2, 2008 at the Armed Forces Retirement Home in Washington, D.C., and was buried at Arlington National Cemetery.

Darrell "Shifty" Powers

One of the most beloved men in Easy Company, and probably the best shot in the Regiment, Shifty Powers passed away nearly two weeks after the 65th anniversary of D-Day on June 17, 2009 at Wellmont Regional Hospital in Bristol, TN. Powers lived on Shifty Lane in Clinchco, VA and was 86 years old when he passed from cancer.

Powers got his nickname from his basketball skills and enlisted in the Army at the age of 19 on August 4, 1942. Shifty served in every campaign involving Easy Company, and he shot a number of snipers who hit men in his unit. Powers was never wounded, so when the Germans surrendered, he did not have enough points to be sent home, an outrage that was noticed by all, including his officers. While Easy Company was in Austria, an announcement was made that one soldier in each unit who did not have enough points to automatically qualify to return to the States would be allowed to go home. Apparently, Winters and the other officers rigged the unit lottery to make sure that Shifty won. Unfortunately, Powers was wounded badly in an accident on the way home, and all of his back pay and German pistols were stolen.

He returned to the US and worked as a machinist for Clinchfield Coal. The coal mines in Dickinson, VA were dangerous and two of the larger mine accidents after the War happened there. Shifty was a charter member of Clinchco Missionary Baptist Church.

Powers was survived by his wife of sixty years, Dorothy, a son and a daughter, four grandchildren and two great-grandchildren. Darrell "Shifty" Powers was buried with military honors at Temple Hill Cemetery.

Robert Rader

Bob Rader was one of the vital sergeants who held Easy Company together during the War, yet his contributions and his remarkable post-War accomplishments were not mentioned much in Band of Brothers.

Bob Rader was born in Ohio to a family that had a military tradition dating back to the Revolutionary War. In desperation due to the Depression, Bob enlisted in the Ohio National Guard because of the food assistance it provided his family. With the declaration of war following the Japanese bombing of Pearl Harbor, Rader's National Guard unit was activated, but he was given an honorable discharge because he was only 16 years old. Rader completed high school, and volunteered for the paratroops and ended up in Easy Company.

Rader was made a squad leader, and he served in all of the major campaigns. Along the way, he made a number of close friends in Easy Company, two of whom died in Europe. To honor their memories, Rader's son was named Donald William Rader, after Don Hoobler and William Dukeman.

After he returned home from World War II, he used the G.I. bill to attend Cedarville College. In 1950, he moved to Paso Robles, CA and taught at the School for Boys. During the Korean War, he worked at Camp Roberts, and afterwards taught school and drove the schoolbus at the Lillian Larsen School in San Miguel, CA. Later, he taught at Glen Speck Junior High School. In addition to teaching, Bob Rader also worked as an assistant manager of the Paso Robles Airport and was a volunteer firefighter as well.

Later in his life, he went back to college and received a teaching certificate from California Polytechnic Institute. His teaching career took him to Paso Robles High School, where he also coached basketball, cross-country and track teams. While at the high school, Rader started a program called "Educationally Handicapped," which taught challenged students. He retired in 1981 due to failing health, and when he passed away in 1997 was buried in the Paso Robles cemetery.

In appreciation of his service during the war and as a teacher and a role model, the Mayor of Paso Robles led an effort to rename the 13th Street Bridge in the town the Robert J. Rader Memorial Bridge. The mayor was one of Rader's former students.

Denver "Bull" Randleman

Dick Winters called Bull Randleman the best soldier he ever had. A recipient of the Bronze Star and the Purple Heart, and a veteran of every Easy Company campaign, Bull Randleman passed away on June 26, 2003 from complications of a staph infection.

Randleman was born in Rector, AR and during the Depression, he moved to Michigan, where he found work at a foundry. He enlisted in the Army in 1942 and volunteered for the paratroops. Following the war, Bull went on to become a successful businessman and he owned a construction business in Louisiana. He retired to Texarkana, AR, where he passed.

Eugene "Doc" Roe

Doc Roe is known to all fans of Band of Brothers as one of the life-saving medics who put himself in harm's way to treat the men of Easy Company. Eugene Roe died at the age of 76 on December 30, 1998 at his home in Denham Springs, LA.

Eugene Gilbert Roe, Sr. (also known as Bud back home) was a native of Bayou Chene, St. Mary Parish, LA. Roe enlisted on December 12, 1942 in Lafayette Parish, LA. After the war, during which he was awarded the Purple Heart and a Bronze Star, Roe became a construction contractor. Eugene Roe is buried in the Resthaven Gardens of Memory in Baton Rouge, LA. He was survived by his wife, Myrtle H. Roe, two daughters, a son, two stepdaughters, a stepson, six grandchildren, seven stepgrandchildren and two step great-grandchildren.

Robert Burr Smith

If Burr Smith was alive when Ambrose wrote "Band of Brothers," it is very likely he would have been an important character. I am certain Ambrose would have been fascinated by this amazing man. Smith died in 1983 at the age of 58 from lung cancer, and perhaps for that reason, he wasn't mentioned in the book much.

Luckily, there is a lot of information about the Easy Company machine gunner who was wounded in Foy by a sniper in the church tower. Don Malarkey wrote about Smith in his book, and there is a legendary (to me) picture of the two of them in Zell Um See that was taken on a hotel balcony there. In the picture, Malarkey looks nearly peaceful, while Smith has an intense look in his eyes that I will never forget.

But the best stories told about Smith come from his daughter Susan, who was interviewed for Marcus Brotherton's book, "We Who Are Alive and Remain." In addition, Susan posted a considerable amount about her father on the Internet. I was fortunate to see some of the letters traded between Smith, in the midst of his fight against cancer, and Dick Winters. The letters are wonderful expressions of friendship between two men who admired each other greatly. Susan posted those letters on her website, "Once I was a Soldier, A Tribute to Robert Burr Smith."

Robert Burr Smith was born in Tacoma, WA on May 2, 1924, to Robert Marquette Smith, a chemical engineer with Eastman Kodak Company, and Wylmarie Laura Bell, an army nurse from Prince Edward Island. The Smith family moved to the Brentwood section of Los Angeles when he was a child, and Burr attended Brown Military Academy and University High School.

Smith, like Hugh Redmond and other paratroopers, joined the CIA after World War II. He was a paramilitary advisor in Laos in the 1960s and 1970s, where he was known as "Mr. Clean" or, simply, "Clean." His bald head made him look like the icon for the cleaning product, Mr. Clean. Later, he served as the CIA liaison officer to the Delta Force team during the failed attempt to free the American hostages in Iran in 1980. Smith completed special forces training and was a Green Beret and was in the Army Reserves.

Susan wrote that her father wanted to be a writer, but never had the chance. Smith had three children, Susan, Sandra and Scott, who often did not see him due to his military service or some of his outdoor hobbies. Burr Smith was survived by his wife and children, and several wonderful grandchildren.

Herbert Sobel

Herbert Sobel, the original captain of Easy Company who unified his men through his harsh behavior died a bitter and alienated man on September 30, 1987 at the age of 75. Sobel was born on January 26, 1912 in Chicago, IL, and attended the prestigious Culver Military Academy. A clothing salesman at the outbreak of World War II, he volunteered for the paratroops and received a commission of Second Lieutenant. Sobel was the original commander of Easy Company at Toccoa and was promoted to First Lieutenant and later to Captain. In England, Sobel was reassigned to the jump school at Chilton Foliat following the famous mass resignation of the company's non-commissioned officers. Later, Sobel was reassigned to the 506th as a supply and logistics officer.

Sobel returned from the War angry about losing his command. He became an accountant, and was recalled to duty during the Korean War, and eventually retired as a Lieutenant Colonel. Following the Korean War, Sobel returned to his job as an accountant for a manufacturer in Chicago, got married, had two sons and later was divorced. Marcus Brotherton, in his latest book, interviewed Sobel's son, and a different picture of the man emerged. His son talked about how Herbert Sobel was a good father and in excellent physical shape, and said that many former Easy Company men thanked him for his father's leadership.

Ronald Speirs

Ronald Speirs was one of the most respected and feared men who served in Easy Company, and passed away suddenly on April 11, 2007 at the age of 86. Speirs was born in Edinburgh, Scotland on April 20, 1920 and a few years later, his family emigrated to Boston, MA, arriving on December 26, 1924. He grew up in Portland, ME, and because he received some military training while in high school, he was commissioned a 2nd Lieutenant. Speirs volunteered for the paratroops, and while at Toccoa, he was assigned to Dog Company, not Easy. Many people forget that Speirs, while the commander of Easy at the end of the war, was not an original company member.

The controversial legend of Ron Speirs began on D-Day. That morning, he earned a Silver Star for his part in the attack at Brecourt Manor. That same day, he was rumored to have killed all but one of a group of German prisoners, first offering each of them a cigarette. As they smoked, he supposedly laced into them with his submachine gun. Whether Speirs actually shot the men is hotly debated, as no eyewitness ever stepped forward. Several men felt certain that Speirs committed the act, while others were skeptical of combat rumors. What is of no doubt is that Speirs was capable of such an act.

One of the lesser-known stories about Speirs is one that was witnessed. Early in the Normandy campaign, Speirs shot and killed a sergeant for disobeying an order. During a night operation with Germans in the immediate area, Speirs tried to keep his men quiet until ordered to move out. However, one of the sergeants started to lead his squad forward. Speirs repeated the order but the sergeant started to move out again. Speirs, fearing the men in the sergeant's squad would be killed, shot the man, who died instantly. One account I read stated that the sergeant was drunk, and had repeatedly disobeyed direct orders, and that Speirs' action probably saved the lives of the men in the squad. Speirs went to his commanding officer, Captain Jerre Gross, and reported his own actions, preparing to accept the consequence, which could have included a court martial. But Gross was killed in combat the next day and Speirs was never prosecuted.

To fans of Easy Company, Speirs is best remembered not for controversy but for sheer heroism and combat leadership during Easy Company's assault on Foy. Dick Winters ordered Speirs, who was observing the attack as a member of Dog Company, to relieve a paralyzed Captain Dike. Speirs became the longest serving combat commander of Easy Company during the War.

After World War II, Speirs endured a personal tragedy. While Easy was in England, Speirs met and married a local woman who was the widow of a British soldier. For much of the war, Speirs accumulated a treasure of looted booty that he dutifully sent to his wife. Upon returning to England, Speirs found that the woman's first husband had not been killed. He was actually in a prison camp and made it home, and the woman refused to stay with Speirs or return any of the loot that he sent her. The marriage was nullified.

Speirs remained in the Army and served in the Korean War, during which he made a combat jump and commanded a rifle company. After Korea, Speirs took a Russian language class and in 1956, he was reassigned to be a liaison officer to the Soviet Army and served in Potsdam, East Germany. Two years later, he became the American Governor of the Spandau Prison, where several Nazi war criminals were imprisoned. He retired as a Lieutenant Colonel.

Ralph F. Spina

Ralph Spina was a beloved medic in Easy Company, and was with Babe Heffron during the famous "Hinckle" incident that occurred in the Bois Jacques during the siege of Bastogne. Spina passed away at the age of 87 on August 12, 2007 and was buried at Bluebonnet Hills Memorial Park, in Colleyville, TX, with military honors.

Born in Philadelphia, PA, Spina had a reputation for being adept at making money around a racetrack, and he enlisted in 1943. After the War, he moved to Fort Worth, TX, and lived in that area until he passed. Ralph Spina was survived by his wife of 64 years, Agnes, a daughter, two grandchildren and a great-grandson.

Floyd Talbert

I never found Floyd Talbert's obituary, but the true story of his post-War life was very different from what Ambrose described in "Band of Brothers." While Talbert did have a drinking problem after the War, he was not a drifter nor was he a loner. Following his discharge from the military, Talbert attended Indiana University and then worked for the Union Carbide Company. He later became a farmer and was also a plant manager for the General Tire and Rubber Company, after which he was a car salesman. Talbert moved from Indiana to a part of California that is known for its mountains, lakes and excellent fishing and hunting. Floyd Talbert died in 1982.

Joseph D. Toye

Don Malarkey provided more insight into Joe Toye in his book than I have seen in any other source. Just learning about what a tough life Toye led made me respect him all the more given how brave he was and how much he cared for the men with whom he served.

Sergeant Joe Toye, one of the toughest and most respected men of Easy Company, died on September 3, 1995 at the age of 76. The son of a Pennsylvania coal miner, Toye worked in a coal mine and also in a foundry, and enlisted in the Army after the attack on Pearl Harbor and in 1942, volunteered for the paratroopers.

Toye was one of those men who had the fierce loyalty of his Captain, Dick Winters, all the way down to the privates who served under him. Incredibly brave, Toye was awarded the Purple Heart four times, the last coming when he lost his leg in the Bois Jacques outside Foy. Toye had just returned from the hospital after being wounded in a strafing attack, and chose to be with his men rather than tend to the healing of his own wounds. Joe Toye was there at Brecourt Manor, where his actions merited the Bronze Star, and was there in the midst of the fighting outside Bastogne.

After his horrific wound in the Bois Jacques, Toye spent about nine months in hospitals, and was discharged from an Army hospital in Atlantic City, NJ. He was unable to return to his previous job because of his injury, but he ended up working for Bethlehem Steel in Reading, PA for whom he was a drill bit grinder at Grace Mines.

Toye was married twice and had three sons and one daughter, and at least eight grandchildren. Dick Winters delivered the eulogy at Joe Toye's funeral.

Harry F. Welsh

First Lieutenant Harry Welsh passed away on January 21, 1995 at the age of 77. Born on September 27, 1918 in Wilkes-Barre, PA, Welsh originally was a member of the 504th Regiment of the 82nd Airborne Division. Welsh was a combative guy and repeatedly lost his sergeant's stripes after being busted for fighting.

Despite his behavior, a number of his commanding officers saw his potential and recommended him for Officer Candidate School. After gaining a commission as a 2nd Lieutenant, Welsh was transferred to Easy Company in May 1943. Welsh was a ferocious fighter, but reading about his behavior in Uden during Market-Garden, it appeared he continued to have discipline issues.

After the War, Harry returned home to marry Catherine "Kitty" Grogan, the woman he mentioned several times during the miniseries and she really did use his reserve parachute to make her wedding dress. Welsh became a teacher, then a tax collector and eventually was the director of students for the Wilkes-Barre school district until he retired in 1983. He and Kitty had a son who died before they did; Kitty passed away in 1998.

. . .

Other Eagles who Have Flown

General William "Bill" Lee

In August 1942, General Bill Lee told the assembled men of the newly-formed 101st Airborne Division that their unit, ". . . has no history, but it has a rendezvous with destiny." Bill Lee was the father of the American parachute infantry, and he passed away on June 25, 1948 at the age of 53.

William Carey Lee was born on March 12, 1895 in Dunn, NC, the fifth of seven children of Eldridge and Emma Jane. In his youth, he excelled as a baseball player. Lee attended Wake Forest and North Carolina State, and graduated from college in 1917. While at NC State, he was part of the ROTC program and elected to pursue a military career.

Commissioned as a second lieutenant in the Army in 1917, Lee fought in World War I as a member of the American Expeditionary Force in France. During the war, he was promoted from platoon leader to company commander.

After World War I, he trained in tank warfare at Fort Meade, MD and in France. During the 1930s, he was promoted to the rank of major, and went on a number of tours, including one in Europe during which he had a chance to view German army parachute and glider demonstrations. Lee returned to the US convinced that the Army should establish an airborne infantry force, but his ideas were met with disapproval and resistance.

Ultimately, President Roosevelt took an interest in establishing an airborne unit, and the Army established the parachute training school at Fort Benning. Appropriately, Lee was named the commander. By the time of the attack on Pearl Harbor, Lee was a major general and was given command of the 101st Division. Lee worked closely with Eisenhower to plan the airborne drop into Normandy during D-Day, and he prepared to make the jump with his unit. However, after a period of intense training for Operation Overlord, he suffered a vascular event that some called a heart attack, and others called a stroke, on February 5, 1944. He was sent back to the US, where he learned of the success of the invasion from his home in Dunn, NC. To honor their stricken leader, many of the men of the 101st yelled "Bill Lee" (not "Geronimo") as they exited their aircraft.

Bill Lee married Dava Johnson in 1918, and they bought a house on West Divine Street in Dunn, NC in 1935. After his ailment, he was visited by many dignitaries, and when he died, his home hosted thousands before he was buried in local Greenwood Cemetery. He earned the Distinguished Service Medal for establishing the airborne.

General Maxwell D. Taylor

General Maxwell D. Taylor, the commanding general of the 101st Airborne Division during World War II passed away at 21:55 on Sunday, April 19, 1987 at the age of 85 at Walter Reed Army Hospital in Washington, D.C. He had been hospitalized for three months, and the cause of death was amyotrophic lateral sclerosis, which is better known as Lou Gehrig's disease.

Taylor was a rare combination of courage, daring and strategic thinking, and he put himself in harm's way. In Normandy, he personally led his group of men in attacks towards Causeway Number 1, and volunteered for a near suicide mission in Italy.

Despite his achievements, Taylor was very controversial, receiving a lot of criticism, from those who served under him. Many of the Screaming Eagles felt that he should have been in Bastogne during the siege but instead was back in the US for a Christmas dinner at home, although officially he was on record as being in Washington, DC for testimony to Congress.

Taylor was also criticized by some for being elitist, choosing to put his own quarters in the nicest buildings and homes, while his men had meager shelters and food. Also, it was felt by some that Taylor felt upstaged by General McAuliffe in Bastogne. McAuliffe received a promotion and was transferred out of the Division shortly after Taylor's return.

Nonetheless, his tremendous achievements were reflected in the tributes from some of the most influential men in American government, including Secretary of Defense, Casper Weinberger, who stated "throughout his life, General Taylor epitomized what it means to be a soldier, a diplomat and a scholar." Senator Edward Kennedy of Massachusetts said, "America has lost one of the greatest soldier-statesmen in its history. . . General Taylor was that rare and gifted military leader in the nuclear age who also understood the importance of nuclear arms control. As chairman of the Joint Chiefs of Staff, his support made the Nuclear Test Ban Treaty of 1963 possible. To President Kennedy, that treaty was the finest achievement of his Administration, the first step back from the nuclear brink, and it could not have happened without Maxwell Taylor. We shall miss his courage, his leadership and his friendship."

Maxwell Davenport Taylor was born on Aug. 26, 1901, in the small town of Keynesville, MO to John Earle and Pearle Davenport Taylor, and was an only child. Taylor was destined for the military, having decided to attend West Point at the age of five, influenced by the stories of his maternal grandfather, who served in the Confederate army during the Civil War. He graduated at the age of 15 from Northeast High School in Kansas City, where he engaged in debating, and went to Kansas City Junior College.

While in junior college, he took the entrance examinations for both West Point and the Naval Academy. According to one obituary, while he excelled in language classes, his lack of knowledge of geography caused him to fail the exam for Annapolis. In later life, he claimed, "If the Strait of Malacca had been in Europe, I might have wound up an admiral instead of a general."

Although rejected by Annapolis, he was accepted to West Point, where he excelled, becoming a cadet captain and editor of the student newspaper. In 1922, he was the youngest cadet in his graduating class and ranked fourth overall academically. He was commissioned a Second Lieutenant in the Corps of Engineers.

Taylor graduated from West Point in a time period that was very difficult for young officers. After World War I, the U.S. military shrank to a mere token force, and it was difficult for career officers to gain advancement. Lieutenant Taylor was not promoted to captain until 1935.

His language skills were honed as a young man, and he had so distinguished himself for his mastery of French, that after West Point, he was sent to Paris to perfect his language skills. He returned West Point to teach French and Spanish. He also attended the Field Artillery School and following a two-year course at the Command and General Staff School at Fort Leavenworth, he was sent to the American Embassy in Tokyo, Japan to learn Japanese. Then in 1939 he served as an assistant military attaché in Beijing. By the outbreak of World War II, Taylor had distinguished himself by his language skills and got to travel worldwide as a result.

Taylor said that he became a paratrooper almost by accident. Following a course at the Army War College in June 1940, then-Major Taylor was assigned to an inspection of defense forces in nine Latin American countries and accompanied General Matthew B. Ridgway. Taylor was given command of a field artillery battalion, and by the time the US entered the war, he was chief of staff to General Ridgway, who had been made commander of the 82d Infantry Division.

In December 1942, Taylor was promoted from colonel to brigadier general and was appointed the artillery commander of the 82d Airborne, shipping to Africa in March 1943. After the Division trained in Morocco, it participated in the invasions of Sicily and Italy in July 1943.

Some of the complaints about Taylor seem quite inappropriate given the general's next act – volunteering for what some historians regarded as one of the most dangerous missions of the war, if not a plain and simple suicide mission.

In the fall of 1943, the Italian Army surrendered to the Allies. General Walter Bedell Smith, chief of staff to Gen. Dwight D. Eisenhower, was concerned about the status of Rome, which was being held by a group of Italian troops who refused to lay down arms, as well as a contingent of German soldiers. Smith was considering an Allied airborne invasion but he lacked reliable intelligence and was not sure if the remaining enemy soldiers would fight or not. He decided that he needed a high-ranking US officer to sneak into Rome and determine the viability and need of an airborne attack.

General Taylor and Col. William Tudor Gardner of the Army Air Corps volunteered for the mission, despite knowing that soldiers of either side could shoot them on sight as spies. Undeterred, the men covertly landed at night at the Italian port of Gaeta, and drove into Rome, crossing through American lines, and not even hiding their uniforms save removing their caps.

Taylor and Gardner found the Italian troops who had just joined the Allies were not strong enough to clear the Germans out of Rome, and they called off the airborne attack, which probably would have resulted in disaster. His mission to Rome earned General Taylor the Silver Star and shortly thereafter, he was promoted to Major General and given command of the Screaming Eagles. Taylor jumped into Normandy and his fluency in French helped him learn from the local citizens where he and his men landed, where the Germans were, and where the objectives of the 101st were. In Holland he sustained a minor wound.

Late in 1944, Taylor was called to Washington to testify about a number of issues to Congress. He was unable to make it back to his unit in time to join the Screaming Eagles in their defense of Bastogne. There is no official record of how Taylor's testimony came to be requested, and it is impossible to document whether Taylor somehow forced this in order to be home for Christmas, as some of his critics contend.

After the war ended, Taylor returned to West Point, but this time as the Superintendent of the Military Academy. At 44, he was the youngest superintendent since General Douglas MacArthur, and he revolutionized the Academy's curriculum and emphasis. He updated the focus of the education, which was science-focused, and he also deliberately de-emphasized football.

Three-and-a-half years later, Taylor was appointed Chief of Staff of American Forces in Europe, and in September 1949 became the first commander of the American Military Government in Berlin as well as of the 3,000-man Berlin garrison. Taylor established himself as a diplomat, handling the situation with the local Soviet commander so well that he was given a promotion to serve as Deputy Chief of Staff for Operations and Administration in the Pentagon from 1951 to 1953.

In 1953, Taylor was sent to Korea, where he became commander of the Eighth Army and United Nations forces, and orchestrated a number of combat operations while at the same time balancing requests from then-President Eisenhower, who was trying to negotiate an armistice. Once a truce was reached, Taylor stayed in Seoul, South Korea to arrange prisoner exchanges, support military efforts and rebuild the country.

In 1955, Taylor succeeded his old mentor, General Ridgeway, as Army Chief of Staff. Quickly, General Taylor came into direct conflict with Chairman of the Joint Chiefs of Staff, Admiral Arthur W. Radford, who believed strongly in a military policy centered on a massive nuclear strike capability.

By contrast, Taylor advocated a military strategy around flexible responses, and he noted that atomic response could not address every type of military situation. Frustrated by Radford's unwillingness to listen to his ideas, Taylor resigned as Army Chief of Staff in 1959 and he requested retirement.

Taylor refused to give up his criticism of the new military policy and wrote the book, "The Uncertain Trumpet." In it, Taylor criticized the Joint Chiefs and he outlined his discrepancies with the military establishment. He also turned his attention to other forms of service, serving on the board of an electric company and as President of the Lincoln Center for the Performing Arts.

Taylor was not fated to stay on the sidelines. President John F. Kennedy asked General Taylor to conduct a full investigation of the CIA and Joint Chiefs following the Bay of Pigs disaster. The President felt that he may have been given faulty intelligence and been led into choosing to invade by the CIA. Taylor investigated and concluded that the CIA should no longer be given a major role in large military operations.

After accepting the recommendation from Taylor, President Kennedy, created a new White House position, Military Representative of the President, and he ultimately persuaded the General Taylor to return to active duty in July 1961. The President also made General Taylor his personal watchdog over the nation's intelligence apparatus. During his service to Kennedy, Taylor provided advice on Berlin and the emerging fighting in Vietnam.

After Kennedy was assassinated, General Taylor continued as role as advisor to the President, and in eventually became American Ambassador to Vietnam, a position he held only shortly before resigning.

After retiring, Taylor remained busy, writing numerous books and articles and testifying before Congress. A decade after the American withdrawal from Vietnam, Taylor wrote of three lessons that he felt should have been learned. His three points are telling given the American experience in Iraq.

First, he stated "before we ally ourselves to another country, we must ascertain to what extent they can exploit our help." In Vietnam he deemed the majority of help offered was unusable. Second, he stated that the President should have declared war, and that the Gulf of Tonkin Resolution was insufficient to galvanize national support. His third point was that television should not be allowed on the battlefield. Whereas in World War II, where the press felt a sense of American pride, in Vietnam reporters sought to undermine the American command, according to Taylor.

General Taylor lived on Washington's Embassy Row and was survived by his wife, Lydia Gardner Happer, whom he married in 1925, as well as two sons, John and Thomas. Maxwell Taylor and his wife Lydia are buried in Arlington National Cemetery.

General Anthony Clement McAuliffe

General Tony McAuliffe, who replied to the German demand for the surrender of the 101st in Bastogne with the infamous, "NUTS," passed away in Chevy Chase, MD on August 11, 1975 at the age of 77.

McAuliffe was born in Washington, DC on July 2, 1898, and after attending the University of West Virginia, entered West Point, from which he graduated in 1918. He spent the years before World War II honing his skills as an artillery officer as he rose through the ranks of the Army.

On D-Day, McAuliffe was the commander of the 101st's artillery, but with the death of General Don Pratt in a glider accident that day, he was elevated to Deputy Division Commander. He commanded the 101st during the siege of Bastogne after the unit was deployed while General Taylor was in

Washington, DC. In 1945, he was given command of the 103rd Infantry Division until the end of the War, which some people attribute to the vanity of General Taylor. One school of thought states that after Taylor rejoined the 101st in Bastogne and saw what a good job McAuliffe did, he felt threatened. So, he "promoted" McAuliffe outside the Division to the 103rd.

McAuliffe remained in the Army until 1956, and held a number of positions, including Commander in Chief of the U.S. Army in Europe. After his retirement, he worked for the American Cyanamid Corporation for several years and also was the chairman of the New York State Civil Defense Commission, 1960-1963.

General Tony McAuliffe is buried in Arlington National Cemetery next to his wife and son. He rests in Section 3, site 2536.

Major General Joseph H. Harper

Joseph H. Harper, the commander of the 327th Glider Regiment, passed away at his Atlanta, GA home on Sunday, August 7, 1990 at the age of 89 due to cardiac arrest. Major General Harper joined the Army in 1923, and rose to commander of the 401st Glider Infantry Regiment, which was somewhat notable given that he was not a West Pointer. The 401st was eventually split in order to accommodate more battalions, and that led to the creation of the 327th Glider Infantry Regiment, which Harper commanded.

One of Harper's most notable moments came during the encirclement of Bastogne. Harper had the pleasure of delivering General McAuliffe's famous "NUTS" response to the German envoys. Harper handed McAuliffe's note to the German officers, and one of them asked if it was a positive or negative reply. Harper translated the intention of the message, saying that it meant "go to hell." Harper retired from the military in 1959.

Lt. General Harry W. O. Kinnard

The man who suggested to General McAuliffe that he use his earlier statement, "nuts," as the reply to the German surrender demand at Bastogne, Harry Kinnard, passed away at the age of 93 on January 5, 2009.

Harry William Osborne Kinnard II was born in Dallas, TX and graduated from West Point in 1939. He rose to the be on the 101st Division staff during World War II and won a Distinguished Service Cross in Holland. In Bastogne, he was a lieutenant colonel and the Division's operations officer. Kinnard stayed in the military after the War and was a pioneer in a new tactic in combat: the airmobile infantry, which used helicopters to transport men to the battlefield in rapid deployment.

He was given command of the 11th Air Assault Division (Test) at Fort Benning to refine the airmobile approach, and that unit became the First Cavalry Division (Airmobile). Kinnard led it in the Army's first major fight in Vietnam, the November 1965 Battle of the Ia Drang Valley. Fighting in Ia Drang was bitter and in some cases, hand-to-hand, and it signaled that the North Vietnamese were prepared for a savage war of attrition.

General Kinnard retired from the military in 1969, and was survived by his wife, Libby, two sons, three daughters, two stepdaughters, 16 grandchildren; and 15 great-grandchildren. Harry Kinnard was buried in Arlington National Cemetery.

Don Brininstool

Sergeant Don Brininstool was Don Burgett's squad leader, and through books such as "Seven Roads to Hell," I have this image of Brininstool as one of the best non-coms in the entire Division.

Donald W. Brininstool, a man I wish I met, passed away at the age of 87 on March 22, 2009 in Bradenton, FL. Brininstool was born on July 12, 1921 to Genevieve and William Brininstool in Jackson, MI, where he lived for his whole life. He graduated from Jackson High School and enlisted in August 1942 in Detroit, and volunteered for the paratroops. Don Brininstool seemed to be an instinctive and ferocious combat leader and he was awarded the Silver Star, the Bronze Star and the Purple Heart among other decorations.

After the War he spent most of his career as a tool and die maker for Sparton Corporation and for the Hancock Corporation, and later was a sales representative for Jackson Janitorial Service. He was a member of the Elks Lodge #113, the American Legion, and the Veterans of Foreign Wars.

Brininstool was preceded in death by his wife, Margaret and a stepson, and was survived by his daughter, a stepson, 11 grandchildren, 18 great-grandchildren and eight great-great-grandchildren. Donald Brininstool was buried in Hillcrest Memorial Park on N. Elm Ave. in Jackson, MI.

Thomas J. Niland, Jr.

Lieutenant Thomas J. Niland, Jr., a member of the 327th Glider Regiment of the 101st Airborne and a hero of a fierce fight outside Marvie during the defense of the Bastogne perimeter, died on March 16th, 2004 at the age of 83. I think about Niland when I visit Marvie today, knowing that is where he won his Silver Star for his defense during a German armor attack.

Born in Tonawanda, NY to Thomas and Mary Louise, Tom Niland was one of 13 children, and was very athletic as a child. When World War II broke out, the Niland family contributed a full squad. Tom and his two brothers, Joe and Mike, enlisted, and his first cousins, Edward, Preston, Robert and Frederick were the inspiration for the movie, "Saving Private Ryan." At the time of his enlistment, Tom Niland was pursuing a degree in business administration at Canisius, and he had to put his studies on hold.

As a member of the 327th Glider Infantry, Tom participated in the major campaigns of the 101st: Normandy, Holland and the Battle of the Bulge. During the fighting around the Marvie, Niland earned a Silver Star for exposing himself to enemy tank and artillery fire while organizing his Battalion's defense.

During that defense, Niland, a First Lieutenant and battalion S-2, organized the intelligence and supply sections and the cooks in a dramatic defense around the battalion CP. He then organized the makeshift team against German tanks and then enlisted two Shermans belonging to Team O'Hara and directed their fire against the enemy. Lieutenant Niland later wrote, "Our previous battle experiences were of great value to us. We could anticipate the situation and did not panic when it happened. Everyone took it upon themselves to stop the attack."

After World War II, Niland returned to Canisius where, in spite of an arm hurt by shrapnel, he excelled in basketball, captaining his team for two years before graduating in 1947. That year, Niland became newly-formed Jesuit Le Moyne College's first men's basketball coach and director of athletics, and stayed at the institution for 43 years. He earned national coaching honors and inductions into the Syracuse University, Le Moyne College and Canisius College athletic halls of fame. He coached Le Moyne for 26 years, compiling a 327-219 record and seven NCAA Division II national tournament appearances, and retired as director of athletics in 1990.

When he passed, colleagues talked about Niland's incredible character, devout Catholicism and commitment to the institution. The President of Le Moyne at the time was quoted as saying, "True to the Jesuit ideal of developing the whole person, Tom cared about much more than success on the field. He cared immensely about nurturing a strong character and a sense of value."

As athletic director, he became a member of the NCAA's basketball rules committee and was part of its infractions committee, the first time a non-Division I athletic director was appointed to that body. A local obituary concluded, "Throughout his time at Le Moyne, Niland proved time and again that he was a good fit, indeed, for the small Jesuit school committed to coaxing the best from its students."

General Steve Archie Chappuis

General "Silent" Steve Chappuis, former commander of the 502nd Regiment, passed away at the age of 94 on August 19, 2008 in Tacoma, WA. Chappuis was born in Rayne, LA on December 28, 1913 to Archie and Elise, and graduated from LSU in 1936. In a recorded interview he gave that is part of the Army archives, Chappuis had many stories from his LSU days.

After graduation from college, he was commissioned as a second lieutenant in the US Army Reserve and in 1941 he joined the paratroopers and was ultimately assigned to the 502nd. By D-Day, he rose to the rank of Lt. Colonel and commanded the regiment's 2nd Battalion. During Market Garden, he assumed command of the 502nd following the death of Colonel Robert Cole. Chappuis was known among his men as "Silent Steve" for his demeanor.

Chappuis returned to the US after the War, and married Kathryn A. Jurjevich on June 6, 1946 at Fort Meyer, VA. He stayed in the military and had a wide range of assignments, including with the Army General Staff, SHAPE, as Deputy Chief of Staff, Operations for the XVIII Airborne Corps; as Deputy Chief of Staff of the 1st Corps Group in Korea; and as Deputy Commander of the 4th Infantry Division Brigade, among others.

He retired from the Army and went into the private sector with the Bank of Washington in Tacoma, not far from one his last assignments, which was as Commander of the X US Army Corps in nearby Fort Lawton.

Steve and Kay Chappuis traveled extensively, and he was an avid tennis player. General Steve Chappuis was survived by his wife of 62 years, daughter, son and granddaughter, and was buried in Mt. Tahoma National Cemetery in Kent, WA.

Harrison Summers

Harrison Summers, sergeant in the 502nd and the hero of the XYZ Complex on D-Day, passed away in West Virginia in 1983. If anyone in the 101st deserved a Congressional Medal of Honor for his actions on D-Day, it should have been Sergeant Summers, but that recognition eluded him.

Summers was so quiet about his accomplishments, that many of the men who worked with him in the coal mines never knew he had even served in World War II. In fact, he was once left out of a veterans' appreciation day at the mine.

On D-Day, he nearly single-handedly knocked out the German stronghold known as XYZ and was credited with killing over two dozen Germans, a feat that was described by Stephen Ambrose and SLA Marshall. Summers was nominated for the Congressional Medal of Honor by his commander, Pat Cassidy, but some accused the Colonel of not pursuing the distinction with enough vigor.

Summers did receive a battlefield promotion to lieutenant and a Distinguished Service Cross, and was also awarded a Purple Heart. He returned to Marion County after the War and worked as a coal miner and later a mine inspector. Harrison Summers was buried in Marion County Cemetery in West Virginia.

Other Screaming Eagles who Made it Home

Robert Vincent Agin

101st Airborne veteran Robert V. Agin passed away at the age of 84 on February 14th, 2008 at Baystate Medical Center in

Longmeadow, MA. He was born on May 26, 1923 in Corona, NY to Herbert S. and Florence (Coll) Agin.

After the war, Agin worked for Medusa Cement Company and then moved to Federal White Cement Co. from which he retired. Agin was a resident of Longmeadow for the last 48 years of his life and was a parishioner of St. Mary's Church, a member of the church's Nocturnal Adoration Society and, with his wife, a teacher of confirmation classes.

After retirement, he volunteered with the Meals on Wheels program for ten years with his wife. Robert Agin was survived by his wife of 60 years, Madeline, three sons, a daughter, five grandchildren, three sisters-in-law, a brother-in-law and many cousins, nephews and nieces. His daughter, Diane L. Agin, preceded him in death in March 1982. Robert Agin was laid to rest with military honor in Gate of Heaven Cemetery, Tinkham Road, Springfield, MA.

Reverend McCurtis W. Allison

McCurtis Allison passed away at the age of 59 on December 25, 1982, at Holy Spirit Hospital in East Pennsboro Township, PA. He served as a chaplain with the 101st in World War II and in Korea. Allison was a graduate of Gettysburg College and the Lutheran Theological Seminary and completed his graduate studies at the University of Pennsylvania. He taught medieval history at Mount Airy Seminary and was chaplain at the Kislyn Industrial School for Boys. Reverend McCurtis Allison was survived by his wife, Elinor Allison, a son, five daughters and a grandchild.

Sam J. Amico

Sam Amico of Rochester, NY was a medic in the 101st Airborne and died on February 14, 2008, at age 87. Amico was taken prisoner during the War after serving in several battles. He was preceded in death by his first wife, Josephine, and was survived by his second wife, Linda, two sons and four grandchildren.

Arnold Keith Anderson

Arnold Keith Anderson passed away at the age of 76 from leukemia at Wake Forest Bowman Gray Baptist Hospital in Winston-Salem, NC on September 14, 2000. He had volunteered for an experimental cancer therapy and passed of heart failure.

Anderson was born on March 14, 1924, in Berryessa Valley, CA and was the great-grandson of pioneers who settled in the Napa Valley area. During World War II, he served with the 101st as a medic, and later parachuted into Japan following the surrender to care for American prisoners of war.

After leaving the military, he continued his education and ultimately gained his medical degree from Loma Linda University School of Medicine in 1953. He practiced medicine in Kentucky, Tennessee, and California. He decided to change careers and got his PhD from the University of Northern Colorado, and in 1967 began a 24-year university teaching career in mathematics. Keith Anderson was survived by his wife, Marcella and a daughter.

John Harvey Anderson Sr.

Screaming Eagle John Harvey Anderson Sr. passed away at his Fridley, MN home from cancer on March 5, 2005 at the age of 83. John Anderson was born on March 16, 1921 and grew up in Spruce, MI. He served in a number of campaigns, including the Battle of the Bulge. After the war, Anderson went into business, and in 1967, he co-founded Northern Printing Ink, Inc. of Golden Valley, MN. In 1992, he retired as CEO and co-owner. He was an avid hunter and fisherman, Clearwater Lake and Emily, MN. He was survived by his wife of 62 years, Fran, three children and six grandchildren.

Jesse Aranda

Screaming Eagle veteran Jesse Aranda died at his home in Bayside, WI on September 10, 2007, of natural causes. Aranda spent his early youth at St. Amelia's Orphanage and attended West Allis High School. Following his return from the War, he received degrees from the University of Mexico City, Clemson and the University of Wisconsin, and he worked for the city of Milwaukee in the department of public works for over 30 years. On a ski weekend Jesse met his future wife, Patricia, and they married in 1962. He spent parts of two decades as President of Milwaukee Lakefront's McKinley Tennis Club, and also enjoyed golf. He and Patricia had three sons, and they also had five grandchildren.

Robert Leaning Ashworth

Bob Ashworth passed away on December 28, 2007 at the age of 93 at his son's home in Boise, ID, only a few miles from where he was born on Aug. 23, 1914. Anderson's parents were the Rev. Thomas and Ella Ashworth, and they lived on a small farm near Payette, ID, where his father was the long-time rector of St. James Episcopal Church. In 1929, his father assumed new duties in Butte, MT as the rector of St. John's Episcopal Church, and the family moved there. In 1932, Ashworth graduated from Butte High School.

Bob Ashworth was a career military man, starting with his entrance into the U.S. Military Academy at West Point in 1934. In World War II, he was a battalion commander with the 17th Airborne Division in Europe. After the War ended, he was assigned to Fort Jackson, SC on temporary duty, and while there, he met Betty Lea Harper, an army captain and nurse assigned to the post hospital. They fell in love and they got married in 1947.

Later in Ashworth's 30-year career, he became the commanding general of the Headquarters Area Command in Vietnam. His service took him to Panama, Pakistan and Korea, and he commanded units of the 2nd Infantry, 3rd Infantry, 82nd Airborne and 101st Airborne Divisions. He also had two assignments to the Pentagon on the Department of the Army staff, a tour as the U.S. Military Academy Chief of Staff, and assignments as the Deputy Commanding General of the U.S. Army Infantry Training Centers at Ft. Jackson. SC, and Ft. Lewis. Ashworth retired from active service in 1968 as a brigadier general.

Following his retirement from the Army, he lived in Columbia, SC and worked for the South Carolina state government. He retired for good in 1975, and he and his wife moved to Whidbey Island, where he spent 30 years before moving in with his son in Idaho. Robert Ashworth was preceded in death by his wife of 51 years, Betty, in 1998, and was survived by two sons, six grandchildren and a great-granddaughter.

Rolland J. Asselin

Screaming Eagle Rolland J. Asselin passed away on November 11, 2007 at the Holyoke, MA Soldiers Home at the age of 80. He was born on November 21, 1926 in Chicopee, MA to Narcisse and Eva, and was a graduate of Chicopee High School in the Class of 1944. Asselin served in both World War II and Korea.

After graduating from the Massachusetts College of Pharmacy in 1952, he worked as a pharmacist and owned the West End Pharmacy in Holyoke for over 30 years. He was also a member of the Western MA Pharmacy Association, and was a registered sanitarian for the Springfield Health Department. Asselin was a communicant of Assumption Church and a member of the Chicopee Elks Post #1849, a member of the Knights of Columbus Elder Council #69, the American Legion Post #452, and the Beavers Club in Holyoke.

He was survived by his wife of 57 years, his son, daughter and grandchildren, and was buried in Precious Blood Cemetery in South Hadley, MA.

Leland A. Austin

Screaming Eagle Leland Austin died in Venice, FL at the age of 88. Born in Williamsville, NY on January 28, 1919, he was survived by his wife, Juann, a daughter and son, and two grandchildren.

Chester Ernest Baker

Chester Baker, a Screaming Eagle who received the Purple Heart for wounds received in Holland on November 5, 1944, passed away peacefully at home in the arms of his wife on January 22, 2008 at his home in Hanover, MA.

Baker was born in Weymouth MA, to Chester E Baker Sr. and Phyllis Marie LeFavor of West Bridgewater, MA, both of whom died when he was young. He was then raised by his grandparents, John and Jeannette LeFavor of Quincy, MA.

After the War, he earned degrees from Northeastern University, Suffolk Law School, and Bentley College, and he worked in accounting and law for over 50 years. Baker worked for the Estate and Gift Tax Division of the Internal Revenue Service and started his own tax practice in Hanover, MA.

While working at a downtown Boston accounting firm, Baker met Patricia Beaver. They grew closer as they shared their passion for skiing and were married for 43 years, settling in Hanover MA, and raising six children. An obituary stated that he would often say of his marriage, "It was the best decision I ever made!" In addition to skiing, Baker loved the outdoors and was an avid golfer.

Chester Baker was survived by his wife, six children and three grandchildren, and was interred at Mt. Wollaston Cemetery in Quincy, MA.

James William Ballentine

James Ballentine, a veteran of the 101st passed away on January 11th, 2007 at the age of 80 in Charlotte, NC. Born on January 31, 1926, in Monroe, NC, he moved to Charlotte with his family in the 1930's. Jim Ballentine was a member of St. John's Baptist Church, Charlotte, from his teen years. During the War, he saw action at Bastogne, and was awarded the Purple Heart and two Bronze Stars.

Ballentine returned to Charlotte after the war, where he met and married Jean Ashcraft of Wadesboro, NC. In 1954, James and Jean bought a small soda shop on Commonwealth Avenue called "The Penguin" and in the next several decades, the place expanded and became a Charlotte institution. His obituary said that all walks of life journeyed to the Penguin to enjoy good food, cold beverages and a unique atmosphere. Known as being generous, witty and down-to-earth, Jim Ballentine rarely talked about his war experience.

Jim and Jean retired in 1999, and they stayed in their Elizabeth neighborhood home where they had raised five children. Jim worked in his garage often and enjoyed walking his Border Collie, Dan. James Ballentine was survived by his wife of 57 years, Jean, five daughters and eight grandchildren. Appropriately, his memorial service was held at his beloved St. John's Baptist Church, and he was buried with Military Honors on Sunday, January 14, 2007 at Sharon Memorial Park in Charlotte.

Donald G. Barlowe

Donald Barlowe died peacefully in his home at the age of 85 on April 27th 2007. Born in Wilmington, DE on April

6th, 1922, Barlowe jumped into Normandy on D-Day, and also served in Holland and through the Battle of the Bulge. He was awarded Four Purple Hearts, Three Bronze Stars, several commendations and a Battlefield Commission. On January of 1983 Don and his wife Jean moved from Decatur, TN to Fort Pierce, FL, where he retired. Survivors included his wife, Jean, a son and a daughter, three grandchildren and four great-grandchildren. Donald Barlowe was buried in Fort Pierce, FL at Riverview Memorial Park.

Clive Bruce Barney

Clive Bruce Barney, a veteran of the 501st Regiment, passed away at the age of 85, on March 6, 2008, in Ronkonkoma, NY after a long struggle with Alzheimer's Disease. He was born in Waitsfield, VT on June 2, 1922, to Harold and Rachel, and enlisted on November 18, 1942. He fought with the 501st from Normandy into Germany, and was awarded the Purple Heart for being wounded at Bastogne. He was discharged with the rank of Staff Sergeant on November 5, 1945.

Barney was employed as a flight test engineer with Fairchild-Republic Corp in Farmingdale, NY until his retirement in 1985. He was a founding member of St. Boniface Episcopal Church in Lindenhurst, NY, and a former member of the School Board in Wyandanch, NY.

Clive Bruce Barney was survived by his wife, Violet, whom he married on August 21, 1944 in Lambourn, England, two sons, three daughters, 14 grandchildren and three great-grandchildren. He was buried in the cemetery in Monroe, MA.

Glenn P. Barr Sr.

Glenn Perkins Barr, passed away on Sunday, March 8, 2008 in Huntsville, AL, where he was a long-time resident, at the age of 84. Barr was born on May 21, 1923 in Mount Pleasant, TN, and served with the 101st, including dropping into Normandy on D-Day and was a recipient of the Purple Heart and a Bronze Star.

Barr graduated from Michigan Tech with a degree in electrical engineering and went to work for Victor Chemical Company in Tennessee. The he moved his young family to Huntsville in the 1950's to work for NASA in the early days of the space program. Ultimately he retired after 25 years with NASA and several years with Boeing.

Glenn Barr was preceded in death by his first wife, Mary Jo Degen and his second wife, Mary Ann Blanton Barr. He was survived by his wife, Dr. Mabry Miller Barr, one son, two daughters, two stepchildren, six grandchildren and eight great-grandchildren and five stepgrandchildren. Glenn Barr was buried in Arlington Cemetery in Mount Pleasant in Huntsville, AL.

Claude E. Barron

Claude Barron was one of the men of Red Falvey's HQ Company of the 2nd Battalion of the 506th Regiment, along with Otto Sykes, Charlie Rhinehart and the rest. Barron passed away at the age of 83 on Monday, June 19, 2006 after an almost three year battle with cancer. Born in Clarkesville, GA on August 8, 1922, to Claude and Ruby, Claude Barron and his twin sister, Carolyn, were orphaned at age nine.

Barron was raised by relatives and attended boarding schools, and he graduated from Blue Ridge School for Boys in Hendersonville, NC in 1942. At the Blue Ridge School, he was an excellent football player and it was expected that he would go on to play in college. However, he enlisted in the Army in June 1942, volunteered for the paratroopers and trained at Toccoa and was assigned to the 2nd Battalion of the 506th.

On his fifth and final qualifying jump, he sustained a serious wound to his left hand. However, he overcame the injury in time to jump into Normandy on D-Day. In France, he was wounded and was awarded a Purple Heart. He also jumped in Holland during Operation Market-Garden, and was severely injured in October, 1944.

Barron was evacuated to the States and returned to service as a Jump Master at the Parachute School at Ft. Benning, GA, preparing troops for the expected invasion of Japan. After the end of World War II, he was discharged in November, 1945, with numerous awards including a Purple Heart, Bronze Star and Good Conduct Medal.

When he returned home he became a licensed First Class Radio/Telephone Operator/engineer and then graduated from Texas Western College in August, 1953, with a BS in Mining Engineering with a Geology Option. Barron worked for Atlantic Richfield and then for the Rare Metals Corporation which became part of El Paso Natural Gas Company.

Barron retired from El Paso Natural Gas in 1981, and he and his wife traveled across the United States, visiting family and spending time at their cabin in Kingston, NM. He was an Eagle Scout Mentor, and a member of the Disabled American Veterans, Veterans of Foreign Wars, 506th Airborne Infantry Regiment Association, 82nd Airborne Division Association El Paso chapter, American Institute of Mining Engineers, the Amateur Radio League, and the El Paso Amateur Radio Club. Claude Barron was survived by his wife of 53 years, their two sons and several grandchildren.

Joseph T. Bass

Joseph T. Bass survived World War II as a member of the 501st Regiment, but was killed in combat in Korea in 1950. He was born in Van Buren, AR and served in the Civilian Conservation Corps in Salmon, ID before becoming a paratrooper during World War II.

Bass was a squad leader in the 1st platoon of Company F of the 501st Regiment, and jumped into Normandy as a Pathfinder. On June 13, 1944, he was shot in the head in a firefight near Carentan, but survived and was awarded the Purple Heart. He healed in time to rejoin his unit for Operation Market-Garden, and he fought at Bastogne. His obituary called him a "one-man army" and one of the best soldiers in his company.

After World War II, he stayed in the paratroops and made a number of demonstration jumps and fought on the Airborne School boxing team. In 1950, Bass was deployed to Korea as a sergeant in the 27th Infantry Regiment, the Wolfhounds, of the 25th Division. While in Korea, he had a number of brushes with the media, including an interview with Jimmy Cannon, who wrote a story about the sergeant in the New York Post. Cannon quoted Bass saying that he preferred hand to hand combat. Later that year, a photo of Bass was printed in LIFE magazine, but it was a posthumous appearance, as it came after he was killed in combat.

Bass was recommended for the Silver Star in Korea for his actions near Chindong. A communist attack pressed within 75 yards of his regimental command post, so Bass took 20 men and launched a flanking attack, during which he was credited personally for 10 kills. Sergeant Joseph Bass was buried in Arlington National Cemetery, with military honors and with a number of his paratrooper comrades in attendance.

Gilman W. Bates

Gilman Bates passed away at the age of 85 at his home in Summerfield, OH on July 19, 2002. He was born on June 30, 1916 in Noble County, OH to Joseph and Violet. Bates served with the 101st during World War II and returned home and worked at the Law & Sons Orchards near Mt. Ephraim, OH until he retired. He was survived by two sisters and several nieces, nephews and cousins. Gilman Bates was buried with military honors in Fredericksdale Cemetery near Sarahsville, OH.

Gaetano "Guy" Barrella

Paratrooper Gaetano "Guy" Barrella passed away on July 30, 2007 at the age of 83 after a long fight with cancer at his home in Boynton Beach, FL. He was born on July 12, 1924 in Stamford, CT to Frank and Mary, who immigrated to the US from Potenza Province, Italy. Barrella raised his family in Stamford and retired to Boynton Beach in 1992. He was survived by his wife, children and grandchildren.

Robert J. Bearss

Robert J. Bearss, a veteran of the 506th, died at Elderwood Health Care at Birchwood, NY on Saturday, March 22, 2008. He spent 33 years after the war as an industrial engineer with Carrier Corporation in the Syracuse area, and was a volunteer with the AARP and with the League of Women Voters. Bob Bearss was predeceased by his wife of 43 years, Jeanne, in 1993 and son, Kim, in 1997, and was survived by two daughters, a daughter-in-law and three grandchildren. He was buried at the Oakwood Cemetery.

Paul John "Jack" Becker Jr.

Screaming Eagle Jack Becker passed away at the age of 81 in Edina, MN on March 16, 2007. He was a graduate of Washburn High School and was a champion golfer. Becker was preceded in death by his wife Joanne, and was survived by three sons and one daughter, and seven grandchildren. He was interred at Ft. Snelling National Cemetery.

George Edwin Beckwith

George Edwin Beckwith passed away at the age of 80 in Maplewood MN on May 4, 2006. Beckwith was born on March 28, 1926 and graduated from the high school in Harrodsburg, KY in 1944. He served with the 101st and was a member of the Counter Intelligence Corps (CIC) in Austria after the war ended.

Beckwith was a Past Master of the University Masonic Lodge #316, and was a member of Unizar Lodge #347, Scottish Rite, Zuhrah Shrine Merrimakers and Knights Templar. He was preceded in death by his wife of 42 yrs, Ruth, and was survived by five children and eight grandchildren.

Carmen Bell

Carmen Bell died at the age of 94 on October 7, 2007 in Cuyahoga Falls, OH. Bell was born in Grove City, PA, and lived in Cuyahoga Falls for most of his life. He worked for B.F. Goodrich as a tirebuilder for 36 years, and retired in 1975.

He was a recipient of the Purple Heart and the Bronze Star and was active in the 101st Airborne Division Association. Also, he was a member of the American Legion Charles Faust Post 281, played minor league baseball and was an avid golfer.

Carmen Bell was preceded in death by his wife, Annabelle, and was survived by his five sons, many grandchildren and great- and great-great-grandchildren. He was buried at Ohio Western Reserve National Cemetery.

Edward Raymond Bell

Edward Raymond Bell passed away on July 19, 2007 at the age of 88 in Sheridan, WY at the VA Medical Center. He was born on July 30, 1918, to Frood and Clarissa in Pine County, MN, where he attended school. Bell enlisted in the Minnesota National Guard in November 1939 and entered active duty in February 1941. During World War II, he served with both the 82nd and 101st and was honorably discharged on July 30, 1945.

Bell returned home and married Rebecca C. Johnson in Minneota, MN and attended Dunwoody Institute in Minneapolis. He took a job in Denver and in 1957, became the South Dakota, Montana and Wyoming district manager for Libby Foods, and he moved his family to Sheridan.

He worked in the food business for Panetta Brothers, then for PKS and Decker Coal, from which he would retired in 1983. Bell was a member of Trinity Lutheran Church, the American Legion, Sheridan Elks Lodge 520 and the Disabled American Veterans. Also, he volunteered at the Sheridan Senior Citizens Center, where he delivered Meals on Wheels, drove the Disabled American Veterans van and worked as an escort at the Sheridan VA Medical Center.

Bell enjoyed traveling with Bots Sots and Good Sams and dancing with the Jeans and Queens Square Dancing Club, working in his yard and garden, refinishing furniture, playing cards, hunting, fishing and camping with family and friends. Edward Bell was survived by his wife, Rebecca, a daughter, three sons, six grandchildren and five great-grandchildren, and was buried with military honors in Sheridan Elks Cemetery.

Salvatore Frank Bellino

Salvatore Frank Bellino, died on October 6, 2005, at Broadmoor Assisted Living in Fort Pierce, FL at the age of 85. He was born in Brooklyn, N.Y., and during the War was awarded the Purple Heart and the Bronze Star. Returning to NY, he lived in Massapequa on Long Island and worked for the town's Sanitation Department for more than 30 years before retiring to Port St. Lucie in 1982. He was a member of St. Lucie Catholic Church, Sons of Italy Lodge 2594 and the American Legion. Salvatore Bellino was survived by his wife, Theresa, stepdaughter and stepson, and was buried in Hillcrest Memorial Gardens in Fort Pierce.

Frederick R. Berkheimer

Frederick R. Berkheimer passed away on Wednesday, August, 10, 1993 at his home in Hanover, PA at the age of 77. He was born on April 15, 1916 to Robert and Clara, in Abbotstown, PA and was predeceased by his wife, Mary, in 1978.

Joe Beyrle

One of the most amazing stories of any paratrooper belonged to Joe Beyrle, who passed away on December 12, 2004 at the age of 81 due to heart failure. Ironically, he passed in a Toccoa, GA hotel room, while on a trip there to talk to students and veterans groups

Joseph Robert Beyrle was born in Muskegon, MI and graduated from Saint Joseph High School where he was voted best informed, most obvious temper, class shark and best dressed. In June 1942, he declined a baseball scholarship to the University of Notre Dame and enlisted in the Army and then volunteered for the paratroops, and joined the 506th at Toccoa.

Beyrle was known as an extremely enthusiastic paratrooper, and earned the nickname "Jumpin' Joe" and he had the distinction of being the only soldier to fight for both the U.S. and the Soviet Union during the ar.

Beyrle jumped into Normandy with the rest of the 101st on D-Day and landed on a church roof in St. Come-du-Mont under fire as he descended. He bounced off the roof, landed in the cemetery, got out of his harness and headed out to complete his mission of destroying bridges that could be used by the Germans for reinforcement. However, Beyrle was captured and marched to the rear. As he marched, he saw German soldiers bayoneting the body of the commander of the 3rd Battalion of the 506th, Bob Wolverton, still suspended from the tree where his parachute had snagged.

German soldiers marched Beyrle and other American captives toward a staging area, but American planes mistook the column for German troops and roared in for a strafing attack. Beyrle was hit by shrapnel, but managed to escape only to be caught again a few hours later. A German soldier stripped Beyrle of his dog tags, which were later found on the body of a man in an American uniform in France, and a case of mistaken identity ensued. The dead soldier was a German masquerading as an American, and in September 1944, Beyrle's parents in Muskegon, MI were told their son died in combat.

After his capture, Beyrle was taken from one prison camp to another, usually by train, and he was beaten, interrogated and starved. After several escape attempts, he finally succeeded in January 1945, and found a Russian tank unit. Beyrle later wrote how he hid in the farm of an elderly German couple. The Soviet soldiers shot the couple and fed them to their pigs, and then ate the pigs. Beyrle joined the Soviets and spent a month as a machine gunner on a Soviet Sherman tank.

The tank unit destroyed one of the POW camps where Beyrle had been imprisoned and shortly afterwards, he was injured by a German dive bomber attack, and he spent time in a hospital in Poland. After recovering, he made his way to the U.S. Embassy in Moscow and presented himself. The Embassy staff did not believe his identity and he was arrested, until fingerprints finally established that he was, indeed, Joe Beyrle.

On September 14, 1946, over a year after World War II ended, Joe Beyrle returned to Muskegon and got married in the church where a funeral Mass was held for him two years earlier after the case of mistaken identity. Beyrle stayed in Muskegon and worked as a supervisor for Brunswick, a manufacturer of bowling balls and pool tables, until he retired in 1981.

He was active with the Veterans of Foreign Wars, the American Legion and other veterans groups. In 1994, Beyrle was honored at the White House, and Russian President Boris Yeltsin presented Beyrle with four medals for his service with the Red Army. In 2002, he worked with military historian Thomas Taylor on a book about his experiences entitled, "The Simple Sounds of Freedom: The True Story of the Only Soldier to Fight for Both America and the Soviet Union in World War II." In 2004, the designer of the AK-47 assault rifle, Lt. Gen. Mikhail

Kalashnikov, presented one of his guns to Beyrle in a ceremony at a Moscow Victory Day celebration.

Joe Beyrle was survived by his wife of 58 years, JoAnne, three children, seven grandchildren and a great-grandson.

Charles R. Bixler

Bud Bixler was a highly decorated Screaming Eagles veteran who made both glider and parachute landings during the War. He passed away peacefully at his home in Lake Elsinore, CA on May 2, 2007, at the age of 83, and was surrounded by his family.

Born on a farm in Quincy, IA on May 18, 1923, he graduated from Corning High School in 1941 and then attended Creighton University in Omaha, NE until he ended up in the Army. He went to Camp Roberts in California for basic training and upon volunteering for the paratroopers, was assigned to the 327th Glider Regiment. He preferred parachute drops to glider landings and during the War, made four airborne and one glider landing. He was awarded the Bronze Star and four Bronze Battle Stars, served in Bastogne and guarded Goering's stolen art collection. He was one of 12 survivors of the original 175 men of his company.

After the War, he returned to Iowa and married Ruth McElroy in 1947. They had a son, Fred, in 1949, and moved to San Diego, CA in 1952. Two years later, they gave birth to a daughter. The Bixlers moved again, a few times before they settled in Lake Elsinore, California in 1983. In 1991, Bud retired after 20 years as a truck salesman from Carmenita Truck Center.

In retirement, he pursued his passion of rebuilding and selling old Chevy trucks, and was internationally-known for his expertise in models built between 1955 and 1959. Bud was preceded in death by his son Fred in 1996, and was survived by his wife Ruth, daughter and two grandchildren.

Roy E. Bjorkman

Roy E. Bjorkman served with the 101st during World War II and passed away in Edina, MN and was buried at Sunset Memorial Park. He was on December 3, 1916 in Lincoln, NE, and was a graduate of West High School and the University of Minnesota and was the founder and owner of Bjorkman Furs. Roy Bjorkman was preceded in death by his wife Evy, two daughters and an infant son, and was survived by a daughter, and was buried at Sunset Memorial Park.

Harry Blackledge

Harry Blackledge passed away on December 5, 1988 at the age of 64 in Throop, PA. He was a 101st veteran and a life member and past commander of VFW Post 227, Rutherford, NJ. After the war, he spent 43 years as a sterilizer for Becton-Dickinson and retired in 1985. He was survived by his wife, Mary

George Blair Sr.

George W. Blair Sr. passed away at the age of 86 on Saturday, March 22, 2008 in Chattanooga, TN. Blair served with both the 82nd and 101st, and received multiple decorations. He returned home and worked for Chattanooga System Operations Division for 29 years and then with the Electric Power Board. He was a volunteer with the VA and was the Senior Volunteer Coordinator for the Chattanooga Outpatient Clinic with over 10,000 hours of service. Blair was a member of the Shriners, the Scottish Rite, York Rite, the VFW Post 1289, American Legion Post 95, 40-8 Box Car Association, the Military Order of the Purple Heart and the 82nd Airborne Division Association Alvin C. York Chapter.

George Blair was survived by his wife, Katherine, one son and daughter, and a grandson, and was buried in Chattanooga National Cemetery

Dawson Bolus

Screaming Eagle Dawson Bolus passed away at the age of 83 on March 12, 2008 in Charleston, SC. Bolus was born on February 27, 1925 in Louisville, KY to George and Mary, and was the youngest of nine children. He enlisted in the Army at 15, and served with the 101st and saw action in Normandy and during the Battle of the Bulge and rose to the rank of Staff Sergeant. He was a graduate of Wofford College, and was survived by his wife of 57 years, Martha , three sons, one daughter and ten grandchildren. Dawson Bolus was buried at Holy Cross Cemetery in Charleston.

Patsy "Pat" Bonvenuto

Pat Bonvenuto passed away at the age of 81, on November 21, 2007, at Joel Pomerene Memorial Hospital in Millersburg, OH, following a lengthy illness. Born on February 12, 1926, to Patsy and Maria, he was a replacement soldier in the 101st, and served in the Rhineland and Central Germany campaigns. He served in Korea as well, and was a lieutenant in 40th Air Division, and held a variety of roles, from squadron adjutant and public information officer to certified personnel management instructor. He also was an ejection seat instructor.

Bonvenuto graduated from West Virginia University in 1951 with a degree in journalism, and later completed graduate work at WVU, California State College of Pa. and Kent State University. He became the city editor of the Dominion News in Morgantown, WV and moved to East Liverpool, OH in 1969, and taught at Beaver Local.

He was a life member of the Disabled American Veterans, the American Legion Post 374 and VFW Post 66. Pat Bonvenuto was survived by his wife, Mary Jane, two sons and a stepdaughter, and was buried with honors in Columbiana County Memorial Park.

Carl M. Boor

Carl Boor, passed away in Kansas at the age of 86 on August 21, 2007. He was a veteran who served with both the 82nd and 101st Airborne Divisions, and after the war, he spent 30 years working for Boeing. He was a member of the Masons for over 50 years, and he loved flying planes, his grandchildren, his dogs, traveling, gardening and, according to his obituary, "pestering his wife." He was preceded in death by a daughter and son, a great-granddaughter and a great-great-grandson. He was survived by his wife of 66 years, Mary, five daughters 18 grandchildren, 24 great-grandchildren and 7 great-great-grandchildren. Carl Boor was buried in the Girard Cemetery in Girard, KS.

Kenneth E. Booth

101st Airborne veteran Kenneth E. Booth, of Middletown, KY passed away at the age of 81 on Tuesday, Jan. 18, 2000, at his residence. He was born in Mount Sterling, KY on November 23, 1918, to Edmon T. and Alma, and was a lifelong resident of the Middletown area. After returning home from the War, he worked for Armco/AK Steel Co. and had also worked in the Streets Department for the City of Middletown for 23 years.

Booth was preceded in death by his wife, Jannie and was survived by two sisters, a brother-in-law, a brother and many nieces, nephews, great-nieces and great-nephews. He was buried at Woodside Cemetery in Middletown.

Joseph Boris

Joseph Boris passed away at 78 on Thursday, May 1, 2003 at the VA Medical Center in West Palm Beach, FL. Born in New York, NY, he retired and lived in Jensen Beach, FL for twenty two years. Prior to his retirement, he was a linotype operator for the Daily News in New York City for over 30 years. Boris was a member of the American Legion Post #0126.

John Batista Bortolon

Gliderman John Batista Bortolon passed away in Dolton, IL at the age of 80. A lifelong resident of Dolton, he was a member of Company E of the 327th Glider Infantry Regiment, and saw action in the Battle of the Bulge.

He retired from the Rexnord Company after 39 years of service. He was a Dolton Volunteer Fireman for 37 years, one-time President of the Dolton AARP, a member of VFW Post #9964 and Past President of the 101st Airborne Chicago Chapter, Member of the Indiana Chapter of the Battle of the Bulge and a long-time member of St. Jude the Apostle Church.

John Bortolon was married to his wife, Armida, for 57 years, and was survived by two children and two grandchildren. His funeral service was held in South Holland, IL and he was buried nearby at the Oakland Memory Lanes Cemetery.

Robert M. Bowen

Screaming Eagle Robert Bowen passed away at the age of 91 on May 9, 2005, in Paris, France, while attending a celebration of the 60th anniversary of the end of World War II. Bowen lived in Linthicum, MD and was born on Jan. 21, 1914, in Baltimore.

Bowen wrote of his experience with the 101st in his book, "Fighting with the Screaming Eagles: With the 101st Airborne from Normandy to Bastogne." Bowen was processed at Fort George Meade in Maryland, and he transferred to Fort Bragg for his airborne training. He was assigned to Company C of the 401st Glider Infantry and he landed in Normandy on D-Day, only to be wounded in the Normandy campaign.

Bowen recovered from his wounds and went on to fight again in Holland and in the Battle of the Bulge. He was captured at Bastogne, and he spent the rest of the war in a

German POW camp. His book was written just after the war, and was based on his memories and the collection of letters he sent to his wife.

Robert Bowen was survived by his wife Christine and was buried in the Lutheran Cemetery in Violetville, MD.

Edgar Bowers

Edgar Bowers passed away on February 4, 2000 in San Francisco, CA at the age of 75 from non-Hodgkins Lymphoma. He was born on March, 2, 1924 in Rome, GA, where his mother was a teacher and his father worked in a nursery garden.

He attended the University of North Carolina in 1942 but left to join the Army and he served in the Counter Intelligence Corps assigned to the 101st and was later was stationed in Berchtesgaden as an interpreter until he was discharged in April 1946. He completed his undergraduate degree at the University of North Carolina, and then went to Stanford University in 1947 to pursue his doctorate on the poems of Yeats's friend T. Sturge Moore. He studied under the critic and minor poet Yvor Winters, and he was a peer of Thom Gunn.

Bowers taught at several universities including Duke, and then spent 30 years at the University of California at Santa Barbara until he retired in 1991. He was a member of the English Faculty and specialized in English Renaissance and modern poetry. Among the benefits of living there was his home overlooking the beach, where he was inspired by dolphins and surfers, especially as he wrote his own poetry.

Bowers received a Guggenheim fellowship in 1959, and a second one in 1969, and was influenced by Winters, especially in his early works. The work of Edgar Bowers first became well-known in England in 1963 when Ted Hughes and Thom Gunn included him in their Faber volume, "Five American Poets," and when he was anthologized by Donald Hall. The second phase of Bowers' work began around 1965, and was influenced by depression and alcoholism. In 1989, Bowers was awarded the Bollingen Prize for Poetry in 1989 for his For Louis Pasteur.

Bowers works included: The Form Of Loss (1956), The Astronomers (1965), Witnesses (1981), Walking the Line (1988), Living Together (1988), Chaco Canyon (1988), For Louis Pasteur (1989) and How We Came from Paris to Blois (1990).

Obituaries written by literary critics described Bowers as somewhat controversial for his writing style, particularly his use of abstractions. He was described as egalitarian but was unfairly accused of being elitist, and he had been attacked for his homosexuality. However, his Collected Poems appeared in 1997, Harold Bloom called Bowers one of the best American poets of the previous 40 years.

Fred O. Brauer

Fred Brauer was not a member of the 101st, but he deserves to an honorary Screaming Eagle because he flew resupply missions to Bastogne and earned the Distinguished Flying Cross. He passed away at the age of 89 from natural causes in Missoula, MT on June 25, 2007.

Brauer was born August 23, 1917, in Butte, MT. His father and mother homesteaded in Divide, MT but the family was forced to move back to Butte in the early 1920s when their place burned down. Shortly afterwards, the family moved to Bonner, MT where Brauer attended Bonner School and then Missoula County High School, from which he graduated in 1937. He then went to the University of Montana, where he played football from 1937 to 1940.

Brauer was not able to complete his degree because of the war, and he became a pilot, earning his medal for his mission to Bastogne. After World War II, he returned to Montana and began a career that made him legendary: smoke-jumping. He placed a high priority on training, and was one of the pioneers of this new method of fighting forest fires. Later in his career, he appeared in several documentaries and History Channel programs, and he finished his 29-year forest service career as a technical director for the "Lassie" television program. Also, he was a technical director and fire expert in the motion picture "Red Skies Over Montana."

In 1963, Brauer returned to Missoula, and built the Lolo View Manor mobile home park by himself. He was known as a man who loved to work with his own hands and he was proud of his accomplishments.

Fred Brauer was preceded in death by his wife of 37 years, Harriett Anne, and was survived by a son, daughter, stepdaughter and eight grandchildren and several great-grandchildren. He was buried at the Sunset Memorial Cemetery and military honors were provided by Malmstrom Air Force Base.

Charles H. Brazeau

Screaming Eagle Charles Brazeau passed away at the age of 82 in Arlington Heights, IL on Saturday, December 13, 2003. He was born on March 2, 1921, in Chicago, and served with the 101st, including in the Battle of the Bulge.

John P. Brighenti Sr.

John P. Brighenti Sr. passed away at the age of 83 on February 15, 2008 in North Huntingdon, PA. He was born on January 26, 1925, in Biddle, PA to James and Marie and served in the 101st during the War. Afterwards, he was a security guard for the Westinghouse Bettis Atomic Plant. He was a member of Strawpump Sports Shop and numerous sportsmen's clubs. John Brighenti was preceded in death by his wife, Margaret and a son, and was survived by two daughters, two grandchildren and a great-grandson.

Bertie Leon Brookover

Bertie Leon Brookover, a captain in the 101st, passed away on Wednesday, May 16, 2001, in Eustis, FL at the age of 87. Brookover was born July 8, 1913, in Fairview, FL, to Learney French and Mary Alice. Slightly older than other men in the 101st when war was declared (he was 28), he had graduated from the agricultural sciences program at the University of West Virginia in 1936. Following the war, he served 17 years in the reserves as a major.

He lived in Stewart, FL and then Tavares, FL, and owned a dairy farm at the site where Federal Hocking High School now stands. He also built, owned and operated Skyline Speedway and was a timber contractor.

He was survived by his second wife, Alice, four daughters, two stepsons, 15 grandchildren, 23 great-grandchildren and four great-great-grandchildren. He was preceded in death by his first wife, Thelma, a son, Bertie L. Jr., a grandson, and a great-granddaughter. He was buried in Coolville Cemetery with military honors.

Edwin Earl Brown

Edwin Earl Brown passed away at the age of 71 on October 5, 1985 in Brookfield, OH. He was born on January 24, 1914 in Elk City, KS and served with the 501st Regiment in Normandy, Holland and Bastogne, where he was seriously wounded and awarded the Bronze Star and a Purple Heart. He survived the war and served again in Korea and then went on to raise a family. Edwin Brown was buried in Arlington Cemetery, Section 18, Grave 1041-1.

George Wilson Brown Sr.

George Wilson Brown, Sr., passed away at the age of 80 on May 6, 2007at Presbyterian Hospital in Charlotte, NC, where he lived. After the war, he served in the Civil Air Patrol. George Brown was predeceased by his wife, Annie Elizabeth, and was survived by two daughters, two sons and a granddaughter. He was buried at Marks Creek Presbyterian Church Cemetery.

Fred Broyhill

Fred Broyhill, a member of the 101st passed away in 1992 in Statesville, NC. He married Catherine Sherrill on December 30, 1940 and volunteered for the paratroopers and served until 1945. After the War, he returned home and worked as a textile engineer. In the 1950s, he and his wife began traveling and working internationally, and they lived in Puerto Rico, Hong Kong, Thailand, Iran, Brazil and Singapore. After retirement in 1975, the couple moved to Florida and also spent time in North Carolina.

Joe Bruscato

Joe Bruscato passed away on June 4, 2007 in Arizona, at the age of 83. He was born on January 28, 1924 in Kansas City, MO to an Italian immigrant family. In 1956, he moved to Phoenix and worked for Thunderbird Freight Lines for 28 years until his retirement in 1985. Joe Bruscato was survived by his wife, Norma, four children, four grandchildren and three great-grandchildren, and was buried at Phoenix Memorial Park.

Earl Robert "Bob" Burgess

Bob" Burgess, passed away on Sunday May 27, 2007 at home in East Hartford, CT at the age of 81. Born in Procter, VT on September 4, 1925, to Earl and Jessie, he lived in East Hartford for many years. Burgess was a demolition specialist with the 502nd Regiment of the 101st Airborne. After the war, Burgess worked for the Fuller Brush Company for 30 years, and then was employed by the State of Connecticut for 16 years.

He was an avid hunter and fisherman, a member of the 82nd Airborne Association of Greater Hartford and raced stock cars at Riverside Raceway in the 1950's with the number 502. Burgess was survived by his wife, five children, eight grandchildren and great-grandchildren, and was predeceased by a son, Richard Burgess. Robert Burgess was buried with military honors in Hillside Cemetery, East Hartford.

Howard V. Bussiere

Howard V. Bussiere Jr., a member of the 1st Battalion of the 506th Regiment, and a long-time resident of Danville, NH died Thursday, March 13, 2008, at Exeter Hospital at the age of 82.

He was born in Stafford Springs, CT to Howard V. Sr. and Marguerite E. (Hetzel) Bussiere. Bussiere enlisted in April 1943, and was attracted to the paratroopers because of the extra pay. He fought in Normandy and Holland, the Battle of the Bulge and through Germany. He received a number of citations, including a Good Conduct Medal.

Upon returning home, he met and married his wife of 58 years, Rose (DeFazio) Bussiere, who died in July, 2007, and he worked as a mechanic for the United Shoe Machinery Co. in Haverhill, NH repairing machinery in various factories throughout New England. Bussiere had a reputation as a guy who could fix anything. He was also known as an avid fisherman, and rented out a garage across the street from his home where he stored 20-foot boat he built himself.

He also had a fondness for horses, especially raising and training them. In addition, he took up the hobby of building and flying remote control model airplanes, but he was the kind of man who loved to tinker with all sorts of things. One of his reported favorite pastimes was traveling with his wife in their mobile home across the country.

Howard Bussiere was survived by his brothers, Eugene of Salisbury, NH and Frank of Victorville, CA, and many nieces and nephews. And was preceded in death by three sisters. Howard Bussiere was buried in St. Patrick's Cemetery, North Broadway, Haverhill, NH.

Harold L. Buttrey

101st Airborne medic Harold L. Buttrey passed away at the age of 84 on January 11, 2008, in the Medway Country Manor, in Medway, MA. Born in Corning, NY on July 19, 1923, to Leroy and Lillian, he was a graduate of Elmira High School. Buttrey lived most of his life in Corning, before moving to Oneonta, NY about 25 years before he passed.

During the War he saw action throughout Europe, and was awarded the Purple Heart, the American Defense Medal, the Good Conduct Medal, the European African Middle Eastern Service Medal, and the Distinguished Unit Badge. Following the War, he served as an official Army photographer and achieved the rank of corporal.

After returning from Europe, he worked as a salesman for many years, and retired from the ZEP Chemical Company. He had an interest in designing and making custom jewelry, buying and selling antiques, and playing golf, and was a member of the American Legion in Oneonta.

He was survived by his wife of 55 years, Simone, and two daughters, as well as three grandchildren. Harold Buttrey was buried in Corning.

Patrick J. Callery

Medic Patrick Callery of the 502nd passed away on May 9, 2007, at the age of 87, in Sandy Hook, CT. Callery was born in West Hempstead, NY, and jumped into Normandy on D-Day. He was survived by his wife Teresa, two children, five grandchildren and five great grandchildren. Patrick Callery was buried at Calverton National Cemetery, Calverton, LI.

Louis J. Cantone Jr.

Louis Cantone, a 101st veteran, passed away in Illinois after retiring from the Chicago Police Department as a lieutenant, and after 32 years and in the Federal Protective Services. He was a native of Illinois, and graduated from Harper High School as well as Northwestern University. He was preceded in death by his wife Margaret and a daughter, and was survived by six children and 18 grandchildren, as well as 14 great-grandchildren. Louis Cantone was buried at Abraham Lincoln National Cemetery.

Norman A. Capels

Norman Capels passed away at the age of 82 on February 17, 2001 at the James Square Health & Rehabilitation Centre in his home town of Syracuse, NY. Capels jumped into Normandy on D-Day and during the War was awarded a Purple Heart and two Bronze Stars. After the War, he spent 37 years as a truck driver with I. Fleischman & Sons Furniture Co. of Syracuse and retired in 1980. He was a communicant of St. Matthew's Church, a life member of 101st Airborne Association and a member of Eastwood Senior Citizens Club.

Norman Capels was survived by his wife, Marion, five daughters, two sons, 10 grandchildren and eight great-grandchildren, and was buried in the Onondaga County Veterans Memorial Cemetery.

Reverend Nicholas Cardell

Dr. Nick Cardell passed away on Monday, October 7, 2002 at the age of 77. He was born on June 23, 1925, in Smith Falls, Ontario, and was educated at Columbia College and Meadville - Lombard. He served with the 101st during the War and was captured during the Battle of the Bulge, but he managed to escape and return to his unit.

Cardell was ordained by the Point Lookout Community Presbyterian Church in Point Lookout, NY in 1952, and in 1957, received a preliminary fellowship in the American Unitarian Association. He was ordained on October 20, 1959, by the First Unitarian Society of Plainfield, NJ and served congregations in that state and in New York. When he retired in 1995, the May Memorial Unitarian Society of Syracuse, NY named him minister emeritus.

He was a well-known social activist, served time in a federal prison for his protests and won many awards, including the Central New York/ American Civil Liberties Union Ralph Kharas Distinguished Service Award. Nicholas Cardell was survived by his wife, Catherine, a daughter and a son.

William Paul Catoe

William Paul Catoe passed away at the age of 68, in Camden, SC on Tuesday, Oct.19, 1993. Born in Kershaw County, to Cora and William, he was awarded a Purple Heart and two Bronze Stars.

He was the retired owner of the Red Top Cab Company in Camden, a member of the James Belk Post 17 of the American Legion, and a charter member of Emmanuel Baptist Church, where he was a former deacon and Sunday school teacher. Catoe also enjoyed a large family, and was survived by two daughters, a son, seven grandchildren and four great-grandchildren. William Catoe was buried in the Emmanuel Baptist Church Cemetery.

Dr. Estill L. Caudill, Jr.

Dr. Estill L. Caudill, Jr. was a doctor who served with both the 101st and the 82nd Airborne Divisions during World War II, and passed away at his home on Pine Hill Road Extension in Elizabethton, VA at the age of 82 on March 1, 1999.

Dr. Caudill was a native of Narrows, VA and was born to Dr. E.L. Caudill Sr. and Flora Weatherly Caudill. In 1941, he graduated from the Medical College of Virginia, and following his internship, he entered the Army, serving in D-Day, the Battle of the Bulge and on into Germany with both the 101st and the 82nd Airborne.

After the War, Caudill returned to Elizabethton, VA and became a family practitioner and served as president of the Tennessee Academy of General Practice, the Tennessee State Board of Registration in Medicine, and was the Carter County Medical Examiner for many years. He also served as Medical Director of Beaunit Fibers until his retirement.

Outside of his medical affiliations, he was a member and past president of the Elizabethton Rotary Club, a former director of Citizens Bank and a charter director of Security Federal Savings Bank. He also was a member of the First United Methodist Church.

Dr. Estill Cadill was preceded in death by his wife, Lucy Bolton Caudill, on October 12, 1987. His survivors included a son, two daughters and six grandchildren. He was interred at Happy Valley Memorial Park.

John W. "J.W." Campbell

John W. ' J.W.' Campbell passed away at 81 on Thursday, June 3, 2004 at the Grace Healthcare facility of Abingdon, VA after a long illness. He was born in Abingdon, the son of D. J. and Kate Gray. JW Campbell was a member of V. F. W. Post 1994 and the American Legion and was survived by his wife of 54 years, Edna, one son, one daughter and two granddaughters. John Campbell was buried at Forest Hills Memory

Gardens with honors conducted by the Highlands Veterans Honor Color Guard.

Charles Louis Carney Sr.

Charles Louis Carney, Sr., passed away on Monday, February 4, 2008. Carney was a 1938 graduate of Milford, CT High School. After the War, he earned a BS in Chemical Engineering at Tulane University in 1950 and an MBA at the University of West Florida in 1972.

Carney was a fire protection and safety engineer for the Monsanto Corporation. He was very active in his community of Gulf Breeze, FL, where he was a volunteer fire chief, a scout master from 1959 to 1967 for Troop 11, and a little league coach for many years.

He was preceded in death by his first wife of more than 22 years, Alma Gruntz, and his second wife of more than 28 years, Berth Webb. He was survived by two sons and a daughter, seven grandchildren and two great-grandchildren.

Richard "Dick" Case

Richard case passed away at the age of 87 on March 30, 2008 at the Nathan Adelson Hospice in Las Vegas, NV. He had been unconscious for several weeks after choking on a piece of steak during dinner at a friend's house.

Richard Haynes Case was born Nov. 17, 1920, in Nanaimo, British Columbia, Canada, and his family moved to the US when he was four years old. He attended college at Georgia Tech, and in 1943, he joined the Army and volunteered for the paratroopers and demolition school. He was in the 502nd Regiment when he jumped into Normandy on D-Day, and also served in Market-Garden and the Battle of the Bulge, and received three Purple Hearts and three Bronze Stars.

After the War, he graduated from the University of California, Berkeley with a political science degree in 1948 and then attended the University of Grenoble in France. In 1950, he returned to active duty serving with the 187th Parachute Infantry Regiment Combat Team in Korea and Japan, and afterwards he served with the 10th Special Forces Group in Bad Tolz, Germany from 1958-1960.

In 1956, Case spent time as a consultant to the makers of the movie, "The Man in the Gray Flannel Suit." That year, he also served as a military adviser for the movie, "Screaming Eagles."

Upon leaving the military, Case ran a travel agency in Las Vegas with his wife Betty, who passed away in 2003. He spent time volunteering with the Boy Scouts and he also was a pilot and once flew an aircraft from the East Coast to the West Coast following railroad tracks.

In addition to being predeceased by his wife and a son, he was survived by his former wife, three sons, a daughter and five grandchildren. Richard Case was buried in Arlington National Cemetery.

William Chartos

William Chartos passed away peacefully on November 5, 2007 at the age of 89. Born April 10, 1918 in Harco, IL, he was a varsity football player for Michigan State University and a veteran of both the 82nd and 101st Airborne Divisions during World War II.

He was a resident of Tucson, AZ from 1948 until his passing, and was a sales representative in southern Arizona for the Johns Manville Corporation for 34 years. An excellent athlete, he was known as a tremendous golfer, and he also loved nature and gardening. William Chartos was preceded in death by his wife, Effie, and was survived by his daughter, Mary Elizabeth.

Chief Charles E. "Ed" Chedd

Ed Chedd passed away on April 6, 2005 at the age of 88 in Florida. He was born on May 9, 1916 in Hartely-Wintney, England. He enlisted in the Army and volunteered for the paratroops and served with the 101st. He received a Purple Heart Award for wounds received in Normandy. After the War, he was the Fire Chief at McCoy Air Force Base in Florida, and he rewrote the Air Force guidelines for fighting fires in the event of a nuclear incident. In the 1960s, he relocated and served as a Fire Prevention Engineer for the Alaskan Air Command. He retired to Florida near Orlando and was preceded in death by his wife on March 13, 2004.

Michael Chwastiak

Screaming Eagle veteran Michael Chwastiak passed away at 84 on April 8, 2008, in the Cedarbrook-Fountain Hill Annex near his home of Emmaus, PA. After the war, he was a self-employed cookware salesman until he retired and was a life member of Macungie Fire Company and Macungie Veterans of Foreign Wars. Michael Chwastiak was survived by his wife of 61 years, Althea, two daughters, a grandson and two great-grandchildren. He was buried in Fairview Cemetery in Macungie.

Cornelius D. "Neil" Clement

Cornelius Clement, passed away at the age of 82 in Pompano Beach, FL on August 18, 2007. He was born on November 11, 1924 in Detroit, MI to Edward and Mary. He spent 40 years in Pittsburgh working in sheet metal before retiring to Florida in 2003. Neil Clement was survived by his wife of 37 years, Rita, three daughters and a son, nine grandchildren and six great-grandchildren, and was buried in Beth Shalom Cemetery near Pittsburgh.

James A. Clemente

James Clemente of O'Hara Township near Pittsburgh, PA, passed away at the age of 86 on December 10, 2007. Clemente participated in the D-Day drop jump on Normandy and was awarded a Purple Heart and a Bronze Star. He was survived by his wife Elnora and two children and was predeceased by two children. James Clemente was buried in Madonna of Jerusalem Church in Sharpsburg, PA.

Prentiss O. Cochran

Prentiss O. "Cotton" Cochran, passed away at the age of 79 on September 29, 1999 at Mease Morton Plant Hospital in Clearwater, FL. He was born on September 13, 1920, in Braxton County, WV to Peter Jackson and Ula Susan Ash Cochran. He was employed at Preston Electric & Telephone Co. (Alltel) in Masontown as a lineman supervisor for more than 30 years, and was a member of the Masontown Methodist Church and the Masontown VFW Post 1589.

Prentiss Cochran was survived by two sons and five grandchildren and was preceded in death by his first and second wives, Allie and Alice, and an infant son. He was buried with military honors at the Masontown Cemetery.

Harold Collins

Harold "Buck" Collins, passed away from heart disease at the age of 82 on March 12, 2008, at East Paso Care Center in Dade City, FL. Born on January 9, 1926, in Lewistown, PA to Wesley and Millie Collins, he was captured during the Battle of the Bulge.

Mr. Collins was a former employee of Diamond Shamrock and a retiree of Rockwell International Brake Division in Ashtabula, OH and spent years living in Madison, OH. He was preceded in death by his first wife, of 58 years, Marcelene and a son. Survivors included his second wife, Marlene, three children and three stepchildren, 12 grandchildren, 22 great-grandchildren and one great-great grandchild. He was buried at the Arcola Road Cemetery in Geneva, OH.

Charles Arthur Conley III

Charles Arthur Conley, passed away quietly in his sleep after a short battle with cancer at the age of 88, on May 21, 2007. A resident of Rockville Centre, NY, for 47 years, he was a co-founder of Walsh/Conley Religious Goods in Hempstead, NY, which he operated for 50 years. Conley was married to his wife Margaret for 60 years, had several children, and was buried at the Gate of Heaven Cemetery in Hawthorne, NY.

Raymond A. Connolly

Raymond A. Connolly passed away at the age of 85 on February 7, 2008, at the MidState Medical Center in Meriden, CT. Born in New Haven, CT on February 13, 1922, to Joseph and Della, he attended grade schools in that city. He participated in D-Day and in the Battle of the Bulge.

Connolly returned home and graduated from Providence College, and was employed as a Special Agent with the Federal Bureau of Investigation for 30 years, serving in the Knoxville, Chicago, Albany and New Haven offices until his retirement. He lived in the Wallingford area for over 30 years before moving to North Haverhill, NH later in life. He was also the proprietor of the Turnpike Package Store and Carvel Ice Cream Store, in Wallingford, and was a parishioner of the Church of the Resurrection there.

Raymond Connolly was preceded in death by his wife, Louise Byrnes, and was survived by his four daughters, seven sons and 18 grandchildren. He was buried with military honors at All Saints Cemetery in North Haven, CT.

Bert Constant

Bert Constant passed away in Springfield, IL in April 2008. He had been a First Lieutenant and was captured twice and was awarded two Purple Hearts. He was buried in the cemetery at Camp Butler in Springfield, IL

Leon Roland Cookson

Leon Roland Cookson passed away at his home in Inverness, FL. He was born on December 7, 1924, in Woodbury, VT to William and Alice. After the war, he was a stonecutter for more than 40 years at Buttura and Sons Granite Co. in Barre, VT. After retiring, he moved from Plainfield, VT to Inverness in 1987. Cookson was survived by his wife of 40 years, Betty, two sons, six daughters, 15 grandchildren and four great-grandchildren.

Merrill L. "Ham" Coup

Ham Coup, a veteran of the 502nd Regiment, passed away in March 2004 at the age of 84. Born on April 12, 1919, in Milton, PA to Merrill and Margaret E. (Hendricks) Coup, he was a 1936 graduate of Hartley Township High School, Laurelton. As a youth, he worked at the Laurelton Foundry, and married Hazel Leola Shirk on April 6, 1941, in Hartleton, PA.

He enlisted in the Army on May 20, 1941, in Harrisburg, PA and was honorably discharged as a corporal at the Indiantown Gap Military Reservation on September 21, 1945. Coup served in every major campaign, including D-Day, Holland and the Battle of the Bulge. He received the Purple Heart and Good Conduct Medal, American Defense Service and American Theater Service medals, as well as the Distinguished United Badge with One Oak Leaf Cluster and the European African Middle Eastern Service Medal with four Bronze Stars and one Bronze Arrowhead.

After World War II, he was employed as the plant manager of Glen-Gery Brick Co. and then was the supervisor of the company's plant in Watsontown, for 23 years before retiring in the early 1970s. He enjoyed gardening, woodworking, making crafts, baseball, football and bowling. He played baseball as a young man, and many elderly residents of the town of Selinsgrove, he hit the longest home run ever seen at the age of 17.

Coup was a member of St. John's United Church of Christ, Mifflinburg, the Good Fellowship Sunday School Class and served four terms on the council as both an elder and a deacon. Also, he was a 69-year member of Loyal Order of Moose Lodge 1396, Mifflinburg, and a member of Thomas H. Clapham Post 410, American Legion, Mifflinburg, starting in 1945 and was the post commander in 1950 and 1951. He was a member of Yoder-Zimmerman Post 1964, Veterans of Foreign Wars, Mifflinburg, since 1945 and a member of the Union County Sportsmen's Club, Weikert.

Ham Coup was preceded in death by his wife and one son, and was survived by a daughter, one granddaughter and three great-grandchildren. He was buried with full military rites by the Thomas H. Clapham Post 410, American Legion, at the Hill Top Cemetery, Mifflinburg, PA.

Stanley Cybulski

"Bucky" Cybulski passed away at the age of 80 on July 26, 2002 in East Lansing, MI. He was born on January 29, 1922 in Detroit, MI and was a trooper in Company F of the 501st Regiment. He stayed in the military after the War and retired from the Army Tank Automotive Command in Warren, MI. He was survived by his wife of 51 years, Erma, a daughter and son, and three grandchildren, Stanley Cybulski was buried in Ft. Custer National Cemetery in Augusta, MI.

Mitchell J. Czarkowski

"Carbide Mike" Carbide Mike" Czarkowski, passed away at the age of 85 in May 2007 in Illinois. He was born to Emil and the Mary Ann and served in both the 82nd and 101st, and dropped into Normandy on D-day. He worked for Illinois Tool Works for 45 years, and was married to Lillian Ondrla, and had a son and a daughter. Michael Carbide Mike" Czarkowski was buried at Memory Gardens Cemetery in Norridge, IL.

Troy Decker

Troy H. Decker, passed away at the age of 85 on July 19, 2007, at his residence in of Connelly Springs, NC after a period of declining health. He was born in Burke County on April 15, 1922, to Max and Cora Lee.

Decker served with the 506th Regiment during World War II and he participated in all of the major campaigns of the 101st, earning the Purple Heart, Certificate of Merit, Bronze Star, Good Conduct Award and Combat Infantryman Badge. After the War, he became a self-employed mechanical contractor. Troy Decker was survived by his wife of 65 years, Margaret, four daughters, five grandchildren and seven great-grandchildren

Paul Dely

Paul Dely passed away at the age of 87 on April 24, 2004 in Richland, GA where he retired. He was born in Roseland, NJ and during the War, was taken prisoner. He worked for Eastern Airlines as a mechanic, retiring in 1979 and moving to Richland from Miami, FL. He was a member of the Dayspring Presbyterian Church in Spring Hill, GA, and was survived by three sons and a step-daughter.

Donald J. Deotte

Donald Deotte passed away peacefully at the age of 83, at his home in New Orleans, LA on October 24, 2007. He was born in Putnam, CT to Mary and Ernest and served with both the 82nd and 101st in World War II, and moved to New Orleans in 1948.

He graduated from Loyola University, and was an adjuster with the Travelers, Commercial Union and Gray Insurance companies. Also, he was the owner and President of the Louisiana Auto Salvage Pool, and an avid tennis player. Donald Deotte was survived by his wife of 52 years, Diana.

Valentino Desiderato

Valentino Desiderato passed away at 83 on December 10, 2002 in Staten Island, NY, where he lived his whole life. He was born in Port Richmond and moved to Westerleigh in the 1970s. He started his post-war career as a marble and tile fitter at Terranova Tile Co., and then spent 25 years as a printer with the J.M. Huber Ink Corp., Edison, N.J., until he retired in 1992.

Kenneth Harold Dill

Ken Dill passed away peacefully at the age of 87 at his home in Sacramento, CA on September 22, 2007 surrounded by his children after a year and half battle with cancer.

Born in Avant, Oklahoma on November 1, 1919 to Pierce and Hester, he moved with his family to Arizona in 1938 where they farmed as they had in the Sooner State. When the War broke out Ken moved to San Diego, CA and worked in aircraft factories until he was drafted. He volunteered to serve in the paratroopers and was a member of the 502nd Regiment.

Dill returned to San Diego from the War, and then moved to Stockton, CA where he met his future wife, Betty Williams. Ken and Betty were married in February of 1949 and they raised three children. The couple moved to Sacramento in 1953, and he worked at Rawson Drug & Sundries for 35 years.

Ken Dill was an excellent athlete. As a golfer, he consistently shot in the 80s and he played third base in fast-pitch softball. He was also extremely well known for his green thumb, and for producing tomatoes and other vegetables year after year. In retirement, he and his wife were members of the

Sierra Treasurer Hunters Club and enjoyed traveling in their RV, especially to Arizona.

Ken Dill was preceded in death by his wife, Betty, and was survived by his two sons and daughter, seven grandchildren and five great-grandchildren. He was buried at Cherokee Memorial Park.

Harry Dingman, Jr.

Harry Dingman, Jr. passed away at the age of 80 on June 17, 2002 at Forsyth Medical Center in Winston-Salem, NC. He was born on February 13, 1922, in the Bronx section of New York City to Harry Sr. and Anna Cecelia Ennis.

During World War II, he was a member of I Company in the Third Battalion of the 506th, and received the Purple Heart after being one of the many men of his unit wounded near Bastogne. He spent the last 30 years of his life living in Winston-Salem, where he worked for AT&T-Lucent Technologies as a technical writer, until his retirement. In Winston-Salem, he was an active member of the Military Order of the Purple Heart and the Disabled American Veterans, the Elks Club and of Holy Family Catholic Church.

Harry Dingman was survived by his wife, Maria, a son, three daughters and six grandchildren and was buried at the National Cemetery in Arlington, VA in Section 67, site 4320.

Frank Domyan

Frank A. Domyan passed away at his Anawalt, WV home on October 24, 2002 at the age of 84. He worked as a coal miner until he retired. Frank Domyan was survived by a sister, and buried with military honors in Woodlawn Memorial Park in Bluewell, PA.

Harold B. Downes

Harold B. Downes, passed away in Little Rock, AR on January 2, 2008 at the age of 82. He was born in Rochester, N.Y., on March 27, 1925, to Edward Samuel and Anna Josephine, and was jumped on D-Day and served in the Battle of the Bulge.

Following his return from the War, he spent years as a sales manager for GTE in its Sylvania subsidiary. Harold Downes was preceded in death by his wife of 52 years, Barbara, who passed on May 21, 2003. He was survived by three daughters, nine grandchildren and six great-grandchildren.

William H. "Bill" Dragon

Bill Dragon passed away peacefully at his home in Independence, MO at the age of 88 on December 7, 2001. Born on February 12, 1919, he was a member of the 502nd Regiment. While on a train leaving Kansas City, Bill met Dorothy Frances Heather. They began writing to each other immediately and were married on New Year's Day 1944 at Camp Mackall, NC. In order to support his wife, Dragon joined the paratroopers for the extra $50 a month in pay. Two weeks after the marriage, he received his orders to ship out, and he did not see his wife again for nearly two years.

Dragon was a member of the Headquarters Company, of the 3rd Battalion of the 502nd Regiment and jumped into Normandy on D-Day and into Holland. During Market-Garden, he was wounded and sent to a hospital in London. After recuperating, he rejoined the 502nd in time to deploy to Bastogne. Dragon was honorably discharged in 1945 with the rank of Technical Sergeant, and had been awarded the Purple Heart and four Bronze Stars, among other awards.

After the war, Bill and Dorothy made their home in Independence, where they raised three daughters, two sons, numerous stray dogs, abandoned cats and a slew of rabbits at their home on North River Blvd. During the summer, he tended his vegetable and flower gardens in the summer. In the winter, Dragon could be found racing around the neighborhood on a toboggan, or building a snow dragon or an igloo fort. In 1981, after 25 years of service, Bill retired from Associated Wholesale Grocers, and he and his wife sold their house and traveled around the country in their motor home. They wintered in Alamo, TX each year until poor health forced them to return back to Independence.

Bill Dragon was a hero and as a friend to many. He treated people well, and was known for an unusual sense of humor, much to the frustration of his wife and family. He was survived by his wife Dorothy, three children and eight grandchildren. He was buried with military honors in "Jackson County Veteran's Field of Honor" in Swan Lake Memorial Gardens, Grain Valley.

William C. Dreesen Sr.

William C. Dreesen, Sr., passed away at the age of 86 on Friday, April 4, 2008 at Clifton Springs Hospital near Rochester, NY. He was a lifelong resident of Canandaigua, NY and served with the 101st on D-Day, and was awarded numerous medals including the Bronze Star and the Purple Heart.

Dreesen enjoyed outdoor activities and was an avid gardener. William Dreesen was predeceased by his wife, Rachel, in 2006 and was survived by a daughter, son, four grandchildren and six great-grandchildren and was buried in Woodlawn Cemetery in Canandaigua.

Ernest C. Drum

"Mouse" Drum passed away at the age of 88 on Friday, Oct. 12, 2007, at Catawba Valley Medical Center in Hickory, NC. Born on July 3, 1919, in Catawba County, to John and Bessie, he was a member of the 326th Engineers and served in the Battle of the Bulge.

He lived in Maiden, NC, worked for Carolina Mills until he retired in 1986, and was preceded in death by his wife, Edwina, and survived by his daughter, a granddaughter and a great-granddaughter. Ernest Drum was buried in the cemetery of Mount Ruhama Baptist Church in Maiden, of which he was a member.

Rene Dussaq

A wonderfully colorful man, Rene Dussaq, a Screaming Eagle, passed away at the age of 84 in June 1996, two years after he celebrated the 50th anniversary of D-Day by parachuting into Normandy in again. He passed away at his Encino, CA home after a short, severe fight with leukemia.

Dussaq loved life and pursued things vigorously. He was at one point a matador, polo player, champion fencer and Davis Cup tennis player for Cuba, where he moved after graduating from the University of Geneva with a degree in philosophy. He became a naturalized U.S. citizen in 1939, and fought for his new country in World War II as a paratrooper.

By the end of the war, Dussaq accumulated an incredible list of distinctions. He was awarded the Distinguished Service Cross, Distinguished Service Medal, Distinguished Service Order and the Silver Star with clusters. He was nominated for a Congressional Medal of Honor for his bravery in a special operation for "landing secretly behind German lines in France to organize French defense resistance, and mine and subvert vital enemy observation stations." Rene Dussaq also was awarded France's highest decoration, the Croix de Guerre with palm leaf.

Following World War II, he became an expert ocean diver, and refined SCUBA gear invented by Jacques Cousteau, before moving on to become a stuntman in Hollywood. Then he settled in for something more traditional, taking a job with the Prudential Life Insurance Co., where he worked until his retirement in 1970.

But his love of adventure didn't stop. One of his long-time friends said of visiting a then-82 Rene Dussaq at his home, "he was out in the back yard doing giant swings on the horizontal bars." That same year, 1994, Dussaq was the oldest of the 41 veterans of the 101st Airborne Division who had gone to Normandy to reenact the D-Day jump. Strong winds blew Dussaq over two miles from the landing zone and organizers frantically scrambled to look for him.

Rene Dussaq was eventually found holding court in a local pub, celebrating the day and sharing stories about D-Day with the local villagers. He was then introduced to the prime minister of France, Edouard Balladur. He later excitedly told President Clinton at the White House that once again, he and the men had accomplished their mission.

Rene and his beloved wife, Charlotte, were married on December 7, 1946. Charlotte and her family spread Rene's ashes on the grounds of a summer cabin they owned in Bear Valley Springs, CA.

Robert E. Engwer

Robert E. Engwer passed away at the age of 80 from lung cancer. Engwer worked as a business manager for District 622 and Mounds View School District 621 in the St. Paul, MN area, and was a past school board member of District 622 and a North High School Distinguished Alumni recipient. He was a member of the Jaycees, V.F.W. Post 1350, American Legion Post 39, the North St. Paul Lions, Mason's, MN Old Timers Football Association and Tamarack Sportsmen's Club. Also, he was inducted into the Macalester College Football Hall of

Fame and was a co-Founding Member of the North St. Paul Historical Society.

Robert Engwer was preceded in death by his wife, and was survived by eight children, 21 grandchildren and ten great-grandchildren, and was buried in Evergreen Memorial Gardens in St. Paul, MN.

Philip J. Ergon

Philip J. Ergon, a Screaming Eagle who served in Bastogne, passed away at his Canton, OH home, surrounded by his family, at the age of 85.

Born in Youngstown, OH, he lived in Canton for most of his life. During the War, he received numerous awards, including four bronze stars and a Good Conduct Medal. After the War, he worked for the City of Canton Urban Renewal Acquisition Division until retirement. He was a member of the North Canton Elks Lodge #2029, McKinley Eagles Aerie #2370 and St. Haralambos Greek Orthodox Church.

Philip Ergon was preceded in death by his wife Honoria and a daughter, and was survived by four children, seven grandchildren and one great-grandchild. He was buried in Forest Hill Cemetery.

Aldridge "Augie" Everitt

Augie Everitt passed away at the age of 87 at his son's home in Bucks County, PA on September 18, 2007, with his family by his side. Everitt was born to Elizabeth and Joseph and raised on a family farm in the area of Levittown, PA. He was an Eagle Scout and graduated from Langhorne-Middletown High School in 1938 where he excelled in basketball, football and track.

After high school he went to work for Rohm & Haas in Bristol, PA where he met his future wife Jean. After serving with the 101st during World War II, he returned to work at Rohm & Haas and ultimately was with the company for 42 years. During the late 1940's and early 1950's, he was the star center on his plant's basketball team in the Industrial League, and the star player on their golf team.

Everitt was an accomplished golfer, racking up four holes in one between 1949 and 1964. In the mid-1950s, his brother-in-law, who lived in Allentown, NJ, announced he planned to leave farming, and Everitt convinced him to turn the farm into a golf course. They created one of the most popular courses in central New Jersey, Cream Ridge Golf Club.

In 1963, Everitt was asked by his neighbors to run for Middletown Township Supervisor. Although he lost the election, he was subsequently appointed supervisor to fill an existing vacancy on the board and went on to serve for 16 years. In 1967, Everitt parted from his party and became the first Independent candidate ever to win elected office in Middletown Township. He was also a volunteer with the Penndel-Middletown Emergency Squad and worked with the Lower Bucks County United Way.

Augie Everitt was preceded in death by his wife only a few months before he passed. He was survived by two sons and grandchildren, and was buried in Our Lady of Grace Cemetery in Humeville, PA.

Frank Facenda

Francis C. Facenda passed away at the age of 84 on November 6, 2008 in Westville, NJ. He born, raised and lived in Philadelphia until he was married and moved to Westville in 1951. During the War he was awarded a Purple Heart and a Bronze Star.

Facenda was a member of the VFW, the Disabled American Veterans, the 101st Airborne Association and an honorary lifetime member of the Westville Fire Dept. Before retiring in 1970, he was an expeditor for RCA in Camden for 29 years. He was a founding member of the Westville Little League and stayed involved for 15 years, and also was a Phillies fan.

Frank Facenda was survived by his wife, Mary, and son Vincent, and was buried in Gloucester County Veterans Memorial Cemetery in Williamstown, NJ.

John M. Faulk

John M. Faulk passed away at the age of 83 on Saturday, March 12, 2005 at Eagle Creek Health & Rehab in Indianapolis, IN. During the War he was awarded a Purple Heart and a Bronze Star, and then returned home to Indianapolis. Faulk worked part-time at Wackenhut Security for 20 years, was a boiler mechanic at Indianapolis Public Schools for 38 years and also worked part-time at the Indianapolis Motor Speedway for 40 years. He was a member of the Calvary Tabernacle.

John Faulk was survived by his wife, five sons, a daughter, 20 grandchildren and 23 great-grandchildren, and was buried in Floral Park Cemetery in Indianapolis.

Thomas J. Ferkler

Tom Ferkler passed away on May 6, 2007, in Lansdowne. PA. He was survived by his wife of 44 years, Eileen, three children and ten grandchildren.

Roy Joe Finnell

Roy Joe Finnell, a veteran who served in the 506th, and who became an Episcopal priest, passed away at the age of 85 on December 24, 2007, at Hospice House in Kansas City, MO. Born on January 31, 1922, near Keytesville, MO, he was the only son of the William Roy and Lilah May (Vance). In 1942, he enlisted in the Army and volunteered for the Airborne and was assigned to the 506th.

A participant in D-Day, Sergeant Finnell was severely wounded in combat near Ste. Mere Eglise, and he was evacuated to the US. For his actions and wounds, he was awarded the Purple Heart, Bronze Star, and the Combat Infantry Badge. In 1946, he was joined in the US by his wife, June King-Hall, of London, England, and their baby daughter, Felicity.

After his discharge, he graduated from Cleveland Chiropractic College in Kansas City, MO, and he then opened a chiropractic practice in Independence, MO. In 1957, he went to work for the Bendix Corporation, where he worked for the next thirty years in quality control.

While he had an active business career, Dr. Finnell was a deeply-religious man, and he was ordained an Episcopal priest in 1988. He served in the Western Missouri diocese, including in his home parish of Trinity Church in Independence. Dr. Finnell was an avid golfer, gardener, and bird watcher.

Following the death of his wife, June, in 1987, he remarried and was survived by his second wife, Gayle, and daughters Felicity and Antoinette and son David Finnell, stepson Jeffrey and stepdaughter Barbara. He also had seven grandchildren, three stepgrandchildren, and two great- grandchildren.

Dominick E. Fiore Jr.

Dominick E. Fiore Jr. passed away at the age of 81 on Thursday, May 5, 2005 at the VNA Hospice at St. Luke's in Fountain Hill, PA. He was born on March 28, 1924, in Middletown, PA to Dominick and Ersilia. During the War, he served with the 101st and earned a Good Conduct Medal.

Fiore was a retired therapy aide at the Middletown Psychiatric Center, a member of the Washington Heights Fire Company and president of the Residents Council at Holy Family Manor Nursing Home in Bethlehem, PA. He was an avid Yankees and NASCAR fan, and was a talented bowler.

Dominick Fiore was survived by his wife of 58 years, Grace, three sons, eight grandchildren and four great-grandchildren, and was buried in Wallkill Cemetery in Phillipsburg, PA.

James Edgecombe (Jim) Fiske

Jim Fiske passed away at the age of 86 on July 8, 2007 Tucson, AZ after a long illness.

Fiske was born in Oakland, CA, to Albert and Helen on July 10, 1921. He served with the 101st during the War and was wounded severely after jumping into Normandy, earning him a Purple Heart. His injury had an upside: while in the hospital in England, he met his future wife Joan and they married on October 24, 1945.

After the War, Fiske was a long-time international sales representative for Robert Shaw Controls until retiring in 1987. He and his wife loved to travel in their RV, and spent their summers as volunteers for the National Park Service, living in Tucson, AZ at The Voyager RV Resort during the winters. Fiske volunteered at El Dorado Hospital for 14 years until he fell ill. Also, he was a member of the Masonic order - F. A & M., Acacia Lodge #243, Hayward, California and the American Legion.

Jim Fiske was survived by his wife of 61 years, Joan, a daughter and a son, as well as several grandchildren and great-grandchildren.

John A. Fitzgerald

John Fitzgerald, passed away at the age of 86 on April 24, 2007, in Stockton, CA after suffering a stroke. He was born on January 16, 1921 in Stockton, and graduated from Stockton

High in 1939. During the War, he earned two Bronze Stars while serving with the 101st.

After the war, he returned home and started Fitzgerald Printing Co. in his parents' basement. He ended up selling the company to his business partner, and it was renamed Snyder Lithograph.

Fitzgerald was a member of the Morning Star Masons for over 65 yrs, a 32nd degree member of Scottish Rite for over 60 years, one of the original members of Stockton Chapter 19 Parents Without Partners; the founder and lifetime member of Stockton Singles and a former member of South Stockton Lions Club. He enjoyed dove and duck hunting, country western music and dancing at the Stockton Singles. John Fitzgerald was survived by a son, a daughter and two grandchildren.

William G. "Bill" Fleck

Bill Fleck passed away at the age of 83 on Wednesday, September 21, 2005 in Hobart, IN. He was a graduate of Hobart High School and a graduate of the School of Banking at the University of Wisconsin. Fleck received the Bronze Star during the War.

He retired in 1983 from Gary National Bank as Comptroller after 36 years, and was past President of Northern Indiana Chapter of National Bank and Comptroller's Association, past President of Northern Indiana Chapter of American Institute of Banking, a member and Past Commander of American Legion Post 54 and past Treasurer of Phi Delta Kappa Fraternity. In addition, he was a member of St. Bridget Church in Hobart, past member of St. Bridget Church Parrish Council, and past Finance Chairman of St. Bridget Church.

Bill Fleck was preceded in death by his wife, Jayne, in January, 2005, and was survived by a son, daughter, six grandchildren and a great-grandson, and was buried at Hobart Cemetery.

Roland A. Foerch

Roland A. Foerch, known to his friends as "Sarge," passed away at the age of 82 on April 6, 2008, at Bay Medical Center in Panama City, FL. Born on March 4, 1926, in Lansing, Mich., he moved to Panama City in 1958. Sarge Foerch was a drill sergeant and then a First Sergeant with the 82nd and the 101st in World War II and during the Korean War.

After he retired from the Army, he bought a boat, and he chartered it out for fishing trips and had the marketing slogan of, "if you don't catch anything, then the next trip is free." In addition to the fish charters, he was also a foreman for Mike Anderson's Construction.

He also constructed a sailboat made entirely out of cement, and after four years of work, he sailed it successfully. He named the boat "Sea-Ment," and it is still used today.

Roland Foerch was survived by his wife of 60 years, Elizabeth, a daughter and two sons, four grandchildren and seven great-grandchildren.

Eugene Ford

Eugene Ford passed away at the age of 95 at 1 PM at Regional Medical Center in Madisonville, KY. He was born Nov. 26, 1912, in Hopkins County, KY to Frank and Margaret. He served with the 101st during the War and was awarded a Purple heart and he was a life member of VFW Post No. 5480 in Madisonville, KY, American Legion Post No. 6, Earlington American Legion Post No. 2 and the 101st Airborne Division Association.

Ford came home and worked as a coal miner until he retired. He was preceded in death by his wife, Hattie, on

January 22, 1992, and survived by three sons, two stepdaughters, a stepson, and several grandchildren, great-grandchildren and great-great-grandchildren; and several nieces and nephews. Eugene Ford was buried with military honors in New Salem Cemetery in Nortonville.

Thomas C. Fracassi

Thomas Fracassi passed away on Wednesday, July 25, 2007 at the Veterans Affairs Medical Center in West Palm Beach, FL. He was a member of the 501st Regiment and served in Normandy, Holland and during the Battle of the Bulge. He lived in Niagara Falls, NY before moving to Florida and was survived by his wife Mary. Thomas Fracassi was buried with military honors in St. Joseph Cemetery, Niagara Falls NY.

Russell J. Franke

Russell J. Franke passed away on Friday, September 28, 2007 at the age of 87. Born on January 7, 1920 to Arthur and Anna, he graduated from Lincoln High School in Manitowoc, WI in 1937. During the War, he served with the 327th Glider Infantry Regiment of the 101st.

On September 1, 1948 he married Eleanore A. Kozaczuk and he graduated from the University of Wisconsin-Madison in 1950. Franke worked for the Allen-Bradley Co. in Milwaukee for 32 years until he retired in 1982.

Russell Franke was predeceased by his wife, and survived by a daughter and a son and five grandchildren, as well as two great grandsons, and was buried in Evergreen Cemetery in Manitowoc, WI.

Carl Worley Franklin

Carl Worley Franklin passed away at the age of 87 on Thursday, Nov. 22, 2007, in Tyler, TX. Franklin was born Aug. 26,

1920, in Winchester, TN to Worley and Elsen, and after the War, he worked for Southwestern Bell for 34 years before retiring. Franklin was a member of the Church of Christ and the Holly Lake Men's Golf Association, served as a scoutmaster in Fort Worth and was a Junior Achievement leader. Carl Franklin was survived by his wife, Maudell, four sons, 11 grandchildren and one great-grandchild.

Jerome Frazes

Jerome Frazes, passed away on September 9, 2007 in Illinois. Frazes was a cantor of the B'nai Torah Congregation in Highland Park, IL for 36 years. He was survived by his wife of 56 years, Clare, two children and four grandchildren. Cantor Jerome Frazes was buried in Memorial Park Cemetery, Skokie, IL.

Gordon S. Friar

Gordon Friar passed away at the age of 86 on Friday, February 22, 2008, in Chattanooga, TN. Friar was a lifelong resident of Chattanooga and was captured and held as a prisoner during World War II. He received the Purple Heart, the Bronze Star, and several other medals.

After returning home, he was the owner and operator of Friars Drive Inn and Restaurant for many years, was an iron worker for several local companies and one in Saudi Arabia, and was a member of the American Legion and the VFW.

He was preceded in death by his wife, Mildred, and survived by several nieces and nephews. Gordon Friar was buried with military honors in the Chattanooga National Cemetery.

Jack E. Galt

Jack E. Galt passed away of natural causes at the age of 84 on September 8, 2007 in Great Falls, MT. Galt was born in

Geyser, MT on April 18, 1923, the fifth child of Errol and Florence, and attended schools in Geyser and Great Falls, graduating from the Ursuline Academy. He graduated from Montana State College, though his college years were interrupted when he enlisted in the Army during World War II. He served in the 101st as a medic and saw action in Holland and the Battle of the Bulge.

After he returned from the War, he completed college and became a cattle buyer and ranch manager for Wertheimer Cattle Co. of South St. Paul, MN until the late 1960s. Galt married Theresa McBride in 1951. He divorced and later married Louise Rankin in 1967. He and Louise were ranchers in south central and eastern Montana.

Long active in Montana politics, Galt served as a Republican in the state House of Representatives in 1973 and 1974, and then in the state Senate from 1975 to 1989. During his 18-year legislative career he played a major role in agriculture, water and land issues. Later, he served several terms as a Republican national committeeman for Montana and was on the executive board of the state party.

Jack Galt was survived by his wife of 40 years, Louise, seven children, and many grandchildren and great-grandchildren. He was buried on the 71 Ranch, in Martinsdale, MT.

Joseph Gambino

Joseph Gambino passed away at the age of 82 on February 1, 2006 at Jordan Hospital in Plymouth, MA after a long fight with heart disease. His life was so accomplished and rich, that the Boston Globe's obituary about him was over 1400 words long.

Gambino's parents were Sicilian immigrants who settled in South Boston, and he attended South Boston High School, graduating in 1941. While in school, he met Catherine Fitzgerald, and they were married in 1942.

He enlisted in 1943, and with his wife expecting, Gambino volunteered to be a paratrooper for the extra pay, and he joined the 101st in time to jump into Normandy on D-Day. During Market-Garden, he was temporarily paralyzed in Eindhoven by a bomb blast and was awarded a Purple Heart, although he was able to return to his unit within several days. Family members said in his obituary that Gambino felt that he cheated death several times and that every day of his life was a gift.

When he returned to Boston, Gambino got on the list to be a Boston policeman, attracted by the job security, which appealed to him living through the Depression. He spent a year working on the fish pier until his name came up on the waiting list, and he entered the Boston police force. He was assigned to Station 11, in the Fields Corner section of Dorchester, and he moved his family near the station house, and they frequently saw him riding by when he became a motorcycle officer. Gambino was involved in a number of notorious arrests, including that of Elmer "Trigger" Burke, who was a hit man tied up in the Brink's robbery.

At night, Gambino studied and got a job with the state as an inspector of food and pharmaceuticals, but he had to retire in his 50s when he suffered a heart attack. In retirement, he focused mostly on his family, and he talked very little of his experiences during the war.

Joseph Gambino's wife of 61 years, Catherine, preceded him in death in 2003. He was survived by three daughters, two sons, 14 grandchildren and seven great-grandchildren and was buried in Mayflower Cemetery in Duxbury.

William "Dee" (Bill) Gammon

William "Dee" (Bill) Gammon, passed away at the age of 88 on April 10, 2008 at his home near Las Cruces, NM, surrounded by his family, after a lengthy battle with Alzheimer's Disease.

Gammon was born on April 25, 1919, to W.W. "Bill" and Nora (Pinckard) Gammon in Alma, AR, and attended Sophie Meyer Grade School and Van Buren High School. Bill Gammon was distinguished from many Screaming Eagles because he enlisted in the Army in 1938, not after the outbreak of war. He was stationed at Fort Sill, Okla., as part of the 18th Field Artillery Unit, and he reenlisted in the Army after Pearl Harbor, and volunteered for the paratroopers.

He parachuted into Normandy on D-Day and into Holland during Market-Garden, and was with the Screaming Eagles in Bastogne, as a sergeant. He was awarded a parachutist's badge, and an artillery insignia, as well as the American Defense Medal, American Theater Medal, European Theater Medal, the World War II Victory Medal and the Occupation Forces Medal from Germany.

Gammon was discharged from the Army for the second time in 1945 and worked in the missile fields at Fort Worth and El Paso, Texas, and retired in 1980. He was a lifetime member of the 101st Airborne Division Association and a member of the TALON Chapter.

Bill Gammon was survived by his wife of 35 years, Linda Anderson Gammon, his son, Geoffrey, his step-daughters Sara and Sandra Swann, and his step-son James. He was also survived by 12 grandchildren

Lee Gardner

Lee Gardner passed away on July 6, 2007 at the age of 84 in Hollywood, FL. Lee and his twin brother Hy were born on May 9, 1923 in New York City to Alex and Tillie. During World War II, he participated in D-Day and the Battle of the Bulge.

After the War, Gardner became a very successful business executive. He was the founder of Kady Industries, and in 1957 started Dyno Merchandise Corp. which became one of the largest sewing notion businesses in the U.S. Gardner's company became the leading national distributor for the Singer Company, and it was ultimately sold to Conagra.

In 1977, he moved to Florida and lived in the Ft. Lauderdale/Hollywood area. Lee Gardner was survived by his wife, Harriett, two daughters, two sons, four grandchildren and two great-grandchildren. He was buried in Beth David Cemetery in Hollywood, FL.

Bernard T. Gaudreau

Bernard Gaudreau passed away at the age of 83 on June 19, 2007, at Penacook Place in Haverhill, MA. He was born in Haverhill on May 31, 1924 to Arthur and Catherine Gaudreau.

Gaudreau served with the 101st from 1942-45 and participated in D-Day. He was injured twice during the War and returned to duty both times, and was the recipient of a Purple Heart and a Bronze Star.

After the War, he returned to Haverhill, and spent the rest of his life in the area. He worked as a supervisor at Western Electric, and retired in 1987. He spent his retirement with his family enjoying their beach house in Maine and cooking blueberry pancake breakfasts for his grandchildren.

Bernard Gaudreau was survived by his wife of 59 years, Eleanor, two daughters, a son, six grandchildren and four great-grandchildren, and was buried in Elmwood Cemetery in Bradford, MA.

Maurice Ghnassia

Maurice Jean-Henri Ghnassia passed away at the age of 82, at his home in Cullowhee, NC on January 4, 2003, after a long illness. He was born in Paris on July 23, 1920, to Ichoa and

Esther, and he was a leader in the French Resistance during the German occupation of France. Ghnassia commanded a group of Francs-Tireurs, and after the liberation of southern France, he became a paratrooper attached to the 101st Airborne. His regiment was commanded by the late senator from North Carolina, Terry Sanford.

After the War he completed his studies at the University of Paris, and he would go on to be a disc jockey known as "Mr. Blues." Ghnassia had a jazz radio program in France, and eventually became a press correspondent for France Observateur and Europe No. 1 to the United Nations and the White House in the 1950s and 1960s. In the 1970s, he was the media manager for the American Institute of Certified Public Accountants and produced an award-winning documentary film, "A Profession Integrates."

He continued his unusual career by moving to New York, NY and Windsor, CT Ghnassia translated the "Peanuts" books by Charles Schultz into French. He also was a was a professor of Western heritage at the University of Hartford until his retirement in 2000, and wrote three best-selling novels, "Un Dimanche Pour Pleurer," "Foule aux Dames" and "Arena," as well as a number of short stories and poems. He was a member of the Author's Guild, Societe des Auteurs et Compositeurs, the Connecticut Academy of the Arts and Sciences and the Alliance Francaise de Hartford.

Maurice Jean-Henri Ghnassia was preceded in death by one son, and survived by his wife, Jill, and was buried in Harmony Cemetery in Milton, PA.

Donald C. Gill Sr.

Donald C. Gill, Sr. passed away at the age of 85 in Glenview, IL. Gill was married for 65 years to Lois Sullivan, and had three children and four grandchildren.

Justine "Tony" A. Gorniak Sr.

Tony Gorniak, Sr. passed away at the age of 84 on March 22, 2008 at his home in Fort Atkinson, WI. He was born in Chicago, IL on September 26, 1923 to Agnatius and Mary Gorniak, and during the War received a number of decorations including a Good Conduct Medal.

Gorniak married Josephine M. Van Hooydonk in Belgium on Sept. 8, 1945, and the two of them returned to the US and raised a family. Josephine preceded him in death on July 30, 2002, and he was also predeceased by a son. However, he was survived by seven children, 21 grandchildren and many great-grandchildren. Tony Gorniak was buried in Evergreen Cemetery in Fort Atkinson.

Wilford James Grant

Wilford James Grant passed away at the age of 84 on January 8, 2007 at St. Clair Hospital in Pittsburgh, PA. He suffered from dementia the last five years of his life and lived in the Beverly Healthcare Mt. Lebanon Manor nursing home.

Grant parachuted into Normandy on D-Day and landed in two feet of water. He also dropped into Holland during Market-Garden, and was wounded by shrapnel from a German artillery attack during the Battle of the Bulge.

He returned to civilian life and worked for the Department of Defense facility on Neville Island, repairing and servicing missiles and artillery. Grant dedicated a significant amount of time to community service, as a volunteer firefighter and Boy Scout leader, and with an animal shelter and local river cleanup. He was willing to talk about his war experiences, but only after someone else initiated the conversation.

Wilford Grant was survived by his wife, Rose, two daughters and six grandchildren, and was buried in the National Cemetery of the Alleghenies in Washington County, PA.

LeRoy Gros

LeRoy Gros passed away at the age of 84 on June 4, 2008 in New Iberia, LA. A native of Labadieville, LA, he served in Company C of the 506th's 1st Battalion, and participated in every major campaign of the 101st, and was awarded multiple decorations including a Purple Heart and a Bronze Star.

He came home from Europe and had a 36-year career with Texaco as a superintendent. He lived in the town of New Iberia for many years, and was buried in Holy Family Cemetery there. LeRoy Gros was preceded in death by his wife, Lilly, and a grandchild, and was survived by four children, several grandchildren and two great-grandchildren.

Stanley Gruber

Stanley Gruber passed away at the age of 82 on November 7, 2001, at his home in Brookline, MA. Gruber was born in Newton, MA, where he attended Newton High School. Later, he attended Colby College where he lettered in three sports, and graduated in the class of 1941. He was wounded in Normandy and spent some time working for the Veterans Administration. Later, he founded several banks in New England, including the North Quincy Co-operative Bank and Chestnut Hill Co-operative Bank. Stanley Gruber was survived by his wife of 47 years, Esther, two daughters and six grandchildren.

Adolphe G. Gueymard

Adolph Gueymard passed away on December 8, 2008 at the age of 95 in Houston, TX. He was a native of St. Gabriel, LA and graduated from LSU in 1935, with a degree in Petroleum

Engineering. He was in the third glider to land in Normandy on D-Day, and was the recipient of two Bronze Stars.

He served as Senior Vice President and Manager of the Energy Division of First City National Bank of Houston until his retirement in 1973. In his retirement, he served on many boards of directors including Zapata Corporation, Camco, Inc., First City National Bank, Harrisburg Bank and Maxwell Laboratories.

He remained dedicated to his alma mater and established the Gueymard Professorship in Geology and Geophysics at LSU. In 2000, he was inducted into the LSU Alumni Hall of Distinction and in 2006, into the LSU Basic Sciences Hall of Distinction.

He was preceded in death by his wife, Josephine, and was survived by many nephews and nieces. Adolph Gueymard was buried in the St. Gabriel (LA) Church Cemetery.

Harry A. Haas

Harry "Bud" Haas passed away at the age of 80 on May 21, 2005. Bud Haas was born on Dec. 31, 1924, in RR1 Klingerstown, PA, to Harry and Helen, and was a 1941 graduate of Hegins Township High School.

Haas was a staff sergeant in the 101st Airborne Division, and fought in Normandy and at Bastogne. He was awarded four bronze stars and Good Conduct Medal, among other distinctions.

Bud was a retired chicken farmer and co-owner and operator of the former Haas Brothers Feed Mill, RR1 Klingerstown. He was a lifelong member of the Salem United Church of Christ Church, Klingerstown, where he was a former deacon, elder, and Sunday school superintendent. In addition, he was also a member of Disabled American Veterans, and the Veterans and Foreign Wars and American Legion, an avid Phillies fan, enjoyed playing cards and visited the sick.

Harry Haas was survived by two daughters, five grandchildren and two great-granddaughters, and was buried with military honors in the Salem Cemetery in Klingerstown, PA.

George Haddy

George Haddy of Mason City, IA, passed away at the age of 78 on December 20, 1996 at the North Iowa Mercy Health Center. He was born on Dec. 27, 1917 to Michael and Andora in Scarville. The family, moved to Mason City in 1926 and again to Kansas. However, the family returned to Mason City where he graduated from City High School in 1937.

Haddy worked for Jacob E. Decker until 1942 when he joined that Army and volunteered as a paratrooper. He was assigned to the 101st Division and jumped into Normandy on D-Day.

Following the War, he married Lucille Haddy in 1946 in Los Angeles, CA, and the two spent 38 years together until she passed away in 1984. Haddy owned and operated a grocery store and restaurant for several years and also worked in Los Angeles. In 1990, He married Lucille Nassiff in Los Angeles and then moved to Mason City to retire.

He was a member of the Clausen-Worden Post #101 of Mason City, John Grantus American Legion Post in Lost Angeles, 101st Airborne Division Association and Syrian Antiochian Orthodox Church in Los Angeles. He also was president of the Mason City Senior Chamber of Commerce.

George Haddy was survived by his second his wife, Lucille, a son, four step-children, and 11 step grandchildren. He was buried at the Forest Lawn Hollywood Hills Cemetery, in Hollywood, CA.

Wilbur Haight

Wilbur J. Haight, a Screaming Eagle veteran passed away at the age of 75 on February 18, 2001 at St. Mary's Hospital in Amsterdam, NY. Haight lived in the town of Broadalbin and was a resident of that town and Amsterdam for his whole life. After the war, he returned to Amsterdam and worked for the rubber mill at Collette Manufacturing Co. for 25 years before working for Mohawk Finishing, from which he retired.

Dr. Oliver Handelsman

Dr. Oliver Handelsman passed away in Pittsburgh, PA at the age of 88 on September 21, 2006. He was born on September 20, 1918 and was a major in the 101st during World War II. After the War, he attended the University of Pittsburgh Medical School on the GI Bill and in 1950, graduated at the top of his class and went into general practice.

He spent 46 years practicing medicine at University of Pittsburgh Medical Center - Braddock, retiring in 1997. He had offices in different parts of the Pittsburgh area, and worked long hours, keeping his office open until 1 AM even at the time of his retirement. Throughout his career, he was known for anonymously delivering clothing and food to the doorsteps of patients he knew needed help, and providing medical care for free.

Dr. Handelsman met his wife of 52 years, Claire Brenner, when she brought her father in for a doctor's visit. As the story goes, Dr. Handelsman required Mr. Brenner to make multiple follow-up visits so he could have a reason to see Claire.

Oliver Handelsman was survived by his wife, Claire, three sons and five grandchildren, and was buried in Temple Sinai Cemetery.

Fayez Handy

Fayez Handy passed away at the age of 84 on January 13, 2008 in Bakersfield, CA. He was born in Bakersfield on December 19, 1923 and attended Lincoln and Washington Junior High and graduated from East High in 1941. He joined the Army in 1942 and volunteered for the paratroopers. He was wounded in both Normandy and Holland and received the Purple Heart with the Oak Leaf Cluster.

He married Dolores Kesterson in 1949 and had six children, and farmed in the Arvin and Lamont areas of California for over 50 years until the passing of his son Rocky. After Rocky's death, Fayez retired and moved to Bakersfield, where he enjoyed working in his garden and reminiscing about World War II. Fayez Handy was survived by five children, 16 grandchildren and 13 great- grandchildren.

Warren T. Ward" Hanna, Sr.

Warren T. ``Ward" Hanna Sr. a member of the 506th, passed away at the age of 87 on June 21, 2007 at his home in Framingham, MA. He was born in Natick, MA to Thomas A. and Eva (Lutz) Hanna.

Hanna was a graduate of Natick High School, where he was a distinguished athlete. He was captain of the football and golf teams and a member of the hockey team. He also served as a swimming instructor and guard for the Red Cross. After high school, he enlisted in the Army and volunteered for the paratroops and he joined the 506th in time for its' march to Atlanta.

Hanna was an inventor and a tinkerer and while in the military, was granted a patent on a quick-release parachute harness that was specifically designed for use when a paratrooper ended up in a tree. During his military service, he suffered significant hearing loss.

He returned home and graduated from the Rhode Island Institute of Technology, where he trained for a career in heating, venting and air conditioning systems. In 1960, he founded Worcester Air Conditioning Co., which became one of the largest HVAC businesses in the northeastern US. Then in 1986, he founded Hard of Hearing Advocates, a nonprofit designed to provide advocacy for hard-of-hearing people.

Ward Hanna was survived by his wife, Patricia, three sons and two grandchildren.

Lt. Col. Harold W. "Hank" Hannah

Harold "Hank" Hannah passed away at the age of 90 on November, 20, 2001 at Crossroads Community Hospital in Mt. Vernon, IL. Hannah was the son of a central Illinois tenant farmer, and was educated at country grade schools and at Monticello, IL Community High School. He attended the University of Illinois colleges of Agriculture and Law, and enlisted in the Army in World War II.

Hannah volunteered for the paratroopers and rose to the rank of Lieutenant Colonel and was General Taylor's G-3. Hannah served in Normandy and in Holland during Operation Market-Garden. During the Market-Garden campaign, Hannah was wounded severely at St. Oedenrode, and was replaced by Harry Kinnard. After spending a considerable amount of time in the hospital, Hannah retired from the military a year later with disability.

Hannah returned to the University of Illinois and was placed in charge of their veterans program, and also was responsible for establishing an agriculture university in India 1955-57. He directed other projects in Nigeria and Michigan, and published a series of articles on agricultural and veterinary law, and for many years authored a regular column in the Journal of the American Veterinary Medical Association. Eventually, he became assistant to the dean, associate dean, and professor of agriculture and veterinary law, and his career at the University lasted 61 years.

He married Verna "Bowie" Buffinger Webb on June 5, 1965, in Mt. Vernon, IL. He had a diverse group of hobbies, including sawmilling, woodworking, vegetable gardening, photography, music, meteorology and nature study. He continued to write throughout his life, including about his military experiences.

Hank Hannah was predeceased by a son, and was survived by his wife, Verna, four children, seven grandchildren; two great-grandchildren, two step-sons and a number of step-grandchildren.

Hugh Harkins Jr.

Hugh Harkins Jr., passed away at the age of 76 on Tuesday, December 1, 1998, in Monongahela Valley Hospital in Carroll Township, PA. Harkins was born April 6, 1922, in Courtney, PA, to Hugh Sr. and Jenny Payne Harkins. He enlisted in the Army and volunteered for the paratroopers and joined the 101st in 1943. He participated in D-Day and was taken prisoner, spending 11 months in a German camp.

Harkins retired in 1971 from U.S. Steel's Gary Works, and then spent several years with Corning Glass Inc. He was a member of Mingo Presbyterian Church in Finleyville, PA, and the American Legion Frank Downer Post 302 and Sutman Yohe Veterans of Foreign Wars Post 1409 of Monongahela, PA and enjoyed hunting and fishing.

Hugh Harkins was survived by his wife, Lucille Thomas, to whom he was married for 55 years, and three sons, eight grandchildren and four great-grandchildren.

Richard H. Harms

Richard H. Harms, passed away at 82 on June 8, 2000 in St. Luke's Hospital in Maumee, OH due to congestive heart failure. Harms lived in the South Toledo area for most of his life, graduating from Libbey High School in 1936, and before the War worked for Community Traction Co., in a meat packing plant and as a bus driver. He was wounded during World War II but returned home to South Toledo, where he worked and then retired as a municipal worker.

John D. Harrell

John D. Harrell passed away at the age of 88, on July 6, 2004 at Sacred Heart Hospital in Pensacola, FL. Known as a Southern gentleman, he joined the 101st and ended up serving from D-Day to the scaling of the Eagle's Nest. He was a successful local businessman and a civic leader and was survived by his wife of 61 years, Frances.

Marlin W. Havig

Marlin Havig passed away at the age of 89 on Friday, August 18, 2006, at the Osage Rehabilitation and Health Care Center in Osage, IA. He was born on August 15, 1917, in Osage to Martin and Olive and graduated from Osage High School. On August 14, 1940, he married Elaine Kleckner at St. Peter's Catholic Church in New Haven, CT. He was with the 101st during the War, and was wounded on Christmas Eve, 1944 near Bastogne.

He returned home and became a rural mail carrier and retired at the age of 65. Havig was a member of Sacred Heart Catholic Church, Osage American Legion Post 278, Osage V.F.W. Post #7920 and Disabled American Veterans of Mason City, and enjoyed woodworking, fishing and coin collecting.

Marlin Havig was survived by his wife, Elaine, three daughters, a son, seven grandchildren, 13 great-grandchildren, three step-grandchildren and five step great-grandchildren, and was buried with military honors in the Sacred Heart Catholic Church in Osage.

Arthur Hawk

Arthur Allen Hawk, passed away on January 16, 2003 at the age of 78 at his home in Holland Township, PA. Hawk fought in the Battle of the Bulge, and returned home to receive his education. He graduated from Lafayette College in Easton in 1950 with a B.S. degree in mathematics, and then worked for 30 years as math teacher, as well as a football coach at Frenchtown High School and Delaware Valley Regional High School. As an assistant coach, he helped lead his team to a state championship in 1960.

Arthur Hawk was survived by his wife of 53 years, Jacqueline, two daughters and five grandchildren, and was interred at the Northampton Memorial Shrine in Easton, PA.

James A. Haynie

James A. Haynie passed away at the age of 84 on February 12, 2008 at Johns Hopkins Bayview Medical Center in Baltimore, MD from cardiac arrest. He was born, raised and educated in Baltimore and was a glider infantryman with the 101st serving in communications during World War II, and saw action in the Battle of the Bulge.

After returning home to Baltimore, he worked as a bicycle messenger in the Baltimore Street Western Union office delivering telegrams. Later, he joined American District Telegraph Co., a security company that was acquired by Tyco International Ltd., and retired as a supervisor in 1986.

Haynie was a lifelong fire buff and collector of fire memorabilia, and in the 1940s was a founder of the Box 414 Association, a volunteer organization that provided food and coffee to firefighters fighting two-alarm or bigger fires. James Haynie was survived by his wife of 54 years, Joyce.

Clark R. Heggeness

Clark Richard Heggeness passed away at the age of 86 in May 2007 in Long Beach, CA. He was born the son of Norwegian immigrants on November 3, 1920 in Fargo, ND, and studied mathematics at North Dakota Agricultural College. During his time in school, he met his future wife, June, and the couple was married in 1943.

After graduating from college in 1942, he enlisted in the Army and volunteered for the paratroopers. He underwent training in Georgia with was commissioned as a lieutenant. He participated in D-Day and in Operation Market Garden and suffered wounds in both campaigns. Heggeness recovered from his wounds in Holland in time for the Battle of the Bulge, during which he earned a third Purple Heart. After another recovery, he rejoined his unit in time to help capture the Eagle's Nest. Heggeness was always proud of his service and remained active in the 101st Airborne alumni association.

Upon returning home, he attended law school at the University of Michigan, and received his law degree in 1948. He then moved to Long Beach, CA with his wife and two young children and joined the law firm of Ball, Hunt & Hart, where he spent the next five decades. As an attorney, he participated in a number of major cases, including the 1966 merger of Atlantic Refining and Richfield Petroleum to form ARCO, was President of the Long Beach Bar Association in 1969 and named Long Beach "Lawyer of the Year" in 1994.

He served on the delegation that brought the Queen Mary to Long Beach, and actively participated in civic and philanthropic organizations in the community, such as the Boy Scouts, the Camp Fire Girls, and the Boys and Girls Clubs, and he served on the Selective Service Board. He was also well-known as a golfer and the Virginia Country Club passed a rule prohibiting golfers from swimming in the club's lake as a response to his antics.

Clark Heggeness was survived by his wife, June, seven children, 14 grandchildren and seven great-grandchildren.

Richard P. Hemmerdinger, Sr.

Richard P. Hemmerdinger passed away at the age of 85 at his home in Woburn, MA. He was born in Boston to Cora and Harold and graduated from Medford High School in 1936. Afterwards, he attended Middlesex Veterinary Academy for three years, interrupting his studies to serve in the Army for five years with the 101st.

Hemmerdinger returned home to raise his family with his Anna. They lived in Medford, MA for before moving to Woburn, and he worked as a quality control inspector at GE in Lynn. He and his wife then started a business called The Pampered Pet Shop, which they ran for forty years.

Richard Hemmerdinger was predeceased by his wife Anna, who passed in 1992, and was survived by his three sons, two daughters, nine grandchildren and seven great grandchildren.

Arthur C. "Art" Hensell

Art Hensell passed away on November 11, 2007 at the age of 79 in Kalamazoo, MI. He was born on March 28, 1928 in Kalamazoo to Clyde and Letha. He continued to serve as a paratrooper after the war, and was stationed in Japan from 1946 to 1947. Afterwards, he worked for Sutherland/James River Paper for 42 years.

Hensell was preceded in death by his wife Arlene, and by a son. He remarried and was survived by his second wife, Ann, as well as three children, four grandchildren and five great-grandchildren. Art Hensell was buried in Ft. Custer National Cemetery.

Dale C. Henry

Screaming Eagle Dale C. Henry passed away at the age of 90 on April 23, 2007, in Fort Worth, TX. He was born Aug. 28, 1916, in New Vienna, OH, to William Martin and Myrtle Eloise Hoskins, and was raised and educated in Jamestown, OH. He served with Screaming Eagles throughout the war, and before he shipped out, he and Ellie Ruth Green were married on July 9, 1942, in Columbus, GA.

After the war, Henry farmed his family's home and was a manager of the grain elevator in Bowersville, in Greene County, Ohio, and later was a HUD housing inspector for the city of Dayton, Ohio. He was known as an excellent horseshoe pitcher and loved dancing.

He was preceded in death by his wife, Ruth, in 2000, and was survived by two sons, three grandchildren and three great-grandchildren. Dale Henry was buried at Italy Cemetery in Italy, TX.

Lewis Keith Herbold

Lewis Keith Herbold passed away at the age of 83 surrounded by his family, on January 16, 2008, at Evergreen Hospital in Kirkland, WA. He was an only child, born in Warren, OH on January 31, 1924. He lived in Montclair, CA before moving to Lynnwood, WA in 1991. Herbold loved fishing, the Seattle Mariners, golfing and the outdoors, was an avid reader and loved to spend time at the Edmonds Pier. Lewis Herbold was survived by his former wife, four children, eight grandchildren and eleven great-grandchildren.

John B. Hickman Jr.

John B. Hickman Jr. died at the age of 83 on March 25, 2008 from complications of emphysema at Methodist Charlton Medical Center in Dallas, TX. Born and raised in Texarkana,

AR, Hickman joined the Army in 1943 and was 19 when he jumped into Normandy on D-Day. Like many of paratroopers, Hickman landed way off target and it took him days to rejoin his unit. He served through Market-Garden, Bastogne and all the way into Germany and Austria. During the war, he was a radio technician and, this skill served him well in one of his first post-war jobs, as a late-night radio engineer and announcer for KSAM-AM in Huntsville, TX. He moved to the northern part of the state and for a while attended Texas Christian University.

Eventually, Hickman joined Mobil Oil Company, where he worked until he retired in December 1987. He was self-taught on a number of subjects, and he rose from a purchasing position to a master technician and he helped research nuclear well-logging tools. In his obituary, he was lauded by one of the physicists and engineers who worked with him for 25 years as a man who could fix anything, even when others were stumped.

Hickman was known for his sense of humor and for receiving the Silver Beaver in honor of 21 years as a Boy Scout leader.

John Hickman was survived by his wife, Joanna, a son and a daughter, two sisters, a brother, seven grandchildren and four great-grandchildren, and was buried at Dallas-Fort Worth National Cemetery.

George J. Hodge

George Hodge passed away at 87 on Sunday, October 28, 2007 in Shawnee KS. Hodge was born on February 12, 1925, in Tuscumbia, MO to Harvey and Lena, and was the oldest of three sons. During the Great Depression, his family lost their farm and his father could not find steady work, and they lived in a shanty house in Eldon, MO. At age 17, he joined the Civilian Conservation Corps (CCC), and was sent to the Lake of the

Ozarks State Park, where he did park maintenance, built a Girl Scouts Camp and roofed cabins.

On December 3, 1942, Hodge enlisted in the Army and became a member of Company A of the 502nd Parachute Regiment. On leave, he married the love of his life, Faye Kennedy, on May 12, 1943, and one week later he shipped out to Europe. He would not return to Faye for 28 months, finally getting home in December 1945.

Hodge's experience on D-Day did not start well. Misdropped into the middle of a German infantry regiment that was dug in along the shore, he was held captive for several days until soldiers of the 4th Infantry Division liberated him. Hodge was able to rejoin his unit and fought in Normandy, Holland and Bastogne. During the Battle of the Bulge, he suffered frostbite on his feet and hands, and lived with complications for the rest of his life.

He retired after working the electric furnace at Sheffield Steel/Armco Steel for more than 40 years. George and Faye lost their first child, Sharon, who was born in September 1946 and survived only nine days. However, they had two more daughters and they bought their first home in northeast Johnson County in 1950.

George Hodge was preceded in death by his wife, Faye, and was survived by his daughters, six grandchildren and 10 great grandchildren.

Robert Lee "Bob" Hoffman

Bob Hoffman passed away at the age of 78 on December 2, 2004 at the Big Bend Care Center in St. Louis, MO. He was born to Elmer and Mina and spent many years in Dexter, MO, where he attended Dexter High School. Later he attended Washington University. He was survived by his wife, Virginia, two sons and three grandchildren. Bob Hoffman was buried in the Jefferson Barracks National Cemetery in St. Louis, the same place where Lt. Tom Meehan lies.

Sammie N. Homan

Colonel Sammie N. Homan passed away at the age of 70 at Walter Reed Army Hospital on May 9, 1989. He was born in Alabama on March 12, 1919 and enlisted in the Army in 1940, receiving his commission later that year. During World War II, he was an officer in 501st Regiment, jumping into Normandy and Holland. During the Battle of the Bulge, Homan let the 2nd Battalion of the 501st and it was his unit that engaged the Germans on Hill 510.

Homan served as a battalion commander and regimental executive officer with the 2nd Infantry Division during the Korean War, and in the 1960s was a senior military adviser to a South Vietnamese Army corps. He also was a regimental commander with the 11th Airborne Division before retiring in 1965, when he was a bureau chief in the Army Combat Development Command at Fort Belvoir. Homan was a 1961 graduate of the University of Maryland, and also of the Army Command and General Staff College and the Army War College.

During his illustrious career, he received many citations, including the Legion of Merit, four Bronze Stars, the Purple Heart, the Master Parachutist Badge and the Combat Infantryman's Badge with Star, and had made 130 jumps.

Sammie Homan was survived by his wife, Sarah, three sons, two daughters and seven grandchildren and was buried in Arlington National Cemetery at Section 66, site 3964.

Wade Eldon Horn

Wade Eldon Horn passed away at the age of 92 on October 5, 2007 in Lakeland, FL. He was born in Princeton, MO on December 8, 1914 to John and Adjia Mae. Horn was a Purchasing Agent for the state of Missouri and after 16 years of service, moved to Lakeland in 1973. After moving to Lakeland he worked for the Polk County School Board as a purchasing agent as well. He was a member of the Masonic Lodge #43 in Jefferson City, MO also a member of the VFW in Fayette, MO and the Victory Church in Lakeland. Wade Horn was preceded in death by his wife of 68 years, Mildred, and was survived by his daughter, son and granddaughter.

John Herman Hubble

John Hubble passed away at the age of 86 on February 14th, 2008 at his home in Brownsburg, IN. He was born April 11, 1921 in Marion, VA to John and Helen, who moved the family a short while later to Beech Grove.

While serving with the 101st, he was seriously wounded in England, and after the War, returned home to earn his B.A. from Butler University and a Masters from Indiana University. Hubble was a teacher and administrator in the Indianapolis Public School System until he retired in 1985.

John Hubble was survived by his wife of 62 years, Nellie, two daughters, nine grandchildren and twenty great-grandchildren, and was buried in Orchard Hill Cemetery

Ernest C. Hurt Jr.

Ernest C. Hurt passed away at the age of 83 on December 18, 2005 in Highland, IN.

He was a graduate of Hammond High School and also of Ball State and served with the 101st during D-Day, Market-Garden and the Battle of the Bulge. After the war, he was a teacher in Hammond and Highland for 38 years.

He was a member of the First Christian Church "Disciples of Christ" of Highland, and loved playing baseball with the

Hammond Braves. Ernest Hurt was survived by his wife of 59 years, Juanita, two sons, two daughters, five grandchildren and six great-grandchildren.

Hubert "Hub" B. Jauquet

Hub Jauquet, passed away at the age of 87 at his Green Bay, WI home on March 28, 2008, after a short illness. Jauquet was born on June 27, 1920 to Frank and Clara (Collard) Jauquet. He served in the Army from August 1940 to September 1945 and fought in every major campaign involving the 101st Airborne Division. During his service, he received a Bronze Star and four Bronze Battle Stars, and was a proud, active member of the VFW Bellevue Post #9677.

Returning home, he married Marian Goltz on Sept. 25, 1946, and worked in farming, construction and millwork and owned Jauquet's Ceramic Shoppe. After retiring, Hub and Marian moved to Mountain, WI for 18 years, during which he got to spend time with his family and pursue gardening, golfing, bowling, Sudoku puzzles, Milwaukee Brewer games and teaching his grandchildren card games.

Hubert Jauquet was survived by his wife of 61 years, Marian, three sons, four daughters, 13 grandchildren and five great-grandchildren, and his dog, Penny. He was buried in the church cemetery at the Prince of Peace Parish, Holy Martyrs site.

John M. Jarvis

John Jarvis passed away at the age of 80 on February 29, 2008 in Cuyahoga Falls, OH, where he lived for most of his life. He was born in Jarvisville, WV and after the war, worked as a crane operator for Ford Motor Co until he retired in 1987, with 32 years of service at the Walton Hills Plant. He was preceded in death by his wife, Wylodean, and was survived by two sons, a daughter and two granddaughters. John Jarvis was buried in Northlawn Memorial Gardens.

Harold Bentley "Hal" Jeffcoat

Hal Jeffcoat passed away on August 30, 2007, in Tampa, FL at the age of 82. Born on September 6, 1924 to George and Alma, he was an engineer during the War. While in Italy during World War II, he met his future wife of 61 years, Valma, of Gloucester, MA, who was serving in the Women's Auxiliary Army Corps (WAAC).

After the war, Jeffcoat began a very successful 12-year career as a professional baseball player. He was signed by the Chicago Cubs in 1946, and after a brief stint in the minor leagues, was called up to the majors. He played centerfield for the Cubs until 1956, and then for the Cincinnati Reds until 1959, and later completed his major league career with the St. Louis Cardinals. Later in his career, he switched from centerfielder to relief pitcher

Jeffcoat returned to the Cubs organization in 1961 as the manager of the Palatka Cubs of the Florida State League. Following his baseball career, he worked for the Continental Can Co. in Tampa, FL until he retired. He remained a big baseball fan and rooted for the Tampa Bay Rays.

A very religious man, he was a member of Holy Trinity Lutheran Church in Tampa, and served in a number of ministry positions and supported the growth and expansion of the church for more than 50 years. Hal Jeffcoat was survived by his wife, Valma, three sons, two granddaughters, a grandson and two great-granddaughters, and was buried in Florida National Cemetery.

George E. Johnson

George Edward Johnson, passed away at the age of 84 on March 25, 2008 in his Fayetteville, NY home with his wife and family at his side. He was born on September 29, 1923 in Chicago, IL, the fourth of five children. Johnson served with the

101st during the war, and was a First Sergeant during the Battle of the Bulge, eventually retiring from the reserves as a First Lieutenant.

After returning home, he attended and graduated from Northwestern University, where he met his future wife, Caryl Lee. After they married, they moved to Oklahoma and later upstate New York while he worked for Clark Equipment Company. While working at Clark, he met a future business partner, and they together founded Thompson and Johnson Equipment Company, and he worked there for 53 years.

Johnson was active in the community, and served as a member of Rotary International, The Bandits, Gyro International, MHEDA, Sigma Nu (Northwestern chapter), Onondaga Golf & Country Club, Century Club and Turtle Creek Club. The Johnsons maintained additional residences in Old Forge, NY and Jupiter, FL. George Johnson was survived by his wife of 59 years, Caryl, two daughters and four grandchildren.

Philippe Jutras

Philippe Jutras has to be considered an honorary Screaming Eagle after spending three decades as the curator of the Airborne museum in Ste. Mere Eglise. He passed away at the age of 87 on April 4, 2004 at a hospital in Valognes, a town in Normandy, after falling in his home.

Jutras was of French Canadian descent, though he was born in Amesbury, MA and served in the American Army during World War II. He did not participate in D-Day, but he did pass through Ste. Mere Eglise in mid-July, as part of an Army supply unit. In that town, the first liberated on D-Day, Jutras found a parachute in a nearby field and asked a local woman to tailor it into a dress for his daughter, Phyllis, who was 10 months old at the time.

He spent 20 years in the Army and retired and settled in Maine, serving as a state legislator in the 1960's and early

1970's. In 1972, Jutras returned to Ste. Mere Eglise to visit the Castels, a family that housed him during his stay in Normandy. While there he was reacquainted with their daughter, Antoinette. Jutras was divorced and Antoinette was a widow and the two fell in love and two years later, were married.

Jutras moved to Ste. Mere Eglise, and became the unpaid curator of a small D-Day museum that had been built in town about a decade earlier. He vigorously set to work expanding the museum and its collection of artifacts and was instrumental in a big construction project there. Under his leadership, the museum aided its famous C-47 transport, a glider from the invasion, a Sherman tank and extensive artifacts from veterans.

For his work at the museum, Jutras was awarded membership in the Legion of Honor by the French government. He even earned a cameo in the opening scenes of "Saving Private Ryan." Philippe Jutras was survived by his wife, Antoinette, two daughters, four grandchildren and three great-grandchildren.

William Parker "B" Kee

Bill Kee passed away suddenly at his home on May 7, 2007 at the age of 82. He was born in Woburn, MA and lived there his entire life. Born to John and Margaret, he was a graduate of the Woburn High School class of 1943.

After graduation, he joined the Army, volunteered for the paratroops and was assigned to the 101st Airborne Division. He served in the Battle of the Bulge and Germany and was awarded the Bronze Star and the Purple Heart. He had remained a member of the Veterans of Foreign Wars since he was discharged in 1945.

Upon returning from Europe, he received his undergraduate degree and law degree from Suffolk University, and had a distinguished career in the insurance industry, working with Maryland Casualty for ten years and One Beacon Insurance for 26 until retiring in 1989. Kee enjoyed cigars, horse races at Saratoga Springs, cardplaying and volunteer work. Bill Kee was buried in Calvary Cemetery in Woburn.

Joseph Kelly

Joseph Kelly, a veteran of the 101st who served from 1942 to 1945, passed away on August 9, 2002 at the Bellhaven Nursing Home in Bellport, L.I., where he had lived for five years. Spending his entire life in the New York City area, he was born in Brooklyn, and then moved to Stapleton, where he lived for 40 years before finally relocating to West Sayville in the 1970s. Kelly was a retired telephone splicer.

Joseph Kettering

Joseph Kettering passed away in his home near Cleveland, OH on October, 1996. He enlisted in the Army after high school and served with the 101st in Normandy, Holland and during the Battle of the Bulge, during which he was captured. He spent more than three months in a POW camp. He was a longtime member of the 101st Airborne Association and was serving as president of the Northeast Ohio Chapter.

Daniel E. Kendler

Daniel E. Kendler passed away at the age of 85 on Thursday, Nov. 22, 2007, at Saint Barnabas Medical Center in Livingston, NJ. He was born in Brooklyn, NY and lived in West Orange, NJ for many years.

Kendler served as a staff sergeant and radioman with the 101st and fought throughout the War. Daniel Kendler was survived by his wife of 62 years, Ethel, two daughters and two grandsons. He was buried with military honors in Beth Israel Cemetery, in Woodbridge, NJ.

Thomas F. Kiernan, Jr.

Thomas Kiernan passed away due to a stroke at the age of 84 on December 28, 2003 in San Francisco, CA. Kiernan was born and raised in San Francisco. He was a graduate of the reserve officers training program at the University of San Francisco. During World War II, he served as a lieutenant with the 101st and saw action in every major campaign involving the Division. He was wounded and received three Purple Hearts, a Bronze Star and the Belgian Croix de Guerre.

After the war, he worked in his family's real estate firm and helped develop the old New Mission Market in San Francisco's Mission District, built homes in Marin County, and developed apartment buildings, shopping centers and gasoline and convenience stores, and finally retired at the age of 82.

Thomas Kiernan was predeceased by his first wife, of 40 years, Patricia, who passed in 1997, and was survived by his second wife, Sheila, a son, two daughters and five grandchildren.

Frank J. Kovacs

Frank J. Kovacs passed away at the age of 86 on April 10, 2008, at Hospice of Northwest Ohio in Toledo, OH. Toledo was where Kovacs was born, on September 19, 1921, to John and Teresa. He was awarded the Purple Heart during World War II.

Kovacs returned to Ohio and was a plumber for many years. He married Frances Banaszak on April 19, 1947, and the two were together until she passed away on May 20, 1997. Kovacs was a member of All Saints Catholic Church, a life member of the VFW Post 4906 and a member of the Rossford Seniors, and enjoyed woodworking, fishing and taking occasional casino trips.

Frank Kovacs was survived by four children, nine grandchildren and six great-grandchildren and his cat, Annabelle, and was buried with military honors in Fort Meigs Cemetery in Ohio.

Melvin Kramer

Melvin Kramer passed away on March 5, 2008 in southwest Minnesota after about 10 years of poor health. He was a member of the 327th Glider Infantry and served in the Battle of the Bulge and a number of other theaters, and was discharged on January 17, 1946. After the War, Kramer returned home to southwest Minnesota and lived a successful small-town life, starting a family and working for his father's bank in Vesta, MN, of which he ultimately became president.

John Kraus

John Kraus passed away at the age of 85on November 27, 2007. Born on June 24, 1922, he was proud of his service with the Screaming Eagles, including the defense of Bastogne. After the war, he went into business in Contra Costa County, California. He owned Alamo Pools and Crystal Springs Pools in San Mateo, and designed and constructed many buildings in the Midwest. He loved fishing and boating on Lake Berryessa with his family and friends. John Kraus was survived by five children and had 20 grand and great-grandchildren.

Evon W. Kruse

Evon W. Kruse passed away at the age of 86 on February 23, 2008, in Louisiana. He was preceded in death by his wife Helen and was survived by three daughters, four grandchildren and one great-grandchild. Evon Kruse was buried in the Metairie Cemetery in Metairie, LA.

Floyd J. Kuehnau, Sr.

Floyd J. Kuehnau, Sr., passed away at the age of 79 on June 1, 2001, in West Bend, IN and was buried on the anniversary of D-Day. He was born May 8, 1922, to Alvin and Isabelle, and after the War was a Merchant Marine on the Great Lakes for many years. He also worked for the city of Marinette for several years and drove, owned and operated a semi for many years. Floyd Kuehnau, was survived by three sons, nine grandchildren and three great-grandchildren.

Gene Kristie

Gene Kristie passed away at the age of 75 on May 20, 1997 at Lutheran General Hospital in Park Ridge, IL. Kristie was awarded the Purple Heart and four Bronze Service Stars during World War II. He spent many years as a building manager.

Robert L. Kvam

Robert L. Kvam was a veteran of the 506th, and passed away at the age of 85 in Atlanta, GA, on April 7, 2005. Kvam was born in Minneapolis, MN and spent many years in Milwaukee, WI. After World War II, he moved his family to Dunwoody, GA. He was preceded in death by his wife, Theone, in 1991; brothers, Keith, Robert, Leonard and John; and sisters Myrtle and Evelyn. He was survived by his children, Mike, Barbara, Peter and Tracee, as well two grandchildren.

William "Bill" Forrest Ladd

Bill Ladd passed away at his home in Siler City, NC on August 17, 2006. He served in World War II and Korea and was in both the 82nd and 101st Divisions. He retired with the 101st and was stationed at Fort Campbell at the time. He served 11 years overseas and was a member of VFW Post No. 7313, DAV No. 5 of Sanford, N.C., and a Mason for 50 years with Lodge No. 181 of Carthage, N.C. He was survived by his wife, Lynda, four daughters, two sons, 14 grandchildren and six great-grandchildren. Bill Ladd was buried with military honors in Loves Creek Baptist Cemetery.

David Laurent

David Laurent passed away in Smithfield, RI on March 25, 2004. He served as a combat liaison officer for the 101st Infantry and then as assistant special service officer for the 8th Armored Division under General George Patton.

Laurent had a distinguished musical career, retiring after 50 years as a vocalist and a professor in Brown University's music department, which he chaired for ten years.

A bass baritone, he began singing professionally in his teens and was recognized for his performances from the oratorio, German lieder, French melodie, and American song repertoires.

He performed in Verdi's Requiem at the Imperial College in London and received the Grand Prix du Disque for his role as the Christus in an early-1950s recording of Alessandro Scarlatti's St. John Passion.

Laurent performed with the Rhode Island Philharmonic and the Rhode Island Singers, which he also conducted, and appeared with major East Coast symphony orchestras and had been the featured artist at Bach festivals. He gave his last full-length recital in 1987. Laurent was also past president and former governor of the National Association of Teachers of Singing, a member of the American Association of University Professors, and former president of the Brown Faculty Club. In recognition of his service, Brown University established a scholarship in his honor.

David Laurent was survived by his wife, Ruth, two sons and four grandchildren.

William J. Lees

William J. Lees Sr. passed away at the age of 69 on March 1, 1992 in the emergency room at the House of the Good Samaritan after being stricken at home in Watertown, NY. He was buried in nearby Glenwood Cemetery.

Norwood Lester

Norwood "Woodie" Lester passed away at the age of 78 on Thursday, April 16, 1998, in Valley Health Village, South Charleston, SC. Lester parachuted into Normandy and received a Purple Heart. He lived in Lake in Logan County, and was a self-employed carpenter and former commander of VFW Post 3668 at Lake. He was survived by his three daughters, four grandchildren, two stepgrandchildren and three great-grandchildren. Norwood Lester was buried in Nelson Cemetery in Lake, with military honors.

Melvin Frank Lett

Melvin Frank Lett passed away at the age of 89 on April 27, 2009. He was born on March 22, 1920 in Willoughby, OH, and served in the Army for 24 years, during which he earned a Purple Heart and Bronze Star. Following his military career he later drove a bookmobile for 15 years for the Penrose Library. He was a life member of the 101st Airborne Division, VFW Post #3917, American Legion Post 38, and the Enlisted Assoc. #1. Melvin Lett was preceded in death by his wife, Freide, and survived by his son.

Marvin Little

Marvin Little passed away at the age of 81 in Leesburg, FL on Tuesday, March 30, 1999. He was a retired coal miner, and was survived by his wife, Florine and two sons.

Charles Lofino

Charles Joseph Lofino passed away at the age of 84 from natural causes on Sunday, March 2, 2008 in Florida. Lofino was born in Dayton, OH on March 6, 1923 to Dominick and Josephine and served in the 82nd's 508th Regiment.

After returning home to Dayton, he worked in his father's produce business and in 1953 established his first grocery store. He went on to have a very successful career in retail groceries and was successful in real estate development and banking in both Ohio and Florida.

Lofino was active in the Beavercreek community in Ohio and donated the land of his family farm to the YMCA to build a complex, and also create the Dominick Lofino Park. In addition, he donated the building of one of his grocery stores for the construction of the Beavercreek Senior Center and Community Theatre, and in recognition, was awarded the Beavercreek Chamber of Commerce's E.G. Shaw award for community service.

In his new home of Sarasota, FL, he continued his philanthropy and helped build the Charles J. Lofino Family Complex at the Sarasota YMCA including the Josephine Lofino Splash Park located on Potter Park Drive in South Sarasota. He was recognized with the 2007 YMCA First Citizens award. Lofino never retired, but he managed to find spare time for boating, and in his younger days, played tennis, motorcycled and piloted.

Charlie Lofino was survived by his wife, Anna, a son and daughter and six grandchildren, and was buried in Woodland Cemetery in Dayton, OH.

Edward J. Lyskawa

Edward J. Lyskawa of Big River, CA, passed away at the age of 86 on February 21, 2008, at the home of his daughter, Donna. Lyskawa was born in Syracuse, NY on August 13, 1921. As a member of the 327th Regiment, he served in all of the major campaigns involving the 101st. Eddie Lyskawa retired after 30 years with the United States Postal Service and was a member of the NALC Branch 134, and was also a lifetime member of the American Legion Pulaski Post 1650 and VFW Post 3146.

Lyskawa was preceded in death by his wife, Dorothy, in 1997, and by his son, David, in 2006, and was survived by his children, Donna, George and Brenda, as well as 15 grandchildren; and three great-grandchildren. He was buried with military honors in the Veterans Memorial Cemetery in Syracuse, NY.

Kenneth Glenn Lytton

Kenneth Glenn Lytton, passed away at the age of 84 on October 10, 1999, at his home in his native Gastonia, NC. Born to Cullen and Hettie Sherrill, he attended Gastonia High School and graduated from Clemson University, where he earned a letter in riflemanship, as a member of the Class of 1941.

Lytton was commissioned as a Second Lieutenant in the Army in 1941, and was assigned to 82nd Airborne Division. He was reassigned to 101st Airborne Division, and was an original member of the Headquarters Company of the 327th Glider Infantry Regiment. He served in multiple campaigns and was awarded two Bronze Stars, the Combat Infantry Badge and a Purple Heart.

He completed graduate work at the University of North Carolina, Chapel Hill in 1946 and became an electrical contractor, salesman and electrical consultant for General Electric Co. He formed Fiber Controls in 1952, and held numerous patents for textile machinery and was known as Father of Belt Blending.

Lytton was a member of First United Methodist Church, Separk Bible Class, United Methodist Men, American Legion, World War II Last Man Club of Gaston County, 101st Airborne Division Association, Carolina Chapter of 101st, Litten-Lytton-Litton Historical Association, Fort Campbell Historical

Association and Le Mirador Country Club of Mont Pelerin, Switzerland. He also served on the board of the North Carolina Textile Foundation, and was a former member of the Kiwanis and Civitan clubs, and the Gaston Country Club, American Textile Machinery Association, N.C. Textile Association, S.C. Textile Association, Georgia Textile Association, Alabama Textile Association and International Textile Machinery Association. He also held a private pilot's license.

Kenneth Glenn Lytton, was survived by his wife, Jane Land, and several children and stepchildren, and was buried at Gaston Memorial Park with full Military Honors by the World War II Last Man Club of Gaston County.

John B. Mantonya

John Mantonya passed away at the age of 85 at his home in Utica, NY on December 18, 2007. He was born on May 26, 1922, in Columbus, NY to Elroy and Blanche and was a 1940 graduate of Utica High School. Later he attended Washington and Jefferson College and received his law degree from Ohio State University.

John Mantonya practiced law for 58 years until the day he died. He was a member of the Utica United Methodist Church, the American Bar Association, the Ohio State Bar Association, the Licking County Bar Association and American Legion Post 92 in Utica. He served as mayor of Utica and was a president of the North Fork School Board, and he was also a lifetime member of the Salvation Army Board. At the time of his death, he was a Salvation Army Lifetime Honoree, and was a long-time Ohio State Buckeye fan.

He was predeceased by his first wife of 40 years, Mary, who passed on May 3, 1987, and was survived by his second wife of 18 years, Carole, three daughters, a stepdaughter, many grandchildren and a great-grandson. John Mantonya was buried with military honors in Southlawn Cemetery in Utica.

Robert Marshall

Robert Marshall passed away at his home in Port Angeles, WA in 2007 at the age of 85.

Born in Fairhaven, MA, he served in the Army from 1940 to 1946, and was a master sergeant with both the 82nd and 101st, ultimately being awarded a Silver Star, two Bronze Stars and three Purple Hearts for wounds. He was with the 82nd when it dropped into Africa, Sicily and Italy, and then was transferred to the 101st in time for D-Day. During the Battle of the Bulge, Marshall was severely wounded, and lost an eye and a finger.

After the war, he went to Japan to help rebuild that country where he met his future wife of 60 years, Betty. He returned home and served in the Army tugboat service between San Francisco and Seattle and worked as a pipefitter at the Puget Sound Navy Shipyard through the Vietnam War.

One of Marshall's great contributions was to help create the first Native American VFW, Post 11481 in Neah Bay, WA. Marshall himself was not Native American. Marshall met a Marine veteran and found out that there was no post in Neah Bay, and he helped use his fundraising contacts to get the organization started. The local tribes found a great friend in Marshall and they appreciated his commitment to them, which began in 1955 when he met local tribal members while salmon fishing.

Robert Marshall was survived by his wife, Betty, two daughters, a son, seven grandchildren and four great-grandchildren.

Denver Earl May

Denver May passed away at the age of 87 on February 26, 2008, at his residence in the Columbus, OH area. May spent years working for the Gahanna, OH Public School system and was a lifetime member of the Whitehall Post #8794 VFW. Denver May was preceded in death by his wife, Marvene.

Joseph T. McNeely

Joseph T. McNeely, a Screaming Eagle who parachuted into Normandy on D-Day passed away on December 11, 1997 in Fair Oaks, CA at the age of 85. He was suffering from severe pulmonary disease and congestive heart failure. During the War he was awarded the Purple Heart for wounds received during the Battle of the Bulge. After he returned to California, he became a California Highway Patrol officer.

Joel Mehall

Joel Mehall passed away at the age of 90 at the Ketchikan, AK Pioneers' Home on Jan. 10, 2008. He served in the Third Battalion of the 502nd Regiment, and he rarely shared his war experiences with friends and relatives.

Mehall participated in D-Day, Market-Garden and in the defense of Bastogne, and he was awarded two Bronze Stars, three Purple Hearts and a Good Conduct Medal. Friends and relatives said that he mentioned being captured by the Germans but that he escaped, and that he was reported AWOL for leaving a hospital when wounded in order to rejoin his unit. Joel Mehall was single all his life, and worked on pipelines in Oregon and as a logger in Alaska.

Jack V. Messina

Jack V. Messina passed away at the age of 80 on February 12, 2002 at the VA hospital in Kerrville, TX. He was born on May 18, 1923 in Chenyville, LA to Joseph and Mary Sircha. Messina had a distinguished military career that included stints in both the Army and THE Air Force. In 1942, he enlisted in the Army and served with the 101st and 82nd Airborne Divisions, and in 1948 joined the Air Force, with which he served until 1972, retiring at the rank of Senior Master Sergeant. In addition to World War II, Messina served in Korea and Vietnam. Messina received a Silver Star in World War II and an Air Medal in Vietnam for a combat mission. He was also awarded the Meritorious Service Medal in Vietnam and a Commendation Medal for outstanding duty in the Air Force in the Philippines. Among his proudest achievements was serving in the Air Force pararescue team, a unit whose motto is "That others may live" and of his service with the S.E.R.F. (Survival Evasion Resistance Escape). He also earned Master Air Crew Wings, Master Jump Wings and a Combat Infantry Badge.

Jack Messina married Inez Lowery in 1948, and was survived by two daughters and one son, two grandchildren and four great-grandchildren. He was preceded in death by his wife. Jack Messina was buried in the Owens Family Cemetery outside Lumberton N.C. with full military honors.

Bernard Meyer, Jr.

Bernard L. Meyer, passed away at the age of 80 at Muhlenberg Regional Medical Center in Plainfield, NJ. Meyer was a lifelong resident of nearby Westfield. After serving with the 101st during the War, he returned home and was a lab technician with Merck & Co. for 40 years before retiring in 1981. Bernard Meyer was survived by his wife, Margaret, three daughters, three sons, 15 grandchildren and two great-grandchildren.

William Miley

General William Miley, the last surviving division commander from World War II, passed away at the age of 99 on September 26, 1997 at his home in Starkville, MS. He was born in Fort Mason, CA and grew up in Washington after his father died while on duty in the Philippines in 1899. Miley came from a long line of accomplished soldiers: his brother, father, grandfather and two great-grandfathers were West Point graduates, and he went on to attend the Academy and graduate with the

Class of 1918. He was a champion gymnast, and was a star of the Army's First Division Circus, which toured the country after World War I.

Like many graduates of the service academies in the years after World War I, there was little room for advancement in a military that was been reduced substantially. He spent 14 years as a lieutenant in the 1920's and 1930's. During the early part of this period, he met his future wife, Julia Sudduth, while teaching military science at what is now Mississippi State University.

In 1940, the US Army decided to experiment with airborne infantry, and created the 48-man provisional Parachute Test Platoon. Miley was not part of the original group of men, but he was given command of the unit, the 501st Parachute Battalion at Fort Benning, GA, in October 1940. He not only trained the men in infantry tactics, but he also helped design their jump suits and helped determine the best way to jump with a rifle.

Miley went through jump training and commanded some of the early pioneers of parachute infantry, including the first leader of the test platoon, Capt. William T. Ryder, Sgt. Aubrey Eberhardt, who was said to be the man to shout "Geronimo" as he left an aircraft, and Sgt. John Swetish, who helped develop training towers.

He set an early example for the men. In one case, he refused to let an enlisted man risk making a test jump with an especially heavy pack. Miley insisted on making the jump himself and ended up breaking his shoulder.

After Pearl Harbor, he and the 501st were assigned to guard the Panama Canal, the first overseas duty for a paratroop unit. Soon, he organized the first paratroop regiment, the 503rd. While he was promoted to brigadier general, he was considered too junior to be given a division, so he was made assistant commander of the 82d Airborne under General Matthew Ridgeway when it was formed in June 1942.

Miley was promoted to Major General, and he organized the 17th Airborne Division, which he led during Operation Varsity, the largest paratroop drop of World War II. Legend has that he was the first man out of the first plane when the 17th dropped behind the Rhine River on March 24, 1945.

The 17th was deactivated shortly after World War II, and Miley ran the Airborne School at Fort Benning, commanded the 11th Airborne Division in occupied Japan, served as the first chairman of the Joint Airborne Troop Board at Fort Bragg, NC and commanded Army forces in Alaska.

After he retired from the military in 1955, he spent 11 years as a stock broker at Merrill Lynch in Washington before retiring to Starkville. General William Miley was predeceased by his wife in 1995, and was survived by two sons, six grandchildren and 11 great-grandchildren.

Paul R. Moukad

Paul Moukad passed away at the age of 81 on September 11, 1993 in Homestead, FL from a stroke. He was born in New Jersey in 1912 and completed three years of high school and worked as a driver. He enlisted in the Army in January 1941 in Jamaica, NY and served with the 101st as a sergeant. During Market-Garden, he and 15 of his men landed outside of a Dutch village and hid in the attic of an abandoned house, attempting to set up an ambush. The next morning, Germans entered the house, but they failed to search the attic and soon left. Moukad led his paratroopers into nearby woods and dodged the German soldiers who opened fire on them, but they avoided being captured with the help of a Dutch priest. Moukad was given the Medal of Valor and Distinguished Service. Paul Moukad was survived by a sister.

Bert Myers

Bert Myers passed away in Little Rock, AR on April 19, 2008 at the age of 82. Myers was provided a final salute by The Patriot Guard Riders, who escorted his hearse on the highway from the Roller McNutt Funeral Home in Conway, AR to the Forrest Hills Memorial Park on Highway 5 in Little Rock, AR.

Hugh Winder Nibley

Hugh Nibley passed away at the age of 94 on February 24, 2005, at his home in Provo, UT. Nibley was considered one of the leading scholars of Mormon history, and he was well known within the Church of Latter Day Saints for his willingness to express his views, even if they were not generally popular.

Nibley was born on March 27, 1910, in Portland, OR to Alexander and Agnes and attended public schools in Portland, Medford, OR and Los Angeles, CA. He graduated from high school at 17 and served a three-year church mission in Germany, and an additional one in the US. In 1934, he gained his bachelor's degree in history at UCLA and in 1938 received a doctorate in classics at Berkeley. After graduation, he taught college at Claremont, CA, but his career was interrupted by World War II. He joined the Army in 1942, and became a military intelligence officer in the 101st, and dropped into Normandy on D-Day.

He married Phyllis Anne Hawkes Draper on Sept. 18, 1946, in the Salt Lake LDS Temple and that year began teaching history, religion and languages at Brigham Young University. While at BYU, he authored several full-length books, scholarly papers and white papers on using ancient languages to interpret scripture. His command of ancient languages was legendary, even to non-Mormon scholars, and he was recognized among the Church of Latter Day Saints for his dedication to the study of the Book of Mormon.

In 1973, BYU created the Institute for Ancient Studies at BYU and Nibley was named its first director. He helped the library acquire an extensive religious studies collection, and was recognized by the University, receiving Professor of the Year in 1973, Distinguished Service Award in 1979, an honorary doctorate in 1983 and the Exemplary Manhood Award in 1991. Nibley officially retired from BYU in 1975 but taught until 1994. Hugh Nibley was survived by his wife and eight children.

Jim Norene

Jim Norene passed away in his sleep on June 5, 2009 at the age of 85. He was in Normandy to participate in the ceremonies honoring the 65th anniversary of D-Day, and traveled despite being terminally ill from cancer. Earlier on June 5th, he visited the American cemetery in Colleville-sur-Mer and wanted to remember the men with whom he served and to meet the other veterans who made the trip.

On the morning of the 6th, President Barack Obama, who met Norene on the trip, discussed the veteran's passing during his speech, saying, "Jim was gravely ill when he left his home, and he knew that he might not return. But just as he did sixty-five years ago, he came anyway. May he now rest in peace with the boys he once bled with, and may his family always find solace in the heroism he showed here."

Jim Norene served in Company G of the Third Battalion of the 502nd Regiment. In 1954 he moved or Heppner, OR and opened a veterinary clinic that he operated until his retirement in 1995. The townspeople of Heppner called him, simply, "Doc." Jim Norene was eulogized by his family as a wonderful man who had to make a trip from which he knew he might not return.

James Norris, Sr.

James S. Norris, Sr. passed away at the age of 91 on February 23, 2009 in Roanoke, VA.

During the War, he earned a Purple Heart and a Bronze Star. He returned home to work as a welder for the Salem VA, from which he retired in 1972, and later worked as a car transporter. He was a long time member of the Northminster Presbyterian Church, and raised vegetables.

He was preceded in death by his wife, Frances, and survived by son, James, daughter, Carolyn and two grandchildren. James Norris was buried in Blue Ridge Memorial Gardens.

Denis Parsons

Denis Parsons passed away at the age of 89 on February 4, 2009 in San Rafael, CA. He was born on December 3, 1919 and served in Company G of the 327th Glider Infantry. He was active in the Northern California 101st Airborne Association and was a National President in 1994, Past President of the Northern California Chapter, Board of Governors for many years, and served on the Donald Pratt Memorial Committee.

Marvin Peyton

Marvin Peyton passed away October 10, 2007, at the age of 85. He was born on June 7, 1922, and after World War II, worked as an engineer for the State of California for 35 years. Peyton was a great lover of the outdoors, especially the North Coast and the Tahoe Basin, an avid reader, and enjoyed hiking, fishing, swimming, golf, gardening, traveling and the Sacramento ballet and symphony. Marvin Peyton was survived by his three daughters and a granddaughter.

Clyde William Phillips

Clyde William Phillips passed away at the age of 81 in Riverdale, GA on March 10, 2006. He was born Feb. 8, 1925 in Fulton County, GA and spent 27 years with the 101st, seeing action in World War II and Korea. After leaving the military, he was a mechanic for the City of Atlanta Fire Department and was a union organizer for the Carpenters Union Local 225. Clyde Phillips was survived by his wife, Ethel, four sons, three daughters, 12 grandchildren and 17 great-grandchildren, and was buried in Westview Cemetery in Atlanta, GA.

Thomas A. Pinon

Thomas A. Pinon, passed away at the age of 76 on June 27, 1997 from cancer. He graduated from Sacramento High School in 1940, and after the War worked for Olmsted & Wood Printers and then spent two decades as a maintenance man for the Sacramento city Department of Public Works.

John A. Pistolis

John A. Pistolis, passed away at the age of 96, at his home in Mountain Home, NC on February 7, 2008. He was born in Fidakia, Greece, to Athas and Georgia K. Pistolis. He moved to the US and enlisted in the Army when the War broke out and served as a sergeant with the 101st from 1941 to 1945.

He lived in West Virginia after the War, and then moved to Henderson County, NC in 1952. He and his wife, Zoitsa, owned and operated Johnny's Restaurant in Mountain Home for 25 years, until they retired in 1977.

Pistolis was a member of the Holy Trinity Greek Orthodox Church of Asheville, NC beginning in 1952 and a member of the Velouchi Brotherhood. He was survived by his wife of 71 years, Zoitsa, a daughter, a son, five grandchildren and six great-grandchildren. John Pistolis was buried in Shepherd Memorial Park in Asheville, NC.

Henry G. Plitt

Henry Plitt, a Pathfinder on D-Day and a Nazi hunter after the war, passed away on January 26, 1993, in Los Angeles, CA at the age of 74. Born on November 26, 1918 in my home town of New York City, he graduated in 1935 from Staunton Military Academy.

Plitt joined the Army and volunteered for the paratroopers and dropped into Normandy on D-Day as a Pathfinder. Plitt was a Jew, which made him a favorite of the press, which loved that he hunted Nazis towards the end, and after, the war.

Plitt was involved in the capture of the high-ranking Nazi, Julius Streicher. He recalled later in his life that he and his unit got a tip that there was a senior Nazi who was living in the town of Waidring, Austria. They were unsure of his identity, but from the description they received, he thought it was the head of the SS, Heinrich Himmler. He borrowed a jeep, driver and interpreter and went up a hill to a chalet, and entered with his pistol in hand. Inside, there was a man sitting facing an easel painting a mountain he could see through the window.

When the man was asked his name, he replied "Joseph Sailer," and produced papers supporting his identity. Plitt didn't think things added up and he asked him a number of questions, and by odd chance, asked him about Julius Streicher and the man confessed his real identity. Plitt loaded him into his jeep and placed his pistol in his ribs, and asked if he was the Streicher who was against the Jews. Streicher was arrogant and calm, and when they arrived at regimental headquarters in Berchtesgaden, Plitt kicked him to hurry the Nazi out of the jeep. A group of reporters was nearby and when they found out Plitt was Jewish, he was besieged with microphones and cameras. The news media loved that fact that a Jew had captured this Nazis, so he received much publicity, and in his words "things started to happen that changed the rest of my life." Plitt's military career would continue later in life, as in 1964, he enlisted in the Army Reserves and attained the rank of Brigadier General.

After the war, he worked for Paramount Pictures, and in 1974, he purchased ABC's motion picture theaters. By 1984 he and his wife, Sedge, made Plitt Theaters, Inc. into one of the largest chains of independent theaters in the nation. Sedge passed away in 2002. Henry Plitt was honored as a Will Rogers Motion Picture Pioneer and in 1991 received an honorary doctorate from Bar-Ilan University in Israel.

Sam Robert Pope

Sam Robert "Bob" Pope passed away at the age of 90 on April 9, 2008 at The G. V. Montgomery Veterans Affairs Medical Center in Jackson, MS. He was born on July 16, 1917 to Samuel and Lucy in Yazoo County, MS, and was wounded in Normandy. He was a lifelong resident of Yazoo County, and a member of the First Baptist Church of Yazoo City, and was preceded in death by his wife of 44 years, Pauline. Bob Pope was survived by three children, five grandchildren and ten great-grandchildren and was buried in the Glenwood Cemetery in Yazoo City.

Galen Ross Potter

Galen Ross Potter passed away at the age of 80 on November 25, 2001 at Colonial Manor in Cleburne, TX. Born on January 22, 1921, in Mammoth Springs, AR, he was a resident of Burleson, TX for over 40 years and after the War was a masonry contractor, and was a member of Hilltop Church of Christ. Galen Potter was survived by his wife of 60 years, Mary, two sons and two daughters, 20 grandchildren and 16 great-grandchildren, and was buried at Laurel Land Memorial Park.

Joseph Pranger Jr.

Joseph Pranger Jr. passed away at the age of 79 on January 23, 2003, at Saint John's Hospital in Springfield, IL. He was born on July 30, 1923, at Daum Station in Linder Township to Joseph and Gertrude. While attending St. John's School, he worked at Alfeld's Grocery Store in Carrollton and later at the Western Cartridge company. He returned from the War to marry Edna Butler on October 14, 1945, in Carrollton, IL.

Pranger spent some timing farming with his father, and from 1970 to 1985, worked at the Greene County Highway Department. He loved golfing, and worked as an assistant greens superintendent at Lone Oak Golf Course and also maintained a pilot's license. He belonged to St. John's Church and the Minutemen of the church, the Knights of Columbus of Carrollton and the Jerseyville Moose Lodge.

He was survived by his wife of 57 years, two daughters, a son, four grandchildren and four great-grandchildren. Joseph Pranger was buried in the cemetery of St. John's Church in Carrollton.

Johnny Presas

Johnny Presas passed away at the age of 83 in Corpus Christi, TX on June 9, 2005.

Presas was a long-time resident of Corpus Christi and enlisted in the Reserves at the age of 18, and ended up serving with the 101st during World War II serving in the Battle of the Bulge, among other places. He was awarded two Purple Hearts and two Bronze Stars.

When he returned home, he married his childhood sweetheart, Patty Galvan, and spent 32 years as a mail carrier and then was a bailiff for the 117th District Court. Johnny and Patty had two sons, John and Raul.

Ralph Pugh

Ralph Bee Pugh, passed away at the age of 84 on Sunday, September 17, 2006, at Midland Memorial Hospital in Midland, TX. He was born on December 19, 1921 to Lee and Myrtle in

Coahoma, TX and served with the 101st as a medic from June 1942 until January 1946.

Pugh married Ruby Sandefer in Muleshoe, Texas on January 25, 1947, and he farmed in Midland and the Tarzan community, managed Planter's Gins and from 1970 until his retirement in 1987, was employed as building maintenance engineer for Wall Towers.

Pugh was preceded in death by a son and a daughter and was survived by his wife of 59 years, one daughter, two sons, six grandchildren and three great grandchildren. Ralph Pugh was buried in Resthaven Memorial Park.

Henry W. Quist

Dr. Henry W. Quist passed away at the age of 89 on November 2, 2007 after a long illness in Minneapolis, MN. He was born in Minneapolis on May 1, 1918 to Henry and Esther and attended the University of Minnesota for both his undergraduate degree and medical school. Quist graduated in 1943 and did his internship at Minneapolis General Hospital, and then entered the Army and served as a medical officer in the 101st.

He married Jean Watson of Farmer City, IL, in 1948 and practiced family medicine in Minneapolis until his retirement in 1991 at age 73. Henry Quist was survived by his wife, a daughter and a son, and was buried in Sunset Cemetery in Minneapolis.

Colonel Edson Raff

Colonel Edson Raff, who led the first combat jump by American paratroopers in World War II, passed away at the age of 95 on March 11, 2003 in Garnett, KS. Edson Duncan Raff was born on November 15, 1907, in New York, NY and graduated from West Point in 1933 with a concentration in mathematics.

Raff wrote of his early airborne experiences in the 1944 book, "We Jumped to Fight."

Raff trained at Fort Benning, GA shortly after the Army opened its jump school, and he soon became a leader in the elite paratroop forces. He led the first American paratroop drop, which was part of Operation Torch, the Allied invasion of North Africa. On the November 7, 1942, Colonel Raff led the 556 paratroopers of his 2nd Battalion of the 509th Parachute Infantry Regiment on the inaugural mission. They took off in the evening from Cornwall in western England for the longest journey for an airborne invasion that had been taken up to that point in military history.

The men flew 1,600 miles to seize two airstrips near Oran, Algeria. The drop was a mess and many planes missed their targets. When Colonel Raff dropped, he landed on top of a large rock and broke two ribs. As he composed himself, he found out that he was 35 miles from his drop zone, the airstrip at Tafaraoui. He hitched a ride by jeep and by the time he arrived at the field, he found that it had been seized by seaborne troops.

The men of the 2nd Battalion then joined up with a hodgepodge of British engineers, a small American anti-tank unit and lightly armed French troops and fought against an experienced German enemy that had a huge numerical advantage. General Eisenhower cited the exploits of Raff's paratroopers, and credited them with completely confusing the German forces.

After the campaign in Africa, Raff trained paratroopers for the invasion of France. On D-Day, he commanded an armored task force that landed at Utah Beach on D-Day, June 6, 1944. During the Battle of the Bulge, Raff commanded the 82nd Division's 507th Regiment. On March 24, 1945, Colonel Raff participated in Operation Varsity, landing near Wesel, and then taking part in the capture of Essen and Duisburg.

After World War II, Raff stayed in the military and in the 1950's, commanded the 77th Special Forces Group, Airborne, and the Psychological Warfare Center, which were both based at Fort Bragg, NC. Raff was an early advocate for having Special Forces troops wear green berets, and despite the objections of many in the Army, the hats became part of the uniform in 1961.

Colonel Raff retired from the military in 1958, having been awarded the Legion of Merit and the Silver and Bronze stars, and inclusion in the French Legion of Honor. In addition to living in Kansas, he also lived in Bora Bora, French Polynesia. Edson Raff was survived by his second wife, Alomah Make, a son, a daughter, 10 grandchildren and two great-grandchildren.

Hugh R. Rafferty

Hugh Rafferty passed away at the age of 68, in September, 1990 at Chester County Hospital near Philadelphia, PA after a long illness. He was born in Fulton, NY and lived in West Chester, PA until he passed. Hugh Rafferty was a medic with the 327th Glider Infantry and served in a number of campaigns, including D-Day and the Battle of the Bulge. He was awarded the Purple Heart.

Leonard A. Rapport

Author of "Rendezvous with Destiny," the history of the 101st, Leonard A. Rapport, passed away at the age of 95 on March 17, 2008 at Sibley Memorial Hospital in Bethesda, MD.

Rapport was born in Durham, NC and studied at the University of North Carolina with R.D.W. Connor, who eventually became the first archivist of the United States. He graduated in 1935 and worked for the UNC Press and also wrote fiction. In 1936, he wrote the short story, "The Night the Bucket Fell." The story was published in the Virginia Quarterly Review and then was reprinted in "The Best Short Stories of 1937" and got reviews that were even better than those received for pieces by literary giants, John Dos Passos, Eudora Welty and Thomas Wolfe.

From 1938 to 1941, he participated in the Southern Writers' Project, and interviewed a number of colorful figures in North Carolina, and compiled a number of oral histories were into publications that appeared in the "Treasury of Southern Folklore," "First-Person America" and The Washington Post.

He served as a paratrooper from 1941 to 1948 and collaborated with Arthur Northwood, Jr. to document the wartime history of the 101st Division in their successfully-received book, "Rendezvous with Destiny," which was published in 1948. While writing "Rendezvous," Rapport honed the documentary skills that he would use later in life as a historian and archivist.

He would go on to become an archivist at the National Archives, and was considered an authority on 18th-century documents, especially ones related to the Constitutional Convention of 1787 and the Bill of Rights.

In 1957, he received a master's degree in history from George Washington University.

He was associate editor of the "Documentary History of the Ratification of the Constitution and the Bill of Rights" from 1958 to 1969 and later studied and collected records from the 1787 convention at which the U.S. Constitution was written. In 1984, he retired from the National Archives.

Rapport received grants from the Ford Foundation and National Endowment for the Humanities and was named a fellow of the Society of American Archivists. After retirement, he took a series of long hikes, including one along the Appalachian Trail through Virginia, Tennessee and North Carolina. He also walked from coast to coast in England, Northern Ireland and Scotland, and slept in a sleeping bag he carried on his back. He made his final long-distance hike at the age of 80, when he was in Ireland.

Leonard Rapport was survived by his wife of 61 years, Virginia, two children and a granddaughter.

Ned Roscoe Reid

Sergeant Ned "The General" Reid passed away at the age of 84 on Tuesday, March 1, 2005 at a military nursing home in Los Altos, CA. He was called "The General" by patients and staff because he wore his army hat and his medals.

Reid was born on December 31, 1924 in Salt Lake City, UT to Samuel and Vera, and was the fourth of eight children. He attended school in Salt Lake City, and graduated from West High, where he was involved with ROTC. He then went on to attend the University of Utah, and eventually joined the 101st.

At Bastogne he suffered severe leg injuries from an artillery burst, but was able to recover and later jump with the 17th Airborne Division into Germany, landing near Wesel. Reid also saw service during the Korean War.

He married Shirlie Phyllis Ohlin on July 12, 1947, and lived in Utah, Idaho and Nebraska before settling in California, where Reid worked as an insurance salesman. Ned Reid was survived by his son and daughter and was buried in Arlington Cemetery, in Section 69, site 660.

Melvin Renstrom

Melvin Renstrom Sr. passed away at the age of 87 on February 17, 2009 in Billings, MT from natural causes. He was born in St. Paul, MN on Dec. 21, 1921, to Melvin and Alma Renstrom and was the oldest of three children. He graduated from Senior High School in Billings in 1940. While attending high school, he met his future wife, Lorina Oster. Mel enlisted in the Army in the summer of 1943 and volunteered for the paratroopers.

After the War, he married Lorina and worked for an oil refinery for 37 years. His obituary stated that he always took the time to visit his co-workers when they were ill or in the hospital. He had many interests and attended all of his children's events, from games to concerts. Also, he attended 101st Airborne reunions regularly, bowled, worked on cars and pets.

Renstrom was survived by his wife of 62 years, Lorina, two sisters, two sons, a granddaughter and four great-grandchildren. Melvin Renstrom was buried with military honors in Sunset Memorial Gardens.

Raymond C. Rhodes

Raymond C. Rhodes passed away at the age of 87 on October 23, 2005 at St. Anthony Hospice, in Crown Point IN. He served with the 101st from 1942 to 1945, and received four gold leaf clusters, the Purple Heart for wounds suffered in Holland and a Bronze Star. He was a lifetime member of the American Legion, Post 20 and the Crown Point VFW.

After the War, Rhodes worked for Arco for 27 years and retired in 1975. Raymond Rhodes was survived by his wife of 63 years, Laura, two sons, one daughter, seven grandchildren and 10 great-grandchildren.

Chelcia "Chuck" Riaden

Chuck Riaden passed away at the age of 77 on January 8, 2004 at his Hammond, IN home after an extended fight with cancer. Born in Fordsville, KY on February 15, 1926 to Lou and Verna, he worked at U.S. Gypsum Co. from 1943 until April of

1944. He joined the Army in 1944 and served in the military until he was discharged in 1946.

He worked for Blaw Knox in East Chicago, IN and retired after 30 years of service, and then worked for Smith Chevy Auto Dealership of Hammond, IN. His hobbies included automotive repair, electronics, woodworking, fishing, model cars and trains and racing.

Chuck Riaden was survived by his wife of 53 years, Esther Ann, a daughter, two sons and two grandchildren and was buried in Chapel Lawn Memorial Gardens, Schererville, IN.

Richard D. Richey

Richard David Richey passed away at the age of 81 on April 29, 2006 at the Princeton Care Center in New Jersey. Born in Lamkershim, CA, his parents, the late Commander and Mrs. Joseph Richey moved to West Windsor, NJ in 1933. His parents built a home called Oaklynn in Grover's Mill, NJ, the setting for the War of the Worlds broadcast by Orson Welles.

During World War II, he was a Pathfinder and fought in Normandy, Germany, the Battle of the Bulge and Italy, and was awarded seven bronze stars and two Purple Hearts.

Richey was a graduate of The Metropolitan School of Furniture Finishing, where he became a certified master restorer and refinisher of fine antiques. He then opened The Little Old Mill on Grover's Mill Pond, was a member of the American Legion and VFW and also volunteered at a nearby soup kitchen. Richard D. Richey was survived by his wife, Catherine, three children and three grandchildren.

Lt. General Elvy B. Roberts

Lt. General Elvy B. Roberts (retired) passed away peacefully at home in Alameda, CA, on October 11, 2005, seven weeks after his 88th birthday. Roberts, a tall, native Kentuckian who was known for his warm personality, positive energy and interest in others, had a long and distinguished military career that began in World War II, during which he served with both the 501st and 502nd Regiments.

Roberts was a West Point graduate who was promoted several times during World War II. He started as a company commander, then became a regimental operations officer and, ultimately, a battalion commander. He jumped on D-Day and as part of Market-Garden and participated in all of the major campaigns of the 101st Airborne Division.

Roberts attended the Command and General Staff College, Armed Forces Staff College, and the Army War College. He served in Iran for two years, and then assumed command of the 1st Airborne Battle Group, 506th Infantry Regiment of the Screaming Eagles in 1961. He became chief of staff of the 11th Air Assault Division and later served in Vietnam as an assistant commander of the 9th Infantry Division.

In May 1969, he became the commanding general of the 1st Calvary Division. He led combined U.S. and South Vietnamese forces in an assault against Cambodian strongholds on May 1, 1970. Following the Vietnam War, Roberts was assigned to posts in Japan, China, Korea, Mexico, Spain and Yugoslavia, before being named the head of the U.S. Delegation for Mutual and Balanced Force Reduction in Vienna. In 1975, he retired from his last post, as the commanding general of the Sixth U.S. Army at the Presidio in San Francisco.

After his retirement from the military, he spent more than two decades in the insurance business with Johnson and Anton, Inc. and in the food services industry with Guckenheimer Enterprises, Inc. He also served on several boards and maintained membership in the Bohemian Club, the St. Francis Yacht Club, the Rotary Club, the Guide Dogs for the Blind, and the Meyer Friedman Institute for Cardiac Research, to name but a few.

General Elvy Roberts was survived by his wife, Kim, two daughters, a son, five grandsons and four great grandchildren.

Rogie Roberts

Rogie Roberts passed away at the age of 85 on March 17, 2008 in Beaumont, TX. He was born on May 26, 1922 in Lake Charles, LA to Marshall and Callie, and served with the 101st, receiving a Silver Star and two Purple Hearts.

He was a member of St. John's Methodist Church in Port Arthur, TX and was a 33rd Degree Shriner. Roberts was preceded in death by his wife, Inez, and survived by his son and daughter, five grandchildren and five great-grandchildren. Rogie Roberts was buried in Oak Bluff Memorial Park in Port Neches, TX.

Leroy Robison

Leroy Robison passed away at the age of 81 on Saturday, July 3, 2004, in Amarillo, TX. He was born on June 25, 1923, in Wheeler County, TX. Before shipping overseas, he married Artie Mullins on Sept. 13, 1942, in Sayre, OK, and after the War, farmed until he retired in 1997, living in Sunray, TX beginning in 1954. Robison was a past president and longtime member of Sunray Co-op, a member and board member of Union Equity and from the age of 12 a member of the First Presbyterian Church of Magic City. Leroy Robison was survived by his wife, two daughters, three grandchildren and three great-grandchildren, and was buried in Lane Memorial Cemetery.

Henry W. Rogers

Henry W. Rogers passed away at the age of 92 in West Hartford, CT on November 4, 2007. Rogers served in the Army from 1943 to 1946, and was wounded in Bastogne. After the War, he worked for the Connecticut General Life Insurance Company and the Hartford Post Office. Henry Rogers was survived by his wife of 60 years, Elizabeth, three sons and a daughter and four grandchildren, and was buried in Fairview Cemetery in West Hartford.

Harry Rollins

Lieutenant Colonel Harry W. Rollins passed away at the age of 90 on January 29, 2008 at Walter Reed Army Medical Center. Rollins was born in Winnemucca, Nevada in 1917 and raised in Chicago. During the 1920s, he worked as a delivery boy in Chicago. He joined the Army in 1942, was sent to Officer Candidate School, joined the 82nd Airborne and parachuted into Grave, Holland in 1944. During the Battle of the Bulge he was captured and held by the Nazis as a prisoner of war, but escaped twice, and by the end of the War had been awarded two Bronze Stars and two Purple Hearts and other military honors.

After World War II, Rollins continued his military career and eventually went from the 82nd to the 101st, and had tours of duty in Alaska, Japan and Germany, among other places. He married Vivian Runyan of Bridgeport, AL in 1947 and he stayed in the Army until 1967 and worked as a civilian at the Pentagon until 1982.

Harry Rollins was survived by his wife, Vivian, two daughters, a son and five grandchildren, and was predeceased by two children. He donated his body for medical research to the Uniformed Services Medical University at Bethesda Naval Hospital.

Eugene C. Root

Eugene Root passed away at St. Elizabeth Health Center near Youngstown, OH. He was born on May 7, 1920, in Girard, OH to Clinton and Sophie and lived in the area his entire life. Root graduated from Girard High School in 1938 and during the War earned a Bronze Star.

After the War, he returned to Ohio and worked for Youngstown Sheet & Tube/LTV Steel, Brier Hill Works for 38 years, and retired as a stocker in the shipping department in 1980. He was a member of Holy Name of Jesus Church and the VFW Post 419. Root was survived by his wife, Margaret, whom he married on June 10, 1950, a son, two daughters, six grandchildren and two great-grandchildren. Eugene Root was buried with military honors in Calvary Cemetery.

George Millar Rosie

George Rosie passed away at the age of 84 on May 14, 2008 at Life Care Center in Plainwell, MI. He was born on September 13, 1923 in Highland Park, IL to Frank and Elizabeth, and as a young man was an excellent golfer in the North Shore area of Chicago.

He joined the 101st and jumped into Normandy on D-Day, but was captured and spent 11 months as a prisoner of war, mostly at a camp in Poland. In 1945, Rosie settled in Kalamazoo, MI and worked as a golf pro at Milham Park Golf Course along with his cousin.

He then operated the Red Arrow course until 1952, and he gave up his pro status to compete in local golf tournaments. In 1951, he found an entry-level job at KVP to supplement his golf earnings, and he eventually retired from that company in the 1970s, after rising to superintendent of the Parchment Division, which was later sold to Georgia Pacific.

In addition to pursuing his love of golf, Rosie also was active in the 101st Airborne Association, and became its national president and served on its board of directors for many years. George Rosie was preceded in death by his wife, Agnes, and was survived by his four children, 12 grandchildren and 10 great-grandchildren.

Robert Wesley Rugg

Robert Rugg passed away on March 27, 2008 at the age of 89. After the War he worked for the Eastman Kodak Company in Rochester, NY until his retirement. He graduated from the University of Rochester and later volunteered at the library there. Robert Rugg was survived by his wife of 64 years, Roberta, five children, twelve grandchildren, thirteen great-grandchildren and two great-great grandchildren.

Francis L. Sampson

The "Paratrooper Padre," Monsignor Francis L. Sampson, passed away at the age of 83 in Sioux Falls, on Jan. 28, 1996 from cancer. He was considered among the most well-known chaplains in Army history, and he wrote about his experiences in his memoirs entitled, "Look Out Below."

Sampson was born Feb. 29, 1912. His father was the manager of a small-town hotel, and his mother was the business manager and cook. The family moved a lot, and Sampson attended high school at Cathedral High in Sioux Falls, SD and then at Franklin High School in Portland, OR, from which he graduated in 1930. Sampson graduated from Notre Dame University in 1937, and he entered St. Paul's Seminary in St. Paul, MN the following year.

Francis Sampson was ordained at St. Ambrose Cathedral in Des Moines, IA on May 31, 1941 and served the St. Joseph Parish in Neola and taught at Dowling High School in Des Moines. When the War broke out, he was given permission to enlist and was commissioned as a first lieutenant in the Army in 1942. Sampson underwent paratrooper training and became the regimental chaplain for the 501st Regiment.

On D-Day, Sampson became the first chaplain to take part in the invasion of France, and he may have had divine intervention on his landing. Sampson splashed down in a river, and he scrambled to cut away his equipment before he drowned. Sampson had the full complement of paratrooper's gear except for two major differences: he didn't have a weapon and he carried a Mass kit. He recalled that he had to dive five or six times to retrieve that Mass kit from the bottom of the river.

Sampson ended up in a French farmhouse and tended to over two dozen American paratroopers who were wounded. Germans surrounded the building and captured all of the Americans, but he was unharmed and later saved when the Germans were forced to flee by a counterattack.

During Operation Market-Garden, Sampson landed in water again, this time in the moat of a castle. He had a more severe experience during the Battle of the Bulge. Sampson was taken prisoner outside of Bastogne, and was nearly shot for being a Catholic and was saved only by the intervention of a German soldier. He and the fellow captives were forced to march 185 miles to Germany in severe winter weather and were then shipped by train without food or water for several days before finally being imprisoned in Stalag II A, north of Berlin. He lost 35 pounds from his 185-pound frame before Soviet soldiers liberated the camp in April 1945.

In his memoir, he scoffed at any notion that he was a hero or brave and wrote, "remember that no pair of knees ever shook more than my own in times of danger."

When combat ended, he returned home and served at a parish and taught math in the Des Moines Diocese before being encouraged by his bishop, Gerald Bergan, to return to military service. In 1946, Sampson re-entered the military, in which he would serve for decades.

In 1950, Sampson parachuted into Korea with the 187th Airborne Infantry Regiment in an attempt to rescue American POWs. During the Vietnam War, Sampson made annual Christmas trips to be with the American troops there. In 1967,

President Johnson appointed Sampson as the Army's chief of chaplains, and he was promoted to major general, a position from which he retired in 1971.

In 1971, he served as pastor of St. Mary's Catholic Church in Shenandoah until March 10, 1972, when he was asked to head the USO for two years. Francis Sampson finally retired to Sioux Falls, SD, where he passed. He is buried in St. Catharine's Cemetery in Luverne, MN, and his grave marker says simply, "Lord, make me an instrument of your peace."

Charles Santarsiero

Charles "Sandy" Santarsiero, a lieutenant in the Third Battalion of the 506th, passed away at the age of 81 on May 10, 2004 in the Moses Taylor Hospital emergency room in Scranton, PA, where he was a longtime resident.

Born in Dunmore, PA to John and Mary Zaccanino Santarsiero, he was a graduate of Dunmore High School and a member of St. Clare's Church. Sandy Santarsiero was involved in some of the bitterest fighting seen by the Screaming Eagles. On D-Day, he landed in the area of Drop Zone D and he was recommended for the Congressional Medal of Honor for his role in the fighting around the bridges in Brevands. A few days later, in the fighting around Bloody Gulch, he received a machine gun bullet in his thigh and recovered in time to jump into Holland.

Santarsiero's platoon was in the lead during the 506th's advance towards Eindhoven after the drop into Holland, and Colonel Sink gave him a personal order: "Charlie, you punch the hole and I will pour in the men." During Market-Garden, he was severely wounded by shrapnel from a German 88 round and it took three years and 17 operations before he was discharged. For his service, he received the Distinguished Service Cross. After the War, he was active in the 101st Airborne Association of Retired Veterans, and as a member of the McHugh-

Bushweller VFW Post 3474 in Dumore, PA. He spent his post-War life working as a lineman and troubleshooter for Pennsylvania Power and Light until he retired.

His wife, Clara preceded him in death on March 12, 1998, and he was survived by two brothers, Tony of Dunmore, PA, and Joseph, of Florida, several nieces and nephews, and his lifetime friend, Anna Mecca, Dunmore. Sandy Santarsiero was buried in Forest Hill Cemetery in Dunmore, PA.

Adrien J. Saucier

Adrien J. Saucier passed away at the age of 84 on Friday, October 12, 2007, at York Hospital in Wells, ME following a battle with cancer. Saucier was born on December 8, 1922, in Wallagrass, ME to John and Modeste, and attended local schools. He served with the 101st during the War and returned to work as a carpenter at the Portsmouth Naval Shipyard. He enjoyed hunting, fishing and gambling and was a member of American Legion Post # 47 for 46 years.

Adrien Saucier was survived by his wife Mary, two sons, two daughters, a stepson, a stepdaughter, seven grandchildren, six great-grandchildren and four step grandchildren, and was buried in Pine Hill Cemetery in Wells Branch, ME.

Jerome Seaver

Jerome Seaver passed away on February 12, 2004 at the age of 88 at his home in Kimberly, WI. He was born on August 5, 1915 to George and Elizabeth, and lived in Appleton, WI until the age of nine, when his family relocated to Kimberly. During the Depression, he worked for one year for the Conservation Corps, and then went to work with Kimberly Clark, for whom he worked for 40 years. His service with Kimberly Clark was interrupted by the war, during which he served with the 101st in the medical attachment. He served in every major campaign of the war, and was awarded a Bronze Star and the Purple Heart.

Seaver returned home t and married Margaret VanDehy, who passed away in 1973. He remarried two years later. He was survived by his second wife, Mary, five daughters: nine grandchildren, seven great-grandchildren, ten step-children, 28 step-grandchildren and 64 step-great grandchildren, and a step great-great-grandchild. Jerome Seaver was buried with military honors in the cemetery of Holy Name Catholic Church.

Michael Sertic

Michael Sertic passed away at the age of 85 in Griffith, IN Michael on June 9, 2007.

Sertic served in the 501st Regiment during World War II, and afterwards worked for Inland Steel. Sertic was survived by his wife, Mable, two sons, one step-son and three grandchildren.

Thomas L. Shamp

Thomas L. Shamp, passed away at the age of 83 at the Rose Lane Health Center in Canton, OH. He was born in Elmore, OH, and during the War, served with the 101st and was awarded a Purple Heart and a Bronze Star and was a prisoner of war.

Shamp spent 32 years as a truck driver with R & W Trucking until he retired in 1981. He spent the last 25 years of his life in Canton, and was a member of VFW Post #10178, Elks Lodge, Moose Lodge #3880, Eagles Aerie #2370, American Legion Post #44, the 101st Airborne Association and the National Teamsters Local of Chicago.

Thomas Shamp was survived by his companion of 20 years, Evelyn, and was buried in Sunset Hills Memory Gardens.

James J. Sheeran

James Sheeran passed away at the age of 84 on July 16, 2007 in Princeton, NJ. Born on Jan. 9, 1923 in Passaic, NJ, Sheeran was a celebrated high school athlete. During his senior year at West Orange High School, he quarterbacked West Orange's football team to its first and only state football title by defeating East Patterson High in 1941.

Sheeran joined the 101st and jumped into Normandy on D-Day, only to be taken prisoner by the Germans. He escaped from the train taking him to a POW camp and joined the French underground, serving with the Maquis until he was able to rejoin his unit. Sheeran would then serve during Market-Garden and the Battle of the Bulge. Sheeran never forgot the French who helped him and after the war, collected more than three tons of food and clothing and shipped them to France via a C-47 airplane whose full use was granted to him by the United States Air Force. In January 2007, in recognition of his actions during the war, Sheeran's name was entered as a Chevalier of the Order of the Legion of Honor, the highest decoration awarded by the government of France. In addition, he was also awarded a lifetime achievement award by the New Jersey Assembly.

After the War, Sheeran graduated from law school and became the youngest mayor of West Orange, NJ at the age of 35. Later, he was a special agent for the FBI, and was later appointed as New Jersey's insurance commissioner. Sheeran was New Jersey's last two-term insurance commissioner (1974-1982), and was widely-recognized as a consumer advocate. After leaving government, he and his wife formed two not-for-profit insurance companies, NJ CURE and NJ PURE.

James Sheeran was survived by his wife, Lena, four daughters, a son, two stepchildren and 15 grandchildren, and was buried in St. Catherine's Cemetery in Sea Girt, NJ.

Robert L. Sherman

Robert L. Sherman passed away at the age of 84, in Blossburg, PA on April 15, 2005. He was married to his wife, Louise, for

44 years until she passed. Robert Sherman was survived by two daughters, two sons, grandchildren and great-grandchildren

John Sigalos

John Sigalos passed away at the age of 86 on July 23, 2007 in Hallandale Beach, FL. Born in Stamford, CT, Sigalos spent his youth in Athens, Greece. He joined the U. S. Merchant Marines and in 1941, enlisted in the Army and volunteered for the paratroops and joined the 101st. He served throughout the war, from D-Day through Bastogne into Germany.

Sigalos married his wife Anna after the War and in 1952 moved to Marietta, GA, where they ran a restaurant until they retired in 1982 and moved to Florida. He was a regular fisherman, and also was a member of the Saint George Greek Orthodox Church in Hollywood, FL. John Sigalos was survived by his wife of 60 years, three children and grandchildren, and was buried at Greenwood Cemetery in Atlanta, GA.

John H. Simson

John Simson passed away at the age of 79 on July 7, 2001 in Houston, TX. He was born in St. Paul, MN, on April 9, 1922, to Anna and Emanuel Swanson, and he spent his early years in Stillwater, MN. He was a member of the 506th on D-Day and shortly after parachuting into Normandy was wounded and taken prisoner.

After returning home, he held several management positions in the restaurant and motel field throughout the eastern U.S., and then spent 22 years working for the Panama Canal Company, retiring as Chief of the Storehouse Division. He was known for his love of fishing in the Bay of Panama and for being one of the early users of home computers.

John Simson was survived by his wife, Marisabel, and his four sons and was buried in Memorial Oaks Cemetery.

Rudy Lee Sloan

Rudy Lee Sloan passed away at the age of 84 on January 29, 2006, at his home in Sanford, FL. He graduated from St. Lucie County High School in Fort Pierce, FL in 1939 and was inducted into the St. Lucie County Sports Hall of Fame. He served with the 101st during World War II and returned home to work as an engineer for the Atlantic Coast Line and Seaboard Coastline Railroad for 42 years.

Rudy Lee Sloan was preceded in death by his two wives, and was survived by two daughters, a son and five grandchildren and was buried in Oaklawn Park Cemetery in Sanford.

Edward D. Smalley

Edward D. Smalley passed away at the age of 84 on May 19, 1998. Born in Akron, OH, he volunteered for the paratroopers, and received a Purple Heart and was taken prisoner during the Battle of the Bulge. Returning to Akron, he worked for B. F. Goodrich for 41 years of service.

Smalley was a member of Trinity Lutheran Church for 32 years, where he served as an usher and helped with the church's Day Center, and was known for his volunteer work at the church and community. Edward Smalley was preceded in death by his son Donald, and was survived by his wife of 52 years, Bernice and was interred at Mt. Peace Cemetery.

Frederick A. Sneesby

Frederick A. Sneesby, died at the age of 84 on June 5, 2001, at the home of his daughter, Frances, of Warwick, RI. Sneesby was born in Pawtucket, RI to Edward and Overlena, and he lived in the town all his life until he moved to Warwick. He was a mail carrier for the U.S. Postal Service for 30 years, and was a member of the National Letter Carriers Association and retired in 1979.

Frederick Sneesby was preceded in death by his wife, Theresa, and he was survived by three daughters, four sons and nine grandchildren. He was a lifelong communicant of St. Edward Church, and was buried with military honors in St. Francis Cemetery in Pawtucket.

Joe M. Spears Jr.

Joe M. Spears passed away at the age of 87 on Wednesday October 31, 2007. He was born in San Benito, Texas on January 14, 1920 to Joe and Ethel, and attended public schools in San Benito, and he graduated from Texas A&M with B.S. degrees in Mechanical Engineering and Industrial Engineering. During World War II, Spears served as a Master Sergeant in the 101st, earning both paratrooper and glider wings. After Bastogne, he received a battlefield commission.

When he returned from the War, he worked for the Central Power and Light Company and retired as Manager of Consumer Research. In 1987 he and his wife, Laura Nell, his high school sweetheart, moved to Wimberley, TX. Spears enjoyed sports and he officiated high school football games. He was active in the Boy Scouts and was the Exalted Ruler of the Elks Lodge in San Benito, Secretary of the San Benito Lions Club, and was a member of the San Benito Consolidated Independent School Board.

He was preceded in death by Laura, to whom he had been married for 63 years. He was survived three sons and three grandsons.

Francis R. "Pug" St. Jean

Francis "Pug" St. Jean, passed away at the age of 83 at his home in Putnam, CT. Born on December 14, 1924 in Norwich, CT to Joseph and Evelyn, he lived in Putnam most of his life. St. Jean served with the 101st and fought in Normandy and the

Rhineland before being discharged in 1946 and received numerous awards including a Good Conduct Medal.

After the War, he operated a plumbing business for several years, was the Superintendent for the Town of Putnam Water Department and retired in 2001 from the Control Concepts Company.

Francis St. Jean was predeceased by his wife of nearly 55 years, Frances, and was survived by a son and two granddaughters and was buried with military honors in St. Mary Cemetery in Putnam.

Louis J. Stanislowski

Louis Stanislowski, who served in World War II with both the 82nd and 101st, passed away at the age of 79 in Columbia Heights, MN on March 23, 2002. He was survived by his wife of 56 years, Olive, two daughters, two sons and nine grandchildren.

Johnie Starnes

Johnie Starnes, passed away at the age of 86 on May 23, 1999 at Livingston Hospital near Marion, KY. Starnes was predeceased by his wife Ann, and survived by a son, grandson and four great-grandchildren. Johnie Starnes was buried in Deer Creek Cemetery near Marion.

Harry F. Staub

Harry Staub passed away on June 26, 2007, in Maryland. He was preceded in death by his wife, Eileen, and was survived by a son and a daughter, three grandchildren and a great-granddaughter. Harry Staub was buried with military honors in Arlington National Cemetery.

Robert Edward Steele

Robert Steele passed away at the age of 84 on April 10, 2006 in Sparta, NC from heart complications. Born in Conneaut, OH on February 2, 1922, he went to school there and was selected to attend All Boys State. After the War he lived in Conneaut until 1955, when he moved his wife and four children to St. Petersburg, FL and worked in the building supply business before joining Fuller Industries, where he was promoted to manager. Steele then started his own lumber and building supply business before retiring to Sparta, NC in 1976.

While living in Naples, FL he was a member of the schools Fellowship of Christian Athletes organization, which gave young people an opportunity to meet famous athletes of the day and hear their testimonies. He also served one term as President of Naples' Optimist Club, and was voted Father of the Year in 1967.

After his wife, Jeanne, passed away in 1986, he moved back to Florida and then returned to North Carolina where he lived in Wilkes, until his death. He was also predeceased by his eldest son, Corporal Robert Hugh Steele. Robert Steele was survived by two sons, a daughter, nine grandchildren and 14 great-grandchildren, and buried in Sparta Cemetery.

Henry Steinmetz

Henry Steinmetz passed away at the age of 76 on October 13, 2001 at Central Florida Regional Hospital in Sanford, FL from a heart attack. Born in Bayonne, NJ, he was raised in Staten Island, NY and was a New York City policeman after the War. The day after graduating from Port Richmond High School on Staten Island, he enlisted in the Army and volunteered for the paratroopers. He retired and moved to Sanford, FL.

Leland Garn Stillman

Leland Stillman passed away at the age of 83 on October 27, 2004 in Salt Lake City, UT. He was born in Salt Lake City on May 16, 1921 to Joseph and Emma. Stillman served in D Company of the 501st Regiment and received multiple decorations, including a Purple Hear and he was a life member of the Disabled American Veterans.

He returned home and married Neva Gene Lemmon on May 4, 1945, and worked for Mountain Fuel Supply Company for 30 years. He also operated his own television repair business for many years, and was an avid fisherman.

Stillman was preceded in death by his wife of 58 years, Neva, on October 1, 2003 and was survived by two daughters, five grandchildren and four great- grandchildren. Leland Stillman was buried in Elysian Burial Gardens.

Chester E. Stotts

Chester E. Stotts passed away at the age of 75 on Tuesday, October 23, 2000, at Montrose Memorial Hospital, near his home of Delta, CO. Born on November 25, 1924, in Olathe, CO to Lewis and Julia Stotts, he spent his childhood in the Olathe and Delta areas, and attended Columbine Grade School and graduated from Delta High School in 1942.

Stotts married Rosemaire Hinton on June 15, 1947, in Delta, attended college at Colorado State University in Fort Collins and then at Oregon State University. After college he moved to Chicago where he worked for Swift and Company in poultry research. In 1967 he returned home to Delta to work for Hinton Auto Parts, until he retired in 1982.

In his retirement, he had many interests. He was a member of the Presbyterian Church of Delta, president of the Grand

Mesa Good Sams RV Club, and past president of Delta Senior Citizens and a volunteer for Meals on Wheels. He loved RVing and he built one of his family's homes and drew the plans for his last one.

Chester Stotts was survived by his wife, Marie Stotts of Delta, a son, two daughters, eight grandchildren; and three great-grandchildren, and was buried at the Delta City Cemetery.

Lewis R. Sutfin

Lewis R. Sutfin passed away at the age of 93 on April 2, 2008 in Bonham, TX. Sutfin was born on January 1, 1915 in Goodland, KS, and fought in Normandy and Holland. He was wounded during Market Garden and healed in time to fight in Bastogne. He was awarded a Silver Star and a Purple Heart.

After the War, he attended a Technical Trade School in Minneapolis, MN and went to work for Braniff Airways. In 1961, he was transferred to Dallas, where he worked for Braniff at Love Field until he retired in 1980. He was preceded in death by his wife and daughter, and spent the last few years of his life at the Veterans Administration hospital in Bonham, TX. Lewis Sutfin was buried next to his wife and daughter at the Restland cemetery in Dallas.

David Talburt

David Talburt passed away at the age of 83 on March 18, 2006 in Harrison, AR. He was born on January 27, 1923 to Noble Essie. After the War, he was a carpenter and millwright, and worked on dams for the Corps of Engineers. He attended Trinity Baptist Church in Capps, AR, and was survived by his wife, Doris, two sons and two grandchildren. David Talburt was buried in Maplewood Cemetery.

Albert Tarbell

Albert Tarbell, the first Mohawk Indian paratrooper in the 82nd Airborne Division passed away on August 24, 2009 at the age of 86. He was from the St. Regis Mohawk Indian Reservation in upstate New York, and became part of the 504th Regiment. He served in Anzio in January 1944, was in the first wave of men who crossed the Waal River on September 20th, 1944 and fought in the battle near Herresbach in the Ardennes. In the Den Heuvel Woods in Holland, Tarbell volunteered to repair a damaged phone line in the middle of a severe artillery barrage to restore communications with his CP. James Megellas eulogized Tarbell and described losing a very good friend, a good soldier and a hero for our country and the Mohawk Nation.

Wilmer L. Thigpen

Wilmer L. Thigpen passed away at the age of 81 on the 63rd anniversary of D-Day, June 6, 2007, in Cochran, GA. He was born in Montgomery County, GA to Louie and Missouri Darley and worked on Robins Air Force Base until his retirement. He was survived by his wife of 56 years, Jean, two sons, a daughter, four grandchildren and two great-grandchildren. Wilmer Thigpen was buried in Pulaski-Bleckley Memorial Gardens.

Breathen Thomas

Breathen Thomas passed away at the age of 85 on January 24, 2005 in Monroe, LA. He was born on February 25, 1919, in Union Parish, LA to Will and Mae. He returned from the War and worked as a machinist for Texas Gas until he retired. Breathen Thomas survived by two daughters, seven grandchildren and twelve great grand children. He asked for no formal service and in lieu of flowers, it was asked that people done to the Ouachita Humane Society or any animal shelter because he loved animals.

Leo Thompsen

Leo Thompsen passed away at the age of 83 on July 24, 2007 from Congestive Heart Failure. A longtime resident of Alaska, he passed at the Providence Extended Care facility. Thompsen was born on June 1, 1924, in Brooklyn, N.Y., and attended school there. In 1942 he enlisted in the Army and volunteered for the airborne.

After he returned from the War, he earned a civil engineering degree from Virginia Polytechnic Institute. In 1953, he moved to Alaska and worked for a fishery in Juneau, where he met his future wife, Harriet Habberstad. In 1965, they settled in Anchorage, and over the next 20 years, he worked for several government agencies before retiring from the Corps of Engineers at Fort Richardson in 1986.

After his retirement, he and Harriet ran a bed and breakfast during the summers and traveled in the winters until she passed away in 1997. Thompsen then met Ileen Ellison who became his inseparable companion for the last 10 years of his life. He was proud of his service with the 101st and spoke frequently about World War II.

Leo Thompsen was preceded in death by his wife of 41 years, Harriet, and survived by two daughters, a son, five grandsons and six great-grandchildren.

John Franklin Tiller

John Franklin Tiller passed away at the age of 86 on December 3, 2007 in Lafayette, LA. He was a born in Boaz, Alabama to John and Mary and served in the 501st Regiment.

He graduated from Birmingham Southern College and moved to Louisiana to work as an electrical sales engineer. He was preceded in death by his wife of 48 years, Betty, and a son and was survived by two daughters and one grandson. John Tiller was buried in Village Falls Cemetery in Mulga, AL.

Charles Timmes

General Charles J. Timmes passed away from a heart attack at the age of 83 on October 22, 1990 at Fairfax Hospital in Falls Church, VA. A 1932 graduate of Fordham Law School, Timmes was a practicing attorney in New York, NY before being called to active duty in 1941.

Timmes was a highly decorated veteran of World War II, leading a Battalion of the 82d Airborne on D-Day, and participating in fierce fighting in an orchard near the Merderet River. That battlefield is known eponymously as "Timmes' Orchard."

He also participated in the Battle of the Bulge and also Operation Varsity across the Rhine in March 1945. He was awarded the Distinguished Service Cross, two Distinguished Service Medals, the Silver Star, two Bronze Stars and two Purple Hearts.

After the War, he was a military adviser in South Korea and in Washington, and served as assistant commander of the 101st Airborne Division. Timmes served in Vietnam from 1961 to 1964, and was chief of the United States Military Assistance Advisory Group there. He then held staff positions before retiring from active duty in 1967. He then worked with the CIA in Vietnam from 1967 to 1975, before returning to the US and working as an attorney in Washington and living in Falls Church, VA.

General Charles Timmes was survived by his wife, two sons, a daughter and 15 grandchildren

Albert Hampton Toler Sr.

Albert Hampton Toler Sr. passed away at the age of 82 on July 16, 2007 in California. Toler was one of 13 children and was born in Baileysville, WV. In 1939, when he turned 16, he enlisted in the Army. At first he was a cook, then became a tank driver and eventually volunteered for the paratroopers, gaining an assignment to the 82nd and then the 101st. He dropped into Normandy on D-Day and he also fought during the Battle of the Bulge. Toler suffered an injury and was confined to a British hospital for some time, and ultimately left the service in 1945.

Toler was known as both a tough bird and also as a very generous person. He moved to California in 1951 and owned Al's Place, a beer bar in Ontario, for years and then started a trucking company called A & G Transport. Al Toler was survived by his wife Joyce, a son, a daughter, a granddaughter and two great grandchildren.

Jack O. Tomlinson

Jack Tomlinson passed away at the age of 84 on March 3, 2008 in Birmingham, AL. Born on May 18, 1923, he was awarded the Purple Heart in Bastogne. He graduated from the University of Alabama and was an active alumni supporter, and had a successful career in the life insurance business that included being a member of the Million Dollar Round Table for 47 years.

He served as Senior Warden at both the Church of the Advent and St. Mary's-on-the-Highlands and was past Chairman of the Board of St. Martins in the Pines. Jack Tomlinson was survived by his wife of 60 years, Jean, two sons, five grandchildren and two great-grandchildren, and was buried at St. Mary's-on-the-Highlands.

Raymond Trost

Raymond Trost, passed away at the age of 92 on June 18, 2007 in Edina, MN. He was predeceased by his wife, wife, Luella, and survived by his siblings, and was buried at Fort Snelling National Cemetery.

Vernon Leroy Troxel

Vernon Leroy Troxel passed away at the age of 90 on July 27, 2007 at his home near Bozeman, MT, surrounded by his family. He spent the last year of his life in poor health.

Troxel was born in Alma Center, WI on March 20, 1917, and left school after the eighth grade to help his family survive during the Great Depression. When his father died, he sold the family farm and joined the Army, and served with the 101st for the duration of the War.

He returned home and worked as a contract timber faller, which suited his interest in nature. Troxel was an environmentalist and a naturalist and believed in harvesting forests rather than exploiting them. He was also an avid fisherman and gardener, a gourmet cook, and a grassroots worker and active humanitarian. Vernon Troxel was survived by his wife of 47 years, Jo Anne, and a daughter.

Richard Eugene Turner

Richard Turner passed away at the age of 84 on August 19, 2007 in Orlando, FL. Born in Rushville, OH, to George and Pearl on June 8, 1923, he was the youngest of seven children and was nicknamed "Boss." He served through all of the 101st's major campaigns.

After the War, he attended the University of Ohio and then got his law degree in 1952 from Miami University in Coral Gables, and like many of his family members, became a Mason. He was admitted to the Florida Bar and practiced law in Orlando before becoming an investigator with the U.S. Departments of State and Agriculture. His job allowed him to live in Washington, D.C., San Francisco, Dallas, Atlanta, and Columbus, OH, and he retired in 1977 and moved back to Orlando. However, he shortly thereafter resumed part-time work with the State Department.

In his retirement, he enjoyed traveling to 101st Airborne reunions all over the country, and was honored as the 2007 Veteran of the Year by his local chapter. He also traveled back to Ohio frequently. Richard Turner was survived by his wife of 56 years, Edith and two daughters, and was buried in Greenwood Cemetery.

Paul Eugene Truby

Paul Eugene Truby passed away at the age of 73 on September 9, 1998, in Washington (PA) Hospital following a lengthy illness. Truby was born on December 25, 1924, in Washington, PA to Elmer and Minnie Frank Truby, and was a member of the Trinity High School class of 1943. He joined the 101st as a replacement and served in Germany. During the Korean War, he served with the 11th Airborne. In his career, he was awarded the Parachute Badge, Combat Infantry Badge, Good Conduct Medal, Distinguished Unit Badge, American Campaign Medal, European-African-Middle Eastern Campaign Medal and World War II Victory Medal.

Truby held a number of jobs, and was employed at McGraw-Edison for 14 years before retiring in 1986 because of ill health. He was affiliated with Trinity Episcopal Church of Washington, and was a member of Washington Lodge 164 F&AM and Coudersport Consistory, was a lifetime member and past commander of Confluence Veterans of Foreign Wars Post 7250, a member of Edwin Scott Linton American Legion Post 175 and Washington Senior Citizens, and was involved with the Thomas Campbell Care Association dartball team and travel club.

On June 25, 1973, Truby married Dorothy Ann Long, who survived him, along with two sons, a stepdaughter, four grandchildren and a great-granddaughter.

David D. Turow

Dr. David D. Turow passed away at the age of 80 on December 26, 1998 at Evanston (IL) Hospital after a lengthy illness. Turow graduated from the University of Illinois Medical School in Chicago in 1942 and trained at Cook County Hospital. He served as a Major in the Army Medical Corps during World War II and was attached to the 101st. He received the Bronze Star three times, and he was one of the surgeons who parachuted into Bastogne to provide medical care for the men trapped during the siege. He also was present when the American Army liberated Dachau concentration camp.

He practiced Obstetrics and Gynecology for over 50 years in Chicago and the northern suburbs, during which time he delivered more than 7,400 newborns. Turow was a clinical professor at Chicago Medical College and a Fellow of the American College of Obstetrics and Gynecology, served as the chairman of the Department of Obstetrics and Gynecology at Edgewater Hospital, Chicago, and later as chairman of the Department of Gynecology at Rush North Shore Hospital, Skokie. He was a member of the Board of the Chicago Medical Society for many years, and authored many medical articles.

David Turow was survived by his wife, Rita, a teacher and a writer, a son and daughter and four grandchildren.

Russell Arlington Tyler

Russell Arlington Tyler passed away at the age of 89 on April 14, 2002 in Escondido, CA from a massive stroke. He was born on September, 1912 in Eau Claire, WI to Myron and Florence and graduated from Milton Union High School.

He married Lois Stoller of Hinsdale, IL on June 14, 1942 before shipping out to Europe with the 101st, in which he served as a medic. He was a surgical technician at Mercy Hospital for nine years in Janesville before moving to Escondido, CA in 1963. Tyler was known for running a popcorn stand at sporting events and fairs in the Escondido area and his caramel corn was well-known. He was a life-time member of the Seventh-Day Adventist Church. Russell Tyler was survived by his wife, Lois, two daughters and two grandchildren.

Robert Francis Vandepas

Bob Vandepas passed away at the age of 89 on January 6, 2008 in El Paso, TX. Born on April 4, 1918 in Bowman, ND, he was a gliderman with the 101st during World War II.

After the War, he worked as a salesman and a corporate officer with the family's business, Neil J. Vandepas and Sons, Inc. of Minneapolis, MN, where he lived for years. He spent 35 years living in El Paso, where he belonged to VFW Post 10354.

Bob Vandepas was preceded in death by a son, and was survived by his companion of 16 years, Jeannie, two sons and four grandchildren, and was buried in Restlawn Memorial.

William Bernard Ventry

William Bernard Ventry passed away on Thursday, May 24, 2007 at the age of 85 in Apalachicola, FL. He was a native of Quincy, FL and moved to Apalachicola in 1943.

Ventry married his wife on April 24, 1943, and shipped out to serve in Europe. Following the War, he worked for DNR as a heavy equipment operator. William Ventry was survived by his wife of 64 years, Erris, a son, grandson and three great grandchildren, and was buried in Magnolia Cemetery.

Robert W. Waller Sr.

Robert Waller passed away in Levittown, NY on January 18, 2008. He worked for years as a business agent and 50-year member of the Local 531 UBC&J of America. He was survived by his wife Helen, two daughters, a son, four grandchildren and one great-grandchild.

Lamar Wansley

Lamar Travis Wansley passed away peacefully at the age of 90 on Wednesday, May 30, 2007 at his Athens, GA home. Wansley was born on June 10, 1916 in Carnesville, GA to Beatrice and John. He graduated from North Georgia College and the University of Georgia, and in 1938 married Ruth Roper.

Wansley was working at Georgia Power Company in Athens, GA when Pearl Harbor was bombed and he became an original member of the 101st, serving from D-Day until the end of the War in the 327th Glider Regiment. He received four Bronze stars and was promoted to captain during the Battle of Bulge and served in regimental communications.

After the war, he resumed his career with the Georgia Power Company, for whom he worked for 41 years. He moved from Athens to Atlanta and then to Valdosta where he was a Vice President until his retirement in 1981. Lamar Wansley was survived by his wife, Ruth, two daughters, a son, seven grandchildren and eight great-grandchildren, and was buried in Allen United Methodist Church Cemetery in Carnesville, GA.

Jack Warden

The Emmy- and Oscar-winning actor, Jack Warden, died at the age of 85 at a hospital in New York, NY on July 19, 2006. Warden was born John H. Lebzelter in 1920 in Newark, NJ and was in high school during the Depression when he tried to become a professional boxer. He fought 14 times as a welterweight before joining the Navy, where he was sent to China and patrolled the Yangtze River. Following his stint in the Navy, he worked as a nightclub bouncer, a lifeguard and a deckhand on an East River tugboat.

In 1941, he joined the Merchant Marine, and worked in the engine room of a ship that traversed the Atlantic in convoys, and had to endure bombings by enemy warplanes. He decided to enlist in the Army and volunteered for the paratroopers. He was serving in the 101st but shortly before D-Day, he broke his leg during a nighttime practice jump in England and was sent back to the US where he spent nearly a year in a hospital. While in the hospital he decided to pursue acting, but not before he recovered in time to participate in the Battle of the Bulge.

Warden attended classes and acted in Tennessee Williams plays before moving on to television. His career flourished in the 1950s as he got steady television work, and he also appeared on Broadway in Clifford Odets' "Golden Boy" and Arthur Miller's "A View From the Bridge." In 1953, he had small roles in "From Here to Eternity" and "Run Silent, Run Deep," and had a breakthrough performance in 1957's "Twelve Angry Men."

He had many movie roles, including as a news editor in "All the President's Men," a lawyer in "The Verdict" and the president in "Being There." Warden was nominated twice for supporting-actor Oscars in two Warren Beatty movies, first as a businessman in "Shampoo" and as the good-hearted football trainer in "Heaven Can Wait." He also had multiple roles on television and appeared in many other movies and plays throughout his career. He won a supporting actor Emmy for his role as Chicago Bears coach George Halas in the 1971 made-for-TV movie "Brian's Song" and was twice nominated in the 1980s as leading actor in a comedy for his show "Crazy Like a Fox."

Jack Warden was survived by his longtime girlfriend, Marucha Hinds, his estranged wife, Vanda, a son and two grandchildren.

Howard A. Webb

Howard Webb passed away at the age of 88 on April 25, 2007 in Cumming, GA. Webb served with both the 82nd and 101st during World War II. He was a member of Clear Springs Baptist Church for 74 years where he served as a deacon and a member of Alpharetta American Legion Post 201 for 50 years. Howard Webb was survived by his wife of 61 years, Vera, a daughter and a son, and one grandchild. He was buried in Sawnee View Memorial Gardens.

Rudolph P. Wedra

Rudolph Wedra, passed away at the age of 83 on July 28, 2007 at his home in Lake Placid, FL. He was born in Osijek, Yugoslavia on September 15, 1923, to parents Joseph and Theresa and was a member of the 501st Regiment.

He spent years working for the Ford Motor Company in Michigan, and moved to Lake Placid in 1985. Rudolph Wedra was a Boy Scout Master, a little league baseball and football coach, belonged to the Masons, Scottish Rites, Shriners, and spent many years, with the Lake Placid Elks Lodge. While living in Michigan, he served on the Recreation Commission of his town, St. Clair Shores, 23 years.

He treasured his association with the military and was a Veterans of Foreign Wars Life Member, American Legion Life Member, 101st Airborne Association Life Member, 501st Airborne Association Life Member, Sun Shine Airborne Chapter Life Member and a member of the Michigan 101st Association. Rudolph Wedra was survived by his wife of 60 years, Pam, and sister, Marie Hybel.

David Sisk Wexler

David Sisk Wexler passed away at the age of 80 in Illinois. He was a publisher and vice president for Cahners Publishing Co. for nearly 30 years. He was survived by his wife Medelin, two children and several grandchildren and was buried at Westlawn Cemetery in Chicago.

David John Whaley, Jr.

David John Whaley, Jr. passed away at the age of 80 on January 15, 2008, at New Hanover Regional Medical Center in Wilmington, NC. He was born on June 22, 1927, in Wallace, NC to David and Geneva, his obituary stated that he served with the 101st during the War (his age would make him quite young).

He was a lifelong member of the Wallace Pentecostal Holiness Church, and an avid gardener. David Whaley was survived by his wife, Genell Whaley, daughter, two sons, five grandchildren and six great-grandchildren, and was buried in Riverview Memorial Park Mausoleum.

Cecil Spencer "Whit" Whitworth

Whit Whitworth passed away at the age of 85 due to cancer at heart disease in his home in Crystal, MN. Born in Atlanta, GA on June 17, 1922 he was a sergeant with the 101st and was awarded a Purple Heart for wounds he sustained in Normandy. He was a church volunteer, sales manager and community leader. Cecil Whitworth was survived by his wife Evelyn, and a son, daughter, three grandchildren and a great-granddaughter, and was buried in Glen Haven Memorial Gardens.

Carl R. Wheeler

Carl Wheeler passed away at the age of 82 on January 1, 2004 at his home in Havre de Grace, MD. Wheeler suffered from Lewy's Disease, a form of dementia. Wheeler was born in Marion, VA and moved to Perry Point, MD when his father got a job at the VA there. After graduating from Perryville High School in 1939, he enlisted in the Maryland National Guard. After the War, he married the widow of a fellow soldier who died in combat.

George Eugene Willey

George Willey passed away at the age of 86 on November 30, 2007 in Oregon City, OR. He was born Jan. 9, 1921, in Ft. Wayne, IN to Robert and Doris Willey. Willey had a very difficult childhood during the Great Depression. His parents divorced and he lived with various relatives and, on occasion, with area farmers. He attended school in Marcellus, MI and then went to high school in Ohio. He graduated from Sunbury High School in 1939 and played football, basketball, baseball and track in high school. After high school, he lived and worked on a golf course and golf was a major part of his life for the next 70 years.

After working at the golf course, he was employed by Allison Aircraft in Indianapolis, IN and enlisted in the Army Air Corps in 1942. However, he decided to transfer to the paratroops, and was assigned to D Company of the 2nd Battalion of the 501st Regiment.

He dropped into Normandy on D-Day and fought in and around Carentan, as did the rest of his regiment, and he also jumped into Holland during Market-Garden and fought in Bastogne and on Vosges Mountain.

After returning home, Willey had a difficult time finding work and re-enlisted in the Army, earning five additional battle stars during the Korean War. He met his wife, Betty, on a blind date and they married Sept. 17, 1955, and stayed together for 52 years. Willey worked for Leonard Refinery in Alma, MI and then he moved his family to Portland, OR in 1969 and worked as a chemical analyst for Rhone-Poulenc, retiring in 1983. The couple bought a winter home in Florida and they traveled to Europe in 1984 for the 40th anniversary of D-Day. He was an active volunteer, especially with the PAL.

George Willey was survived by his wife, Betty, three sons, seven grandchildren and two great-grandchildren, and was buried in Willamette National Cemetery.

Jesse L. Williams Jr.

Jesse Lyonia Williams Jr., passed away at the age of 85 on January 22, 2002, at his home in Suffolk, VA. Born on November 25, 1916, in Nansemond County to Mignon Delane Johnson and Jesse Lyonia Williams Sr., he was a member of Providence United Methodist Church and a sixth generation farmer. Survivors include his daughter, two sons and three grandchildren. Jesse Williams was buried in Holly Lawn Cemetery in Suffolk, VA.

Leo Wesley Wilson

Leo Wesley Wilson passed away at the age of 87 on November 5, 2004 in Bakersfield, CA. He was born on January 15, 1917, in Fairfield, IL and served as a glider infantryman in the 101st during the War. Wilson resided in Kern County, CA for 63 years and was the owner and operator of Fryes Market in Bakersfield for 45 years. Wilson was preceded in death by his wife of 63 years, Reno, on September 18, 2004, and was survived by many nieces and nephews and grandnieces and grandnephews.

John McLean Wilson

Dr. John McLean Wilson passed away in his sleep in his home at the age of 89 on June 14, 2006 after a long illness. He was born on June 3, 1917, in Darlington, NC, one of six children of Bertha and Thomas. Wilson earned his Bachelor's Degree from the Citadel and a Doctor of Medicine Degree from the Duke University School of Medicine.

He served as a Captain in the US Army Medical Corps during World War II as a Battalion Surgeon and paratrooper in the 517th Airborne Infantry Regiment of the 17th (later 13th) Airborne Division. His last military assignment was as chief of the contagious disease department at the Hospital in Fort Bragg, NC.

Dr. Wilson practiced medicine in Darlington for 53 years. With his wife, he founded the Wilson Clinic and Hospital in 1947, which grew into a substantial medical business that included Wilson Senior Care, Inc., the parent company of Oakhaven Nursing Home, Medford Place Nursing Home, Morrell Memorial Nursing Center, and Med Center Pharmacy. Dr. Wilson remained President and Chairman of the Board of

Wilson Senior Care, Inc., until his death. In addition, he was a lifelong member of St. Matthew's Episcopal Church, a championship golfer and an outdoorsman.

Dr. John Wilson was survived by his wife, Betty, one daughter, three sons, nine grandchildren and one great grandchild, and was buried in Grove Hill Cemetery.

Ralph Wilson

Ralph Wilson passed away at the age of 87 on August 11, 2005, at his home in Anthon, IA. He was born on July 4, 1918 in Anthon to Raymond and Anna, attended St. Joseph's Catholic School and graduated from Anthon Public High School in 1936. The year of his graduation, he was on the baseball team that went to the state tournament, and he remained a baseball fan his life, and enjoyed watching the Cubs.

Wilson started working at Garrison's Grocery Store when he was ten years old until 1943, when he went to Alaska to work on the Alcan Highway. Three years earlier, on August 19, 1940, he married Grace Irene Jones in South Sioux City.

He spent little time in Alaska, as he joined the U.S. Army and served with the 101st from April 1944 until January 1946. Wilson fought in the Battle of the Bulge and attained the rank of Sergeant before receiving his honorable discharge.

After the War, he returned home to work for his father and purchased the Wilson Motor Company. In 1966 was appointed Anthon postmaster, a spot he held until he retired in 1988.

He was an Anthon City Councilman and was a member of the Anthon Lions Club, volunteered with the Anthon Fire Department and was a member of the American Legion McNiff Post #389 of Anthon. Wilson also enjoyed golfing, drag racing and ballroom dancing.

Ralph Wilson was survived by his wife of 64 years, Grace, four sons, a daughter and many grandchildren and great-grandchildren, and was buried with military honors in St. Joseph's Catholic Cemetery.

Joseph P. Zamparelli

Joseph P. Zamparelli passed away at the age of 87 on April 27, 2007 at Massachusetts General Hospital. Zamparelli lived in the Boston area his whole life. He was raised in Medford, MA and graduated from Medford High School in 1939. He received a degree from the Massachusetts College of Pharmacy in 1943 and in 1959 received a master's degree in education from the former Calvin Coolidge College.

Raymond A. Zastrow

Raymond A. Zastrow passed away at the age of 85 in February 2003 at his home in Brooklyn Park, MN. He was born in Bock, MN, and worked for Ford for 20 years, and was preceded in death by his wife of 51 years, Ruth. Raymond Zastrow was survived by his son, two grandchildren and two great-grandchildren. He enjoyed waking up every Sunday at 5AM and going fishing with his son.

Michael Zelicskovics Sr.

Michael Zelicskovics Sr. passed away at the age of 87 on January 18, 2009. During the War, he was a member of the 501st Regiment. He was a life member of the General Anthony C. McAuliffe NY NJ Chapter of the 101st Airborne Division. Michael Zelicskovics was survived by his wife of 62 years, Helen, who passed only a few months later. Survivors include a son, three daughters and five grandchildren.

Louis Zotti

Louis "Duke" Zotti passed away at the age of 90 on July 14, 2008 from cancer at his daughter's home in Norristown, PA.

Zotti grew up in the Norristown area and had eight siblings. He dropped out of school in the sixth grade, and spent a lot of time criss-crossing the country by jumping onto trains in order to find work.

He served with the 101st during the War, and participated in Normandy, Holland and the Battle of the Bulge. He was wounded during Market Garden and in Bastogne and was awarded two Purple Hearts. Returning home, he married Lucy Romano and worked as a painter and a maintenance worker. He worked for the Star Dental Manufacturing Company when he retired in 1982.

Zotti was proud of his military service, and he visited Europe frequently. In 1954, he was honored by the Dutch government at a ceremony with other members of the 101st. He was a member of the Philadelphia chapter of the 101st Airborne Division's veterans organization and the Catholic War Veterans Post 1182 in Norristown. His hobbies included woodworking, and spending time at his family's beach house in New Jersey.

Louis Zotti was predeceased by his wife of 56 years in 2001, and he was survived by a son, daughter and three grandchildren and was buried in St. Patrick's Cemetery in Norristown.

Edward M. Zroskie

Edward Zroskie passed away in January 2008 in Chicago, IL. He was predeceased by his wife Marion, and survived by three children, ten grandchildren and 12 great-grandchildren. Edward Zroskie was buried in Resurrection Cemetery in Chicago.

Walter J. Zych

Walter J. Zych passed away at the age of 80 on May 1, 1999 at the Rose Hawthorne Lathrop Home in South Dartmouth, MA.

He was born in New Bedford, MA to Peter and Katazyna and lived there his until moving to Dartmouth, MA four years prior to his death. He and worked for Revere Copper & Brass until he retired.

Walter Zych was survived by his wife, Doris, a son, a daughter, three stepchildren, 12 grandchildren and four great-grandchildren, and was buried in the Massachusetts National Cemetery in Bourne, MA.

VIII
Recommended Resources

Tour Guides

Ardennes

Hans Wijers

Bastogne

Reg Jans: http://www.facebook.com/people/Reg-Jans/1183323562

Holland

National Liberation Museum (I toured with Frank van den Bergh)

Normandy

Battlebus Tours: http://www.battlebus.fr/Staff.html

Overlord Tour: http://www.overlordtour.com/ (I toured with Olivier)

Online Resources

Mark Bando's authoritative site: http://www.ww2airborne.com

The 506th Regiment website: www.506infantry.org

327th Glider site: http://www.327gir.com/Home.html

101st site: http://www.airborne101st.com/

Toccoa Museum: www.toccoahistory.com

Other Online Resources

Site where I read the piece by Tom Meehan's daughter: http://www.awon.org/awfather.shtml

Site to search for soldiers by cemetery: http://www.abmc.gov/search/wwii_unit_detail.php

Veteran's Websites

Don Burgett: www.donaldrburgett.com

Recommended Reading

- Any of Mark Bando's books (Screaming Eagles at Normandy, Vanguard of the Crusade, Avenging Eagles)

- Battle: The Story of the Bulge by John Toland

- A Time for Trumpets: The Untold Story of the Battle of the Bulge by Charles B. MacDonald

- Noville Outpost to Bastogne: My Last Battle by Don Addor

- Alamo In The Ardennes: The Untold Story of the American Soldiers Who Made the Defense of Bastogne Possible by John C. McManus

- A Bridge Too Far by Cornelius Ryan

- Down to Earth: The 507th Parachute Infantry Regiment in Normandy by Martin K. a. Morgan

- Brothers in Battle, Best of Friends by William "Wild Bill" Guarnere, Edward "Babe" Heffron, and Robyn Post

- Easy Company Soldier: The Legendary Battles of a Sergeant from World War II's "Band of Brothers" by Don Malarkey and Bob Welch

- We Who Are Alive and Remain: Untold Stories from the Band of Brothers by Marcus Brotherton

- Call of Duty: My Life Before, During and After the Band of Brothers by Lt. Lynn "Buck" Compton, Marcus Brotherton, and John McCain

- Beyond the Rhine: A Screaming Eagle in Germany by Donald R. Burgett

- Seven Roads to Hell: A Screaming Eagle at Bastogne by Donald R. Burgett

- Currahee!: A Screaming Eagle at Normandy by Donald R. Burgett and Stephen E. Ambrose

- The Road to Arnhem: A Screaming Eagle in Holland (World War II Library) by Donald R. Burgett

- Parachute Infantry: An American Paratrooper's Memoir of D-Day and the Fall of the Third Reich (Dell War Series) by David Webster

- A Tour of the Bulge Battlefield by William Cavanagh

- D-Day Then and Now by Winston G. Ramsey

- Battle of the Bulge: Then and Now by Jean-Paul Pallud

- The Battered Bastards of Bastogne: The 101st Airborne and the Battle of the Bulge, December 19, 1944-January 17, 1945 by George Koskimaki

- D-Day with the Screaming Eagles by George Koskimaki

- Hell's Highway: A Chronicle of the 101st Airborne in the Holland Campaign, September-November 1944 by George Koskimaki

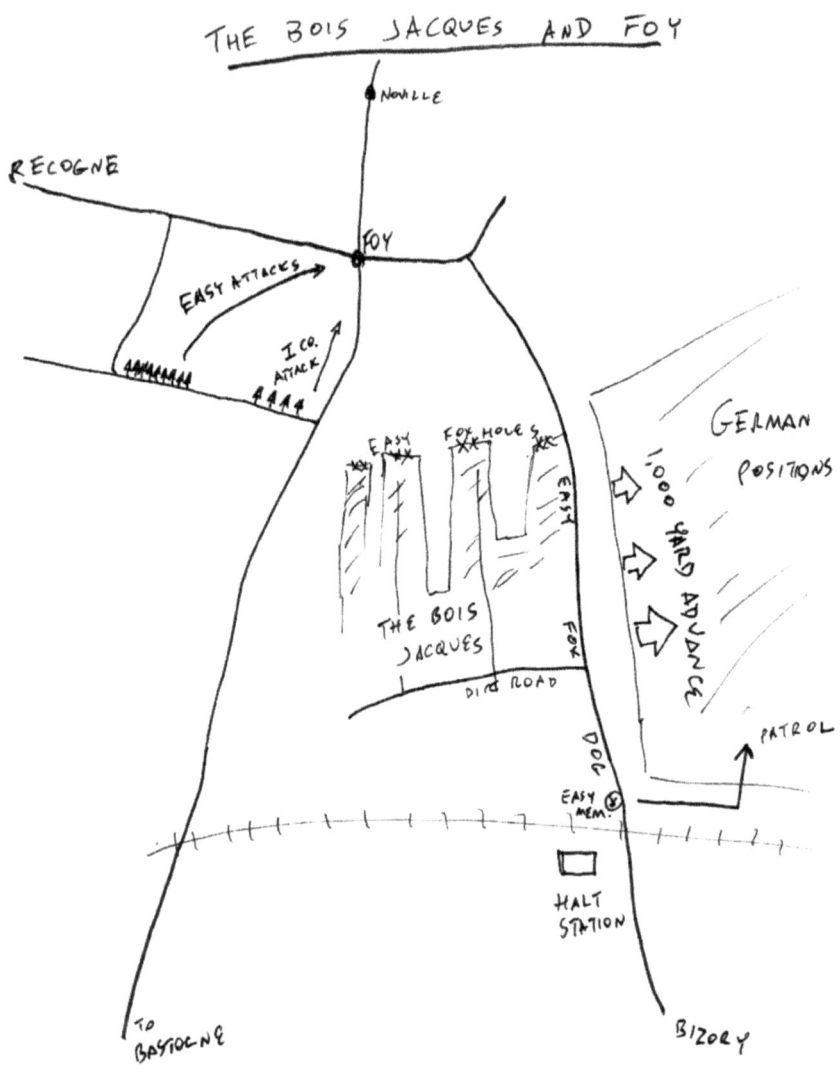

My Map of the Bois Jacques

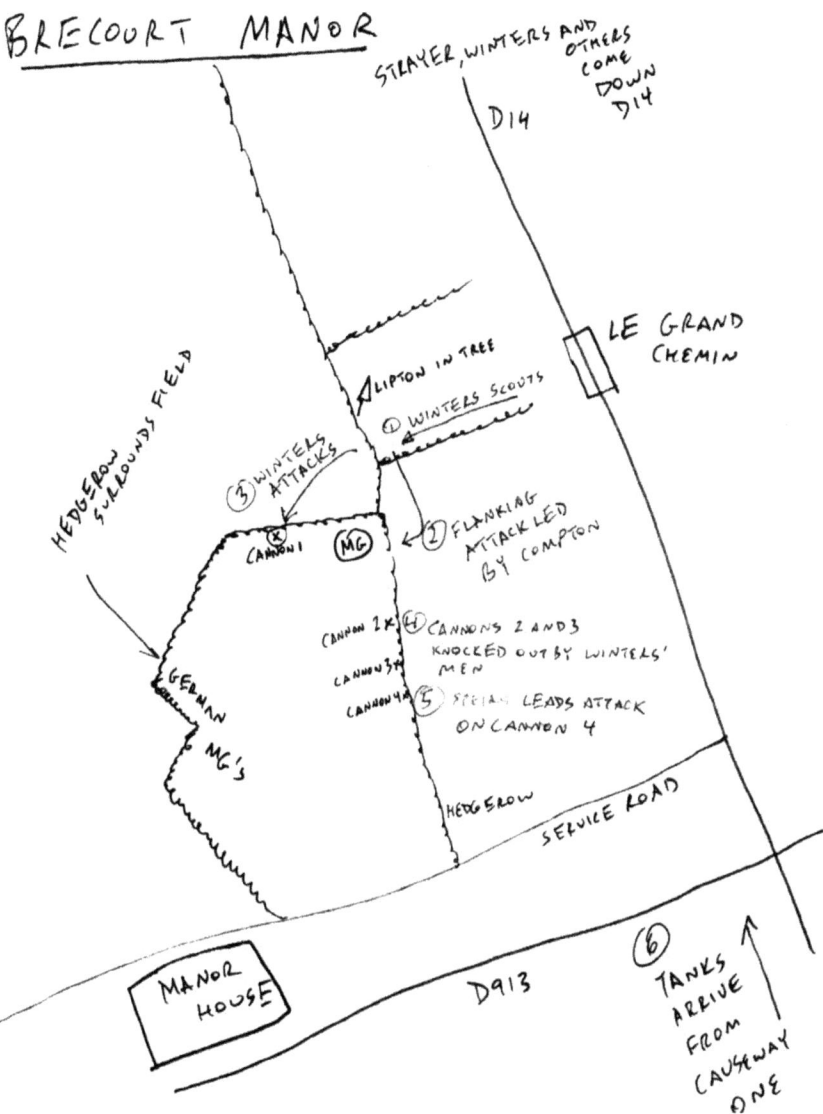

My Map of Brecourt Manor

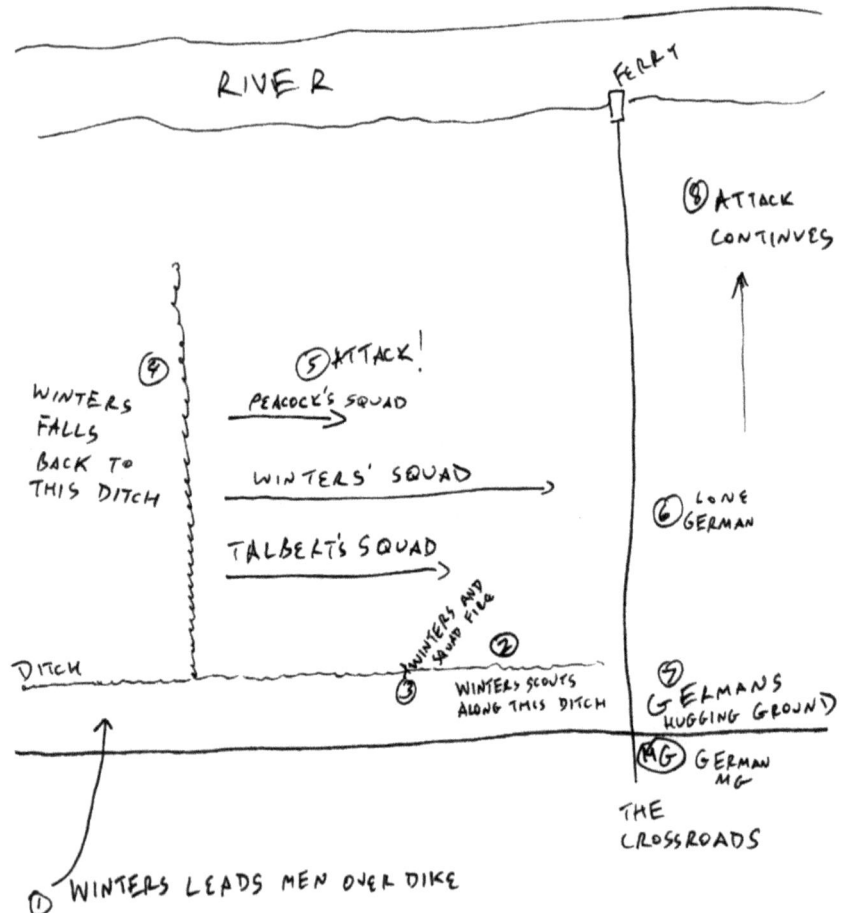

My Map of the Crossroads